D1031681

Argentina is notable for its long history of strong counterrevolutionary organizations. By tracing the development of the first significant and long-lasting far-right group, the Argentine Patriotic League, Sandra McGee Deutsch examines the conditions and motives that gave rise to Argentina's counterrevolutionary movement.

Founded in 1919, the Argentine Patriotic League was a bourgeois reaction against the largely immigrant working class and the left. To counter the doctrine of "class struggle," League spokesmen formulated a "nationalist" ideology. The League appealed to broad segments of the Argentine populace, attracting upper- and middle-class women to administer social welfare programs designed to co-opt laborers into the capitalist system and recruiting men to break up strikes, unions, and leftist meetings. Such were the native origins and persistent appeal of the Argentine Patriotic League. Its precedents for populism, Peronism, and the military juntas of 1976–83; its anticommunism and repression of dissidents—all these topics make *Counterrevolution in Argentina, 1900–1932* a valuable and timely book.

Sandra McGee Deutsch is an assistant professor of history at the University of Texas at El Paso. Her articles have appeared in the *Hispanic American Historical Review, South Eastern Latin Americanist*, and elsewhere.

COUNTER

University of Nebraska Press: Lincoln & London

Sandra McGee Deutsch

COUNTERREVOLUTION

in Argentina, 1900–1932

The Argentine Patriotic League

The paper in this book meets the
guidelines for permanence
and durability of the Committee
on Production Guidelines for
Book Longevity of the Council on
Library Resources.

Library of Congress
Cataloging-in-Publication Data
Deutsch, Sandra McGee, 1950 –
Counterrevolution
in Argentina, 1900-1932.
Bibliography: p.
Includes index.
1. Argentina – Politics and
government – 1860-1910.
2. Argentina – Politics and
government – 1910-1943.
3. Liga Patriótica Argentina.
4. Counterrevolutions –
Argentina – History – 20th
century.   I. Title.
F2847.D48 1986   982'.061   85-16388
ISBN 0-8032-1669-6 (alkaline paper)

To My Parents

Contents

viii *List of Illustrations*

ix   *Acknowledgments*

I   *Introduction*

ONE
9   *Background to Counterrevolution: Society and Politics till 1916*

TWO
33   *The Ingredients of Counterrevolution, 1900–1918*

THREE
66   *The Rise of the Argentine Patriotic League*

FOUR
112 *The League Keeps Order, 1919–1922*

FIVE
153 *Practical Humanitarianism: The League's Strategy of Class Conciliation*

SIX
187 *The League and the New Forces of Counterrevolution*

SEVEN
225 *The League in Comparative Perspective*

243 *Notes*

281 *Bibliography*

303 *Index*

ILLUSTRATIONS

following page 150

Gustavo Franceschi

Miguel de Andrea

Insignia and motto
of the Argentine
Patriotic League

A festival for the
Señoras' free school

The League celebrates
Caseros

Leading Señoras

Julio Irazusta

Leopoldo Lugones

The Argentine Civic
Legion

Acknowledgments

I would like to reverse the usual order of acknowledgments and first thank my husband, David, for his support and word-processing expertise. Next, I wish to express my deep appreciation to David Bushnell for his perceptive comments on the various drafts of this manuscript and for the model of exemplary scholarship, modesty, and perennial good humor which he sets. I am indebted to Max Kele, whose challenging seminars and questions aroused my interest in counterrevolution. Charles Hale and Ronald Dolkart read the manuscript and offered many valuable suggestions. Richard Walter and Leonardo Senkman were very helpful in providing additional material and ideas; Charles Bergquist expanded my theoretical perspectives. Néstor Tomás Auza contributed insights and helped me locate important sources. I am grateful to my colleagues at the University of Texas at El Paso, especially Kenton Clymer and Oscar Martínez, for their encouragement. I could not have carried out this project without the generous assistance of the late Julio Irazusta, who offered his hospitality and kindly let me consult his papers. Finally, I thank the following persons for their ideas and aid: Clodomiro Araújo Salvadores, Marifran Carlson, James Diehl, Mark Falcoff, Félix Fares, María Feijoó, Martha Ferretti, Ezequiel Gallo, Abel Geoghan, Ernesto Goldar, Adela Harispuru, María Constanza Huergo, José Luis de Imaz, Francis Korn, Boleslao Lewin, Carlos Mayo, Arnaldo Musich (h.), María Teresa Piragino, Oscar Risso, Eduardo Saguier, Lynn Stoner, Judith Sweeney, and my anonymous readers.

Many organizations also contributed assistance and financial support. A Fulbright-Hays dissertation grant from the U.S. Office of Education and a Summer Stipend from the National Endowment for the Humanities enabled me to conduct the research for this study. I am very grateful to the Center for Inter-American and Border Studies of the University of Texas at El Paso for its generous support of scholarship, and to the Graduate School of the same institution, both of which helped fund the publication of this book. For their kindness and cooperation, I am indebted to the staffs of the Biblioteca Nacional, Archivo General de la Nación, Instituto Torcuato Di Tella, Archivo de *La Prensa*, Colegio de Escribanos, Biblioteca Tornquist, Biblioteca Juan B. Justo, Jockey Club, Biblioteca del Consejo Deliberante, and Sociedad Rural Argentina, all in Buenos Aires; Biblioteca Mayor de la Universidad Nacional de Córdoba; and the libraries of the University of Florida, Manchester College, and DePaul University.

The many persons who helped me are not responsible for any deficiencies in this work, nor do they necessarily agree with my findings.

Introduction

The far right—or the counterrevolutionary tendency in politics—and its seemingly irrational appeal have intrigued observers since the birth of Italian fascism.[1] The meaning of counterrevolution is evident in the term itself. It signifies opposition to liberalism, democracy, feminism, and the various strains of leftism; in other words, revolutionary ideologies that dissolve traditional hierarchies and particularisms and thus undermine old, familiar ways of life. The result of such ideologies, according to counterrevolutionaries, is the destruction of personal ties and, eventually, of the social order. In contrast to their ideological opponents, counterrevolutionaries seek to promote stability and their vision of society by strengthening family, morality, religion, authority, property, ethnic loyalties, and nationalism. Researchers have examined these counterrevolutionary traits and, in many cases, have spent entire careers trying to answer one fundamental question: Why have beliefs such as resistance to liberal freedoms, subordination to the nation as the highest authority and moral value, and racism—beliefs antithetical to Western civilization—attracted so many ordinary church-going and law-abiding citizens?

The issue of counterrevolutionary appeal is not limited to European interwar movements. A counterrevolutionary resurgence in the United States, Europe, and Latin America in recent decades has brought new urgency to the quest for understanding this political tendency. French intellectuals have extolled racism, paganism, and social inequalities in prominent newspapers and magazines, and extremists throughout Europe have assaulted Jews, foreigners, and other targets. In the United States, groups such as the Ku Klux Klan have grown in numbers and activism, and fundamentalist Christians and other rightists have criticized "secular humanism" and domestic policies that the government has followed since the 1930s. In southern South America during the 1960s and 1970s, counterrevolutionary military officers established brutal dictatorships supported by large segments of the upper and middle classes. Moreover, counterrevolutionary movements, some of long duration, preceded these regimes and influenced their leaders. Such groups in Latin America have received little scholarly attention, compared with the left, although governments of the former persuasion have far outnumbered those of the latter in twentieth-century Latin America. Researchers have also avoided comparing Latin American counterrevolutionaries with those elsewhere.

Among Latin American countries, Argentina is well known for its prominent twentieth-century counterrevolutionary wing. Important exponents of counterrevolutionary ideas have been found elsewhere: the Brazilian Integralists, Mexican Sinarquistas, National Socialist party of Chile, and recent military dictatorships in Brazil, Uruguay, and Chile, among other examples. In general, however, such movements have had periods of importance and then have faded from view, whereas Argentine counterrevolutionary forces, although rarely large in number, have included leading intellectuals, politicians, military officers, and priests throughout the century.[2] The Revolution of 1930 transformed Argentine government from that of a liberal republic to a short-lived corporatist-leaning dictatorship. The conservative regimes of the "Infamous Decade," intermittent military and Peronist rule from the 1940s to the present, and the activities of fervent counterrevolutionaries throughout these years have further demonstrated the weakness of liberal democracy and the left and the vigor of the right. As of 1983 Argentina was once again a democracy, but counterrevolutionaries were carefully watching the elected government, waiting for it to falter.

Yet another point illustrates the importance of counterrevolution in Argentina. Nationalism has been a significant factor in the political evolution of many Latin American countries, but it has been predominantly leftist-oriented in some of these settings.[3] In contrast, Argentine counterrevolutionaries have succeeded in convincing most of their fellow citizens that they alone should be identified with the cause of national autonomy from foreign domination. For this reason, scholars have usually referred to them as "the nationalists." The fact that they have appropriated the term further demonstrates their strength.

The following, then, is a case study of a counterrevolutionary movement in a country where that political tendency has assumed hegemony since the 1920s. Other studies on Argentine counterrevolutionaries have concentrated on the Revolution of 1930, which scholars have regarded as the birth of the Argentine right, and the years thereafter.[4] Although Marysa Navarro Gerassi and Juan José Hernández Arregui, among others, credited the right with uplifting the national consciousness to a certain extent, they and other researchers have tended to view it as an exotic movement tied to European models and divorced from Argentine realities. Few historians have examined the conditions and motives that led to the formation of counterrevolutionary groups, or the social and economic content of their ideas. Instead, they have generally assumed that the groups represented upper-class responses to the threat of growing middle-class power, and therefore that counterrevolutionaries were primarily antiliberal and antidemocratic.[5] Students of Argentine counterrevolutionary groups also have insisted on the limited nature of their appeal—principally to small numbers of upper-class men in the cities of Buenos Aires and Córdoba. For this reason, Jorge Abelardo Ramos called them "oligarchical nationalists," distinguishing them from "popular nationalists" like Juan Domingo Perón, who attracted a mass following and addressed the problem of economic dependency.[6]

In demonstrating that the early twentieth-century Argentine counterrevolutionaries did not conform to these images, I trace the roots of counterrevolutionary sentiment back to the turn of the century. The key events that triggered its formation were the labor mobilizations of 1909–10 and particularly 1919–21. Founded in 1919, the Liga Patriótica Argentina (Argentine Patriotic League or the League) became the first significant, long-lasting counterrevolutionary organization and one of the most powerful political associations in the country during the 1920s. Despite its importance, the League has received no full-length scholarly treatment.[7] I focus on this group and its predecessors, examining the local ideological forces and circumstances that nourished the League; its formation and membership; its social, economic, and political views; and its activities. It was primarily antileftist, not antiliberal, although the difference between the two stances was vague at times, and its composition was broader than previously believed. Finally, the League and its predecessors manifested concern for poverty and underdevelopment, but little interest in European counterrevolutionary political theory. In fact, they frequently accused the left of following European models inapplicable to Argentina—a charge that later would be hurled against counterrevolutionaries.

Those who mention the League in broader works on the right usually treat it as fundamentally different from subsequent counterrevolutionary groups, implying that it had little influence on the latter.[8] Was the League the origin of oligarchical nationalism, as Jorge Abelardo Ramos suggested?[9] To answer this question, I explore the shift from the League's philosophy to that of new counterrevolutionary circles coalescing in the late 1920s. Although counterrevolutionary ideology and practice changed over the years, the League had a long legacy. In the Argentine political spectrum, the League bears certain resemblances to Peronism and the recent dictatorship, and in the international counter-revolutionary spectrum, it is related to European fascism and other contemporary movements.

I avoid using the words *right*, *nationalism*, and *fascist* because, for several reasons, they are not the best terms available to describe the phenomenon under consideration. The first two are broad and vague, and they obscure the variety of outlooks and social backgrounds represented by groups categorized as such. In contrast, fascism narrowly designates the most extreme groups of the right, whose opposition to modernism and egalitarian-ism assumes a radical, antibourgeois character appealing to the masses. One can only determine whether the League was fascist after detailed study of that organization.

Furthermore, the meaning and ancestry of such movements are not apparent from the terms themselves. Fascism is particularly deficient, for one immediately grasps that the right differs from the left, although not necessarily how, and that nationalists identify themselves with local traditions, although it is not clear which of these they chose to follow. The word fascism in itself, however, denotes little more than a tightly knit group. In fact, the brutal images it evokes may obfuscate rather than clarify its significance. Scholars have refused to call Argentine groups fascist partly on the grounds that they were insufficiently "heartless," systematic, or technological in their use of violence and torture.[10] Yet those who have objected to using this term have never defined fascism. It is true that violence was a component of fascism, serving to reinvigorate old symbols of loyalty, honor, and nationalism. To my knowledge, however, no specialist in European fascism has considered sadism or sophistication in torture methods as essential traits of that generic phenomenon, and most would separate German National Socialism and the Romanian Iron Guard from other, less repressive variants. I do not object to the word fascism per se, as long as one carefully defines it. Although I avoid the word in the first six chapters, I will consider its applicability in the concluding chapter.

At first glance, *nationalism* seems appropriate, particularly as the persons under study often called themselves nationalists and most Argentines have accepted their self-designation. So, too, have most scholars, although they sometimes call it "nationalism of the right," or "oligarchical nationalism." On the other hand, Argentinists never cite leftist proponents of nationalism without the use of qualifiers, such as "national left" and "popular nationalism."

The right's intellectual hegemony and preference for the title of nationalist are not, however, sufficient reasons for independent scholars to adopt the term. One must determine whether concern for the nation's good was the counterrevolutionaries' overriding preoccupation. In this regard it is useful to examine the definition offered by the nationalist Enrique Zuleta Alvarez in his history of the movement. The essential trait of nationalism, according to Zuleta Alvarez, is that it seeks to preserve *lo nacional* in the economic, cultural, and political spheres; it opposes all forms of internationalism, from Marxism to liberalism to foreign business interests. He noted that nationalism was originally tied to liberal forces of revolution, but with the appearance of socialism in the second half of the nineteenth century, it became defensive and moved to the right. Thus, the author linked his nationalism to the right, implying that this was the only legitimate kind given the foreign ties of the left as well as historical developments. Zuleta Alvarez defined nationalism as "the defense of order, hierarchy, authority and Catholic tradition united intimately and essentially to the autonomous and free affirmation of the diverse elements that configure the national personality." [11]

These views can be questioned on several grounds. Can an emphasis on order, hierarchy, and authority coexist with the "free affirmation of the diverse elements?" Have Argentine nationalists, for example, truly respected diversity—that is, the autonomy of non-Catholics? Have they consistently opposed all forms of internationalism, or only some forms (such as Marxism) more than others (such as foreign capitalism)? Finally, one must determine the motives behind "nationalism." Zuleta Alvarez legitimately questioned the depth of left-wing nationalism, pointing out that for the left, national economic independence is a mere step along the path to a proletarian revolution in an underdeveloped country. Yet he did not subject right-wing nationalism to the same scrutiny. Did the right have no underlying motives? As his phrase "the defense of order, hierarchy, authority and Catholic tradition" suggests, social preoccupations influenced the way in which nationalists framed their ideology. The terms used to refer to the persons under study should pinpoint these concerns more accurately than "nationalism" does.

In my opinion, the concept of "counterrevolution" best describes the phenomenon and avoids the dilemmas posed by the other terms. Unlike the latter, its meaning is immediately apparent. The persons under study also used this concept to refer to themselves, although not as frequently as nationalism. Even so, they described their mission as one of repressing revolutionary change, thus indicating their main concern. Moreover, calling them counterrevolutionaries ties these Argentines to a framework of historical change and European thought, which many of them after the League's heyday recognized and accepted.

The roots of counterrevolution in the West can be traced back to the aristocratic opposition to the French Revolution and its guiding principles of rationalism, liberalism, and human equality, principles that also inspired leading figures of the May Revolution of 1810 in Buenos Aires. As liberalism shed its progressive character after the mid-nineteenth century, counterrevolutionary activity became increasingly directed against the danger of a proletarian revolution inspired by Marxism, other forms of socialism, or anarchism. The European counterrevolutionary ranks were strengthened by the addition of the liberal bourgeoisie and landowning peasants, anxious to defend their property and status against the threat from below. As time passed, members of the lower middle class and other groups that had not benefited from industrialization also joined the forces of counterrevolution. The groups in Argentina that opposed equality and the expansion of freedom were not necessarily the same, however, as the ones in Europe.

Counterrevolution does not always mean the suppression of a specific revolution, nor must a revolution immediately precede a counterrevolutionary movement. National Socialism came to power in Germany not at the point of acute revolutionary crisis in 1919 but fourteen years later. Similarly, Benito Mussolini's March on Rome took place in 1922, after the postwar revolutionary threat had been quelled. Instead of saying that counterrevolution follows revolution, one might posit that the same economic and social problems that cause revolutions can also cause counterrevolutions.[12] The problems that gave rise to counterrevolution in Argentina will be discussed at length.

The movements described here will be called counterrevolutionary, although occasionally to avoid repetition I will employ the term *right wing*. I will use the word *nationalist* to refer only to

ONE

Background to Counterrevolution: Society and Politics till 1916

In January 1919 a general strike broke out in Buenos Aires, followed by a week of mass demonstrations, labor violence, and vigilante action against workers. The impact of the Tragic Week, as these disturbances came to be known, was great. Many Argentines believed that a bolshevik-style revolution had nearly taken place and that the danger had not yet receded. To counter this threat, the first antileftist and antilabor group to organize itself on a permanent basis arose—the Argentine Patriotic League. This movement, however, did not simply spring up overnight in response to the events surrounding the Tragic Week. The roots of counterrevolution lay in the tensions associated with the economic development of the previous forty years. To understand the origins of the twentieth-century right, one must look first at the evolution of Argentine society before 1916 and the responses of different groups to the path of change.

From 1880 to 1914, the Argentine economy expanded dramatically and became thoroughly integrated into the world market. Presiding over this dynamic era was a network of leading families which historians have alternately called the elite or oligarchy. An important characteristic of the elite and the upper class from which it came was liberalism. Within these groups there was a consensus in favor of the classical liberal program and an export economy, although support of liberal principles ranged from mere lip service to unequivocal enthusiasm. The aim of liberal ideologues, known as the Generation of Eighty, was ruthlessly secular and rationalistic: to transform backward, disunited Argentina into a prosperous, centralized modern nation.

The positivist slogan "Order and Progress," which won much favor among the elite, revealed its attitude: order for the masses and progress for those few individuals who could successfully compete in a free-market economy.[1] Skeptical of the masses' ability at self-government, the elite claimed that its policies would lay the groundwork for true democracy at some unspecified time in the future. The elite believed that rule by a self-appointed enlightened minority was necessary until the masses were prepared to enter the political system. From 1880 to 1912, the traditional liberal emphasis on liberty mainly translated into liberty for the upper class. In addition, the elite became so convinced of its cultural superiority and its right to rule that it refused to share power even with other factions within the upper class. The oligarchy's arrogant self-perpetuation has led some scholars to characterize its ideology as liberal-conservative, rather than simply liberal. Another, better reason for this characterization is that with the passage of time and the growth of mass consciousness, the elite's classical liberalism became outmoded. By the early twentieth century the elite had become conservative in the sense of resolutely opposing progressive change. However hollow its liberalism, the elite generally used that term to describe its own beliefs, as its descendants (and observers) continue to do today.

Yet the elite's brand of liberalism or liberal-conservatism differed markedly from classical conservatism. Indeed, exponents of traditional conservatism in late nineteenth-century Argentina were few. Only a small but vocal minority resisted the official creed from this perspective, and it preferred to identify itself as Catholic rather than conservative. Far from advocating a dictatorship in the style of Juan Manuel de Rosas, this group considered itself part of a world Catholic movement charged with providing moral leadership for modern republics. The Catholics shared some of the elite's views, such as the belief in the class hierarchy and the basic economic structure, disdain for popular rule, and concern for order. Like the liberals, Catholic spokesmen such as José Manuel Estrada and Pedro Goyena revered the heritage of the 1810 Revolution and a republican form of government, but for different reasons: not because these were rational or liberal, but because the revolution had undermined Bourbon liberalism, and a republic fit Argentine traditions better than a monarchy.[2]

According to the Catholics the defect in the Argentine political system was not its elitist structure, but its secularism. Lacking Christian virtue and humility, the ruling liberals had degenerated into a greedy oligarchy that kept itself in power through fraudulent elections and force. The Catholic statesmen decried the anticlerical, materialistic, and authoritarian tendencies of liberalism. They feared that liberalism would destroy religion, the family, and other mediating institutions, creating in their stead a despotism serving only the rich. Although Estrada and others criticized Social Darwinism and the excesses of capitalism (as well as socialism), the dynamic period of growth had barely begun by the 1880s, nor had leftist activities. Thus at this time they primarily directed their attention to Church–state relations and the abuses of the elite. Successful in their campaign against divorce, Catholics did not fare as well against laical primary education, which became law in 1884, the civil register (1884), and civil marriage (1888), and their discontent continued. In succeeding decades they would increasingly focus on socioeconomic matters.

The elite was not necessarily hypocritical, nor was it exclusively concerned with advancing and safeguarding its power. The Generation of Eighty genuinely believed that its liberalism was the ideology best suited for tackling national problems. Whether its members were correct is debatable, but the fact that similar strains of liberalism characterized other regimes throughout Latin America and Europe at this time probably reinforced their assessment. Except for the North American, the French, and the English cases, most contemporary liberal governments in the late nineteenth century were no more democratic than the Argentine, at least in the sense of permitting mass political participation. The liberal economic model—an export-oriented economy emphasizing agricultural development, open to foreign trade and investment, with limited government intervention—

was widely considered the most suitable for developing nations. Therefore, it is not surprising that Argentines found it attractive. Moreover, the results of these policies seemed to justify this belief.

One of these policies was to stimulate immigration. Liberals from Bernardino Rivadavia to the Generation of Eighty had recognized that development of the agricultural and pastoral industries and the establishment of a modern republic required a substantial influx of laborers. According to many liberals, fulfillment of their ideals depended not only upon a quantitative but a "qualitative" change in the population; they deemed that its improvement through "Europeanization" was essential in order to achieve stability and progress.[3]

Legislation designed to promote immigration, to set up agricultural colonies, and to distribute land to newcomers, combined with the economic prospects available in a rapidly developing area, attracted millions of foreigners. From 1870 to 1910 about 2,200,000 immigrants settled permanently. The foreign-born constituted about 30 percent of the national populace in 1914, representing a higher proportion of immigrants to total population than that of any other major country, including the United States. Immigrants and their children accounted for even a higher percentage of the economically active population in Argentina's industrial and political center, the capital city and the littoral provinces.[4]

Other factors besides immigration, internal and external, fueled Argentine development. One was the increased availability of land for livestock raising and agriculture resulting from the conquest of the Indians and the expansion of the railroad network. Heavy investment in infrastructure and the establishment of flexible exchange rates also facilitated production and trade. The expansion of the export sector occurred within the context of the worldwide Second Industrial Revolution, which brought improvements in the technology of food production, processing, preservation, and shipping. One important result of these changes was the decline of transportation costs from Argentina to European markets and within Argentina itself. Finally, rising external demand for foodstuffs served as further impetus to economic growth.

As a consequence of these factors, Argentina became the greatest showcase of the liberal economic model in Latin America. By 1915 Argentina had become the second largest producer of corn and wool in the world.[5] It had also added chilled and frozen beef, wheat, and other grains to the burgeoning list of exports. Furthermore, rising agricultural production had stimulated the growth of processing and other industries. From 1895 to 1913 the number of industrial enterprises in Buenos Aires doubled, and capital investment increased fivefold.[6] Little data on personal income are available for these years. Judging by their opulent consumption habits around the turn of the century, however, landowners and other privileged groups reaped enormous profits.

The benefits of an open-door, agricultural export economy appeared to be many. It attracted foreign investment, new technology, and workers; it enlarged the internal market; it provided employment opportunities for the lower classes and ample revenues for the upper. The disadvantages of an export-oriented economy—lack of diversification, dependence on world market conditions beyond local control, high foreign debts, regional imbalances—were present, but they were not yet apparent to most Argentines.

Some of the consequences of economic development were unexpected. Liberal advocates of immigration had assumed that foreigners would settle in the countryside and become small farmers and peons. Yet the upper-class monopoly on good land, combined with urban opportunities, drew many immigrants to the cities. These changes altered the traditional social structure, which had consisted of a small upper class of landowners, professionals, and bureaucrats, a tiny urban middle sector, and a large rural lower class. The landowning elite and the rural proletariat remained mostly native-born, whereas the middle-level tenant farmers and colonists were immigrants. Foreign-born white-collar workers, businessmen, craftsmen, and industrialists now composed about 66 percent of the middle class of Buenos Aires, and foreign-born manual laborers constituted about 86 percent of the lower class of that city.[7]

The pattern of immigration was also responsible for a demographic imbalance which had important consequences. Many more men than women had come from abroad; in the capital, for example, 539 of every 1,000 persons were male. Of nineteen countries surveyed in 1914, including European nations, the United States, and Australia, Argentina had the smallest percentage of married men and women out of the total adult population, although this figure did not differ radically from that of, say, Mexico.[8] About 22 percent of the children born between the years of 1914 and 1919 were illegitimate, although again, this was not a high proportion by Latin American standards.[9] Probably many of the legally unmarried adults had stable common-law arrangements, and many "illegitimate" children were the offspring of these relationships. Nevertheless, the *golondrinas* (workers who sailed annually from Europe for the harvest) and widespread seasonal unemployment must have contributed to the incidence of illegitimate births and the abandonment of wives and children. In addition, the large number of single men created a high demand for prostitutes, and Buenos Aires became a world center of the so-called white slave trade. Observers of diverse ideological backgrounds perceived the low percentage of married adults and the large numbers of homeless children, prostitutes, and self-supporting women as evidence of the decline of the family.[10] This perception would affect counterrevolutionary thought and practice.

In the eyes of the upper class, the old familiar culture and social structure were giving way to a new and sometimes threatening mix of peoples and customs. A quiet *aldea* in 1869, Buenos Aires in 1914 was a bustling, cosmopolitan center of industry, commerce, and bureaucracy. In it one could find all the attendant evils of a large modern city: inadequate housing and public services, noise, pollution, disease, crime, extremes of wealth and poverty, broken homes, and discontent. Members of the upper class tended to identify these problems, in all their complexity, with the presence of foreigners.[11]

Meanwhile, another group was forming which blamed capitalism for these problems and saw the creation of a classless society as the eventual solution: the labor movement. It is important to understand the characteristics, strengths, and weaknesses of this group and its feminist allies—the main targets of counterrevolutionary action. For the workers, this was not necessarily a "golden age." Although wages in the period before World War I often were higher than those in Southern Europe or other parts of Latin America, the high costs of shelter and other necessities sometimes canceled out this differential. Currency depreciation in the late nineteenth century benefited the exporters and the speculators, but the workers who received fixed wages suffered. The real wage scale fluctuated markedly throughout the decades preceding World War I, climbing from 1883 to 1899, declining steadily after that year till 1909, and then improving slightly by 1912. Nevertheless, even in the best of times many workers, particularly those in construction and on the docks, could only count on working 200 days a year.[12]

Few male workers could maintain their families on their income, let alone achieve upward mobility. For many working-class families, the wages contributed by women and children spelled the difference between a precarious existence and dire need. Other women had no spouses to depend on for financial support. These conditions forced married and single women into the ranks of workers. In 1914, females constituted 22 percent of the total national labor force over fourteen years of age. As many as 30 percent of all industrial and manual laborers were female, as were 52 percent of instructors and educators, and 84 percent of those providing personal services, a category including maids, laundresses, ironers, and seamstresses. Women industrial laborers were particularly common in dairies and in textile, chemical, tobacco processing, and match factories. As the demand for their labor rose during World War I, female employment figures for the years after 1914 were probably higher than those just given. The fact that women tended to work longer hours under worse conditions for less pay than men led some of them to participate in the labor and feminist movements.[13]

The foundation of the first workers' mutual aid society in 1857 marked the beginning of the labor movement, which grew in numbers and militancy with the arrival of immigrants.[14] During the 1870s and early 1880s, foreign laborers who brought anarchist and socialist ideas with them from Europe established affiliates of the First Workers' International in Buenos Aires and Córdoba. Socialists began to publish the important newspaper *La Vanguardia*, under the editorship of Juan B. Justo, a native-born doctor, in 1894. Justo became a leader of the Partido Socialista Obrero Internacional (International Socialist Workers' party), which was founded about this time and eventually was called the Socialist party.

Although party doctrine initially reflected some revolutionary aspirations, such as socialization of the means of production, it stressed short-term reforms. Socialists aimed to improve living and working conditions by limiting the workday to eight hours, regulating female and child labor, setting a minimum wage, replacing regressive indirect taxes with income and inheritance taxes, and lowering the prices of necessity items. Through the establishment of honest elections, universal suffrage, women's rights, a simplified procedure for naturalization, minority representation in Congress, and such measures as the initiative, referendum, and recall, Socialists hoped to democratize Argentine public life. They also planned to carry out the full liberal program by abolishing the death penalty, standing army, and remaining ties between Church and state. They emphasized political activity within the system rather than labor organization and strikes, although Socialists certainly did not reject such tactics. Though Justo and other party leaders were familiar with Marxism, it never constituted the primary ideological influence on Argentine socialism. Liberalism, Darwinism, positivism, and the revisionist views of European socialists such as Jean Jaurès and Eduard Bernstein exerted far more sway.

The social composition of party activists influenced their ideology and practice. The most visible Socialist leaders tended to be well-educated professionals of middle-class backgrounds. Yet the top Argentine Socialists had fewer aristocratic antecedents than their counterparts in other political parties. Although largely of immigrant descent, by 1910 they mostly were native-born. The party's secondary levels of leadership and the ranks primarily consisted of skilled workers and artisans. The immigrant middle class found the Socialists' consumerism, advocacy of honest democratic government, and lack of chauvinism appealing. Thus, the Socialist party attracted the urban middle class and "labor aristocracy."[15]

The Socialists faced serious obstacles, including a low naturalization rate that limited their potential constituency, electoral fraud, other forms of government repression, and competition from other working-class groups. Nevertheless, their accomplishments in the years before 1914 were substantial. In 1904 the party sent Alfredo J. Palacios to the Chamber of Deputies. The passage of the Sáenz Peña Law in 1912, which guaranteed universal male suffrage and secret ballots, along with minority representation, enabled Socialists to elect party members to both chambers of Congress, where they persistently advocated social legislation and defended workers' rights. By this time the Socialists had established themselves as a major political force in Buenos Aires and other littoral cities, and as the strongest such party in Latin America.

Socialists were less successful at labor organizing, particularly beyond the local union level. When attempts to establish their own labor federation failed, Socialists joined with anarchists to form the Federación Obrera Argentina (FOA, Argentine Workers' Federation) in 1901. Squabbling between the two groups caused the Socialists to leave FOA and set up another organization, the Unión General de Trabajadores (UGT, General Union of Workers), in 1903. There, they gradually lost support to the syndicalists, and at the local union level to both syndicalists and anarchists. Still, Socialists continued to influence the working class through their affiliated unions, *La Vanguardia*, and legislative and political activity. Their social projects, including consumers' cooperatives, workers' libraries and schools, mutual aid societies, and housing programs helped inspire working-class consciousness and provided needed services.

The anarchists, whose ideas reached Argentina as early as the 1870s, competed with the Socialists for working-class loyalties. At first, the prevailing strain of anarchism advocated the complete autonomy of the individual and terrorist tactics, but the collectivist tendency, or anarchocommunism, won out over the individualist by 1900. The collectivists envisioned a society based upon a loose federation of communes, permitting the greatest scope possible for individual decision making and self-realization. To attain this goal, workers would have to strive altogether to destroy the state, privately owned property, and other authoritarian institutions. They deemed no political action legitimate, as this entailed working within the system and thus perpetuating it. For this reason, among others, the anarchists saw the Socialists as traitors to the working class. Anarchists believed that workers would gain class consciousness and valuable experience through direct action—boycotts, sabotage, strikes—and would eventually bring about social revolution through a cataclysmic general strike. With the revolution all fetters would disappear and the federation of communes would spontaneously rise into being.

To lay the groundwork for the future, anarchists founded militant unions, or *sociedades de resistencia*, and other communal institutions from the mid-1880s on. Even so, their inherent lack of cohesion, rigid opposition to compromise, and emphasis on violence impeded organizational efforts.

Anarchism appealed to the majority of organized workers in the period up to World War I. This tendency found its core support among immigrants from Italy, Spain, France, and Russia—countries where it had traditionally exercised a strong appeal. Although they recruited among many types of workers, anarchists tended to attract the unskilled, the day workers, and laborers in small business concerns and on the docks. The anarchist unions joined together with Socialists in FOA, which, after the Socialists departed, changed its name to the Federación Obrera Regional Argentina (FORA, Argentine Regional Workers' Federation) in 1904. In its Fifth Congress in 1905, FORA agreed to formally adopt the principles of anarchocommunism. *La Pro-*

testa, originally founded in 1897, became its mouthpiece and, in addition, the most important anarchist newspaper in South America.

The syndicalists rivaled both the Socialists and the anarchists. They emerged at the beginning of this century, when they took over some of the unions belonging to the UGT, and by 1906 they dominated that federation. Like the anarchists, the syndicalists hoped to overthrow the state and capitalism through a general strike. Their disdain for a coherent ideology and glorification of direct action led them to hold Socialists in low esteem. They advocated no specific program beyond that of creating a society composed of syndicates—workers' organizations that would control production and the distribution of goods and services.

An important feature of syndicalism was its interest in promoting worker unity. Syndicalists planned to bring all unions under one central authority, free of partisan political ties, in order to guarantee harmony of working-class action and purpose. With this aim in mind, the UGT began to negotiate with FORA. Representatives from these groups and from unaffiliated unions created a new federation, the Confederación Obrera Regional Argentina (CORA, Argentine Regional Workers Confederation) in 1909. Its architects allowed much liberty of action to the constituent unions. However, this was not enough to satisfy the most intransigent FORA members, who remained outside the new federation. Finally, CORA members voted to disband their organization and join FORA, which at its Ninth Congress in 1915 agreed to welcome them. This accord proved to be transitory. FORA split into FORA V, which adhered to the anarchocommunist principles declared at the Fifth Congress, and FORA IX (named for the Ninth Congress), which became syndicalist.

Although their long-term goals were revolutionary, in the short run syndicalists acted pragmatically within the system, like the Socialists and unlike the anarchists. Despite their emphasis on organizing workers, they admitted the importance of electing sympathetic public officials and of negotiating with businessmen to win limited economic gains. Their lack of ideological baggage and formal partisan ties would permit them to make deals with political leaders. Significantly, they appealed to native-born workers in larger industrial concerns and in crucial export-related activities such as transportation. As the percentage of the native-born among the working class grew, so, too, did syndicalist strength.

Women were also found in the labor movement, although not in the numbers that their presence in the work force warranted. Cultural strictures, as well as the fact that many women worked in their own homes through subcontracting arrangements or in other people's homes as domestics, inhibited their mobilization. Still, from the late nineteenth century on, females participated in unions of diverse ideological orientations: those of tobacco workers, box makers, match workers, scrubwomen, laundresses, retail salesworkers, telephone workers, domestics, needleworkers, and textile workers. They attended UGT and FORA congresses and were active in strikes. The most important manifestation of female involvement in worker protest in the early twentieth century, however, was the Tenant Strike of 1907, a movement tied to neighborhood rather than any specific union or labor federation. Here, women were instrumental in organizing more than 100,000 slum dwellers of Buenos Aires in a rent protest. Performing their chores as housewives, laundresses, and sweatshop laborers together in the congested tenements, women had formed networks that served as a base for strike action. The largest social conflict in pre–World War I Argentina, the strike nevertheless failed to win a lasting reprieve from rent hikes. The tenant movement alerted reform-minded members of the upper class to the workers' need for adequate housing, and it demonstrated that under the right conditions, working-class women could mobilize themselves to bring about change.[16]

Despite such potential and the presence of some charismatic female unionists, such as Juana Rouco Buela, a self-educated laundress and fiery speaker, women tended to remain in the background of a male-dominated labor movement. A visiting U.S. feminist observed in 1919 that though males and females belonged to the same unions, at meetings females set apart from their male comrades and were rarely as vocal. The principal arenas for anarchist and Socialist women were their own sections of these movements, rather than general activities. Anarchist women participated in women's centers that coordinated discussions, propagandizing, and other actions. They also disseminated anticlerical and individualistic ideals as teachers in the free-school movement. Socialist women, however, outnumbered their anarchist sisters. Women joined the Socialist party because they supported its planks of equal pay for equal work, equality under the law, and regulation of female labor conditions. Also, some prominent Socialist women were related through blood or marriage to male party members. Middle-class professionals and workers were found among female Socialists.[17] Socialist women were best known for their participation in feminist activities, however, rather than in party affairs.

The women's movement at least initially included persons of more exalted social background as well as Socialists. The roots of upper-class female participation can be traced to their socialization patterns. Aristocratic families raised their daughters to become good wives and mothers, to be pious and charitable, and "to know as little as possible of fundamentals, but to make a brilliant appearance in society."[18] Largely secluded from men and from the outside world, girls studied at home with tutors or at prestigious Catholic schools. There they received the minimum education required by law, plus instruction in languages, music, and the arts. This additional preparation, followed by a European tour, was considered necessary to "finish" an upper-class woman's training. Such women did not attend universities or become professionals. Their isolated upbringing led them to form strong attachments to female relatives and schoolmates. After marriage, young society women bolstered these friendships through frequent visiting and philanthropic ventures.

Writing of the early twentieth century, one upper-class matron recalled that women could influence the public good only through "amiable suggestions to men in power, in salons or private interviews, and charity works." The second influence, however, was far from negligible. Women had participated extensively in philanthropic and educational activities since national independence, setting up many institutions to care for the poor, the sick, the indigent, and the orphaned. Public welfare in Argentina was chiefly in their hands, until the rise of professional health bureaucrats—mostly male—by the early twentieth century and Peronist reforms in the 1940s. In such organizations as the Sociedad de Beneficencia (Beneficent Society), founded in 1823, which received government financing and administered many different services for the poor, upper-class women exercised considerable independence and power. To be elected to the society was a social and even a political honor. As U.S. Ambassador Frederic Stimson observed in the early 1900s, the society was "the one power which the government fears and defers to." He claimed that through such organizations, women wielded more clout than their sisters in the United States.[19]

Nevertheless, these powerful women did not challenge society's definition of gender roles. Usually religiously oriented, their many institutions concentrated on health problems and on the needs of impoverished women and children—tasks customarily related to those of motherhood. These "social housekeepers" were content to expand their traditional duties beyond family boundaries, rather than change them. Feminists, who sought to end some of the separation between male and female activity, were found in the left and, together with social housekeepers, in the Consejo Nacional de Mujeres (National Council of Women), established in 1900.[20]

A federation of upper-class charities, middle-class professional associations, women's schools, and clubs of divergent social origins, the council was an uneasy coalition. It could agree only on a vague objective: to expedite the "cultural progress" of womanhood. Under this rubric, the council sponsored such projects as factory inspections, literary and musical events, and a vocational school in Buenos Aires, which trained working-class women in homemaking and industrial skills. As time passed, society matrons began to dominate the leadership and exclude feminist goals from the council's agenda. Other council members, including one of its founders, Dr. Cecilia Grierson, the first Argentine female physician, became disenchanted with these leaders' elitist and pedestrian concerns. When the ruling faction declared in 1910 that "the Argentine woman's action concurrent with progress is neither feminism nor socialism," Grierson and the university-educated contingent left the organization.[21]

A sympathetic observer described the orientation of the resulting council, stripped of its progressive component, as a "tender and tutelar feminism which serves as a refuge to those who suffer hunger for bread, for love, for wisdom," as distinguished from a "combative and sectarian feminism."[22] Class sentiments had never been absent from Argentine social housekeeping, and as labor conflict spread, these concerns began to outweigh the simple humanitarian motives, as will be seen in the next chapter.

The Socialists and the council defectors set up an array of feminist organizations. They publicized their support for related legislation and the women's struggle in the periodical *Unión y Labor* (1909–13). Three noteworthy groups included the Socialist Unión Gremial Femenina (Union of Feminine Trade Unions, 1903), the nonpartisan Asociación de Universitarias Argentinas (Association of Argentine University Women, 1904), and the Partido Feminista Nacional (National Feminist party, 1920), which ran a candidate in the congressional election of that year. The University Women and other groups sponsored a feminist congress in Buenos Aires in 1910, which attracted delegates from all over Latin America. By 1920, the various feminist organizations had recruited about 400 active members and several thousand followers.[23]

Like the upper-class women, the feminists directed their efforts toward manual laborers, abandoned wives, prostitutes, and other impoverished women. They lobbied for higher wages and improved working conditions, opportunities for prostitutes to reform themselves, and expansion of facilities for unwed mothers and homeless children. They established vocational and domestic education classes to train proletarian women to become better workers and mothers. Like other, more conservative members of Argentine society, feminists placed great emphasis on the family and on the mother's role within it. In contrast to social housekeepers, however, they justified their demands for female equality by claiming that the healthy, skilled, and self-confident woman was a better mother who strengthened family and country. In this context, they hoped to improve the legal status of women by revising the civil code, which relegated married women to the level of dependents. Some feminists also wanted the vote, but this issue did not gain widespread support within the women's movement until the 1930s.

There were other important differences between the two groups of female activists. One of these was the feminists' disinterest in, if not hostility toward, religion. Moreover, they did not dispense aid to the poor with the same sense of noblesse oblige that characterized upper-class charities. This difference was attributable not only to the more plebeian origins of the feminists, but to the fact that the latter were more likely to have received professional training than the society matrons.

This panorama of labor, the left, and feminism—targets of future counterrevolutionary action—would not be complete without a consideration of the countryside. Here the union movement faced its greatest challenge. Stimson noted in 1919 that rural workers "in some localities live under conditions comparable to those under which the Russian peasants lived before the overthrow of the Empire."[24] To a far greater extent than other laborers in Argentina, the landless peons suffered from arduous working conditions, woefully substandard housing and diet, low wages, seasonal unemployment, and domination by powerful employers. Laborers in the livestock sector were few in number and widely dispersed. More numerous were the landless farm workers, who included the *golondrinas* and native-born laborers who migrated continually in search of work. After 1900, the latter composed a majority of the landless agricultural labor force. Their migratory life-style and extreme poverty, as well as a rural labor surplus, inhibited organizational efforts.

Conditions differed somewhat for other members of the rural proletariat—laborers in the sugar, tannin, and maté works in the northern periphery of the republic. Except for Indian harvest workers, the employees of these industries formed a more permanent labor force than did other landless rural workers. Moreover, their living and working conditions in an isolated area of Argentina generated a sense of community that other agricultural laborers lacked. Significant organizational feats would take place in this zone after World War I.

Before 1914, the only rural group to mobilize itself with some degree of success was the tenant farmers. Although they did not belong to the rural proletariat, they also suffered from transience and a low standard of living, albeit to a lesser extent than landless peons. The elite's interest in foreign colonization in practice meant converting immigrants into peons and tenants. Governments ceded or sold at nominal prices large stretches of land to colonization companies or favored individuals. The former resold the land to colonists at high profit, and forced them off the land when they were unable to keep up the payments, as was often the case. At the same time, the growth of the livestock and grain sectors, combined with speculation, caused land prices to soar. Few immigrants now had sufficient funds to buy land. Therefore, absentee landownership and tenant farming became the rule, particularly in the cereal belt.

Tenant farmers faced many difficulties. Cultivating grain for export, they were dependent on the vagaries of nature and fluctuations in world demand alike. They also suffered from short leases and harsh contractual terms, debt burdens, and inadequate credit, transportation, and storage facilities. They accepted such adversities because, nature permitting, they still could earn a living. Catastrophe hit in 1911–12, however, when low prices left many tenants unable to pay their rent and other obligations. In protest, beleaguered farmers left fields throughout the cereal zone in 1912. The strike lasted about two months and attracted considerable support from small businessmen and journalists in the affected provinces, the Socialist party, and even anarchists, who carried out (unsolicited) sympathy strikes.[25]

The strikers achieved some gains. The opposition Radical government of Santa Fe province forced landowners to compromise with tenants. In contrast, the federal government refused to help the strikers, although some members of the upper class urged such action. Still, the strike left a legacy of a cohesive farmers' movement, organized into the Federación Agraria Argentina (FAA, Argentine Agrarian Federation). The FAA did not yet propose radical changes in the landowning system, nor did it invite the participation of landless laborers.

This account of organized labor and its partner, feminism, reveals the strengths and limitations of the movement. On the one hand, except for certain years of severe repression, it was the largest and most active in Latin America before World War I. It included the most sizable labor federation (FORA), Socialist party, anarchist contingent, rural organization (FAA), and the most influential workers' newspapers in the region. Moreover, the Socialists, feminists, and FAA recruited potential middle-class allies for labor. These very real successes, however, should not obscure the obstacles that the labor movement faced. Structural factors impeded organizational efforts in the critical export sector, except in the ports and in transportation. Even in the cities, unions often lacked the financial resources necessary to sustain long strikes. Ethnicity, ideology, and differing levels of skill divided the urban working class, although these cleavages were not irremediable. More serious was the great power wielded by employers. The surplus of male workers, together with the availability of inexpensive female and child labor, enabled employers to replace troublesome male "agitators" and strikers. Significantly, the immigrant origins of many workers permitted opponents of organized labor to decry it as foreign. And, when these tactics failed, employers called upon government forces for assistance. For all these reasons, the various labor federations in 1908 represented only about 10 percent of the total labor force, and their activities were mainly limited to the littoral cities.[26] Perhaps 20 to 30 percent of all workers in 1912, however, had belonged at one time to a union, labor party, or other type of labor-sponsored organization.[27]

Aside from the labor threat, the elite also faced challenges from those who wanted to enter the political system. Through electoral fraud, cooptation, and the use of force, leaders had restricted the circulation of elites. They had also prevented immigrants and their lower- and middle-class descendants from participating in politics, although one of the ostensible purposes of immigration had been to expand and stabilize the political system. Many foreigners, however, manifested little interest in becoming citizens or voting. To discourage the handful who did, the government encumbered a theoretically simple naturalization procedure with lengthy police investigations, paperwork, and bureaucratic delays. Meaningful expansion of the political system and removal of the old political elite from power took place only after a momentous struggle, lasting from 1890 to 1916. This quarter-century of conflict engendered new political parties whose conduct would, in turn, affect the rise of counterrevolution.

These crucial events can be traced back to the late 1880s, during the corrupt administration of Miguel Juárez Celman (1886–1890). Dissatisfied with his incompetent handling of the economy and with the closed political system, some members of the upper class and persons of other backgrounds formed a protest movement in 1889, the Unión Cívica (Civic Union). The Civistas regarded the authoritarian rule, cosmopolitanism, and opulent life-style of the elite as perversions of national republican traditions. They espoused purification of the corrupt political system, including suffrage reform. These idealists included Justo, who would soon search for more radical solutions to Argentine problems, and the young Manuel Carlés, future president of the League.[28] The Civistas included aspiring students and politicians from Buenos Aires who felt excluded from power, as Julio Roca (1880–86, 1898–1904) and his handpicked successor Juárez Celman had awarded top posts to fellow provincials. Catholic militants such as Goyena and Estrada opposed the reigning spirit of anticlericalism. The Civic Union also recruited native-born shop owners and artisans severely affected by the economic crisis. They were found mainly in the group of Autonomists, a provincial party of Buenos Aires whose populist roots lay in federalism, which congregated around the figure of Leandro N. Alem. Great landowners and distinguished provincial politicians were also found, however, in Autonomist ranks.

When the economy crashed in 1890, Civic Union, with some military and popular support, rose up against the Juárez Celman regime. Although the elite quelled the rebellion, it was forced to grant complete amnesty to the rebels and to end the Juárez Celman presidency. After this partial victory, the Civistas split into the Unión Cívica Nacional (National Civic Union) and the Unión Cívica Radical (UCR, Radical Civic Union). The first group proclaimed itself satisfied with the results of the revolution and allied itself with the ruling Partido Autonomista Nacional (PAN, National Autonomist party). Alem and the UCR continued to oppose the government and demand suffrage guarantees. The Radicals refused to participate in the fraudulent electoral system and hoped to reach power by erecting a strong national organization and carrying out a revolution. Their second tactic failed, but the first strategy ultimately reaped benefits under the leadership of Alem's successor, Hipólito Yrigoyen.

Yrigoyen took over the helm of the party after breaking with his uncle Alem and helping to bring about his downfall. The reasons for this rift are not very clear, but the antagonism probably grew out of personality differences and conflicting ambitions. Alem, an intellectual familiar with European culture, was a spellbinding orator, whereas Yrigoyen, the diligent behind-the-scenes manipulator, was a man of few ideas—and poorly articulated ones at that. Yrigoyen believed that the Radicals' mission was to save Argentina from the perfidious and decadent forces that ruled it, or what he called *el régimen* (the regime), and that he was destined to lead this struggle. Alem was a casualty of these powerful ambitions.

How did the *régimen* differ from Radicalism? Yrigoyen's definition of this sinister body excluded any conception of class; in this way it presaged future counterrevolutionary descriptions of it. Selfish materialism, dishonesty, and utter disregard for popular national sentiments characterized the *régimen* and at the same time nullified its right to rule. He challenged its political monopoly, but he never questioned the monopoly on landownership and other economic privileges exercised by the upper class, to which he and most Radical leaders belonged. What distinguished important Radical figures from their *régimen* counterparts was not wealth differences but the fact that the Radicals' ancestors had generally arrived in Argentina later than those of the elite, and therefore had enjoyed less social prestige and occupied fewer public offices.[29] At this time the Radicals represented a rival faction within the upper class challenging the elite for power, although they also worked to enlarge the political system by incorporating other groups.

The party appealed to disenchanted members of the upper class and, increasingly, to the middle sectors. The latter found its stance on suffrage rights and public morality compelling. Yrigoyen's nationalism attracted Creoles and the descendants of immigrants, eager to prove their *argentinidad* (Argentinism). The middle class also found other reasons for supporting the UCR. In quest of greater prestige and power, children of foreigners began to enter the universities, liberal professions, and political patronage network, opportunities the upper class regarded as its own. Yrigoyen hinted that he would support their aspirations. Thus the native-born middle class became staunchly Yrigoyenist, and it obtained rewards for its loyalty after 1916.

Radicalism represented no economic threat to the upper class. Yrigoyen did not object to the economic status quo; he only hoped to redistribute some income to the middle class. Furthermore, he strongly supported the export economy. His intentions toward the lower class were paternalistic and far from revolutionary. Before 1916 his main response to the existence of poverty was to direct the Radical machine to distribute food and other favors to potential voters. Indeed, before his election to the presidency, Yrigoyen rarely mentioned social questions, nor did he devise socioeconomic programs. His overriding concern was to clean up the political system.

By the early years of the new century, some reform-minded members of the elite began to realize that there was little to fear from the Radicals, although they continued to view them as social upstarts. After the abortive Radical revolution of 1905, these leaders recognized the necessity of promoting cohesion within the upper class and preventing these periodic uprisings, particularly in view of the growing labor movement. President Roque Sáenz Peña (1910–14) and a few others understood that curbing the leftist threat would require bringing the masses into the established political order. This would entail stealing the Radical platform and guaranteeing universal male suffrage, the secret ballot, and minority representation. By coopting the reformist cause, perhaps the official parties would manage to stay in power. If not, the Radicals would win, but this was preferable to a future leftist victory. With these considerations in mind, Sáenz Peña and a few other prominent politicians discreetly maintained ties with Yrigoyen. The long-awaited electoral reform law of 1912 which bore Sáenz Peña's name emerged out of conversations between the latter and the Radical leader.[30]

The Socialist triumph in the federal capital and Radical gains throughout the nation in the 1914 congressional election revealed the possible shortcomings of the elite's reformist strategy. Alarmed, President Victorino de la Plaza (1914–16) labeled the two victorious parties "extremist" and sought to change the fledgling Sáenz Peña Law, to no avail. The 1916 presidential race, however, would prove the crucial testing ground. The main obstacles the *régimen* faced were of its own making: paucity of ideas and disunity. The old ruling party, PAN, had long since fragmented into personalistic and regional factions widely characterized as "conservative." Most were conservative, however, only in the sense of clinging to outmoded, self-serving beliefs, as described earlier, rather than in the classical sense. Many heirs to PAN's mantle, as well as other anti-Yrigoyenists, realized the need to unite in order to defeat the Radicals. Some of them also recognized that in order to compete effectively with leftist reformers (Socialists) and democrats (Radicals), the old elite would have to create a truly modern national party that was cohesive ideologically as well as structurally. Such a party would synthesize the best features of the elite's liberalism and a concern for social welfare, along the lines of the British Conservative party. These reformers met in 1914 to forge a coalition of provincial parties, the Partido Demócrata Progresista (PDP, Progressive

Democratic party), picking a national deputy from Santa Fe, Lisandro de la Torre, as its standard bearer.[31]

This choice demonstrated that party leaders, if not most party adherents, genuinely hoped the PDP would combine the best features of the old oligarchy with a reformist spirit. A man of impeccable upper-class credentials, de la Torre was nevertheless a political maverick. The iconoclastic *santafesino* had participated in the 1890 Revolution and followed his close friend Alem into the Radical party. In 1898, a bitter quarrel with Yrigoyen, whom he regarded as overly ambitious and dictatorial, precipitated his exit from the party. De la Torre's hatred of Yrigoyen was almost matched by his antipathy toward the *régimen*. De la Torre's anticlericalism and lack of rapport with the Creole masses resembled traits of the elite, yet his veneration for civil liberties, the rights of immigrants, and federalism did not win him friends from the *régimen*. Moreover, the provincial party he led before 1916, the immigrant farmer-based Liga del Sur (League of the South), consistently supported the protective tariff—the only contemporary party to take such a stand against free-trade liberalism.[32]

Drafted by Carlos Ibarguren, a former minister under Roque Sáenz Peña, the PDP platform, like de la Torre's record, contained some novelties. Indeed, only the Socialists and the PDP had a platform; the Radicals did not even announce their ticket until the eve of the election. The PDP unequivocally supported guaranteed universal male suffrage, secret balloting (which other members of the old elite opposed), and open party conventions (to which Radicals objected). Other planks included tariff protection, government stimulation of investment in industry, creation of a national merchant marine, and some state controls on exports. If elected, the PDP government would buy good land from private owners for division and sale to colonists at reasonable terms. It favored taxing incomes and large unexploited estates over taxing consumption and small productive properties. On social welfare issues, it supported regulation of working conditions and government funding for worker mutual aid societies, kindergartens for children of working mothers, and workers' housing. One cannot assume that these proposals were the main attraction for those who joined the PDP, but they are significant nonetheless. In their platform, party leaders manifested far more concern for economic nationalism and labor than did the Radicals.[33]

The progressive platform did not, however, bring certain important members of the old elite into the fold. They distrusted de la Torre, their rival. Conspicuously absent from the PDP was the Partido Conservador (Conservative party) of Buenos Aires, the most powerful regional successor of PAN, founded in 1908 and led by Marcelino Ugarte. Many would-be presidents had courted this former governor of Buenos Aires, a notoriously corrupt political boss who epitomized the most unsavory aspects of the *régimen*. Ugarte, Victorino de la Plaza, and other figures nursed ambitions of their own. Together they withheld support from the PDP and divided its ranks, delivering victory to Yrigoyen in a close election. The opposition, however, retained control of the Senate and considerable strength in the Chamber of Deputies.

The fact that Ugarte and others ultimately preferred Yrigoyen to de la Torre demonstrated that they did not fear the Radicals. It also revealed their indifference to the creation of a unified, modern conservative party combining aristocratic leadership with an interest in the masses. No such party would emerge in the democratic era of Argentine politics (1912–30), although, paradoxically, the Radicals came closer to this goal than did the "conservative" opposition. Nor would one develop after 1930. The *Buenos Aires Herald* noted in 1977 that "Argentina's tragedy has been the lack of a genuine and intelligent conservative movement in the twentieth century."[34] Many would not agree that this has been the nation's principal misfortune. Nevertheless, the existence of such a party might have channeled the energies of disaffected reformers and other members of the elite, energies that instead were absorbed by counterrevolution.

TWO

The Ingredients of Counterrevolution, 1900–1918

The integration of Argentina into the world market dramatically altered its society by the early twentieth century. One of these changes was the growing desire of the masses to improve their standard of living and to help make the decisions that affected their lives. Church people and members of the upper class began to devise means of defusing the worker threat and coping with other social ills related to the path of economic development. Although these individuals often belonged to establishment parties, the evolution of their ideas and actions generally took place outside these groups, which were indifferent to reform or incapable of carrying it out. Underlying these measures of repression and cooptation was a belief in the legitimacy of the class hierarchy. Except during moments of acute crisis, this view remained implicit and often found expression in words and deeds that at first glance may appear unrelated to the issue of class structure. In this chapter, I will trace diverse manifestations of this belief in the status quo that merged into the ideology and practice of counterrevolution.

Workers' attempts to promote class consciousness, wrest economic gains from employers, and, in some cases, prepare for revolution provoked a variety of government countermeasures. Calling a state of siege and closing down workers' institutions were some of the government's weapons. Because such a high percentage of the urban proletariat and the labor movement was foreign-born, immigration restriction and deportation were also used. A large anarchist-led general strike in 1902 inspired the passage of the first immigration restriction bill. According to the Residence Law, the executive branch could deport any foreigner convicted of a crime by a foreign court, or one "whose conduct compromised national security or disturbed public order." The law also enabled the government to deny entrance to foreigners likely to fall into these categories.[1]

Despite such measures, workers continued their efforts to organize and strike, reaching a height of militancy in 1909 and 1910. On May Day 1909, police fired upon a FORA parade in downtown Buenos Aires, killing between five and ten persons and wounding forty to a hundred. Almost all the victims were of foreign birth—Spanish, Italian, and Russian. Enraged at Police Chief Ramón L. Falcón, who had ordered the attack, about 200,000 workers participated in a general strike supported by the Socialists, UGT, and FORA. In response to the strike, which paralyzed the capital from May 3 to 10, the government closed workers' meeting places, deported labor leaders under the Residence Law, and sent troops into the city. The so-called Red Week ended when the government agreed to some of the strikers' demands and reopened union and federation headquarters, but it refused to fire Falcón.[2]

Working-class anger over the May Day massacre smoldered and flamed anew on November 14, 1909, when a young anarchist, Simon Radowitzky, hurled a bomb at Falcón and his secretary, killing them both. Despite the insistence of CORA and FORA that Radowitzky had acted on his own, the government swiftly retaliated against the labor movement. It imposed a two-month state of siege, detained and deported activists, and shut down union headquarters and leftist newspaper presses. A police report ominously identified Radowitzky as a member of an alleged Russian anarchist group—and, as most *porteños* (inhabitants of the capital) realized, the overwhelming majority of Russian immigrants in Argentina were Jewish. Upper-class hostility against Jews and other foreigners grew. A group of young intellectuals met the night after the assassinations to form a club dedicated to opposing socially disruptive, "foreign" ideas. Affiliated with the ruling PAN, the group called itself the Juventud Autonomista (Autonomist Youth). That evening, a group of citizens—perhaps the same Autonomist Youth—broke into the offices of *La Protesta* and destroyed printing machines.[3]

Prominent figures referred to this antileftist theme at Falcón's funeral. Speaking for the Chamber of Deputies, Manuel Carlés praised the fallen police chief as a devoted supporter of "the dignity of the social order." Julio A. Rojas, head of the Autonomist Youth, warned that "the nationality is in danger, and we of the native group must unite ourselves in a movement of common defense." Argentines had to understand that the "improvised cosmopolitanism" of their laws had led to extremes. The first duty of "genuine Argentine parties," above and beyond electoral politics, was to enforce "the principle of authority, the unity of the race, . . . and the patriotic work of functionaries like the unfortunate . . . Falcón."[4]

Individuals continued periodically to assault union headquarters and *La Protesta* through the beginning of the following year. According to the anarchist paper, the participants in one of these forays included eighteen policemen, sons of prestigious families, deputy Juan Balestra, and two future members of the League: Emilio Lamarca, president of the Catholic labor organization Círculos de Obreros (Workers' Circles), and Juan Carlos Gallegos, politician and landowner.[5]

Mobilizations of the left and the right reached a climax in 1910. Protesting against the Residence Law, workers mounted huge demonstrations, one of which, on May 8, attracted an estimated 70,000. Anarchists decided to begin a general strike on May 18 if the government did not meet their conditions: repeal of the law, freedom for those imprisoned for "social matters," and a generous amnesty for army deserters. The government ignored these demands, and the police began to illegally detain throngs of activists. Meanwhile, the government invited guests from Europe and the Americas to join Argentines in celebrating the hundredth anniversary of the May Revolution. Fearing that the proposed general strike would disrupt the festivities, the government declared a state of siege on May 14—an ironic setting for the centennial of the birth of liberty. Despite the state of siege and attendant mass arrests, anarchists carried out their general strike. In the first week under the state of siege, over 150 persons died in clashes between the strikers and forces of order. Several public officials, including the minister of war, stated that it was necessary to destroy anarchism, once and for all.[6]

The size of the demonstrations and their timing both frightened and infuriated many upper-class *porteños*. Civilian groups
arose to counter the anarchists. Starting before and continuing
throughout the celebrations, students paraded through the streets
carrying the national flag, singing patriotic songs, and compelling passersby to remove their hats in the presence of the flag.
Several observers reported bloody encounters between students
and strikers in workers' neighborhoods and the downtown area,
resulting in several deaths. The left, however, was not the students' only target. The fact that Argentina's main Latin American rival, Brazil, did not send representatives to the independence celebrations until the last minute incensed the youths.
Flags of many nations, including Brazil, were displayed all over
the capital, and students demanded that the Brazilian banners be
taken down—in several cases, successfully.[7]

Catholic women also joined the antianarchist forces. In 1908,
the Congregations of the Daughters of Mary, organizations of
female alumnae of prestigious Church-run schools, had formed a
federation. The group included the descendants of women who
had donated their jewels to the original independence cause.
Under Father Miguel de Andrea's guidance, in 1910 its members
dedicated themselves to the "sacred duty" of defending the legacy inherited from their forerunners: "love of God and the fatherland." On May 21, the eve of the centennial, they sponsored
a mass commemorating independence at the downtown church
of Nuestra Señora de la Merced, patron saint of the Argentine
army. Also attending were the Beneficent Society, Liga de Damas
Católicas Argentinas (League of Argentine Catholic Ladies), and
other Catholic and charitable groups. Andrea delivered a patriotic speech at the mass, and then led the women on a short
march from the church to the tomb of José de San Martín, the
liberator of southern South America. Singing the national anthem as they marched, the women embodied upper-class resistance to the left.[8]

More ominous than the student and female activity was that
of paramilitary groups. General Luis Dellepiane, who became
police chief of Buenos Aires after Falcón's death, organized the

Policía Civil Auxiliar (Auxiliary Civil Police) to help the forces of order during the celebration. This group may have participated in the events of May 14, the same day the state of siege was declared. That night, members of the exclusive Sociedad Sportiva Argentina (Argentine Sport Society), other prominent citizens, and policemen destroyed the much-beleaguered offices of *La Protesta* and *La Batalla*, another labor paper. They also launched attacks against *La Vanguardia*, Socialist party headquarters, and the building that housed CORA and several other workers' organizations. Among the alleged vigilante leaders were the Italian Baron Antonio Demarchi; deputies Juan Balestra, Pedro Luro, and Carlos Carlés, Manuel's brother; a police inspector Reynoso; and one Dr. Aubone, probably Carlos Aubone, a former assistant chief of the federal police who later joined the League. Head of the Sport Society, Demarchi was also President Roca's son-in-law and future leader of the Argentine branch of an Italian fascist organization.[9] Civilians carried out other destructive activities in Buenos Aires, La Plata, and Rosario, where policemen either joined them or watched in silence.

Vigilantes also entered Barrio Once, an area inhabited by many Russian Jews. There they looted and destroyed a grocery store and raped several women. Another object of attack was the cultural center and library of a Jewish socialist organization. Marauders destroyed some of the books on the premises and carried the rest to the Plaza del Congreso, where they burned them. This was not the first manifestation of anti-Semitism in Argentina, but it was the first incident marked by violence. Furthermore, it demonstrated the widespread identification of Russian Jewry with leftist politics, a consequence of Radowitzky's crime. Even the humble sectors of society made this identification. One visitor to Buenos Aires during the centennial found three or four newsboys beating a little Jewish boy. When he made them account for their actions, their excuse was that their victim was Russian. He concluded that everything that "savored of the anarchist was in those days in bad repute in Buenos Aires, and the Russian Jews were not in good odor."[10]

One month after the centennial, on June 26, a bomb exploded

in the Teatro Colón and injured about fourteen people. Police accused a Russian anarchist named Romanoff of the deed; anarchists, on the other hand, insisted that the police had set off the bomb, giving authorities an excuse to pass harsh legislation. The next day Congress did in fact approve the Law of Social Defense. This measure prohibited the residence of foreigners who favored using violence against national governments or institutions. Anarchists could not hold meetings, issue propaganda, or form groups. Severe penalties would be imposed for bombing or otherwise damaging property and lives. The authorities would punish those who defended subversive threats against property and lives by spoken or written word, or tried to force others to participate in strikes and boycotts. The law also granted other sweeping powers to the police.[11]

This legislation led swiftly to further arrests and deportations, as well as the shutting down of labor headquarters. Labor organizations continued to recruit new members and to strike, albeit at a reduced level. By 1913, the more overt phase of police persecution had ended, and FORA gradually reasserted itself.[12]

This period of repression only temporarily hampered the left. Its significance for the history of counterrevolution, however, was far-reaching. The events surrounding the centennial brought together groups of men and women whose composition foreshadowed that of the League. Their words and actions also presaged the future conjunction of antileftism, anti-Semitic and antiforeign sentiments, and Catholicism. At this time and later, the upper class claimed to defend the spirit of the May Revolution and liberal freedoms. Yet the vigilantes' illegal acts, police complicity in such infractions, the "legal" assault on political rights, and the authorities' indiscriminate persecution of all labor activists demonstrated the rift between nationalism and its original liberal moorings. The vigilantes subverted their own cry for order by attacking other citizens and private property. They implicitly defined "order" not so much as obeying the law, but as maintaining the existing social hierarchy. Also significant was their association of Argentine identity with their own class identity, and of radicalism with immigration. Their claim that the nationality was in danger really meant that the foreign proletariat threatened upper-class interests. The fact that the working class was overwhelmingly foreign in composition enabled the predominantly Creole upper class to make these linkages.[13]

Such views on immigration emerged as a central theme of counterrevolutionary thought. Attitudes on this subject had changed since the Generation of Eighty, and this change mirrored the growing defensiveness of the ruling class. When liberals in the nineteenth century had advocated Europeanization of the population, they had deemed some Europeans better than others. Only a minority of the immigrants who arrived after 1860, however, were the preferred English, French, Swiss, and Germans. Italians and Spaniards composed the vast majority, and they were accompanied by Russian Jews, Syrians, Lebanese, and other "undesirables." The newcomers' origins provoked much criticism even from the original supporters of immigration. Another cause for dissatisfaction was the fact that foreigners increasingly preferred to settle in the cities rather than the countryside. Argentine commentators usually overlooked the reasons for this situation and instead blamed foreigners for their lack of agricultural skills, their supposed laziness, and their "parasitism."

At the turn of the century, however, attitudes toward immigration had not yet crystallized. This ambivalence surfaced in the popular mobilization against Chile. In 1898 and 1901, boundary disputes between the two countries threatened to escalate into full-scale war. Eager to improve the nation's defenses and determined not to capitulate to Chile, people throughout the country held public assemblies, practiced target shooting, and set up local volunteer militias. These diverse groups of men, youths, and foreign residents joined together in December 1901 under the title of Liga Patriótica Nacional (National Patriotic League). The group also had female adherents, but their activities were confined to planning fund-raising events. In an editorial entitled "The Nation of Immigrants," *La Prensa* extravagantly praised the many foreign members for their contribution to Argentine life and their loyalty to their new homeland, noting that they were indistinguishable from the native-born in the patriotic meetings.[14]

The National Patriotic League resolved to stimulate citizen

defense efforts and interest in foreign affairs, and to convince the
government to strengthen Argentine influence on the continent.
It would also campaign to increase the size of the navy and army,
as well as the people's admiration for the armed forces. Considering its large immigrant component, one of its other objectives
was puzzling: to reinforce the ties of immigrants to their adopted
homeland and to encourage naturalization. Apparently the foreigners' display of patriotic sentiment had not convinced league
leaders of their sincerity, for they viewed the large numbers of
aliens as a threat to the nation. The league, however, did nothing
to remove the bureaucratic obstacles toward becoming a citizen.
The group went on to fight other perceived internal threats to the
nation, carrying out counterdemonstrations against anarchists
and Socialists after 1904.[15]

The potential inner threat to national defense continued to
preoccupy some Argentine intellectuals and leaders. Class conflict divided the nation and weakened its resistance to attack, in
their view. Moreover, many leftists were pacifists or opposed
fighting for their country against the workers of other countries.
The Socialists' stand against militarism, obligatory military service, and military expenditures roused nationalistic ire. On the
eve of World War I, General José F. Uriburu wrote an article criticizing that party. The Socialists, he noted, objected to what they
considered the Argentine army's imitation of the Prussian model,
and yet, paradoxically, they applied a European theory of class
struggle to a country bereft of capital, industry, and inhabitants,
so unlike that continent. Uriburu believed that only the threat of
force, not "progress" or universal benevolence, could prevent
war. Moreover, despite Socialist rhetoric, the army represented
no danger to Argentine civil tradition. Uriburu maintained that
the Socialists wanted to weaken the military because it was the
main organization that society could pit against the revolutionary masses. For this reason Socialists also lashed out against the
military spirit and all manifestations of vitality, discipline, and
cohesion.[16] Many other officers probably shared Uriburu's view
of the left as antinational.

The desire for national unity translated into a reaction against cosmopolitanism and an attempt to revindicate the Argentine cultural heritage, particularly its Hispanic roots. Around the turn of the century some historians and essayists began to disagree with the liberal historians' version of the past, with Domingo Faustino Sarmiento's "Civilization versus Barbarism" dichotomy. Some intellectuals blamed foreigners for class conflict, urban blight, and the immature political system. The fact that most of them favored minority rule evidently did not strike them as contradictory. Viewed with hindsight, the gauchos and caudillos no longer seemed reprehensible. The revisionist works on Juan Manuel de Rosas, in which Ernesto Quesada and other historians judged the dictator more objectively than had previous scholars, exemplified the new perspectives.[17]

The gaucho and the Hispanic past found their greatest defenders in the writers whom historians have called the cultural nationalists. Lured by the attractions of the metropolis, this new generation of writers had left their native provinces for Buenos Aires in the 1890s. Yet conditions in the capital repelled them and aroused their nostalgia for the interior and for bygone days. Cultural nationalists rejected the previous generation's arguments for immigration and stressed the native contribution to national culture. Their reasoning proved to be as racist as that of their predecessors, except that now the tables were turned; they denounced foreigners in harsh terms once reserved for describing Creoles and saved their praise for the latter. Paradoxically, they sometimes combined love for native traditions with pride in Argentine "whiteness"—a legacy of immigration.

Manuel Gálvez, Ricardo Rojas, and Leopoldo Lugones (after his initial leftism had faded), the three most prominent cultural nationalists, had backgrounds similar in respects other than their common provincial origins. All were members of important political families whose destinies had been hurt by modernization. Lugones came from a poor but distinguished family whose military forebears had arrived in Argentina in the late colonial period. A political boss in northern Córdoba, his father lost his ranch in the depression of 1890. Reduced to poverty, the young poet and his family found alternative employment through political connections. In contrast, the Gálvez and Rojas families possessed wealth and the top political offices in their respective provinces of Santa Fe and Santiago del Estero. The Gálvez family was old and patrician, however; the more plebeian Rojas family gained its stature only in the 1880s. Although members of these families and their friends still held power by the time of the centennial, national-level leaders were chipping away at their control. Furthermore, new local political forces tied to immigration and economic change, such as the League of the South, challenged the Gálvez family and its allies.[18]

Therefore, it is not surprising that of the cultural nationalists Gálvez directed the harshest comments against immigration and cosmopolitanism. He complained that first the Argentine nation imported "hordes of Italian peasants"; then it imitated English and French culture; finally it received Jews and anarchists. Compounding the problem, the newcomers injected utilitarian, materialistic, and skeptical attitudes into Argentine life. Now that the arrival of alien groups and ideas had "denationalized" the country, to govern no longer meant to populate but to "Argentinize." Argentina could not and should not expel the immigrants who had helped build the country, but it would have to absorb them completely. Assimilation could only be one way; the Hispanic, Catholic, idealistic national culture would temper the character of the foreign masses. The task of Argentinization faced powerful enemies, for example anticlericals (such as the Socialists); normal school teachers, whose Sarmiento-influenced antinational policies set the tone for the educational system; and mulattoes, whose hatred for Spain was "the hatred of the dark for the white." The Argentinization that Gálvez advocated would somehow preserve and strengthen the soul of the "race" against the determined opposition of these Hispanophobes.[19]

The cultural nationalists defined the Argentine character in terms equivalent to traditional society—terms that did not threaten the existing order. In an ironic about-face from Sarmiento's position, the hitherto reviled gaucho now became a model for the masses to follow. Loyal to his employer, content with his station in life, opposed to thrift, rational behavior, and planning, the idealized gaucho was the antithesis of the successful foreign-born enterpreneur and the labor activist alike. In a famous lecture series in 1913, Lugones captivated a large prestigious audience in Buenos Aires with this image of the gaucho. Significantly, he combined these remarks with attacks on the left and democracy—and then praised the upper class for opening up the political system against its own interests. The popularity of these lectures, later published under the title of *El payador*, reflected the extent to which cultural nationalism and intertwined xenophobic and antimodernist sentiments had permeated the upper class.[20]

Education was another important issue for cultural nationalists, one that had previously concerned liberals. The political elite had viewed education as a means of consolidating the nation and enlightening the masses. This was the reasoning behind the famous law of 1884 which established a public network of obligatory, free, and secular primary schools. Liberals removed Catholic religious instruction from the program because they thought it interfered with the goal of instilling allegiance to the nation and to the reigning ideal of progress. In addition, liberals claimed that it would not please the Protestant immigrants they hoped to attract to Argentine shores.

The purposes of public secular education changed somewhat after the beginnings of mass immigration. By stressing courses with Argentine content, teaching only in Spanish, and instilling patriotism, the schools attempted to forge one nationality and also combat radicalism. Educators hoped that immigrants would adopt the national values and symbols presented by the schools, signifying their acceptance of the hierarchical class structure. According to one foreign visitor in 1912, such preoccupations dominated Argentine education.[21]

The schools in immigrant colonies and ethnic communities seemed to remain outside the community of national values that liberals and then cultural nationalists wanted to create. The latter charged that in these schools foreign-born teachers taught in foreign languages and ignored Argentine studies. Sarmiento had been the first to point out this problem in 1881, when he wrote that the Italian schools impeded the formation of Argentine citizens and of a national culture. Ricardo Rojas, perhaps the most influential of the cultural nationalists, followed this line of thought. In his seminal work, *La restauración nacionalista* (1909, The Nationalist Restoration), Rojas charged that the private (ethnic) schools in Argentina had served as agents of "national dissolution." He described them as colonialist or imperialist institutions that attacked the Argentine nationality, especially its language and national character, and obscured the source of its republican virtues. The Argentine government would have to reclaim the schools on its soil, but Rojas recognized that this would be a difficult task. "A half century of cosmopolitanism in the population, of European capitalism in business enterprises, of abdications in political thought, of Encyclopedism in the public school and internationalism in the private school, do not favor . . . the diffusion of nationalist ideas." And yet the reassertion of nationalism, beginning in the schools, was urgently required, for Argentina faced constant humiliation. Jewish and British capitalists considered Argentina their colony, and the Italians were beginning to view it the same way, while other Europeans did not even know where the nation was located.[22]

Rojas insisted that the restoration of nationalism did not signify liturgical patriotism or unequivocal hostility to everything foreign. Nor did he advocate reimplanting gaucho customs or old economic and social forms. Instead he favored accommodating European ideas to Argentine experience and creating a "mature sense of nationality." Furthermore, his brand of nationalism also included protecting Argentine economic interests and keeping the major share of profits earned by foreign capital in the country.[23] These sentiments seemed rational and constructive, yet his attitudes on "Encyclopedism" and "cosmopolitanism" suggested intolerance.

Moreover, his identification of Jews with capitalism implied an anti-Semitic attitude. To understand his viewpoint, one must examine it in the context of Argentine reactions to Jewish settlement. Although Jews had lived in the country since the colonial period, their numbers were small until the 1890s, when thousands of Russian Jews fled from pogroms to Argentina, among other countries. Many settled in agricultural colonies established by the Jewish Colonization Association (JCA) in Entre Ríos, Santa Fe, western Buenos Aires, and eastern La Pampa. Others, along with coreligionists from Eastern Europe and the Mediterranean region, became artisans, workers, store owners, and small industrialists in the cities. Nevertheless, in 1909 most of the 35,950 Jews in the country were of Russian origin, and 19,360 of them lived in the colonies.[24]

Influenced by the favorable attitude toward immigration and European racist theories, both characteristic of the era, Argentines reacted ambivalently to Jews—even before their arrival. In the 1880s a French newspaper in Buenos Aires reproduced the anti-Semitic arguments of Edouard Drumont for its *porteño* readers. At the same time, *La Nación* praised Jewish accomplishments in the arts, sciences, and business and claimed not to oppose Jewish immigration per se, but it criticized proposed plans for Jewish colonization in the interior. The editors predicted that the Jews would not adapt themselves to Argentine conditions and would form an isolated enclave. Their opinions reflected those of the newspaper's founder, Bartolomé Mitre, who had long opposed both the foundation of colonies based on one ethnic group and Jewish immigration.[25]

More significant for the course of Argentine anti-Semitism was Julián Martel's widely read novel *La bolsa* (The Stock Exchange), set during the boom years of the 1880s and the crash that followed. Writing in 1891, when few Jews resided in the country, Martel nonetheless blamed the corruption and the financial disaster on Jewish avarice. His villains were unsavory Jewish financiers and the unwitting non-Jewish Argentines who were their dupes. Martel's loathsome character, Filiberto Meckser, not only belonged to the supposed international Jewish capitalist establishment, but headed the Jewish white slave society. Martel also tied Jewish capitalism to world socialism, although he did not describe this nexus in detail. The author ignored the main beneficiaries of speculation and rampant inflation, namely the local landowners and British investors. In this manner he avoided criticizing the socioeconomic system that was at fault. Indeed, he defended the landed class and distinguished "good" capital from "evil": respectively, the constructive and benign British influence, and the Jewish monopolizing instinct, which sought to corrupt and control all of society. In general, Martel attributed Argentine problems to the arrival of Jews and other foreigners and the subsequent weakening of the Argentine "race." Despite its virulent racism, or perhaps because of it, *La bolsa* was and remains popular among Argentine readers.[26]

La bolsa exemplifies two strands of anti-Semitism: the traditional and the ideological.[27] The first consists of stereotypical impressions and prejudices handed down through the ages. Traditional anti-Semites assign Jews such traits as materialism, certain physical ("racial") characteristics, exclusiveness, leftism, and unethical business practices. Although their charges are false or exaggerated, such persons still see Jews as human beings, members of a particular religious and ethnic group. The Jew envisioned by ideological anti-Semites, however, is not a real person but a demon figure, an embodiment of modern social forces that they hate and fear. Typically they attribute complex problems to Jewish-led conspiracies. In contrast to traditional anti-Semites, for whom Jews have little importance, the Jews occupy a central position in the world view of ideological anti-Semites.

Although it included some features of traditional anti-Semitism, *La bolsa* also contained all the contradictory tenets of the ideological variety. The Jews pursued world domination through capitalism and socialism. They formed separate enclaves, but they penetrated all groups and sectors of society; they were simultaneously bold and cowardly. Rootless and international in orientation, for some obscure reason they had chosen Argentina as a center of operations. Not content with exploiting the country economically, Jewish pimps exploited female flesh. Here Martel referred to the fact that Jewish criminals played prominent roles in the prostitution rackets, although not so much so in 1890 as later. By 1909 Jews controlled about half of the licensed brothels in Buenos Aires, and the percentage of Jewish prostitutes was even higher.[28] Nevertheless, other "white slavers," compliant law enforcement officials, and most clients were non-Jews, and most Jews denounced these illicit activities. Martel's accusation contained some truth, but his lumping together of high-level finance and low-level crime in one conspiracy was irrational. Similarly, it was true that some of the leading grain exporters were Jewish in origin, yet they tended to convert to Catholicism and intermarry with local aristocratic families.[29]

Rojas did not share Martel's violent resentment toward Jews, and he did not attack them for white slavery or venality. Nevertheless, Rojas praised Martel's work, and the two authors held some assumptions in common. Rojas revealed these thoughts in his discussion of Jewish education in *La restauración nacionalista*. A newspaper campaign in 1908 against the JCA schools in Entre Ríos inspired his remarks. *La Prensa*, *La Nación*, and Argentine educational authorities charged that the JCA schools emphasized Hebrew and Jewish studies in the exclusion of Spanish and Argentine subjects, and they characterized the schools as agents of foreignization. *La Prensa* blamed the JCA, rather than the Jewish immigrants, for administering the schools and the colonies as its own possessions, in disregard of Argentine sovereignty.[30]

Adding to the controversy, Rojas stated that though in principle the Jewish schools were no different from those of other immigrant communities, in actuality they posed additional dangers to the nation. If they did not owe allegiance to another country, they did, however, serve a "nomadic Church and a theocratic family" difficult to incorporate into Argentine life. Jewish learning fostered a sense of separatism in first-generation Argentines, who chose to be Jews rather than Argentines "in complete communion with the people and the soil" of their birthplace. This separatism could inspire anti-Jewish feeling and destroy the spirit of religious and political tolerance which until then, according to Rojas, had characterized native Argentines.[31]

One could criticize these remarks on a variety of grounds, the first being that they did not coincide with the facts. A patriotic citizen of a young, heterogeneous country, Rojas was justifiably concerned about national unity and identity. The real question, however, was not whether the immigrant schools were antinational, but whether the public school system was equipped to serve the masses of immigrants, some of whom had settled in zones newly opened to settlement. Few public schools existed in the countryside and even fewer in frontier areas, and the province of Entre Ríos, where many of the Jewish colonies were located, could not afford to build more. The JCA schools were established in a void; for this reason, they received Christian pupils and the support of local governments. Education officials in Entre Ríos and some federal authorities refuted the charges against the JCA schools and praised the JCA's efforts to "Argentinize" its pupils. The Spanish language and Argentine studies classes were not of high quality, but they usually met minimal standards. Furthermore, to have ignored these subjects and encouraged separatism would have contradicted the JCA's assimilationist goals. Indeed, Alberto Gerchunoff demonstrated Jewish assimilation into Argentine rural life in his popular *Los gauchos judíos* (1910, The Jewish Gauchos). Still, the separatist stereotype persisted, and the JCA handed over its schools to local boards of education in 1914.[32]

Rojas's statements were objectionable for other reasons. He saw Jews as essentially rootless beings who had migrated from country to country without forming ties to any. They reserved their allegiance for their religion and ethnicity, an allegiance strengthened by their schools, endogamous marriage patterns, and family life. Being a Jew meant holding this loyalty above all other sentiments, including patriotism, which the "wandering Jew" was not accustomed to feeling. Rojas believed that one could not be a Jew and an Argentine at the same time; one had to choose between them. He did not seem to recognize that his price for assimilation was rejecting one's religion, or that pluralism could coexist with national unity. Evidently only Catholics, Protestants, or nonbelievers could be Argentine, because their religious identity, or lack thereof, would not compete with their nationality. *La restauración nacionalista* illustrated one of the principal shortcomings of Argentine liberalism which would carry over into counterrevolutionary thought: the desire to forge a firm national identity without tolerating any deviation from the norm.

Rojas's claim that there were no Argentine anti-Semites was naive, if not deliberately evasive. In fact, a strong undercurrent of traditional anti-Semitism—probably unconscious—lurked beneath his own words, as when he blamed Jews for provoking anti-Jewish sentiments. Economic factors had originally helped stimulate his nationalism, and they also affected his attitude toward Jews. In his own words, when he arrived in Buenos Aires he experienced shock; "the sensibility of a traditionally creole provincial could not mold itself to the mercantilism of the port." In light of this distaste for commerce, it is significant that he would go on to link Jews with banking and capitalism. These comments were peripheral to the main threads of his argument; nonetheless, they suggest a perspective not too distant from that of Martel, who tied Jews to international finance. When he wrote *La restauración nacionalista*, in the midst of the labor unrest of 1909, Rojas did not recognize its conservative and chauvinistic implications, but others would adapt his cultural nationalism to justify the existing social order. Years later, Rojas fled from the consequences of his ideas, asserting that his aim had been to incorporate the nationalism, freedom, and individualism of the gaucho into a new form of liberal democracy appropriate to Argentine circumstances. In the 1930s he isolated himself from the Rosas school of thought and joined the persecuted Yrigoyenist wing of the Radical party.[33] Nevertheless, some of the ingredients of counterrevolution were present in his work.

Other liberal democrats and even Juan B. Justo held views similar to those of Rojas on Jewish separatism.[34] However, not all non-Jewish intellectuals or even all the cultural nationalists coincided in these beliefs. A significant but temporary exception was Leopoldo Lugones, who seemingly held no view for long. Yet below the surface this contradictory figure was consistent in a few respects. Somehow Lugones reconciled his long career as a minor bureaucrat with his lifelong distaste for the bourgeoisie and for government. First, as a Socialist, he despised class rule; as an anarchist, any rule whatsoever; as an aristocratic liberal, rule of the masses; finally, as an admirer of fascist and military dictatorships, civilian rule. Other constants were his anticlericalism, his aestheticism, his Darwinism, his individualism—and his fervor for his ideological predilection of the moment. Of all these beliefs, perhaps his individualism was the strongest. His faith in the individuals who made up the masses evolved into the exaltation of the superior man or men who led them. Belief in the self-determination of all evolved into a justification of unrestrained liberty for the few who, in his view, merited it. His experiences in Europe, where many intellectuals followed similar trajectories, may have accounted for his changing political views.

During his aristocratic liberal phase, Lugones defended the Jewish schools. In the Jewish newspaper *Vida Nuestra*, in 1908, he insisted that the campaign against the schools, like any manifestation of anti-Semitism, was based on fiction. The so-called Jewish question was a false dilemma that distracted Argentines from the real problems besetting their country. Religious fanatics and tyrants who persecuted Jews for their love of freedom had created the "Jewish question," not the Jews themselves. Jews formed no attachments to countries where they knew only oppression, such as Russia, but they cherished the lands where they knew liberty. For this reason there was no Jewish question in the United States or England.[35] These enlightened attitudes, however, did not prevent Lugones from attacking democracy and the left in his lecture series five years later.

Lugones was one of many Argentines who reexamined their views on foreigners during the years around the centennial. The question of maintaining order in the face of lower-class discontent preoccupied the upper class. Official repression and vigilante action were not enough to neutralize the labor movement and leftist groups, and cultural nationalism had only an indirect effect. Some businessmen, politicians, clergymen, and intellectuals considered other possible solutions to the social question, including employers' organizations, alternative forms of unions, economic nationalism, limited recognition of workers' rights, and social welfare programs. These plans differed in many respects, but all opposed the main goals of the radical left and even an autonomous labor movement.

The most influential ideas of this type emerged from the Argentine branch of the Social Catholic movement. Social Catholicism was the Church's response to the worldwide challenges posed by modernization, liberalism, and leftist doctrines. The Industrial Revolutions had split society into the mutually antagonistic bourgeoisie and proletariat. Representing the former, liberal governments had ruthlessly pursued free-market policies and chipped away at Church privileges, which they regarded as obstacles to progress. Liberals and workers coincided in their anticlericalism or religious indifference, if in nothing else, and Catholic congregations diminished everywhere. Workers' adherence to trade unions, socialism, and anarchism eventually pushed the Church into action. Although the Church had a stake in the status quo, it had no particular affinity for laissez-faire economics. Hence it could support paternalistic legislation, working-class organization for strictly economic ends, and other humanitarian measures with less qualms than its liberal foes. Pope Leo XIII recognized this and urged Catholics to help the poor in his encyclical *Rerum Novarum* in 1891.[36]

Meanwhile in Argentina, the anticlerical measures of the 1880s forced clerics and laypersons to organize in defense of Catholic principles and social ideals. Estrada, Goyena, Lamarca, and other activists discussed such matters at a national congress of Catholics in 1884. Delegates resolved to establish, among other projects, local employment services and Workers' Social Circles. The organization of these Workers' Circles, however, did not get under way until the 1890s, when Father Federico Grote and other members of the Redemptorist order began to work with the poor. Grote founded the first Workers' Circle in 1892. Others arose throughout the country until by 1912, when Father Miguel de Andrea replaced Grote as spiritual director of the Federation of Workers' Circles, there were seventy-seven with a combined membership of 23,000.[37]

Grote stated that his main purpose was not to insure the workers' material well-being, important though this was, but to win souls back to the Church at a time when traditional religious appeals had lost their efficacy. He aimed to save Argentines from the harmful influences of positivism, liberalism, and especially

socialism and anarchism, and to bring them under the benevo-
lent wing of the Church. As he viewed the concept of class
struggle as the principal foe, Grote did not want the Workers'
Circles to become combative arms of the proletariat. Furthermore, he hoped to attract and educate the rich as well as the poor
and to encourage them to work together, breaking down the
rigid division of society into two implacable enemies. For these
reasons, plus the difficulty of finding receptive workers in each
job category, the circles opened their doors to professionals,
businessmen, employers, and laborers of differing levels of skill.
They resembled medieval guilds more than unions. Mutual aid,
education, employment services, and lobbying for social legislation became the circles' main tasks, and their adherents from the
upper class boosted these efforts.[38]

Circle members and their Social Catholic partners worked
with other groups for social reforms. For example, Catholics
and Socialists secured passage of laws granting Sunday rest and
regulating child and female labor in the federal capital in 1905
and 1907, respectively. Joaquín V. González, Roca's minister of
the interior, took suggestions from Socialist and Workers' Circle
leaders when he drafted his proposal for a national labor code in
1904. While Catholics favored this code, businessmen and industrialists opposed it as radical, Socialists and anarchists condemned it as repressive and conservative, and President Roca did
not support it seriously. The bill was defeated.[39]

While Catholics pursued their goals in Congress, Grote and
his colleagues established the Liga Demócrata Cristiana (Democratic Christian League) in 1902 to supplement the Workers'
Circles' action. It formed several unions, including those of dock
workers and weavers, which altogether attracted 5,000 members.
Strictly economic and "moral," the goals of these confessional
unions would be attained through legal, nonviolent means, for
the organizations disavowed opposition to private property and
the constitutional authorities. Employers obstinately refused to
concede even these limited goals, however, and formed counter-
unions to weaken the Catholic ones. Hindered by the disapproval
of many Catholics, including members of the Church hierarchy,
the league folded in 1908.[40]

A more successful venture was launched that year—the Liga Social Argentina (Argentine Social League). Its president and founder was Lamarca; its leading members included future Argentine Patriotic League member and Deputy Santiago O'Farrell, Alejandro E. Bunge, and Fathers Gustavo J. Franceschi and Miguel de Andrea. President of the Central Junta of the Workers' Circles from 1912 to 1916, Bunge also enjoyed a long career as an economist, statistician, and astute critic of Argentine development. He tirelessly studied economic and social problems and publicized the need for reform in his influential *Revista de Economía Argentina* (Review of Argentine Economy).[41]

Franceschi and Andrea had worked closely with Grote in the Workers' Circles, and they would succeed him as leaders of Social Catholic organizations. Franceschi would gain more fame through his subsequent teaching and publishing activities, which were not, however, unrelated to Social Catholicism. At the time of his participation in the Argentine Social League, Andrea was already a Church figure of considerable stature. Best known as an opposition spokesman for "democracy" in the Peronist years, before then his main battle was against the left. His lifelong suspicion of labor autonomy and mass rule influenced these not wholly inconsistent stands and would also lead him into the Argentine Patriotic League.

The organization to which these men belonged at this time, the Argentine Social League, aimed to "sustain the Christian organization of society," fight against "subversive tendencies," and "intellectually and economically lift up" the social classes. It hoped to accomplish these goals through publications, conferences, and its own library system. By 1914 it had 5,743 members and 184 centers around the country.[42]

A unique aspect of the Argentine Social League was its interest in the countryside. Its rural organizers, in particular José Serralunga Langhi, a future Argentine Patriotic League member, tried to convince small farmers to set up cooperative credit unions (*cajas rurales*). Such institutions would provide more loans for farmers, who would not have to turn to foreign sources of financing. Serralunga also believed it necessary to settle remaining government-owned lands and end the latifundia system in order to develop the nation. Setting up cooperatives, he thought, would expedite this process.[43]

It was no coincidence that the year of greatest Catholic rural activity was the one that witnessed the tenant farmer strikes and the rise of the Argentine Agrarian Federation. Fearful of anarchist-led social upheaval in the countryside, although at that moment its worries were groundless, the Argentine Social League organized a rural congress in November 1912, just after the end of the strikes. Eventually it established more than thirty cooperatives, but these groups had little influence on rural life.

Social Catholic priests and laypersons also turned their efforts toward Argentine women. All sectors of opinion in Argentina agreed upon the importance of the family, motherhood, and womanly virtues. Catholics and other traditionalists, however, placed more emphasis on the family's role in preserving stability than did feminists or leftists. Catholics and other traditionalists believed that the social order was based upon the principles of private property, respect for authority, and morality. Mediating institutions such as Church and family spread these principles and thus tamed unruly human instincts. Without the constant vigilance of these institutions, humanity would sink back into barbarism. Echoing Leo XIII, the Catholic activist and future Argentine Patriotic League member Celia La Palma de Emery noted that socialists and anarchists threatened the nation, not only through their aversion to capitalism, but through their desire to end marriage and to curtail family authority. She added that the Catholic family and religion could serve to prevent social revolution.[44]

If the nationality had its roots in the home, then, as Andrea noted, women were "the custodians of our traditions."[45] Throughout the ages they had dedicated themselves to maintaining the family and inculcating children with the virtues of obedience, patriotism, and faith in God. Moreover, women tended to be more pious than men and more heavily involved in charity work. Their roles and their image of love and self-sacrifice resembled the roles and image of the Church itself. Upper-class women could help the Church restore order in society and bring sheep back to the fold. Furthermore, the Social Catholic priests believed that while destructive leftist doctrines had captured the minds of many working-class men, the traditional female qualities had helped immunize working-class women against their ruinous appeal. Thus, even women of humble social origins were natural allies of the Church and counterrevolution—despite their participation in the Socialist party, anarchism, and the Tenant Strike.

Social Catholics held ambivalent views on female autonomy. The political activities they advocated for women did not appear to threaten the prevailing division of sex roles, but simply represented an extension of women's traditional duties. Their stance against female labor outside the home seemed to confirm their conservatism, yet in this regard their attitudes mirrored those of most Argentines, even feminists. Andrea believed that the base of the family was paternal authority. The ideal was for men to work outside the household and for women to "reign at home," renouncing "inappropriate" jobs in factories and offices. He recognized, however, that many women had to work in order to survive and that they deserved an opportunity to acquire skills and self-confidence.[46]

Moreover, Andrea and Franceschi did not necessarily oppose feminism—as long as they could influence it. Andrea realized that women would eventually attain the vote and thus acquire political power. As working women would be the likely leaders of feminism, it would be expedient to prepare them for these roles and, implicitly, insure that they held conservative views. These women could informally spread "healthy" ideas among their female co-workers and thus contribute to "social tranquility." Franceschi noted that voting and other political activities would not necessarily remove women from the home for lengthy periods, at any rate.[47] This paternalistic but ambivalent position on female independence from the private sphere demonstrated that Social Catholics assigned a higher priority to defending property relations than to maintaining gender relations. They were willing to sacrifice some male prerogatives to the cause of containing revolution.

In pursuit of these goals, Social Catholics tried to recruit poor and rich women alike. Their earliest efforts can be traced back to the 1890s, when a German Redemptorist priest, Santiago Barth, established shelters, apprenticeships, and other programs to help protect young female workers from anti-Christian influences and demoralization. In 1891 he founded the Hogar y Asociación de Domésticas (Home and Association of Domestics), which offered shelter and apprenticeships for unemployed women. Male and female delegates to national Catholic meetings in 1906, 1907, and 1908 urged Catholic women to work with female laborers and participate in the Workers' Circles. La Palma de Emery, for example, noted that the circles offered a "beautiful promise of social pacification." She advised fellow Catholics to provide alms to female workers only at moments of desperate need. By stepping in and giving sustenance at those crucial times, Social Catholics would win over the grateful recipients and eventually their whole families from leftist influence.[48]

In response to these appeals, a Jesuit priest, R. P. Segismundo Masferrer, founded the League of Argentine Catholic Ladies in 1911. Its aims were to encourage female factory workers to save their earnings, accumulate a dowry, and fulfill their "Christian social duty," that is, spurn leftism and prepare for marriage. Preservation of the family and the female domestic sphere clearly fit into these goals. Workers' savings, contributions, and proceeds of benefit functions were deposited in the Catholic Ladies' bank, which in turn financed workers' restaurants, a lodging house for homeless women, and other projects.[49] Another, more combative arm of Social Catholic womanhood was the Daughters of Mary, discussed earlier.

The Catholics also organized confessional unions among women. The first of these, established by the Democratic Christian League in 1904, was the weavers' union, which survived the Democratic Christian League's collapse in 1908. Bartolomé Ayrolo, a priest in Avellaneda, a working-class suburb of Buenos Aires, created a more important all-female union in 1917: the Sociedad "La Cruz" de Obreras Fosforeras ("The Cross" Society of Female Match Workers). The original membership of 175 match workers from four factories grew to 650 and fifteen locals in Avellaneda and Buenos Aires within a year. The union refused to accept former members of "anti-Catholic" or militant workers' groups, and it denied being a "society of resistance," but it did not abjure the strike weapon. Nevertheless, it met more opposition from other laborers than from employers.[50]

Young upper-class women led another attempt to organize their lower-class sisters. Franceschi awakened their interest when he spoke on the social mission of women at a prestigious Catholic high school in Buenos Aires in 1916. Inspired by his message, a group of students decided to meet regularly with Franceschi to read and discuss Catholic doctrine and its application to modern problems. The Centro de Estudios "Blanca de Castilla" ("Blanca de Castilla" Studies Center) was thus founded. The center also conducted research on such critical issues as female and child labor, women in unions, child vagrancy, and the working and living conditions of the poor. The results of these investigations appeared in pamphlets, short monographs, and legislative proposals, which the girls distributed in the streets and even sent to members of Congress, including the Socialist leader Alfredo Palacios, a former Workers' Circle member.[51]

Organizing confessional unions proved to be the center's most important achievement. Its members went to considerable lengths to talk to female laborers, pursuing them from their workplaces to their homes and eating meals with them. These efforts bore fruit between 1917 and 1918, when the center created "Catholic syndicates" of female laborers in Nueva Pompeya (an industrial neighborhood of Buenos Aires), female store employees, and seamstresses. The three syndicates offered employment, medical, educational, legal, and religious services to the 719 members they attracted by 1919. Their goal was to further the economic and professional interests of their constituents in a legal, peaceful, and nonrevolutionary manner. Employers did not resist the syndicates, perhaps because they never resorted to strikes. Center members deliberately retained the leadership positions in the first two syndicates, and advisory status in the seamstresses' union. The unions' requirements for affiliation also manifested the counterrevolutionary sentiments of their founders. Only applicants with "good conduct" records from employers were accepted, and the seamstresses' union emphasized respect for "Religion, Fatherland, Family, and Property" as a qualification for membership. The center's free classes on home economics and religion, as well as its church services, also reinforced the social housekeeping tendency of the Social Catholics. Nevertheless, center members had entered the public sphere to attain their conservative goals. Female control over the fledgling unions ended abruptly in 1922, when Andrea's Federación de Asociaciones Católicas de Empleadas (FACE, Federation of Catholic Associations of Female Employees) absorbed them—to the bitterness of the union founders.[52]

Andrea's assertion of control over the syndicates revealed the limits of his "feminism." It was also consistent with his disapproval of worker mobility and self-rule, however imperfectly the syndicates embodied these principles. He revealed these sentiments in a sermon in 1912, in which he noted that laborers commonly visualized work as a humiliating consequence of their social inferiority. Many believed that once their standing improved, work would become pleasurable. Such persons would always be seeking increases in salary and pleasure. The true Christian knew that labor was the legacy of man's fall from grace, and that man could redeem himself spiritually by patiently bearing this cross. Far from being inferior, the common laborers occupied a dignified and hallowed position in the social hierarchy, for Jesus, venerated by rich and poor alike, had been one of them.[53] Workers should not strive to change the natural order of things; to do so would be un-Christian and immoral. Instead, they should content themselves with improving their circumstances within the existing order and receiving charity from the rich, who were obligated to extend it to them.

Although Andrea claimed to welcome mass rule, the type of democracy he envisioned was a limited one. In 1913 he wrote that democracy carried within it the seeds of danger. Anarchy would accompany the fall of social and political barriers to the masses if the practice of Christian morality did not temper democratic rule. Christian morality meant individual sacrifice in emulation of Christ on earth.[54] In Andrea's view, therefore, the masses should not assert themselves or protest against the system, for to do so would evince greed and egotism. His model of "democracy" denied autonomy to the lower class. As such, it harked back to statements by earlier Catholic spokesmen such as Estrada, and it presaged future remarks by other Argentine Patriotic League members.

Andrea's paternalism demonstrated the chasm between the Social Catholics and those who sought to radically transform society. Nevertheless, his five decades of accomplishments attested to a genuine social concern. Despite the counterrevolutionary aims of his program, many priests and members of the upper class viewed it as radical, unnecessary, or both. Before the Radicals came to power, Congress passed few concrete measures to alleviate the ills that spawned leftism. It established a national labor department (1907), which gathered information on working-class conditions, formulated legislative proposals, and helped arbitrate disputes between labor and capital. Catholic Deputy Juan F. Cafferata's potentially important law of 1915, setting up government-sponsored low-cost housing construction, did not receive adequate funding. Other legislation included a workers' compensation act (1915) and a legal aid law (1913), but these measures, as well as a Sunday rest law and regulation of child and female labor, were not well enforced.[55]

Social legislation received support from a small reformist sector within the upper class. Its prime motivation was to conserve as much of the existing social system as possible in the face of working-class demands. Social Catholic views influenced many of these reformers, as did simple nostalgia for the traditional society in which the extremes of wealth and poverty had not been as evident. This paternalistic viewpoint characterized some figures of officialdom as well as some Radicals, including Yrigoyen. Before Yrigoyen became president, however, his party showed little concern for the foreign-born proletariat which, when it voted at all, favored Socialism.

These reformers also manifested their interest in the social

question outside of government, through research on the condition of the masses. One influential group that carried out such
investigations was the Museo Social Argentino (Argentine Social
Museum), founded by Tomás Amadeo, a leading agronomist,
landowner, and public servant, in 1911. His many works on
trade unionism, agrarian reform, and urban social problems reflected his lifelong concern for these issues. Amadeo also was a
PDP activist and future Argentine Patriotic League member.

According to Amadeo, the Social Museum aimed to forge
solidarity between all human beings "through the economic perfecting of the proletarian classes and the moral perfecting of all
the social classes." He admitted that the workers' question did
not represent an exotic import irrelevant to Argentine conditions, for inflation, unemployment, and poverty were realities
there as well as in Europe. His view of anarchism as a "social
disease suffered by a nucleus, unfortunately numerous, of degenerates and criminals," was not as unique.[56] Still, Amadeo stressed
the need for research and not repression. The museum's collaborators included such future Argentine Patriotic League members as Lamarca, General Proto Ordóñez, Manuel A. Montes de
Oca, Eleodoro Lobos, and Joaquín de Anchorena. Carlos Ibarguren and Gustavo Martínez Zuviría were two other museum
members who became counterrevolutionaries. Other groups
such as the Workers' Circles, the aristocratic Jockey Club, and
the Unión Industrial Argentina, the industrialists' lobby group,
helped fund the museum's research, social projects, and publications.

The museum's monthly bulletin was an excellent source on
strikes, feminism, immigration, the cost of living, workers'
needs, agricultural development, and other social matters. Although some of the journal contributors opposed measures that
would strengthen the workers' sense of class consciousness, the
museum did not come out against workers' organizations per se.
Most of its collaborators advocated the formation of mutual aid
societies, cooperatives, and even unions for workers and other
social groups, as long as they aimed at specific economic improvements and not the restructuring of society. Mutualism in

particular received the museum's endorsement, and its leading spokesman within the institution, and within the upper class, was Carlos Ibarguren.

Member of an illustrious family of Salta, Ibarguren was tied to the Generation of Eighty and the elite through his father, a close friend of Roca, and through his relatives the Uriburus. Despite these connections and the government positions he held before 1916, he never identified himself completely with the *régimen*. Echoing the Catholic politicians and the revolutionaries of 1890, he frequently criticized what he considered its egoism, skepticism, and materialism. Ibarguren first manifested his social preoccupations in an article he wrote in 1897, at the age of twenty. He noted that the liberals' much-vaunted equality did not exist for the workers. Although the old social barriers had fallen, a new upper class had arisen that was worse than the old feudal nobility—the capitalist bourgeoisie. Faced with this enemy, labor had resorted to class struggle. Ibarguren hoped that social measures would dissuade the proletariat from carrying out a violent revolution.[57]

The Radicals and other upper-class politicians believed instead that electoral reform would suffice to heal society's ills. Ibarguren, like Andrea, did not share this faith. In 1912 Ibarguren declared that enlarging the electorate would not insure the proper functioning of democracy. Democracy would be achieved only when organizations capable of responding to "concrete," "collective" interests would participate in government without upsetting the social equilibrium. Many years would pass until this structure would form, he warned, and meanwhile Argentina would be prey to "disoriented oscillation." Even Ibarguren did not realize how long this process would take.

A new factor had entered Argentine society and politics, Ibarguren continued. Justifiably seeking a more equitable distribution of wealth, the workers had united. No one had any reason to fear their struggle, as long as strong moderate forces operated to halt any possible excesses. In Ibarguren's opinion, unity of the "conservative classes" could ward off the extremist threat. He believed, however, that this unity was sadly lacking. The real

danger did not come from the proletariat but from "utopian theories," which could capture the minds of judges and legislators as
easily as those of workers. The former could translate them into
imprudent reforms rather than allow social processes to evolve
into viable solutions.[58] Ibarguren's organic concern for social equilibrium, ambivalence toward democracy, and advocacy of organizations representing "real" interests indicated his counterrevolutionary sentiments.

Ibarguren's speech won praise from President Sáenz Peña, who
appointed him to a succession of positions in his government.
Ibarguren commended Sáenz Peña for his efforts to purify the
political system, but he advised him to bolster the structures of
political democracy with those of social democracy. He wanted
the government to recognize and fund the institutions that immigrants had erected to help each other in cases of illness, old age,
and want. In 1914 there were 214 such institutions with more
than 250,000 members in Buenos Aires.[59] By supporting these
thriving mutual aid societies, the government would work in
harmony with the natural social processes that had brought them
into existence, instead of imposing new artificial institutions.
With the president's approval, Ibarguren drafted a social assistance law and presented it to Congress in 1913. A few months
later Sáena Peña died, and without his presence and support the
bill died as well.

Ibarguren joined de la Torre and other friends in the PDP and
wrote its platform, which included a plank on mutualism. He remained in the PDP after it lost the 1916 election and continued to
press for government recognition of mutual aid societies. In
March 1918, Ibarguren organized a conference on mutualism
sponsored by the Social Museum. Delegates from about 300 labor, employee, professional, and ethnic associations, as well as
a few university departments and government agencies, met to
discuss legislation. The three-day proceedings did not attract
government attention nor did they achieve any concrete results.[60]

Ibarguren continued his activities in the museum and in politics, running unsuccessfully as the PDP candidate for president in
1922. The *régimen*'s hostility toward his party and its poor elec-

toral record disillusioned him, as did what he labeled the "demagoguery" of the Yrigoyen administration. The politicians' greater
interest in narrow partisan concerns rather than in community
welfare convinced him that politics was inevitably corrupt and
inefficient. Governments of neither the liberal-conservative stripe
nor the democratic would ever solve the social question or truly
represent the people. Dismayed with the inertia of the Argentine
political system—and with their own inability to unite and exert
influence—Ibarguren and other reformers moved into the ranks
of counterrevolution.

It is not surprising that reformers and cultural nationalists preoccupied by foreign cultural and ideological influences, like
Ibarguren, Rojas, and Gálvez, were also concerned about foreign
capitalist inroads. They favored promoting domestically owned
enterprises and regulating or even expelling foreign capital, all in
the interest of national sovereignty. Economic nationalism was
not inherently counterrevolutionary, for the Latin American left
has supported home industries more loudly and consistently
than has the right. Sometimes, however, economic nationalism
was linked with other attitudes: exaggerated conceptions of the
nation's needs and defenses, racism and chauvinism, antileftist
sentiments, and a conspiratorial frame of mind. In these con-
texts, as in the case of Martel, economic nationalism was counterrevolutionary.

For example, some capitalist spokesmen combined economic
nationalism with conservative viewpoints on workers' rights and
social mobility. They noted that before mass immigration, relations between employers and laborers were harmonious. Now,
however, foreign workers influenced by their European experiences believed that their interests were directly opposed to those
of the capitalists. Perhaps this was true in industrialized Europe,
but in Argentina it was not the case. Beleaguered by high costs,
low tariffs, and foreign competition, Argentine industries were
young, small, and insecure. Labor demands and strikes added to
these costs and made it even more difficult to stay in business. If
industries and other enterprises closed, workers would starve.
Clearly, their natural interest coincided with that of manage-

ment: to raise production. If workers would accept this view, employers would set equitable wages and insure laborers' well-being. If, however, workers persisted in consolidating themselves as a hostile, falsely separate class, they would deliberately thwart national development and invite employers' retaliation.[61]

When workers organized themselves, some firms created counterassociations, thus contradicting management's "individualism." These employer groups used all means at their disposal to destroy unions so they could treat workers on an individual basis. Adhering companies locked out and blacklisted union members, while simultaneously hiring strikebreakers and organizing them into "yellow" unions.

Because anarchist activities focused on the ports, the vital links of the import–export trade, the most important yellow unions also arose there. In 1905 six railroad companies and the powerful Centro de Navegación Transatlántica (Transatlantic Navigation Center), a group of maritime firms, established the Sociedad Unión Protectora de Trabajo Libre (Protective Union Society of Free Labor). The Protective Union's regulations governed the hiring, firing, and work conditions of the laborers who constituted its pool of strikebreakers in Buenos Aires, Rosario, Bahía Blanca, and other ports. In 1917 the largest coastal shipper, the Mihanovich firm, created a similar company union, the Sociedad Obrera Marítima Protectora del Trabajo Libre (Protective Maritime Worker Society of Free Labor), as a counterweight to the syndicalist Federacion Obrera Marítima (FOM, Maritime Worker Federation). Both of these yellow unions, however, disbanded in the face of labor militancy.[62]

These "free labor" societies set precedents for another, bolder management initiative. Huge waterfront and railroad strikes in 1917 and 1918, as well as Yrigoyen's seeming partiality to labor (discussed in the next chapter), convinced the Transatlantic Navigation Center of the need for an organization broader than the old strikebreaking groups. The new body would continue these activities, but it would also extend them to businesses other than transportation.

To meet these needs, in July 1918 the Asociación del Trabajo

(Labor Association) was created. Pedro Christophersen, a Norwegian landowner, shipper, and head of the stock exchange, was its first president, and its other founding members included delegates from the Transatlantic Navigation Center and firms supplying shippers; five railroad companies; wool and grain exporters; the tram company and electric utilities; organizations of import–export firms and food-processing companies; the Argentine Industrial Union; and the powerful Sociedad Rural Argentina (Argentine Rural Society). The deceptively titled group aimed at improving "moral" and material standards for workers through better salaries, old-age pensions, and workers' compensation. The Labor Association would also lobby for business interests among government officials. Its main priority, however, was to protect the employers' right to freely hire and dismiss workers. The Labor Association represented the union of landowners and businessmen whose interests depended on a docile labor force.[63]

Labor Association members saw their concerns as synonymous with Argentine progress; they viewed an assertive labor movement as alien, antinational, and harmful. This perception of labor, combined with the other attitudes discussed here, formed the basis for counterrevolution. Laborers refused to be compliant in the difficult years during and after World War I. Without a strong conservative party to defend them, property holders reacted violently to the threat of massive social upheaval. This reaction, embodied in the Argentine Patriotic League, is the subject of the next chapter.

THREE

The Rise of the Argentine
Patriotic League

All the ingredients of counterrevolutionary thought were present in Argentina by 1918. Missing was a catalyst that would act upon these ingredients and convert them into action, although one had briefly appeared in 1910. The universal political, economic, and social crisis at the end of World War I served as this catalyst, impelling persons from a variety of backgrounds into the ranks of counterrevolution. Convinced that the Radical government was incapable of defending the status quo against the leftist threat, or unwilling to do so, the Argentine Patriotic League stepped in to fill what it perceived as a power vacuum. Its relationship with the regime, which did not share this perception, was filled with tension and ambivalence.

During the years immediately following World War I, Europe was the scene of convulsion. The demands of war, the massive destruction of lives and property, and the frustrations of peace-making weakened the political, social, and economic structures of the combatant nations. Thrones toppled and the old European empires splintered into new republics lacking firm national identities and experience in self-government. The bolshevik takeover seemed to herald a frightening new era in world history: that of the socialist revolution. Inflation and unemployment greeted the veterans returning from the front and created hardship throughout Europe. Inspired by events in Russia, workers struck, rioted, and occupied factories, while peasants seized landed estates. The specter of revolution became reality in Germany and Hungary. Civil guards formed all over Europe to contain labor radicalism. Even in the United States, a wartime legacy of hyperbolic patriotism and a series of strikes promoted hysterical fear of leftism. Organizations such as the American Protective League and the American Legion expressed these anxieties and contributed to the "Red Scare."

Argentina did not enter the war. Linked through trade, investment, and culture to Europe, however, Argentina also experienced its share of economic dislocation, labor disturbances, and revolutionary stirrings. From 1913 to 1917 the nation suffered through a severe depression, probably worse than that of the 1930s. The lack of new investment and the inability to import machines, fuel, and primary materials hampered industrial growth. Construction, transportation, and most branches of industry slumped during the war years, only to begin a slow recovery in 1918. From 1914 to 1918 the cost of living in Buenos Aires climbed 71 percent, while salaries fell 38 percent.[1] Urban workers faced a huge gap between salaries and the spiraling prices of necessity items, or at worst, unemployment. According to one estimate, unemployment among workers in the capital reached at least 30 percent in 1917.[2]

Bleak conditions also prevailed in the countryside. Grain prices jumped during the war, but lack of cargo space and shortages of machinery and other essential items caused grain exports to decline, resulting in acreage reductions. After the war, grain exports revived briefly, but sank again under the force of world overproduction. Prices for livestock and livestock products shot up during the war. Meat and wool exports soared and the ranching interests profited enormously. Overseas demand declined after the war, however, and the prices and sales of livestock products fell accordingly. These conditions, combined with the rising cost of living, spelled low wages and unemployment for landless rural workers in the littoral region and Patagonia and high indebtedness and eviction rates for tenant farmers in the grain zone. Large landowners in the postwar period were justifiably anxious about the future.

The economic and social climate also preoccupied other groups. The rising cost of living affected all consumers, while the slump in commerce and industry hurt businessmen and their employees. Furthermore, this stagnation limited already narrow employment opportunities for the middle class.

The news of radicalism abroad served as further cause for alarm among the middle and upper classes. Dramatic newspaper headlines reminded readers daily of European events and of massive strikes in neighboring countries. The increased momentum of labor activity suggested the gravity of this threat. By the war's inception, the labor movement had recovered from the earlier period of repression, and a few years after that point it again demonstrated its strength. Tremendous strikes broke out in the crucial transportation and meatpacking sectors from late 1916 through 1918. Inspired by the Russian Revolution and the first signs of urban recovery, workers' confidence grew, as did their unions and protests. By early 1919, the most vigorous federation, FORA IX, claimed 83,000 affiliates, or about 16 percent of the labor force in the capital, growing to 24 percent by the end of the year.[3] The number of strikes and strikers in the capital increased from 80 and 24,300 in 1916 to 367 and 309,000 in 1919, respectively.[4] Perhaps most threatening to the landowners was the spread of conflict to the countryside. Assisted by both FORAS, landless rural workers were mobilizing for the first time.

Significantly, Yrigoyen's stance on labor differed from that of his predecessors in office. Like previous presidents, he was no advocate of unions. Nevertheless, he saw the role of the state as one of promoting social harmony between classes, rather than one of simply repressing labor. Manuel Gálvez later concluded approvingly that in its opposition to class struggle, among other features, Yrigoyenism was more rightist than leftist and, indeed, resembled Italian fascism. It also was pragmatic, for one of its aims was to attract working-class votes. Yrigoyen appealed to workers by manipulating his image. As he had done before assuming the presidency, he donated his salary to charity. Moreover, he lived austerely in a small apartment, which his opponents dubbed "the cave," in an unfashionable neighborhood. Aristocratic critics claimed that at the end of the day he left the Casa Rosada (Pink House, the presidential palace) for "the cave" through the service exit. Yrigoyen's views on class conciliation, however, found little expression in social legislation before 1919. In mid-1918 he proposed bills reforming the Sunday rest law and regulating labor in the home. The opposition-dominated Congress refused to act on the first law and approved the second. During the same year, his government bought foreign sugar and sold it to the public at low prices, yet Radical deputies also backed a law doubling the tariff rate on imported shoes, thus undermining the party's consumerism.[5]

The upper class found his dealings with organized labor more disturbing than his populist image or social legislation. To take votes away from the Socialists, Yrigoyen extended some qualified support to workers in the capital. He limited his dealings with labor to this location, reasoning that rural laborers either did not vote or followed their employers' electoral preferences, and that the Socialists posed little challenge to the Radicals in other cities. He further restricted his ties to syndicalists, who constituted a pool of potential voters because they attracted the native-born and, unlike anarchists, did not unequivocally oppose participation in elections or compromises with the system. Moreover, by this time syndicalists formed the strongest labor faction.

Before 1919 the Yrigoyen government did not deport activists nor did it call a state of siege. No longer were the police and army necessarily at the employers' disposal. Unlike previous presidents, Yrigoyen met with labor representatives and invited them to talk with his ministers. He and other officials personally intervened in major strikes between 1916 and 1918, sometimes to labor's benefit. In the meatpacking strike of 1917, however, the government favored the interests of the powerful foreign companies, indicating the circumscribed nature of Yrigoyen's *obrerismo* (proworkerism), as his critics called it.

Yrigoyen's support for labor was, therefore, conditional and largely symbolic. Nevertheless, the elite which already disdained him took seriously his public image as the friend of the common man, perceiving him as being further to the left than he really was. His more evenhanded approach to capital–labor disputes annoyed important businessmen and stimulated the formation of the Labor Association. Reflecting these sentiments, a U.S. diplo-

mat observed in August 1918 that the president's "greatest interest has been to support labor."[6] Seemingly shortsighted, these
perceptions were nonetheless crucial in determining the rise of
the Argentine Patriotic League.

The Radical president also antagonized opposition parties
in other ways. The intransigence which had served him well
through decades of struggle against the *régimen* continued to
characterize his policies after his victory in 1916. Lacking control
over Congress or provincial governorships, Yrigoyen entered the
presidency from a position of weakness. The party's mandate
could not be filled under these circumstances. Therefore, he frequently intervened in the provinces to reduce opposition fraud
and consolidate his backing, continuing a nationalizing trend begun by Roca. He pursued confrontational tactics in Congress in
order to circumvent initiatives of rival parties. His blatantly partisan motives irritated Socialists, conservative reformers, and
régimen hacks alike. Only a few years into Yrigoyen's term, his
offensive began to alarm members of the old political elite. They
responded in kind to Yrigoyen's political maneuvers. Ambassador Stimson noted that although the ideological differences between the UCR and the *régimen* forces were superficial, the latter
dedicated themselves to obstructing Yrigoyen's proposals, "sometimes in the most inconceivably puerile manner."[7]

Another Yrigoyen stance that irritated the elite was his neutrality. Traditional ties to Western Europe and to French culture
converted many Argentines—and not only those of the upper
class—into sympathizers of the Allies. His nationalistic motives notwithstanding, Yrigoyen's neutrality struck them as pro-
German and as an affront to Western civilization. Some Argentines went abroad to help France in the war effort, while others
formed associations supporting the Allies. One of these was the
Comité pro Aliados (Pro-Allies Committee), which attracted
6,000 adherents. Young journalists and intellectuals including
Gerchunoff, Rojas, Palacios, and future counterrevolutionary activists Lugones, Alfonso de Laferrère, Francisco Uriburu, and
Mariano Villar Sáenz Peña formed its youth branch, the Comité
Nacional de la Juventud (National Youth Committee), in Octo-

ber 1918.[8] Villar Sáenz Peña, its leader, was a landowner and former federal police bureaucrat who was closely related to two past presidents and sympathetic to the UCR; Uriburu and Laferrère were PDP leaders.

During the last weeks of the war, the Youth Committee organized rallies and public speeches supporting the Allies. After the armistice, it planned a mammoth demonstration in the capital on November 13 to celebrate the Allied victory—and to protest against the government. Rumors spread that members of the various pro-Allies groups would try to force Yrigoyen to resign. The night before the demonstration, the president declared November 14 an official holiday in celebration of peace, forestalling plans for his ouster.[9]

Despite the end of the war, the Youth Committee was reluctant to disband. Hatred of Yrigoyen and enthusiasm for the Allies had not been its members' sole motivations. Their enthusiasm was part of a wider feeling characteristic of young, educated Europeans and Argentines in this period: idealism, desire for participation in a larger cause, elevation of action above rational judgment.[10] To members of the Youth Committee, neutrality had cut Argentines off not only from traditional loyalties, but from an absorbing and uplifting activity in which they longed to participate. Their idealism and vitalism were also tied to patriotism and nationalism; citizenship, in their view, meant belonging to a dynamic entity, the state, which was greater than the sum of its human components. This represented a change from classical liberalism, which held that the nation represented merely a pact of individuals.

Some of these young idealists—Lugones, for example—had previously flirted with socialism and anarchism. With their discovery of nationalism, a process speeded by the war, they shed their leftist allegiances. Juan Carulla, a former philosophical anarchist and doctor who served in France, described his shift from left to right in his memoirs. His wartime experiences showed him the dark side of human nature and taught him that humanitarian utopianism was illusory. The only reality was the nation, not abstract notions such as mankind or class. Carulla ignored the patriotism of most German and French socialists, asserting that such parties had not contributed to the war effort and therefore nationalists would have to oppose them. Embracing nationalism did not mean giving up all ideas of revolutionary change; the (temporary) alliance between Georges Sorel's syndicalists and the disciples of Charles Maurras, the French monarchist, proved to Carulla that action and revolution could be harnessed to the cause of the nation.[11]

With the armistice, the Youth Committee lost an outlet for its members' activism. It searched for another raison d'être and soon found it in internal rather than foreign affairs. In a speech entitled "The New Generation's Profession of Faith," Rojas told a large audience at the San Martín Theater, on January 2, 1919, that the Youth Committee would become a political party. He declared that critical economic and cultural issues demanded new responses. The Sáenz Peña Law and the election of 1916 had destroyed the "conservative" parties, the UCR was a mere personalistic clique, and the Socialists emphasized materialism to the detriment of the spirit. The heterogeneous "mercantile" population lacked ideals and faith, which it was unlikely to receive from these bankrupt parties. In contrast, the Youth Committee was prepared to carry out the essential renovation of society. It was the mouthpiece of a new generation that opposed aggressive militarism, a hereditary aristocracy, economic individualism, immorality, imperialism, utilitarian pragmatism, and mechanistic theories of progress. Gerchunoff, Laferrère, and others left the Youth Committee in opposition to its new orientation. (It is not clear whether Palacios or Rojas ever resigned from the group.) Rojas explicitly pitted the group against the ruling party—again setting the scene for counterrevolution without actually joining its ranks himself. A week after the speech, the group further clarified its anti-Yrigoyenism by criticizing the government's attacks on provincial autonomy, its disorderly financial policy, and its "empirical and shortsighted social policy toward labor questions."[12]

The reoriented Youth Committee claimed to oppose the old liberal conservatism as much as it did "antispiritual" socialism.

Supposedly it favored democracy, but not Yrigoyen's personalistic version. In late 1919, Youth Committee leaders united
with other forces against the Radicals, and they supported the
PDP in the 1920 elections, a losing venture.[13] Nevertheless, the
group had already left its mark on Argentine politics through its
activities during the Tragic Week of January 1919.

One can trace the origins of the Tragic Week back to the fervent labor mobilization of the period and, specifically, to a strike
at a large metallurgical factory in the capital which began in December 1918.[14] The Vasena company hired strikebreakers, and
the government assigned policemen, firemen, and soldiers to
guard its installations. Throughout December and the first week
of January 1919, security forces and strikers regularly exchanged
fire. In one of these incidents a policeman died, arousing the ire
of his cohorts. Their anger erupted on January 7, when police
gunfire killed four laborers, three of whom were in their homes,
and wounded twenty to forty others; the security forces suffered
no casualties.

This unwarranted bloodshed angered the working class. On
January 9 thousands marched to the cemetery for the funeral of
the slain workers. Numerous incidents occurred along the way,
climaxing in a battle between them and police at Chacarita.
Nearly 1,000 workers surrounded and attacked the Vasena factory offices, where management and Labor Association officers
were conferring. An entire day passed before policemen, firemen, and soldiers quelled the workers, and about a hundred persons were injured in the battle.

On January 9, in response to the metallurgical union's plea, a
general strike began. It did not receive immediate or unqualified
support from the FORAS, but it did attract many individual
workers. Giant demonstrations, looting, street fighting, and the
paralysis of commerce and transportation accompanied the general strike. Sympathy strikes also broke out in the provinces of
Buenos Aires, Córdoba, Santa Fe, and Mendoza.

Labor Association President Christophersen demanded government intervention after his rescue from the besieged Vasena
offices. About this time, General Luis Dellepiane entered the city

leading troops from nearby Campo de Mayo. It is not clear whether the government requested his participation or whether Dellepiane took the initiative. Fortunately for Yrigoyen, the powerful general was an old Radical sympathizer and had no intention of overthrowing the government, although other officers and civilians may have urged him to do so. The former federal police chief did intend, however, to impose law and order. The government accepted his presence and named him head of all forces in the capital.[15]

Not long after troops arrived on January 9 and 10, the worker-led violence ceased. A few days later, metallurgical union members, government officials, and FORA IX leaders formulated terms for ending the strike, which Yrigoyen convinced company officials to accept. Not all the strikers, however, returned to work according to this timetable. The events of the Tragic Week revealed the divisions and weaknesses in the labor movement, as well as the masses' discontent.

Nevertheless, the violence and mass mobilization convinced many frightened *porteños* that the government had lost control and that revolution was around the corner. News of the Sparticist revolt in Germany, strikes and rallies in Chile, and an alleged "maximalist" (communist) plot in Montevideo fed their fears. The economic problems and labor threat also fueled anti-Semitic sentiments. Many *porteños* now suspected the Jews of bolshevik as well as anarchistic tendencies, again because of their largely Russian origins.

In the early hours of January 10, civilians and police vented these feelings by attacking working-class neighborhoods, destroying labor offices, libraries, newspaper presses, and cultural centers and beating, shooting, and arresting thousands, including many innocent bystanders. Similar actions occurred in Barrio Once, Caballito, and Villa Crespo, areas with many Jewish residents. There, the marauders destroyed community organization sites and private property; they killed at least one person and wounded seventy-one others.[16] The excesses of this foray embarrassed Dellepiane, who attempted to restrain the men under his command. He sent a note to police precinct headquarters, pointing out that most Jews were peaceful, hard-working members of society and asking them not to equate Jews with strikers. One police official later recalled that Dellepiane warned against civilian actions and asked private citizens not to carry out arrests.[17]

Yet the Radical general and his party bore some responsibility for the persecution of workers and Jews. According to another policeman's account, Dellepiane authorized the infantry's security squadron to distribute revolvers and ammunition to numerous civilian volunteers, presumably with Yrigoyen's approval. Officers passed out arms quickly and carelessly, without asking for identification or receipts. These white guards resembled the Auxiliary Civil Police that Dellepiane had created in 1910. Radical organizations may have recruited some of the vigilantes who attacked Jewish neighborhoods specifically for that purpose. Moreover, disproportionately high arrest rates among Jews and the detention of the Russian Jewish leaders of the "First Argentine Soviet" seemed to confirm the traditional anti-Semites' identification of Judaism with communism.[18] Later the authorities admitted that the "soviet" had been imaginary and that its supposed president was a moderate, pacifistic socialist opposed to bolshevism. These delayed disclosures, however, received markedly less publicity than the arrests and had little effect on public opinion.

The white terror continued from the tenth to the fourteenth. Young Radicals joined Youth Committee members as they roamed the city searching for action, or, as they put it, "maintaining order." Such persons also numbered among those who gathered in police precinct headquarters to form neighborhood patrols. Francisco Uriburu organized the first of these patrols on the night of the tenth. Guarding the first precinct, which included much of the business district, this militia consisted solely of Youth Committee members. Others, like the patrol of the seventeenth precinct, the prestigious Barrio Norte, included naval officers and prominent older citizens. So, too, did the thirteenth precinct militia, formed on January 11. Although this neighborhood, Caballito, contained many Jews, none belonged to the militia. Future Argentine Patriotic League president Manuel Carlés was a member, but whether he or other militia members participated in the pogrom of the tenth is unknown.

The Navy had begun to coordinate civilian actions. Since the beginning of the general strike, naval officers and hundreds of youths, many from the Youth Committee, gathered at the Centro Naval (Naval Center), a club for active and retired naval officers on fashionable Florida Street. Rear Admiral Manuel Domecq García ordered the distribution of arms and vehicles to the young men, and other officers, including Captain Jorge Yalour and one Malbrán, of unknown rank, instructed the volunteers on the use of arms.

As the Argentine military had traditionally repressed violent strikes and rebellions against the government, these actions represented little departure from the past. Movement from the officer corps into the top ranks of the federal police, another vital order-keeping force, was common. Agreeing with Uriburu that leftists undermined national security, many of his fellow officers became impatient with Yrigoyen's relative restraint—particularly when they discovered the existence of two soviets in army ranks. Moreover, the same yearnings for action found in young civilians may have characterized younger officers, considering the long time that had elapsed since the military's last foreign engagement. Yrigoyen's propensity for casting himself as labor's friend, while diverting blame for repression onto the armed forces, was also beginning to irritate military leaders.[19]

As the army had usually shouldered the major burden of internal defense, it is not clear why the navy took the initiative in organizing the vigilantes. Perhaps the administration's tactics had alienated the navy more than the army because Yrigoyen had ordered the marines to repress the meatpacking strike of 1917, the most significant case of UCR labor repression up to that point and the last important strike before the Tragic Week. Also, naval officers may not have wished to leave the entire task of keeping order to their interservice rivals. Finally, army leaders tended to sympathize with Germany, whose officers had trained them, whereas the navy emulated Great Britain and, like the Youth Committee, tended to favor the Allies.

The Youth Committee also helped coordinate the vigilantes. On the night of January 10, almost a day after the civilian repression began, some of its members gathered in the Confitería París, on the edge of the wealthy Barrio Norte, to discuss the general strike. Claiming to support the administration, they wrote to the federal police chief and Radical leader Elpidio González requesting deputization as a special order-keeping force. González rejected their proposal. The next day, Youth Committee members and many sympathizers, including Radicals, met at the Naval Center and decided to offer their assistance to Dellepiane. The general's response to this offer is the subject of conflicting reports, but it seems that he told Villar Sáenz Peña that their help was unnecessary. Dellepiane also advised the Youth Committee leader to work together with the Naval Center. That same day, Domecq García and Yalour presented Yrigoyen with a statement signed by many "gentlemen" pledging their support in maintaining order.

Throngs of young Radicals and government opponents alike wrote Yrigoyen, appeared at police headquarters, the Naval Center, or at Youth Committee offices downtown, or tried other means to volunteer for service. Domecq García invited more than 500 of these persons to the Naval Center on Sunday morning, the twelfth, to join a standing citywide guard. Inscription of volunteers began at the meeting and continued through the next few days; by Monday evening alone, 1,000 men had signed up. With the formation of the guard, Villar Sáenz Peña announced that the Youth Committee's mission was complete. Belatedly accepting Dellepiane's suggestion, he placed his men and lists of sympathizers at the disposition of the navy. Domecq García was now the undisputed head of the counterrevolutionary forces.

The night of the twelfth, following the meeting of volunteers, Domecq García and other directors of the Naval Center planned the organization of the new group. They decided to bring the other branch of the military into these deliberations. The next day Domecq García asked the Círculo Militar (Military Circle), the army officers' club, to send a delegate to a meeting in the Naval Center on January 15. The meeting would focus on affairs of "social interest" related to recent events.[20] Keeping Dellepiane informed, Domecq García gave him lists of the civil guard members registered in the Naval Center on the thirteenth and fourteenth. The general assured Domecq García that the government commanded sufficient forces, but he approved of the civilian mobilizations in precinct headquarters. Whether he genuinely favored this idea or simply accepted it as a fait accompli and avoided antagonizing the navy was not clear.

The Tragic Week ended, but many Argentines continued to fear a revolutionary outbreak. Demonstrations against maximalism took place in Santa Fe and other parts of the interior. In the Buenos Aires area, citizens continued to patrol the streets, and threats against Jews persisted. Fear for their personal safety and possessions even drove Jews into the forces of counterrevolution. Anxious to distinguish themselves from radical elements, some community leaders spoke with Dellepiane, insisting that most Jews were dependable, law-abiding merchants, professionals, farmers, and artisans. These same men formed the self-styled Comité Oficial Israelita (Official Jewish Committee), which on January 15 published an appeal from "150,000 Israelites to the People of the Republic." The committee described leftist doctrine as "dissolvent" and extremist. Argentine Jewry regretted "the misdemeanors of a minority whose nationality is not exclusive and whose flaming crime could not have been conceived in the womb of any particular community, but in the negation of God, of the fatherland and of the law."[21] Jewish leftists bitterly accused the group of slander. This did not, however, stop the Official Jewish Committee from meeting with Yrigoyen on January 25. It complained that Jews were in constant danger of attack, and asked for quick government action.[22]

By this time the Chamber of Deputies had discussed the recent occurrences and the Jewish appeals, and it demanded an explanation from the government. Beset by mounting criticism, Yrigoyen publicly disassociated himself from the anti-Semitic aspects of the repression and promised to ask the minister of the interior for an investigation. Anti-Jewish sentiments were incompatible with Argentine tradition, he claimed, and racism was the philosophy of only certain sectors, not of the entire country or of its government. He concluded that in the eyes of the nation, Jewish immigration had been a "beneficial and important element."[23]

Yet Yrigoyen neglected to explain the anti-Semitic statements in the Radical press, the vigilantes' ties to the police and military, and the part that individual Radicals had played and continued to play in the civil guards. In addition, his words and those of the Official Jewish Committee failed to assuage the suspicions of those "certain sectors." In the weeks following the Tragic Week, anti-Semitic posters appeared on the streets of Buenos Aires, some bearing the signature of the Comité Pro Argentinidad (Pro-Argentinism Committee). One of this group's posters characterized the appeal from 150,000 Jews as "crocodile tears" over the slaughter. It insisted that the Russian Jews who infested the country were totally responsible for the blood and lives of so many Argentines, as they also were for the "Revolution of 1910" which had nearly ruined the centennial. The manifesto ended by exhorting the government to free the nation of the Jewish contagion. In response to such threats, leaders of the JCA, Zionist groups, and other organizations continued to assure Yrigoyen and the public that the majority of Jews supported the social order.[24]

By January 14, citizens had formed groups to collect funds for the families of men killed or wounded by workers. The UCR caudillos participated in the numerous collections and ceremonies honoring the fallen. The most important fund-raising group was called, suggestively, the Comisión Pro-Defensa del Orden (Commission for the Defense of Order), headed by the ubiquitous Domecq García. The commission consisted of groups seeking donations from various branches of commerce, the financial sector, transportation, universities, meatpacking plants, cereal exporters, landowners, and newspaper staffs. Among its 111 members were powerful businessmen, including Christophersen, Joaquín de Anchorena, and Luis Zuberbühler, president of the Argentine Industrial Union, and many *régimen* figures. It also, however, included such Radicals as Leopoldo Melo, Vicente

Gallo, Delfor del Valle, and Arturo Goyeneche, men who would join the Antipersonalists in the 1920s. Many members were affiliated with the Labor Association and a few with the Workers' Circles and other Catholic organizations. General Dellepiane and several naval officers numbered among commission adherents, as did participants in the neighborhood civil guards and the Youth Committee, such as Villar Sáenz Peña. Surprisingly, the Youth Committee contingent urged the commission to distribute funds to families of fallen workers and thus assuage class conflict. Eleven Youth Committee members resigned in protest against this stance. Nevertheless, the commission ignored this request.[25]

Other organizations concerned with the defense of order were mushrooming throughout the city and surrounding areas. Precinct militias arose daily. The Liga Pro-Patria (Pro-Fatherland League), under Nicolas A. Calvo, a wealthy landowner, was broader in scope. Its object was to unite Argentines of all classes and fortunes under the national banner. The Pro-Fatherland League announced that it would use all means at its disposal to impede the diffusion of theories that subverted the nation.[26]

These overlapping groups coalesced into the permanent guard that Domecq García was organizing. Delegates from the navy and Major Justo E. Diana of the army attended the meeting he called for January 15, where they discussed the institutionalization of the growing citywide militia. A committee headed by Domecq García sent out a circular to prestigious figures and associations in Buenos Aires, imploring them to come to the defense of order. In the circular the committee referred to the recent traumatic events in the capital, caused by elements from the "dumping grounds" (*escoria*) of Europe, whose germs had infected the weak-spirited. It proposed creating a permanent organization of Argentine citizens to guard against similar occurrences in the future. Its motto would be "Fatherland and Order" and its name the Argentine Patriotic League. The organizers of the League had chosen a broader title for the group than the originally suggested "Civic Guard," implying that its objectives would transcend the mere defense of neighborhoods.[27]

Delegates from many groups, as well as individual priests, students, politicians, army and naval officers, and other citizens attended the League's first organizational meeting on the morning of January 20, 1919, in the Naval Center. Captain Yalour represented the Naval Center, and Major Diana the Military Circle. Elitist groups such as the Jockey Club, Círculo de Armas (a fencing club), Club del Progreso (Progress Club), Yacht Club, and Asociación de Damas Patricias (the upper-class Association of Patrician Ladies) sent spokespersons; Andrea and a Monsignor Piaggio represented the clergy. Domecq García, not surprisingly, became provisional president of the League. Dr. Rodolfo Medina, a professor and government bureaucrat, and naval Lieutenant Pedro Etchepare became its secretaries.[28]

These participants approved a statement of purpose which declared that the group would serve no narrow partisan interest. Instead it would defend the Argentine nationality and maintain the unity of the populace. Above all, it would stimulate the feeling of Argentinism among inhabitants of all religions, political parties, ages, and income levels. Another task would be to lobby for the welfare of teachers and for more schools, where children learned to love and respect their country. League members would encourage the celebration of national holidays and award prizes for the best works on Argentine history, liberalism, and social harmony, in order to counter anarchist propaganda. The group would instill love for the armed forces and convince the public that it was an honor to serve in the institutions that protected Argentine homes, order, and liberty. In addition the League would help uplift the poorer classes economically and morally. It would remind the people that all "healthy ideas" and "political solutions" fit within the framework of the liberal Argentine constitution, which did not "hinder social evolution within the given order, because within it exist no privileges other than those relating to work, talent, and fulfillment of duties to the fatherland." The statement warned "foreigners" that although Argentina was the most hospitable country in the world, its citizens valued their liberty and would defend it by arms if necessary. Accordingly, when anarchism or violent strikes threatened the public order, the League would help authorities prevent property destruction and maintain peace in the home.

After January the League focused on organizational matters.

Members of the Commission for the Defense of Order joined the leadership; the precinct guards formed the core of the ranks. The League renamed these guards "brigades" and numbered them according to police precinct; the organization began with brigades in forty-three of the capital's forty-five precincts.[29] Other urban brigades were organized by livelihood or professional association. One unusual example was the Liga Israelita Pro Argentinidad (Jewish Pro-Argentinism League), an existing organization that affiliated en masse with the League. Its twenty to thirty members were wealthy businessmen with close ties to the Argentine upper class and few, if any, to the Jewish community. This brigade, however, was short-lived.[30]

Brigades outside the capital were established in a number of ways. During and after the Tragic Week, guards similar to the precinct militias arose in other parts of the nation where labor was active. They, too, joined the League as the brigades of their locality. Members of the temporary executive communicated with acquaintances in the interior and entrusted them with the task of raising brigades, or sometimes prominent individuals contacted the executive and volunteered their services. Fearful of strikes by landless peons, farmers asked the League to help them organize brigades, and often the League sent recruiters to scenes of rural labor strife. The League also formed "free labor brigades" of nonunionized workers.[31] Eventually brigades were found in each province and national territory.

The League created its governing authorities in the federal capital. At the end of January 1919, Domecq García asked twenty-two men to form the provisional Central Junta: among them, Andrea, Carlos Aubone (of the 1910 pogrom), Nicolás Calvo, Manuel Carlés, Major Diana, General Eduardo Munilla, Vice Admiral Justo P. Sáenz Valiente, diplomat and conservative intellectual Estanislao Zeballos, and several Radical and opposition politicians. In its first meeting on February 3, the junta set up committees to publicize the League's goals and activities, raise funds, and formulate statutes. During February and March the junta discussed organizational matters and possible social welfare projects. On March 31 it approved the statutes drawn up by a committee and set the first election of permanent officials for April 5.[32]

The statutes restated more explicitly the general goals approved on January 20. The League's first and foremost aim was to inculcate "respect for the law, the principle of authority and the social order." Five of its fifteen goals focused on "Argentinizing" schools in a manner reminiscent of cultural nationalism. The aim of stimulating patriotism in other cultural institutions received attention throughout the document, as did the need to incorporate immigrants into national life. The League recommended naturalizing several categories of foreign residents, excluding those who opposed the constitution. It also favored industrialization and policies that would "guarantee social justice and the wellbeing of the proletarian and his family." It explicitly eschewed any role in electoral politics. Last yet far from least, the League would organize its members into neighborhood groups which would "cooperate in the repression of all movements of anarchistic character." [33]

The statutes also delineated the structure of the new organization. The League would consist of a central association in the capital and local associations throughout the republic. The central association (that is, the brigades of the capital) would select eighty persons, and the local associations (the brigades of each province or territory) would each choose one to serve in the Central Junta, the League's supreme authority. In turn, the Central Junta would elect presiding officers. These eight men, together with seven others chosen by the junta, would form the Executive Council, five of whose members had to be provincial delegates. All of these officials would serve two-year terms and could be reelected; in fact, the composition of the central authorities would change little over the next ten years. The Executive Council would formulate policy, recognize new brigades and coordinate their activities, hold national publicity campaigns, supervise the funds, and report annually to the Central Junta on the "state of the League." [34]

The sole prerequisite for forming a brigade was agreement with the League's aims. Brigades were free to organize themselves as their members wished and petition the central authorities for recognition and funds. Similarly, the statutes specified few requirements for brigade membership. All adult citizens by naturalization or birth, female or male, were eligible, even if they could not afford the recommended annual dues of three pesos. Nevertheless, they had to disclose their profession, employment history, military service background, other affiliations, telephone number, and the vehicles in their possession when they applied for membership, at least in Buenos Aires. Presumably the League used this information to disqualify applicants of lower-class or dubious backgrounds, as well as to determine their potential usefulness to the organization. Civil guards in Germany at this time used similar means to exclude members of the lower class.[35]

The hierarchically organized brigades enjoyed a wide degree of autonomy but were ultimately responsible to the Central Junta and Executive Council, with whom they corresponded on local activities. The junta often sent representatives on investigative or coordinating missions to the provinces, and brigade presidents periodically met with the junta in Buenos Aires. In addition, delegates from the brigades gathered at annual congresses, the first of which was held in 1920, to present papers on national issues. In these congresses, members of the junta and of the various League commissions reported to delegates. The junta probably chose the members of these commissions, a duty not mentioned in the statutes. One of these commissions, that of finance, included some of the country's leading entrepreneurs, who solicited funds for the League among businessmen and employers' associations. As in the national level of the organization, each brigade had its own elected officers, commissions, and treasury. Each brigade also constituted its own paramilitary force, which in the cities were called "neighborhood defense commissions" and in the countryside, somewhat ironically, "commissions in defense of rural labor."

If the national organization's charter emphasized the milder aspects of the League's program, brigade statutes focused on the central issue of capital–labor relations. According to its code, the brigade of Gualeguaychú, Entre Ríos, also called itself the "Organization for the Defense of Production and Industry." The brigade's sole object was "to coordinate and harmonize" the action of businesses "in all matters related to work." It proclaimed "freedom of labor" and the independence of capital as "fundamental principles," while it refused to accept the existence of any workers' group or syndicate "that requires its members to recognize its delegates and that declares boycotts or strikes." Other articles provided for the establishment of a registry of nonunion workers, an employers' tribunal to judge disputes, and mutual aid for laborers. All of the organization's stated functions and principles related to the labor question.[36] These statutes demonstrated that the League would oppose all independent unions, not only those that sought to overturn capitalism.

By the beginning of April 1919, the League was ready for its first national elections. On April 5 the brigades chose a new president, Manuel Carlés, as Domecq García had previously announced his decision to relegate the leadership to a civilian. Domecq García, however, remained a member of the council, which also included a general, a naval lieutenant, and "men of more than average importance in the community," as Sumner Welles put it.[37] Carlés kept the presidency from 1919 until his death in 1946.

Carlés was born in Rosario in 1872—fittingly, near the Plaza de Mayo. Both parents were socially prominent; his mother was the leading philanthropist in Rosario. After her death, a plaza in that city was named for her. His father was known for being a learned gentleman and the first inhabitant of Rosario to export grain to Europe. From an early age, Carlés attended his father's intellectual gatherings, which awakened in him an abiding interest in Argentine studies.[38]

Carlés's career would manifest talent and civic concern. It began when, as a youth, he journeyed to Buenos Aires to seek his fortune. He began to collaborate in Sarmiento's newspaper, *El Censor*, and to discuss issues with the former president, with whom he shared such liberal values as reverence for education. At the same time he initiated his political career in 1889 by attending the first meeting of the Civic Union. The young law student participated in the Revolution of 1893 and, as a result, spent some time in exile. He became a friend of such reformist figures within the *régimen* as Carlos Pellegrini, Figueroa Alcorta, and Roque Sáenz Peña, and he served as a national deputy from 1898 to 1912. He also headed the postal service under President José E. Uriburu and was active in Sáenz Peña's election, although the passage of the suffrage law precipitated his exit from the Chamber. After 1912 he devoted himself to his law career and teaching; for many years he taught Argentine history, geography, constitutional law, and "civic morality" at the University of Buenos Aires, the National High School of Buenos Aires, and several military schools including the Higher War College. A gifted teacher, he made many contacts with military officers in the classroom and inspired students with his patriotic enthusiasm. His speaking ability—and opposition to anarchism—had already won renown during his days in Congress.

In the years between the electoral reform law and the birth of the League, Carlés did not remove himself completely from politics. He initially favored Yrigoyen's policies, especially those related to the provinces, and for this reason the Radical president appointed him to head the 1918 intervention in Salta. During February 1919, while Domecq García, Carlés, and others were openly organizing the League, Yrigoyen was considering naming Carlés to the post of minister of the navy. Carlés's amicable relations with the ruling party continued during the presidency of his close friend Marcelo T. de Alvear (1922–28), who appointed him interventor in San Juan in 1922. The League president's reformist sympathies influenced his friendly ties with Radicals, particularly with what would become the party's Antipersonalist wing. Although some authors have called Carlés a Radical, he never formally joined that party. Indeed, in December 1919 the Conservative Coalition of Buenos Aires considered him for its slate.[39]

Carlés's political experience, intellectual talent, wide contacts, and oratorical skills served him well as League president. He helped shape an effective organization, formulate a counterrevolutionary agenda, and raise publicity for the League's cause. He also shared traits with Andrea and Franceschi; namely, an interest in and ability for recruiting women. Before he became its president, the League did little to attract this group, although it did not shun the possibility of doing so. It had invited the Association of Patrician Ladies to the founding meeting, and the statutes authorized the affiliation of both sexes. After Carlés's election, the recruitment of women began in earnest. The League president initiated a lifelong practice of addressing women's groups and delivering speeches in churches, knowing that the most faithful worshippers were female.

In one such talk, given to the Beneficent Society, Carlés revealed some of his motives for seeking out women. He reminded his audience that his mother, a former society president in Rosario, had incarnated the "virtue of the lady of the Argentine home." Such noble women were needed today to undo the evil legacy of immigration and secular education. Conditions within the "foreign home" led to its members' denial of fatherland, society, and tradition. Harking back to the views of the late nineteenth-century Catholics, Carlés criticized "godless" education for its arrogance and its denigration of family, work, womanhood, and other values. Beneficent Society members should spread the message that only "the home with Fatherland" and "the school with God" could prevent harm to the nation. Carlés later clarified this idea by noting that the disruptive elements tended to have families outside of matrimony, and that "moral disunity" in the family contributed to national disunity.[40] In other words, the social order depended upon the viability of the family, an institution weakened by modernization, immigration, and leftism. The logical implication was that by strengthening the family, the League could also buttress the social order. Moreover, this task would require female participation.

Echoing sentiments expressed earlier by Andrea, Carlés believed that home, school, work, military discipline, and religion constituted the "moral forces of the nation," which maintained authority and unity. The "factors" behind these moral forces were mothers, teachers, workers, soldiers, and clerics. Of these, mothers were particularly important because they educated children and imparted moral precepts. Thus, they were suited for the job of forming the Argentine social conscience by "moralizing the home" and guarding the people from the perversions brought by immigrants. Argentine mothers would teach foreign mothers to instill in their children such "Argentine virtues" as integrity, nobility (*hidalguía*), and love of glory, work, and country. Indeed, Argentine women were the most patriotic of all inhabitants. With their patriotism, Carlés believed that the League would solve the social question, which was a moral dilemma rather than an economic one.[41]

Assigning women this duty, however, presented risks. It seemingly would bring women into the male realm of politics, which Carlés opposed. When asked his opinion of equal rights and the vote for women, Carlés replied that only political opportunists raised this question. Women themselves were uninterested in acquiring what they did not need. Most Argentines were content to view the woman as the "enchantress of the household." He added that the interior of the country (the repository of nationalism) viewed feminism and even the term *woman* (*mujer*), rather than *señora* or *señorita*, with repugnance. Carlés despised feminism, which he defined as "the fight against men in order to masculinize women and feminize men."[42]

Carlés never specifically explained how female Liguistas would avoid trespassing into the male sphere, but the League circumvented the problem by assigning women tasks related to their traditional duties as mothers and wives. Carlés and other spokesmen also were careful to describe the League as a moral and patriotic association, rather than a political one. This designation served two purposes. First, female participation in a moral crusade fit easily into women's traditional sphere of activity. Second and perhaps more important, "politics" meant partisanship, and League officials denied any such intent.[43]

With these motives, League officials set out to attract women to the cause. Periodically Carlés invited various female organizations to meetings at League headquarters. Two of these groups, the National Council of Women and the Asociación Nacional

Pro-Patria de Señoritas (National Pro-Fatherland Association of Señoritas), announced their adherence to League principles. The president of the second group, Mercedes Pujato Crespo, wrote Carlés that the Pro-Fatherland Association would be happy to work for the League's "noble objectives that elements foreign to our soil plan to destroy, enthroning disorder and anarchy." Upper- and middle-class women's clubs and teachers' groups around the country also sent letters of praise to the central authorities. The League invited the Pro-Fatherland Association, Association of Patrician Ladies, Beneficent Society, other female charitable and civic groups, and even the Sisters of the Congregation of the Santa Unión, who taught many upper-class girls in their elite school, to participate in its independence day parade on May 24, 1919, scheduled one day before the official parade. Carlés and the female guests led the procession.[44]

The Central Junta resolved to create a Patriotic League of Señoras (hereinafter, Señoras), inviting representatives of charitable groups in the capital to a meeting on June 29. Sixty-five society matrons and twelve young women attended and listened to speeches by Carlés and several prominent female philanthropists. On July 20 the Señoras elected a permanent Executive Junta and a president, Julia Elena A. de Martínez de Hoz, a sponsor of many Catholic charities and the wife of wealthy landowner and Liguista. Another prominent officer and future president was Hortensia Berdier, an artist and member of an old military family. In early October young women decided to form a group separate from that of their elders. More than a hundred attended the first meeting of the Patriotic League of Señoritas (hereinafter, Señoritas), held in Martínez de Hoz's home on November 1, and elected a provisional junta.[45] Although not among these early leaders, two upper-class Señoritas later became important officers: Jorgelina Cano and Celina de Estrada (related to José Manuel de Estrada).

The Señoras and Señoritas initially declared that their aim was simply to help the poor. In other statements, however, League women clarified their motives. The founders of the women's brigade of Córdoba proclaimed that "the moment has arrived for the Argentine woman to incorporate herself into the movement of defense . . . against the designs of demolition that are fermenting in the nation's bosom." From their vantage point in the home and in society, women discerned a "fertile ground for action in which to contribute to the formation of collective sentiments, the education of new generations in the real love of the fatherland. . . ." Female brigades would oppose class hatred through humanitarian projects.[46]

In 1922 President Jorgelina Cano of the Señoritas added that women could not remain indifferent to the task men faced of ending social convulsions. Being the "other wheel of the wagon in life," women should accompany men not only in times of happiness but in times of struggle. "The voice of the woman, voice of peace, of love and resignation, should make itself heard in the present tumult; her idealistic brain and her believing heart should vibrate . . . searching for solutions of equity and justice" to the social question.[47] By using the "feminine virtues" and performing traditional female duties, women would extend their usual roles of helping their menfolk and protecting their families into the fight against the left.

Women began to join and form brigades, at first adhering to male brigades. In one such case, that of the city of Mendoza, some of the officers were women. Brigades of Señoras and Señoritas, based on locality and marital status, however, became the rule. The first of these were formed in August 1919 when the Señoras' Executive Junta appointed members to establish brigades in eighteen precincts of the capital.[48] Generally the founders of these brigades became their presidents. Individuals created other brigades through their own initiative. Catholic parish groups and other existing organizations transformed themselves into the brigades of their respective neighborhoods, or, in the interior, their respective cities. Although the Señoritas first organized themselves in brigades based on locality, in the 1920s they tended to base their chapters on their main projects—factory schools for female workers. Sometimes female officials in Buenos Aires asked male brigade presidents to set up female auxiliaries, or male brigade leaders suggested to women of the same area that they form such organizations. Thus men and women both helped form the feminine brigades.

In contrast to men, League women created only a handful of free labor brigades, perhaps because few important workers' conflicts involved women. Significantly, a brigade for female department store employees in Buenos Aires arose in 1919 at the same time that some of these workers carried out a strike.[49] Furthermore, although men established more than a dozen professional brigades, female Liguistas formed only one category of professional brigades, those of primary and secondary school teachers (*magisterio*). This was not surprising, given the fact that few women were professionals, and even fewer of this small group were sympathetic to the League. Teaching was one of the few professions easily accessible to women; moreover, Carlés had great interest in education and considered it to be one of the nation's moral forces. As teachers as well as mothers, women profoundly influenced the upbringing of future Argentines and could easily spread the League's ideals.

In January 1920 a teachers' association joined the League, founding the Patriotic League of Argentine Teachers (hereinafter, Teachers). Its original proponent (and an officer in the Association of Patrician Ladies), María Contreras Feliú, was elected president. The provisional authorities were entirely composed of women, but men gradually joined the organization and its governing body. The presidency remained in the hands of women, as did most of the seats in the Directive Commission, which, from Buenos Aires, headed Teachers' brigades organized by sex and province. Nevertheless, the branch's main spokesperson was Justo P. Correa, a high school professor and member of an old Catamarcan family. The fact that this branch was subordinate to the male Central Junta may also have limited women's power within it. At any rate, Teachers' brigades arose only in the federal capital and provinces of Buenos Aires and Mendoza. As in the case of the female free labor brigade, the Mendoza brigade was formed during a teachers' strike. Correa urged teachers to create a brigade in Rosario, but they ignored his plea.[50]

The Teachers' branch and the female free labor brigades were

responsible to the male central authorities, but the Señoras and
Señoritas had their own, largely autonomous, governing bodies:
the Señoras' Executive Junta and the Señoritas' Central Commission. Although the League never explicitly outlined the chain
of command, Carlés clearly considered himself president of male
and female Liguistas, and women accepted his leadership. As if
to underscore his supremacy, the League head appeared at important women's functions. Women in the organization regularly
elected their own brigade and national level officers, just as the
men did. Carlés never explained why he thought it permissible
for women to vote within the League but not outside it; presumably he considered it acceptable for them to choose their own
leaders, as long as these leaders had no authority over men. The
internal organization of the women's leadership and brigades also
resembled those of the men, except that women did not have
paramilitary commissions.[51]

The League's ability to attract women caught the attention of
its foes. *La Protesta* observed in October 1919 that hardly a day
passed without the announcement of a new female brigade.
What the anarchist newspaper considered to be Carlés's single-
handed mobilization of female Liguistas demonstrated his "inclination for women." Hinting that the lifelong bachelor was
effeminate, the authors attributed his interest in recruiting women
to his failure to recruit men. The fact that women now constituted the most militant sector of the League indicated that this
organization, with its "sinister and grotesque" president, would
soon collapse.[52]

The anarchists' forecast was inaccurate as well as biased against
women. The growth of its female sector was only one sign of the
League's dynamism. In mid-April the League claimed to have
9,800 members in the capital.[53] By early May a U.S. diplomat estimated that there were 12,000 Liguistas in the capital and 40,000
in the provinces.[54] Later that month, a sympathetic reporter
noted a continual stream of people flowing in and out of the
League office at the Naval Center. League officials decided to
move their headquarters from these palatial surroundings to an
even larger space in a building on Florida and Lavalle streets,

whose multimillionaire owner, Saturnino Unzué, a Liguista, would charge only half the usual rent.[55] This appearance of bustle and growth contrasted, at least in the opposition's view, with the inertia of the Yrigoyen regime, which delayed filling many diplomatic posts and tended to postpone decision making.

The League's independence day parade on May 24, 1919, demonstrated its strength to the public and the government. About 120,000 persons, including congressmen, judges, and Church officials, marched in the procession led by Carlés and society women. Significantly, even Yrigoyen felt compelled to join the parade. Liguistas distributed small flags and texts of national songs to the crowd as the parade looped around downtown Buenos Aires. When it passed the League office on Florida Street, the marchers cheered. League spokesmen admitted that only a sixth of the participants belonged to the organization, and even this proportion was exaggerated. Nevertheless, the fact that it could mobilize that many people disturbed the government, particularly as the official parade on the following day lacked the luster and enthusiasm of the League's.[56]

The League continued to grow. By November its membership in the capital had dipped to 2,991, but its emblem appeared in 833 localities around the nation.[57] These figures reflected an organizational shift from Buenos Aires toward the provinces, scene of serious labor conflicts. The League claimed to have 1,251 brigades in 1920, 1,400 in 1921, 1,527 in 1922, down to 1,000 in 1925, and up again to 1,200 in 1927. Also, according to the League's statistics, there were 600,000 registered members in the last year mentioned. This number, representing approximately 6 percent of the national population, wildly overshot the mark, and the brigade figures were also extravagant.[58] One can measure League strength more accurately by counting the number of brigades regularly mentioned in the press and represented at the annual congresses, along with their officers. Without including the small circles of Señoritas organized around their schools, one finds 41 women's brigades and 550 men's brigades. Each brigade elected between seven and forty-one officers. Assuming an average of twenty officers per brigade, I estimate that the League's

militant core consisted of about 820 female and 11,000 male activists throughout its first decade of existence.[59]

The League's flexible and essentially reactive nature partly jus-
tifies its spokesmen's exaggeration of membership and brigade
figures. The organization constantly expanded and contracted in
response to its perception of the worker threat. Male brigades
were prepared to draft additional persons and set up branches in
outlying districts. When the League and employers succeeded in
quelling labor disturbances, the newly formed brigades would
fade from sight, and the older standing brigades would shrink to
their cores. In this fashion many male brigades arose and then
disappeared, according to necessity. As it addressed social problems of a more permanent character, the women's sector was
more stable.

Its alternating size notwithstanding, the League extended its
roots widely. The 550 male brigades were spread throughout the
provinces and territories, as shown in Tables 1 and 2. Not surprisingly, they tended to concentrate in heavily inhabited areas.
The Andean and Patagonian regions, however, were exceptions
to this rule, demonstrating that organized labor activity influenced brigade formation more strongly than population. Labor
conflicts were more common in the cereal zone, the littoral ports
and lowlands, and the far south than in the northern Andean areas,
where high unemployment, police vigilance, and traditional paternalism limited unionization and strikes. The prevalence of
small, family-owned landholdings and the possibilities for upward mobility helped limit rural labor conflict in Mendoza.[60]

Slightly over half of the male brigades were rural, centered in
railroad junctions, *estancias* (ranches), sugar plantations, tannin
mills, and towns with less than 5,000 inhabitants. If one adds the
brigades located in *cabeceras* (local seats of government) with
populations below 5,000 to the rural category, the percentage of
rural brigades was much higher. On the other hand, only four of
the female brigades were located in the countryside (see Table 3).
Half were found in the capital and 17 percent in cities and towns
of Buenos Aires province. Aside from these areas, only in the ur-
banized provinces of Córdoba and Mendoza did women create

Table 1. Male Brigades, 1919–1928

Location (province or territory)	No. of urban brigades[a]	No. of rural brigades	Total no. of brigades	% of total brigades	Terr. or prov. population as % of nat'l population, 1920[b]
Buenos Aires	96	69	165	30.0	26.8
Patagonia[c]	18	57	75	13.6	1.6
Federal capital	61	0	61	11.1	19.4
Santa Fe	16	39	55	10.0	11.6
Entre Ríos	12	39	51	9.3	5.3
Córdoba	11	29	40	7.3	9.3
Corrientes	12	5	17	3.1	4.1
La Pampa	6	8	14	2.5	1.4
Santiago del Estero	4	6	10	1.8	3.1
Chaco	4	3	7	1.3	1.1
Misiones	3	2	5	0.9	0.8
San Juan	4	1	5	0.9	1.5
San Luis	4	1	5	0.9	1.4
Mendoza	4	0	4	0.7	3.6
Catamarca	4	0	4	0.7	1.2
Salta	2	1	3	0.5	1.7
La Rioja	3	0	3	0.5	0.9
Tucumán	2	0	2	0.4	3.9
Jujuy	1	0	1	0.2	1.0
Formosa	1	0	1	0.2	0.3
Unclassifiable	0	22	22	4.0	
Total	268	282	550	99.9	99.6

Note: Percentages do not add up to 100 because of rounding.

a. Includes rural seats of government with fewer than 5,000 inhabitants.

b. Source: Vásquez-Presedo, *Estadísticas*, 2:43–45.

c. I have added up all Patagonian brigades because many operated across provincial and territorial lines.

Note: Some of the data in Tables 1–3 are found in McGee, "Gender Roles," 248–49.

Table 2. Male Brigades, 1919–1928, by Region

Region[a]	Urban brigades No. %		Rural brigades No. %		Total no. of regional brigades	% of national brigades	Regional population as % of nat. population, 1920[b]
Pampas	133	(48)	146	(52)	279	50.7	50.4
Federal capital	61	(100)	0	(0)	61	11.1	19.4
Andean	20	(91)	2	(9)	22	4.0	13.8
Northern lowlands and Mesopotamia	36	(40)	55	(60)	91	16.5	14.8
Patagonia	18	(24)	57	(76)	75	13.6	1.6
Unclassifiable[c]	0	(0)	22	(100)	22	4.0	—
Total	268	(49)	282	(51)	550	99.9	100.0

Note: Percentages may not add up to 100 because of rounding.

a. Pampas: Buenos Aires, Santa Fe, Córdoba, La Pampa, San Luis. Andean: Mendoza, Catamarca, San Juan, La Rioja, Salta, Jujuy, Tucumán. Northern lowlands and Mesopotamia: Misiones, Corrientes, Entre Ríos, El Chaco, Formosa, Santiago del Estero. Patagonia: Neuquén, Río Negro, Chubut, Santa Cruz, Tierra del Fuego.

b. Source: Vásquez-Presedo, Estadísticas, 2: 43–45.

c. I could not find the locations of these brigades on the maps; I have assumed they were rural for the purposes of Tables 1–2.

more than one brigade apiece. Female brigades were largely urban because that was where the social problems they hoped to resolve were most evident. Thus, the male and female brigades' regional strengths neatly complemented each other.

The League's base in the early 1920s was comparable to that of Argentina's three national political parties: the Progressive Democrats, Socialists, and Radicals. Competing with rival "conservative" parties, the PDP had little support outside Santa Fe and Córdoba. Although it had centers across the country, the Socialist party was strongest in the city and province of Buenos

Aires. It underwent several schisms just before and during the early 1920s; in 1921 it had only 8,339 members.[61] The broad powers of the executive branch, combined with decades of grass-roots mobilization, gave the ruling party great strength throughout Argentina, although it, too, faced schisms at the provincial and national levels. Nevertheless, with its sphere of influence and centralized national organization, the League resembled a party of the Radical's scope—and it was more tightly knit than the UCR.

From the Tragic Week on, the relationship between the incipient civil guard movement and the regime was ambiguous. The League and its immediate predecessors were founded on the perception that the government lacked the will or force to repress the workers. Although the military officers, members of the opposition, and Youth Committee members who joined these groups may have also opposed the government on other grounds, their Radical comrades did not. The white guards and precinct militias were not necessarily hostile to the administration.[62]

Table 3. Women's Brigades (Señoras and Señoritas), 1919–1928

Location (province or territory)	No. of urban brigades	No. of rural brigades	Total no. of brigades	% of total brigades
Federal capital	20	0	20	48.8
Buenos Aires	5	2	7	17.1
Córdoba	3	1	4	9.8
Mendoza	3	0	3	7.3
Entre Ríos	0	1	1	2.4
Santa Fe	1	0	1	2.4
Santiago del Estero	1	0	1	2.4
Tucumán	1	0	1	2.4
Chaco	1	0	1	2.4
Tierra del Fuego	1	0	1	2.4
Catamarca	1	0	0	2.4
Total	37	4	41	99.8

Note: Percentages may not add up to 100 because of rounding. The groups of Señoritas organized around factory schools are not included.

The Yrigoyen regime's attitude toward the guards and the early League ranged from mild dissuasion to active encouragement. Here one could cite the careless dispersal of arms and Dellepiane's ambivalence toward the vigilantes. In fact, the Radical general eventually joined the League, although his name did not appear in its proceedings until 1926. Referring to the combined efforts of the army, police, and vigilantes, the Radical newspaper *La Epoca* stated approvingly on January 11, 1919, that "the firm attitude of the conservative forces of order kept the antisocial elements from going too far astray." On February 8 it praised the League's "learned patriotism" as healthy and worthwhile. On February 4 *La Vanguardia* called the vigilante groups *patotas radicales* (Radical hooligans) and "Yrigoyen's white guards," but the Socialists, clearly biased against the ruling party, may have overestimated the extent of government involvement.

The League's own version of its origins, however, corroborated the Socialist view. In a pamphlet issued in 1950, the League claimed that the government itself appointed Captain Yalour to form groups in all the neighborhoods of the capital to help the police. The League was born when Yalour discussed his task with other naval officers in the Naval Center. Satisfied with the new organization it had sponsored, the regime permitted the militias, and then the brigades, to meet in police precinct headquarters.[63] Although it is not possible to confirm the League's statement on Yalour, newspaper accounts and a policeman's memoir referred to the meetings in police stations. Indeed, the government initially permitted policemen to become members. In March 1919 Minister of the Interior Ramón Gómez even agreed to allow the League to display its signs in post offices.[64] These facts indicate some collusion between the regime and the early League, although perhaps not to the extent the League later claimed.

As long as the League seemed to confine itself to helping official forces against workers, or planning for such action, the government viewed it favorably. The League's rapid growth, however, alarmed the regime, which began to question the group's motives. Supported by upper-class interests around the country, the League assumed the trappings of a national conservative

party. The conspicuous presence of *régimen* figures in its ranks, as
well as that of upper-class Radicals who were beginning to oppose Yrigoyen, lent credence to administration suspicions that
the League represented a new anti-Yrigoyenist coalition of the
right, more dynamic than the PDP. Some U.S. diplomats shared
this perception. A few days after Carlés's election, Sumner Welles
reported that a profatherland party had just formed and had
chosen Carlés as its president. (Evidently he confused the League
with the Pro-Fatherland League, which the former had absorbed.) Nicolás Repetto and other Socialists also changed their
minds and decided that, in part, the League represented an elitist
attempt at "electoral resurrection," and the anarchists agreed. Yet
Conservative Deputy Julio A. Costa stated that he never joined
the organization, although he supported its aims, because he
thought it was Radical![65]

The League itself later admitted that the Radical government
eventually turned against it because it saw the organization as a
political rival, although the League denied that this was true. National League officials did not intend to form a political party or
officially support opposition candidates, at least during the early
postwar years. Conservative deputy and Liguista Luis Agote
noted that the League contained members of different political
parties who agreed on the need for social harmony.[66] Implicitly,
League members recognized that though their counterrevolutionary message attracted many adherents, including Radicals,
much of this following would evaporate if the appeal became
partisan. The leaders also understood that they could not compete effectively for votes against the Radicals. Moreover, as the
next president, Alvear, fit their taste, there was no reason to
organize against him. Therefore the League contented itself with
its lobbying, alms-dispensing, and order-keeping roles. By the
end of Alvear's term, however, Carlés seriously considered transforming the League into a party in order to campaign against
Yrigoyen's reelection, as will be seen.

The League did not constitute itself as a formal opposition
party in its early years; nevertheless, it genuinely undermined the
regime. The League usurped the government's rightful functions.

It claimed the responsibility to protect Argentine borders, "nationalize" the educational system, and promote the welfare of the laboring classes. Unafraid of alienating supporters, in contrast to the broader-based Radicals, the Socialists continually drew attention to the League's assumption of official duties. On the day of the League's independence parade, Socialists argued in the Buenos Aires City Council that it was hardly the appropriate organization to lead a civic procession including municipal and national officials, let alone represent the patriotism of all Argentines.[67]

Socialists on many occasions also decried the League's extralegal paramilitary forces. In the Chamber of Deputies in June 1919, Repetto insisted that no independent group be allowed to set up its own military organization, substitute itself for the police, or liberate workers from supposed "anarchist tyranny." Even if one could prove that this tyranny existed, the task of liberation belonged to the government or the workers themselves, not to the League. Significantly, both a Radical (Rogelio Araya) and opposition figures (Conservatives Rodolfo Moreno, Matías Sánchez Sorondo, and Luis Agote) defended the League against Repetto's accusations.[68]

The extent of military involvement in the League particularly alarmed the Socialists—and the government. By the end of July 1919 the League claimed 6 generals, 18 colonels, 32 lieutenant colonels, 50 majors, 212 captains, 300 lieutenants, and more than 400 sublieutenants as members, and this was only the army contingent.[69] At its head were retired and active military officers. Members of the armed forces made public displays of allegiance to the League, military aviators transported League officials and spread League propaganda, and League speakers instructed officers on socioeconomic issues. The Central Junta sent officers to the interior on investigative missions. The League was less successful, however, in influencing the ranks. *La Vanguardia* reported that in late February 1919 a sergeant read a League manifesto to his company and asked the soldiers to sign it. Only one corporal responded to his plea, which angered the sergeant, who called the soldiers socialists and maximalists. One soldier stepped forward and insisted that he was a patriot but not a papist, and that

he did not want his name to appear next to Andrea's. (The anticlerical Socialist paper naturally approved of his sentiments.) The
sergeant sent him to the stockade for his impertinence and punished the company by confining it to quarters.[70]

Antimilitaristic Socialists recognized that the widespread support for the League among officers, if not among the ranks,
threatened civilian rule. After Repetto's speech and press reports
of the League's growing military following, the government's
position hardened. Near the end of July 1919, the Ministry of
War prohibited military personnel on active duty from joining or
openly declaring adherence to any patriotic association, stating
that such action was redundant. The Ministry primarily directed
the resolution toward officers, whose defiance forced the government to back down. Yet in August it forbade League members to
meet in police stations and recruit policemen.[71]

The Yrigoyen government could not sever the ties between
the League and the official forces of order. Policemen continued
to belong to or collaborate with the League. Disgruntled by
Yrigoyen's continued use of troops against labor, his interference
in military affairs, and other grievances, active and retired military officers remained prominent in League affairs throughout
the 1920s. More than one hundred served as members of the central authorities and as brigade delegates to the annual congresses,
who usually were high-ranking brigade officers. Participation in
the League may have helped prepare officers for future anti-
Yrigoyenist activity and outright political intervention in 1930.[72]

Unwilling to alienate propertied groups, Yrigoyen bowed to
the League's wishes and moved to the right. Although the Radicals continued to advocate social legislation, the government also
returned to the pre-1916 methods of harassing labor. It banned
some leftist demonstrations and unleashed the police, authorizing them to use the Residence and Social Defense laws, to im-
prison activists, and to prohibit the display of anarchist and Socialist flags. Yrigoyen manifested little concern over League
violence against workers in the provinces, areas poorly covered
by the national press. Radicals, especially Alvear, appointed
League officials to public positions, but when this occurred,

Liguistas resigned their posts in the organization.[73] The desire to appeal to all groups and thus survive politically forced Radical governments to accept the League's existence.

The prominence of the League's leaders was one reason Radical administrations accepted the organization. A study of 146 brigade delegates to the annual congresses from 1920 to 1928 and 71 members of the Central Junta and Executive Council for those years revealed that the League's internal structure was highly stratified, with men of high social rank bunched among the leadership. Information was found on 92 percent of the Central Junta and Executive Council members. Of the national leaders studied 48 percent belonged to the Jockey Club, 51 percent were listed in prestigious social registers, and 31 percent belonged to the Rural Society or local rural associations. If one equates upper-class status with one or more of these affiliations, including membership in the exclusive Circle of Arms, 69 percent of the national male authorities belonged to this class. Also, 51 percent owned land or were closely related to landholding families.[74]

The antecedents of brigade delegates were not as exalted. Information was found on 36 percent, strongly indicating that the majority of this group did not come from high socioeconomic strata. Only 4 percent of the brigade delegates belonged to the Jockey Club, 10 percent were listed in social registers, and 10 percent belonged to a rural association. Eighteen percent could be considered upper-class, and at least 19 percent owned land or were members of landholding families. Because brigade delegates usually were brigade presidents and officers, they probably enjoyed higher status than the rank and file, which will be discussed later. Still, the delegate's backgrounds already demonstrate some of the League's popular appeal.

One can compare Liguistas with members of political parties seated in the Chamber of Deputies between 1916 and 1930, as studied by Peter Smith.[75] Although the two sets of data are not completely analogous, the comparison is suggestive. Thirty-five percent of all the male Liguistas studied were upper-class, which would place them between deputies from provincial "conservative" parties, 44 percent of whom Smith characterized as aristocratic, and Radical Personalist (Yrigoyenist) deputies, 31 percent of whom were aristocratic. The aristocratic percentage of the League central authorities corresponded closely to Smith's figure of 73 percent for Conservative party deputies. Leaders of the League, like those of the Conservatives, numbered among the most prominent members of society.

As noted earlier, many observers viewed the League as the refuge of *régimen* hacks. The degree of overlap between the two is difficult to measure because biographical sources rarely revealed party affiliation. However, one can learn whether persons were elected or appointed to office before 1916; if so, they probably were not Radicals, who abstained from electoral politics until 1912. Significantly, at least 31 percent of the national leaders fell into this category. Although some Radicals helped form the League, and such prominent ones as Leopoldo Melo, José Camilo Crotto, and Carlos Noel remained members, only two turned up in the sample. Both Francisco Bavastro, of the capital, and Luis Juareguiberry, of Entre Ríos, were brigade delegates, and neither was upper-class.

Though the League attracted men of different ages (see Table 4), the largest number were between forty and fifty years of age in 1920, and the average age was forty-seven. This figure was close to the average age of successful politicians; in 1916, national deputies tended to be in their mid-forties, and national senators in their mid-fifties.[76] The fact that I found information on only

Table 4. Age of Male League Members in 1920

	30 and under		31–40		41–50		51–60		61–70		71 and over		Total
	No.	%	No.	%	No.	%	No.	%	No.	%	No.	%	
Central Junta, Executive Council (45)	3	7	6	13	16	36	10	22	8	18	2	4	45
Delegates (18)	6	33	4	22	4	22	1	6	2	11	1	6	18
Total (63)	9	14	10	16	20	32	11	17	10	16	3	5	63

Note: Average age = 47.

Table 5. Primary Occupation of Male League Members in Number and Percentage

Occupation	Central Junta Executive Council (62)	Delegates (63)	Total (125)
Priest	1 (2%)	4 (6%)	5 (4%)
Liberal professions[a]	18 (29%)	18 (29%)	36 (29%)
Bureaucrat/liberal professions	4 (6%)	5 (8%)	9 (7%)
Bureaucrat/politician	2 (3%)	3 (5%)	5 (4%)
Military officer[b]	12 (19%)	4 (16%)	16 (13%)
Workers' brigade member	1 (2%)	6 (10%)	7 (6%)
Commerce, publishing, real estate	4[c] (6%)	2 (3%)	6 (5%)
Banking, finance, utilities, transport	4 (6%)	1 (2%)	5 (4%)
Manufacturing	1 (2%)	0 (0%)	1 (0.8%)
Combination of business activities	2 (3%)	1 (2%)	3 (2%)
Business and agriculture/ranching	8 (13%)	5 (8%)	13 (10%)
All business activities	19 (31%)	9 (14%)	28 (22%)
Agriculture/ranching	6 (10%)	14 (22%)	20 (16%)
All agricultural activities	14 (23%)	19 (30%)	33 (26%)

Note: Percentages may not add up to 100 because of rounding.

a. Includes medical doctors, lawyers, writer-journalists, engineers, professors.

b. In the cases of military officers who also engaged in other professional activities, the military was considered their principal occupation. One officer in the central authorities was also in the liberal professions, three were in agriculture, and one was in business.

c. Two of these men were employees in managerial positions.

29 percent of the sample, however, limits the utility of the age variable.

A variety of occupations was represented in the League, as indicated in Table 5. The largest number of members were in the liberal professions and bureaucracy, followed by agriculture and ranching or a combination of rural and commercial activities, and then by solely business pursuits. Considering the continuities between Social Catholicism and the League, the number of clerical members is surprisingly low. Aside from the five priests who appeared in the group studied, however, at least eleven other prominent Liguistas in the sample participated heavily in the Workers' Circles and other Catholic organizations. As will be seen, women forged the crucial link between the League and the Church.

The only important professional differences between the national leaders and brigade delegates emerged in the categories of military officers and business. Military officers were much more heavily represented in the central authorities than among delegates. The Central Junta and Executive Council members in the sample included two rear admirals, an admiral, a naval captain, three generals, a lieutenant general, a colonel, a lieutenant colonel, a major, and another senior officer of unknown rank. Probably half of these were retired. The three lieutenant colonels and one major among the delegates all came from Buenos Aires province. Perhaps the fact that officers in the capital and surrounding areas had helped create the League accounted for their large numbers at the national level, whereas the moving forces behind the provincial brigades were local employers. Nevertheless, the percentage of delegates in business pursuits was markedly lower than that of national leaders in these occupations. In actuality, the first percentage was probably much higher; many delegates were small-town merchants who escaped the notice of *porteños* who compiled biographical dictionaries. Their status contrasted with that of the eighteen members of the central authorities who were owners or board directors of large corporations and banks, at least five of whom were closely tied to foreign companies. Noting these connections, *La Vanguardia* dubbed the organization the "Anglo-Argentine Patriotic League." [77]

Included in the sample were two representatives each from the stevedores', bakers', and taxi drivers' brigades and one representative of the beltmakers' brigade. Whether these seven men were genuine workers, employers, foremen, or lumpen is not clear.

The brigades they represented were only four of the many categories of "free labor" brigades the League claimed to have: aside
from the ones mentioned, telephone operators, bricklayers, paint-
ers, shoemakers, carpenters, peons, firemen, cigarmakers, and
metallurgical, dock, electrical, sanitary, and railroad workers.
The urban labor brigades were concentrated in the federal capital, although there were such exceptions as the Rosario railroad
workers. The artisan groups such as the bakers seem to have created corporatist-style brigades including both small employers
and their employees, but the majority of these brigades included
nonunionized workers already employed by League members or
hired by them to break strikes or otherwise impede labor mobilization. They came from the labor reserve of the wartime unemployed and immigrants. Peons and sometimes artisans and
mechanics formed the ranks of free labor brigades in the countryside, commanded by employers and foremen.[78] These strikebreakers constituted the League's lower-class contingent, which
clearly had no voice or power within the organization.

As if to symbolize worker powerlessness in the group and outside it, the League held a well-publicized meeting celebrating the
formation of a free labor brigade at the Vasena factory, where the
Tragic Week had begun. The central authorities designated a
commission to represent the new brigade at the festivities and
"explain the significance of the event to the workers."[79] They
deemed the workers incapable of speaking for themselves.

Given the workers' limited roles in the League, the middle
and lower-middle classes constituted its popular component—
perhaps as much as 31 percent of the central authorities and
82 percent of the delegates, and a larger percentage of the ranks.
These individuals, according to *La Vanguardia*, were the "excellent citizens who feared that others doubted their patriotic sentiments." Professionals, teachers, independent businessmen,
employees, minor bureaucrats, and military officers filled the
brigades in the capital. There also were the professional brigades
of medical doctors, high school teachers, pilots, and government
employees. In the cities of the interior, the local chapters usually
attracted schoolmasters, lawyers, physicians, merchants, land-

owners, a few policemen, and priests. Tenant and small independent farmers (*chacareros*), *estancieros*, and their employees and
peons formed rural brigades. The officers of the rural San Salvador, Entre Ríos, brigade, for example, included the following:
a retired colonel (president); two threshing-machine owners
(commission presidents); two farmers (commission president
and secretary general); brick-oven owner (commission president); dairy owner, rancher, agricultural machinist, and two supposed rural workers (junta members).[80]

Recruiting the middle sectors was important to Carlés. His
frequent assertion that no classes existed in Argentina did not prevent him from appealing just as frequently to what he called the
"forgotten class" of professionals, employees, military officers,
priests, small farmers, and retail merchants. His rhetoric, as well
as the social welfare projects for white-collar workers discussed
in the congresses, attested to the League's interest in attracting
these groups. From its earliest manifestos, the League exhibited
particular concern for organizing teachers. Teachers formed a
natural constituency, according to *La Protesta*, as most of them
held an exaggerated view of their status. They saw themselves as
a caste apart from and above the manual workers they disdained,
although both teachers and laborers were salaried employees.
(Perhaps for similar reasons, teachers would also figure promi-
nently in Brazilian and European fascism.)[81] Carlés's interest in
this group owed more to his eagerness to "nationalize" the educational system, however, than to any awareness of its self-image.

The League and the Radical party cast their nationalistic appeals to a similarly broad spectrum of the populace. For this reason, as well as the others previously discussed, the UCR under-
standably viewed it as a potential competitor. There is little
evidence, however, that the League attracted native-born male laborers of their own free will, unlike the Radicals. Moreover, the
Radical focus on democracy won longer-lasting support from
the middle sectors than the League's defense of capitalism. The
League's social base was not as wide as the Radicals'.

Nevertheless, the League, unlike the Radicals, enthusiastically
recruited women. The social backgrounds of female Liguistas

differed in some ways from those of their male counterparts. I classified women as upper-class if they were mentioned in a social register or society album, or if their husbands, fathers, and/ or sons were of that rank. All 45 members of the Junta of Señoras and 69 of the 71 members of the Commission of Señoritas (97 percent) during the years 1920 to 1928 fit this category, compared with 69 percent of the male leaders. Only fragmentary data can be found on the status of the brigade members and Teachers. The League frankly admitted that most Señoritas came from "high society," and observers said the same for the Señoras. This again differed from the lower social standing of male brigade delegates and rank and file. Teachers, however, seemed to come from the middle sectors.[82]

Family relationships and prior affiliations influenced women to join the League. Thirty-six percent of the Junta of Señoras and 23 percent of the Commission of Señoritas were closely related to men in the organization. Their husbands and relatives probably acquainted them with the League's goals and encouraged them to become members. At least 40 percent of the Junta of Señoras and 86 percent of the Commission of Señoritas were closely related to other League women, indicating that female kinship networks particularly influenced the Señoritas to join the League. Membership in philanthropic, Social Catholic, and civic associations proved a more decisive determinant in the case of the Señoras. Fifty-eight percent of the Junta of Señoras came to the organization with such backgrounds, while most of the leading Señoritas were too young to have had this experience (see Table 6 for a list of these associations). The average age of Señoras (n = 7) was fifty-two in 1920, and of Señoritas (n = 20) was twenty-four, but I found information on very few women. In contrast, charity work and Catholic affiliations were not important determinants for male participation in the League, nor were family ties. Only 8 percent of the male central authorities were closely related to female leaders, and 17 percent to other male Liguistas.[83]

These variations between the sexes reflected the different ways in which men and women created networks. Before their participation in the organization, male Liguistas had met each other and

Table 6. Social and Charitable Organizations to Which League
Women Belonged in the Early Twentieth Century

Acción Católica Argentina (Argentine Catholic Action). Large organization of men and women, founded in 1928, devoted to a variety of
aims. (Two Señoras and one Señorita.)
Archicofradía Consolación (Consolation Cofraternity). Built a church,
school, and workshop serving mostly retarded youth. (One
Señora.)
Asilo del Niño Belgrano (Belgrano Children's Asylum). Day-care cen-
ter for children of working mothers. (One Señora.)
Asociación Conservación de la Fe (Conservation of the Faith Associa-
tion). Provided schooling for children in working-class suburbs of
Buenos Aires. (Two Señoras.)
Asociación de Damas Patricias (Association of Patrician Ladies).
Founded in 1912. (One Teacher.)
Asociación El Centavo (The Cent Association). Helped female laborers
to become self-supporting. (One Señora and one Señorita.)
Ayuda Social (Social Aid). Sold goods made by female workers with-
out commission. (One Señora.)
Caja Dotal para Obreras (Dowry Savings Bank for Female Workers).
Affiliated with League of Argentine Catholic Ladies and founded in
1911. Provided credit and other services to working women. (Three
Señoras.)
Cantinas Maternales (Maternal Canteens). Provided services for
mothers and infants of the working class. (Six Señoras.)
Casa de Huérfanas (House of Orphans). (One Señorita.)
Confederación Nacional de Beneficencia (National Beneficent Con-
federation). Founded in 1921. (Two Señoras.)
Consejo Nacional de Mujeres (National Council of Women). Founded
in 1900. (Three Señoras.)
Comisión Inspectora Hospital Rivadavia (Rivadavia Hospital Inspec-
tion Commission). (One Señora.)
Comisión Inspectora Hospital y Consultorio Oftalmológico
(Ophthalmologic Hospital and Clinic Inspection Commission).
(One Señora.)
Comisión Pro-Casa de Empleadas (Commission for the House of Fe-
male Employees). (One Señorita.)
Cooperación Salesiana (Salesian Cooperation). (One Señora.)
Dejad que los Ninos Vengan a Mí (Let the Children Come to Me).
(One Señora.)
El Divino Rostro (The Divine Face). Housed and taught homeless
children. (Three Señoras.)
Escuelas y Patronatos (Schools and Patronships). (Four Señoras.)
Gran Colecta Nacional (Great National Collection). Founded in 1919.
(Sixteen Señoras and two Señoritas.)

Table 6. (*continued*)

Obra de Don Bosco (Don Bosco Work). (One Señora.)

Patronato de Infancia (Patronship of Infancy). Housed and schooled abandoned, abused, and orphaned children. Founded in 1892. (Nine Señoras.)

Patronato de Leprosos (Patronship of Lepers). (Four Señoras and one Señorita.)

Providencia Femenina (Feminine Providence). Helped homeless, impoverished women. (One Señora.)

Sociedad de Beneficencia (Beneficent Society). Founded in 1823. (Four Señoras and one Señorita.)

Sociedad Conferencias de Señoras de San Vicente de Paúl (Conferences of Women of St. Vincent de Paul Society). Provided a variety of services for the poor and for workers. Founded in 1889. (Four Señoras.)

Sociedad Damas de la Misericordia (Ladies of Mercy Society). Services for the indigent, the elderly, and orphaned children. Founded in 1872. (Two Señoras.)

Sociedad Madres Argentinas (Argentine Mothers' Society). Schools, clothing, medicine for impoverished children. Founded in 1905. (One Señora.)

Sociedad San José (San Jose Society). Provided vocational education for girls. (Three Señoras.)

Women's Institute. (One Señora.)

Other, unnamed charities. (Four Señoras and two Señoritas).

---

had formed common goals in university and professional life, social clubs, interest groups, opposition parties, and the military. These contacts and joint concerns, drawn from a broad base of activities, led them into the League. Secluded from public life and denied higher education, women had less opportunities than men to widen their networks. As Jorgelina Cano noted in 1922, the Commission of Señoritas included no professionals.[84] Indeed, only one of the seventy-one ever became a professional (a social worker), and none of the leading Señoras did, although three belonged to the Rural Society. Carlés first campaigned among women by appealing to those of the upper class, precisely because of their philanthropic experience. These women then brought their relatives and friends, with whom they had grown up, attended school, and engaged in charitable activities, into the

League. Recruitment efforts did not extend beyond the narrow bounds of class, except perhaps when male brigades helped establish sister brigades and when Carlés and other leaders appealed to teachers.

Although the composition of the male and female membership differed, the main goal of both sexes was the same: to defend the existing socioeconomic order against the left. As founding member Yalour declared, "the Argentine Patriotic League has one function . . . that of maintaining order."[85] Their middle- and upper-class backgrounds, their statements, and the circumstances surrounding the birth of the organization demonstrated this overriding concern. This was not necessarily the only reason for joining the League. The desire of men and particularly of women to help the poor and strengthen the family led them into the group, but this motive was related to maintaining the status quo. Recruitment efforts among women and the "forgotten class" also made these groups feel important (although not enough so to convince the middle sectors to forsake the UCR). Finally, women found the League's message compelling because it confirmed and exalted their traditional roles. Through their activities described in the next two chapters, Liguistas of both sexes manifested all of these concerns, but the first remained paramount.

FOUR

The League Keeps Order, 1919–1922

Postwar Argentina witnessed an unprecedented unionization effort. Tremendous strikes broke out in the littoral ports, the grain zone, Patagonia, and the northeastern lowlands. Thus the League had much to do. Supported by allies in the Labor Association, police, and military, the League spread antileftist publicity, crushed strikes, and replaced unions with free labor associations. Without serious hindrance from the government, the League helped weaken the labor movement for decades to come.

At first the League's effectiveness seemed doubtful. After the foundation of the League until the end of 1919, its paramilitary groups in the capital appeared superfluous, if not comical. Despite labor mobilization and the fear of bolshevism, there was no labor-led violence on the scale of the Tragic Week. When Liguistas anticipated labor disturbances, Stimson reported, they contented themselves with "riding ostentatiously" in cars from one police station to another, wearing white arm bands, checking to see if the police were doing their duty. The diplomat doubted whether these vigilantes would be able to prevent any real trouble. Other observers, including the Socialists, similarly underestimated the League.[1]

Except in emergencies, the male brigades based in urban residential areas directed most of their efforts toward spreading the League's message through public events and propaganda. A favorite technique was to hold a parade, dance, or other ceremony to commemorate a national holiday or institution. Often female brigades worked behind the scenes, helping to organize these festivities. One example was the Córdoba brigades' day honor-

ing the military on October 31, 1921: the "biggest triumph" of
the League in that city, according to the "local conservative"
paper *Los Principios*. A regiment stationed in the city returned
from maneuvers and marched to the Plaza San Martín, where
male and female Liguistas awaited them. Spectators along the
streets and in balconies watched the League and the soldiers sing
the national anthem and the brigade of Señoras present gifts to
the conscripts.[2]

Not all League events resulted in success. During the previous
year, the same brigades had invited the governor, provincial and
municipal officials, schools, officers from the local garrison,
men's and women's associations, and other groups to attend their
independence day parade. Few of these guests were among the
estimated 200 marchers. Angry over the low turnout, a League
member concluded that the honored gentlemen and ladies had
chosen instead to drink in the governor's mansion or dance in private clubs. Nevertheless, *Los Principios* insisted that despite "indifference and antinationalistic opposition," the celebration had
been pleasant. The mildly leftist *La Voz del Interior*, on the other
hand, embarrassed League members by ridiculing their pom-
posity, provoking the male brigade's junta into denouncing the
paper as subversive and "dangerous." The junta warned all Liguistas and members of society to refrain from reading the paper
or cooperating with its reporters. The ban had little effect.[3]

Brigades also held festivities largely for the purpose of inviting prominent officials. The League hoped to impress them with
its strength, and to influence policy and form tacit alliances. For
example, the brigade of Banfield, Buenos Aires, held a banquet
and parade in 1921 for provincial and capital officials, many of
whom were Radicals, as were some brigade members. *La Vanguardia* observed that the sizable automobile contingent of the
parade did not back up the brigade's claim that it included workers, for none could afford a car.[4]

Brigades spread publicity by putting up placards in cities,
railroad junctions, and country stores (*pulperías*). The League
even created a "poster-fastener" brigade in the capital. Sometimes these poster campaigns provoked controversy. In mid-

January 1920, brigades posted an estimated 50,000 signs entitled "Defense of the Fruits of Labor" in towns and rural areas. Responding to a widely disseminated anarchist placard, the signs quoted Article 81 of the Penal Code, which defined the right of defense against attacks on life and property. Fearing that citizens might misinterpret this clause and take the law into their hands, the municipal intendant of Bahía Blanca ordered the League to take down the posters. Two local newspapers opposed this decision, as did Carlés and the local brigade. In a resulting city council debate, one Radical faction criticized the intendant, while another, seconded by Socialists, supported him. The discussion degenerated into open fighting, joined by League members and other spectators in the galleries. One council member asked the "Argentines present" to meet in the municipal plaza to protest. There, League members and sympathizers gathered to sing the national anthem and demand the intendant's resignation. Brigade leaders sent a formal protest against the order to take down posters to the city council. A few days later Carlés traveled to Bahía Blanca, spoke with the intendant, and invited him to his public speech. Before Carlés left the city, he and the intendant toasted each other, and the League leader declared that they had cleared up the misunderstanding. The Central Junta then sent thousands of extra posters to Bahía Blanca. A similar chain of events took place in Junín and Zárate, Buenos Aires.[5]

In these instances the League favored freedom of speech, but it opposed this right when it threatened its interests. The Socialist schism that supported the Third International, or Comintern, had scheduled a public meeting in the Plaza of General Viamonte, Buenos Aires, for the evening of October 27, 1920. That afternoon the local brigade issued a manifesto to the townspeople, asking them to prevent the event from taking place. Two hundred armed Liguistas and hired thugs, including Radicals, drove to the plaza. When the main speaker asked the police chief for protection, he refused, claiming that he did not have enough agents. Fearful for their lives, the speakers fled when shooting broke out between the League's forces and the audience, mostly consisting of regular Socialists. Two workers and three Liguistas were wounded, and policemen (now, apparently, in sufficient numbers) detained several Socialists and one League member. Both groups sent lawyers to attain their comrades' release. On two other occasions, police and Liguistas in Bahía Blanca in 1921 broke up meetings of the local labor federation which authorities had given permission to hold.[6]

In one incident, the League prevented its own members from exercising their rights. The brigade of Colón, Buenos Aires, held a public assembly on May 16, 1921. A few members asked the speaker some questions about the brigade statutes. Enraged, the brigade president took out a revolver and warned them against further interruptions. Shooting broke out, leaving two dead and many wounded. Backed up by reinforcements from Junín, police arrived and disarmed the opponents.[7]

Such occurrences gave the League the kind of notoriety that its leaders did not desire. To raise more favorable publicity, the League frequently awarded prizes to policemen, firemen, soldiers, and workers who had distinguished themselves in public service—including breaking strikes. These ceremonies also served the purpose of cementing the bonds between the League and the official forces of order. In accordance with this goal, League members proposed pensions for worthy policemen, a holiday commemorating Falcón's death, inexpensive housing for policemen, and other projects.[8]

As education was one of its special concerns, the League directed much of its propaganda toward teachers, education officials, students, and parents. In November 1919 the Central Junta asked parents of normal school students in the capital to subscribe to the following principle: that any woman who opposed "the moral principles or constitutive norms of the nationality, without possibilities of reforming herself," was unfit to teach. The League claimed that parents had agreed, but it offered no proof. As part of this campaign, the Teachers' branch of the League arose in early 1920 (see Chapter 3). The formation of these brigades roused some protest. In March 1920 an association of school principals declared that it was unnecessary for educators to join leagues "whose ends subvert the mission of the teacher." Liguista Teachers replied that their mission was just the opposite.[9] Perhaps this opposition was responsible for the small size of the Teachers' branch.

In 1921, rumors of leftist teachers worried the Mendoza brigade. Its president suggested that parents attend classes to check for subversive lessons. He also advised mothers to form a committee to examine children's textbooks and assignments and insure that the school was the "continuation of the Argentine home." Members of the brigade spoke on civic topics in the schools. Meanwhile Carlés wrote to provincial governments, requesting that their education departments administer loyalty oaths to teachers, like the one given in the national school system. The governments agreed.[10]

Few university students responded to the League's message. The opposition of some League members to the reform movement, along with widespread student sympathy for labor, prevented the League from establishing more than a handful of student brigades. The League's denunciations of student newspapers in Córdoba and Rosario also did not boost its popularity. When administrators in several universities invited Carlés to speak, students walked out and sent notes of protest to rectors and newspapers. Student federations throughout the country loudly criticized the League's repression of labor and asked citizens to boycott its events.[11]

Undaunted by such challenges, the League proceeded with its most crucial task: to break strikes and cripple organized labor. The League employed various tactics to reach this goal. Sometimes, as in several cases discussed later, residential brigades attacked worker targets. Brigades also traced the movements of "agitators" and reported on their activities to the Central Junta.[12]

Perhaps most important, the League asserted control over the supply of laborers through the formation of free worker brigades. Workers' brigades were supposed to provide the same services to their members as unions, such as mutual aid, education, and the improvement of working conditions and economic benefits. In theory they recognized the right to strike against abusive employers but not against the capitalist system. Only on rare occasions, and contrary to the League's wishes, however, did free laborers actually protest. The principal service these brigades performed was to replace strikers with scab laborers. Julio A. Quesada, a prominent real estate auctioneer, headed the League's Dirección de Gremios (Union Governing Board), which placed workers. He and other board members asked employers who belonged to the League to hire only those workers who could present identification cards issued by his office. The League's self-styled "job placement" activities or "mediation" of strikes meant the introduction of free workers.[13]

The registration and meetings of free workers took place at League headquarters at 524 Florida Street. Significantly, the Labor Association also registered its strikebreakers at this location, although it housed them at 735 Sarandí.[14] Nor was address the only feature the two groups had in common. Some of the most prominent Labor Association members also belonged to the League: among them, Joaquín de Anchorena, Labor Association vice-president until 1921, and then president; Secretary-General Atilio del'Oro Maini; Ricardo Aldao, a shipowners' counsel and future Radical governor of Santa Fe; and Santiago O'Farrell, former Catholic deputy and railroad corporation board director. More important, the Labor Association's views on labor issues were virtually identical to the League's. The League and Labor Association worked together, as the latter hinted at in its *Boletín de Servicios*. In the distant future the League would deny this connection and, indeed, its own repression of labor, which it would blame on the Labor Association.[15]

The most important cases of League intervention in labor conflicts in the capital occurred in the simultaneous port and taxi drivers' disputes in May–August 1921. The taxi drivers' union, including drivers of publicly and privately owned vehicles, had carried out a strike in early 1920. Their militancy prompted Carlés to call the union a "soviet." Members of the Liga Propietarios de Automóviles Particulares (League of Private Automobile Owners), affiliated with the Labor Association, met several times in January 1921, agreeing to drive their taxis themselves if the chauffeurs again struck. A handful of Liguistas of-

fered to drive along. Meanwhile, the federal police imprisoned
union members for allegedly committing bombings and other
crimes. In protest, the union announced that a general strike
would start on May 25, which angered patriotic Argentines of
the upper classes.[16]

Early on May 25, a group of young Liguistas forced their way
into the union office with revolvers. At gunpoint, they compelled unionists to kneel, salute the national flag, and then rise
and write "Long live the fatherland" on a blackboard. Breaking
windows as they left, the youths promised to return. During the
day Carlés met with the Automobile Owners and discussed
means of countering the strike. They decided to fire strikers, enter the names of troublemakers on a blacklist, and drive the taxis
themselves, if necessary. They also asked nonaffiliated drivers
to display the national colors (blue and white) on their cars. In
the afternoon, owners and nonunion drivers met in the Plaza
San Martín and drove their vehicles, filled with the families of
League and Automobile Owners members, through the downtown streets to the League office. There, from a balcony, Carlés
addressed the occupants of approximately 300 cars. After the
speech, the self-styled "automobile brigade" continued to recon-
noiter the city, defying union efforts.[17]

That evening, groups of well-dressed young men wearing
blue and white insignia in their lapels gathered at the corner of
Bermejo and Mitre streets, where the taxi drivers' and other
unions were located. Six or seven cars from the "automobile brigade," all with their headlights out, joined them. Their pas-
sengers and the men already there fired at the union office, killing two workers. The young Liguistas poured gasoline on the
building and ignited it, but firemen arrived quickly and doused
the flames. *La Vanguardia* believed that the League had fore-
warned the police, for not only did the firemen arrive almost immediately, but police also had circulated through the area shortly
before, telling residents to remain indoors and avoid the corner in
question. Nevertheless, the police arrested two League members,
whom a judge freed two days later, saying there was no evidence
that they had committed wrongdoing. The judge also ordered

the police to close union headquarters—which the police had actually done immediately after the assault. At that time, the police had carried off union documents, destroyed the furniture and library, and arrested about 300 drivers. Claiming that the union operated outside the law, Police Chief Elpidio González forbade it from meeting. The joint League, Labor Association, and police actions left the taxi drivers in disarray.

The strikebreaking effort continued. The League insisted that 500 federated drivers left the union for the "taxi drivers' brigade" by the end of May. *La Vanguardia* tacitly confirmed these desertions on June 3, noting that the strike continued against great odds. The choice was either to betray one's comrades by returning to work or, increasingly, to face imprisonment, according to the paper. Brigades from the interior also sent "Argentine drivers" to join the new brigade. They were aided by young upperclass Liguistas, licensed by the police, who drove dozens of cabs and remitted fares and tips to the taxi drivers' brigade fund. Thanks to these efforts, the number of privately owned taxis in circulation approached normal levels. On May 30 the League asked the municipality to revoke the licenses of "undesirables," and the Radical intendant, José Luis Cantilo, agreed. The League also asked the city to hire drivers only from its recommended list.

Union representatives met with police authorities in vain to try to work out a truce. Instead, the police closed down *La Protesta* on May 28 and continued to detain federated drivers. Finally, on June 7 the defeated chauffeurs returned to work. This did not, however, end the League's involvement. A week later, the League stopped trams to put blue and white insignias on them, without police interference. In the early morning hours of June 8, League members attached an insignia to a tram at Callao and Santa Fe streets, and then they entered the car and beat the driver, without any provocation.[18]

The League and the Labor Association enjoyed an even greater triumph in the port, scene of almost continual labor strife since 1916. The main port union, the FOM, had won tacit government support and some control over hiring, and it had brought prestige to FORA IX, with which it was affiliated. In early 1921, two stevedores' unions formerly tied to FORA V fused and overpowered the two other such unions affiliated to FOM. The anarchist-influenced group declared in late April that it would only work with the anarchist carters' union. This boycott angered shippers and the Labor Association, who asked the government to settle the problem. When authorities proved unwilling or unable to do so, the Labor Association and the League seized upon the boycott as an opportunity to reassert their control over port workers. They began to send nonunion laborers into the ports, creating a "stevedores' brigade." Knowing that such action would spark violence, Yrigoyen closed the port on May 9 and guarded it with troops.[19]

For the next few weeks the government tried to mediate the dispute and seemed to lean toward the workers' side. Its policy shifted, however, when foreign shippers threatened to boycott Argentine ports unless the government allowed free laborers to work there. Yrigoyen capitulated to this threat. The fact that the "better Argentines" voted, unlike the dock workers, also may have influenced his decision. This meant that Yrigoyen had moved from trying to coopt the Socialist vote to placating the League.[20]

On May 23 the executive branch opened the port to all "fit" laborers, and scuffles between unionized workers and strike-breakers (*crumiros*) sent by the League and Labor Association broke out the next day. José Elías, whom FORA IX claimed was Anchorena's bodyguard, was killed.[21] His funeral a few days later gave Carlés and other orators an opportunity to denounce the brutality of organized labor on the docks. The government sent in troops and reinforced the police on the twenty-seventh to protect "freedom of work." That same day League members and Automobile Owners accompanied about 200 of the stevedores' brigade to the port and guarded them as they worked. Carlés and other League leaders had arrived early at their headquarters that morning, prepared to respond to any calls for keeping order. Carlés personally toured the port twice that day to make sure that the situation was peaceful.

On May 28 the FOM refused to work with nonunion carters. The next day rumors circulated that disturbances would break out in La Boca, a working-class neighborhood along the River Plate, where FOM and other port unions were headquartered. Fifty seven car owners of the automobile brigade responded to Carlés's call, conveying themselves and other League members to La Boca. As the area remained peaceful, Liguistas eventually left.

At this point the FOM committed itself to the contest against nonunion personnel, declaring a general port strike beginning on May 31. The military, under the command of General José F. Uriburu, once again guarded the port, permitting more than 1,000 free laborers to work. After police closed down the FOM headquarters in early June, the union realized that it could not win the struggle. On June 6, its members decided to return to work.

Nevertheless, the struggle between the League and the dock workers continued. In July in the neighboring port of San Fernando, Jesús Huanca, an FOM member, was tying a boat to the pier when a League scab, Agustín Minué, began to harass him. After the two exchanged angry words, the strikebreaker shot Huanca four times and killed him. The police chief and police doctor, both League members, took Minué into custody and treated him well. The FOM gave its fallen comrade a large funeral, at which workers vented their rage against the League.[22]

The League terrorized federated workers and uncooperative shippers alike. Employers' groups affiliated with the Labor Association forced captains and officers to use only League hirelings to load and unload. Armed League "inspectors" prevented union men from getting close to the ships, despite the fact that all qualified laborers, "free" or otherwise, were supposed to be able to work in the port. On August 11, a League inspector boarded the U.S. vessel *Arani* and commanded an officer to choose stevedores from among his forty men waiting alongside on the dock. The officer chose seven strikebreakers, but when he saw how poorly they performed their duties, he replaced them with union men. The inspector protested, and when the officer refused to back down, the former ordered his men to attack him. Only the intervention of the captain and other shipmates prevented violence. The next day the officer again refused to pick

League strikebreakers, and the inspector threatened him. The Maritime Prefecture detained the latter, who was, however, freed by three other League members. Accompanied by fifty men, the persistent inspector returned to the *Arani* on August 13 and shouted insults at the federated stevedores. That day unknown assailants struck the ship captain with a cudgel, rendering him unconscious. Later that month, when the officer of a Spanish ship, *Infanta Isabel de Borbón*, tried to hire union stevedores, another League inspector ordered a policeman to lead the federated workers away from the vessel. A scuffle ensued in which several men were hurt.[23]

Nor did the League treat its own stevedores very well. Poor and unskilled, they often were migrants from the interior. At the beginning of the port struggle in May, the League gave them food and lodgings, but by August it left them to their own devices. As the League and Labor Association had flooded the port with free laborers, many did not actually receive jobs. To secure employment, *crumiros* had to pay League inspectors. In December a free worker, Eleodoro Silva, publicly complained that he had to pay his League boss, Eduardo Schiavino, two pesos a day for work. Angered by this insubordination, Schiavino shot at Silva three times but missed; a nearby policeman witnessed the action but did not interfere.[24]

The government's decision in May to open the port to all laborers in effect had handed it over to the League and its allies. Theoretically the more experienced unionized stevedores were still assured of employment, but the League, with government collusion, prevented this from happening. The employers' interests now controlled the supply of labor in the port, having overpowered FOM, one of the strongest unions in the country.

Aside from the taxi drivers' strike and the port struggle, the League generally left labor management questions in the capital to its partner, the Labor Association. Outside Buenos Aires, however, the League reigned supreme in such matters, indicating that the two groups divided the responsibility for policing the nation. Nevertheless, the Labor Association helped finance League activities in the provinces and recruit strikebreakers.[25]

Before its interventions in the capital, the League had found challenges in the most remote corners of Argentina. Journeying up the rivers as far north as Misiones, El Chaco, and Formosa, FOM militants spread syndicalist literature and gave inspiration to workers in the port towns after 1916. The Socialists established centers in the same region. Aided by FORA IX and FOM organizers, the newly awakened workers created unions even in the landholdings of the foreign-owned La Forestal company, which dominated northern Santa Fe province. Not unexpectedly, League representatives followed the trail of the labor movement, setting up brigades along the same path. The League augmented La Forestal's private police force with mercenaries to repress the strikes of 1919–21. The brigades of Villa Guillermina and Villa Ocampo were within company lands, and Lorenzo Anadón, a prominent Liguista, was a vice-president of La Forestal. The League's more important collaboration in the northeast, however, was with another powerful company, Las Palmas del Chaco Austral.[26]

Like the better-known La Forestal, Las Palmas was a state within a state, with sugar and tannin mills, cattle ranches, port, village, and company stores. The original British owners sold the lands, located in northeastern El Chaco, to a consortium including Argentines in 1909, and national interests took over the firm completely in 1925. At the time of League involvement, most of the firm's directors were Argentine, including the president, Carlos T. Becú, a prominent Radical. They delegated their tasks to a handful of resident administrators, who constituted the upper class of the area. Although little more than sharecroppers, immigrant colonists formed a middle sector. At the bottom of the social scale were 2,000-odd field laborers and stevedores of Creole, Paraguayan, Brazilian, and Indian origins. The most exploited of these workers were the Indians, who migrated from as far away as Misiones for the harvest. *Caciques* (tribal leaders) contracted with the administration for their tribesmen's services and received part of their wages, as well as a fee from the company.[27]

Oppressive working and living conditions affected all workers below the level of administrators. The company paid low wages in scrip and charged high prices for the low-quality goods it sold in its stores; it would not permit independent shops to operate on its property. Laborers who rested during their fourteen-hour workdays or bought goods elsewhere were punished. To change these and other conditions, skilled and unskilled laborers formed a workers' federation in 1918 and maintained strong ties with FOM and FORA IX. The union struck successfully the following year, winning higher wages, extra pay for overtime, and a shorter working day for mill laborers in December 1919. The company also agreed to pay workers in national currency, but for an extra fee. In early 1920, however, management began its counterattack by bringing thugs into Las Palmas. They fired guns into the air at night to frighten the inhabitants and tried to provoke union members in the mills during the daytime.

These agents provocateurs were incorporated into the League brigade of Las Palmas, which arose in May 1920 under President Alberto Danzey, a company administrator, and thirty-six junta members.[28] During the brigade's independence day celebration on May 25, its first activity, Liguistas shouted "Long live the fatherland," while anonymous voices added "Long live the workers' federation!" Offended, brigade leaders demanded that union leaders be punished for this incident, and police obliged them by imprisoning five activists.

Soon the League and Labor Association were collaborating with management to provoke a confrontation with labor. On June 4 Becú asked the Labor Association to send fifteen men to Las Palmas to disrupt the union. The FORA IX discovered this contract and alerted the workers' federation. The nonfederated workers arrived, and provocations against unionists continued. On July 12 a mechanic and brigade officer, Luis Brunet, drew a gun on four union activists in the sugar mill. The four men complained to the police and local judge, who suggested they speak to the highest resident company administrator, Robert Young. When Young dismissed their protests, the union called a strike on July 14, demanding Brunet's expulsion and the payment of wages in national currency without fees. Noting that the strike would fall during the sugar cane harvest, the brigade accused workers of deliberately planning to ruin that operation.

At the union's request, FORA sent a representative, Pedro Alegría, to reason anew with Young. Arriving in Las Palmas,

Alegría found the port filled with armed League *crumiros*. He reported that on July 14 and 15 these men beat some strikers and fired their guns intermittently after dark. Alegría presented the union's demands to Young on the twenty-first, and Young agreed to dismiss Brunet. Later that day, however, the company directorate in Buenos Aires ordered Young to cut off negotiations, and the strike continued. A few days later, Becú told two FORA delegates that he would not fire Brunet. He also admitted that he had dispatched the fifteen agents provocateurs and that he had requested fifty-two more. Becú explained his actions as "a matter of principle."

Tensions mounted in Las Palmas as the strike dragged on. Running short of food, workers labored for colonists for little pay and stole sugar, oranges, and cattle from the company. On August 9 a company administrator, a judge, and several policemen, surrounded by League bodyguards, headed toward the village to enforce a company decision to eject about 1,000 workers and a few colonists from their homes. A throng of armed workers manning a trench accosted them and refused to comply. Retreating, the administrator and others decided to ascertain the strikers' intentions. They sent a group of Indians carrying sugar cane toward the trench where workers had stationed themselves. It was rumored that the League had contracted with *caciques* to hurl their Indians against the strikers. Believing that the Indians were the advance guard of an attack, the workers fired on them. Company and League forces behind the Indians responded with their guns, killing most of the Indians in a crossfire.

The battle continued into the next day, when workers tried to take over the sugar mill. Their enemies repelled the attack and threw the ranks of strikers into confusion. Some escaped from the village, a few ran back to the trench, and others took over the post office and cut telegraph lines. Despite the lack of communication with the outside, the combatants learned that forces of the Ninth Infantry Regiment in Corrientes were on the way. The inhabitants of Las Palmas later claimed that the nonfederated workers burned the fallen strikers in the mill furnaces so as not to leave evidence for the troops, who arrived on the eleventh.

The League was also involved outside the battleground. During the fighting on the ninth and tenth, Danzey encouraged his men to sack workers' homes. Lorenzo Arpellito, an Italian foreman, accused Danzey of instigating the theft of 6,000 pesos worth of goods and currency from his household. A *cacique* told him that Indians and white guards had shared the spoils, the latter taking the most valuable items. Arpellito's denunciation of the League to the police of Las Palmas landed him in the local jail. The entire judicial branch of the Radical-ruled territory appeared unwilling to help him. Fearing for his safety, Arpellito fled to Corrientes after leaving prison. Socialist Deputy Fernando de Andréis divulged this and other tales of League doings in Las Palmas to the Chamber, and asked the minister of the interior to explain League activities. Radical deputies helped defeat his request for an interpellation.[29]

The League did not cease its activities after the troops' commanding officer, Captain Gregorio Pomar, imposed an uneasy ceasefire. The FORA received word that Danzey was recruiting men in Corrientes and Resistencia, arming them, and sending them to Las Palmas. An additional hundred scabs carrying rifles and ammunition left Labor Association headquarters in the capital on August 18. When they reached the beleaguered area, they camped out in company buildings. Administrators and their families poured out of the zone, indicating the likelihood of another battle. At this time, Becú publicly thanked the League for its support.[30]

Captain Pomar, a loyal Radical, arbitrated a solution favorable to workers. When the regiment returned to Corrientes on August 20, however, the company disavowed the agreement, and the union renewed the strike. Police again detained activists "fingered" by Liguistas. When the company tried to starve workers into submission by refusing to sell them food, FOM sent the strikers supplies. The FOM also demonstrated its solidarity when, in a half-comic incident, the hundred strikebreakers sent by the Labor Association begged the maritime union for help. Complaining of League maltreatment, the scabs wanted to return to Buenos Aires, and FOM paid part of their passage. Despite the company's inability to retain nonfederated workers and its consequent loss of the harvest, it remained intransigent.[31]

Then, in early 1921, the directors of La Forestal unwittingly aided the Las Palmas company. The former closed one tannin mill after another, firing thousands of former strikers. La Forestal's policemen and Liguistas drove protesters and the unemployed masses out of company lands. Many of these workers and their families fled to El Chaco, where they searched for food and jobs. This labor surplus enabled Las Palmas del Chaco Austral to replace the strikers. The strike ended in June, and brigades in that province, northern Santa Fe, and Misiones reported that unions in their areas had given way to free labor associations. The workers' federation in Las Palmas, however, aided by the Unión Sindical Argentina (USA, Argentine Syndical Union, discussed later), held on and achieved a long-awaited concession in 1923: payment of wages in national currency without any fees. The arduous struggle that led to this victory exhausted its militancy. The union movement in the northeast declined, and conditions for workers continued to be bleak. Despite the achievement of the Las Palmas union and the passage of Law 11,278 in 1925, guaranteeing wages in national currency, some companies in the region continued to pay laborers in scrip.[32]

The League was also active in the grain zone, where conditions were ripe for protest among small farmers and peons alike. Unrest broke out in 1917 and again in 1919, when prices declined, natural disasters occurred, and a port strike impeded the transport of grains to markets. The FAA asked Yrigoyen for a rent moratorium and government loans but received no answer. Seventy thousand tenant farmers responded to the FAA's call for a rent strike by March 1919. Radicalized by government indifference and a steady worsening of conditions, FAA members also destroyed machinery and crops and even demanded land redistribution. Fearing a revolution, the government repressed the strike severely and broke it by mid-June. To prevent further discord, Socialists, Progressive Democrats, and dissident Radicals proposed a stiff land tax and contract reform in Congress. Yrigoyen, however, favored authorizing the National Mortgage Bank to make more funds available to potential smallholders. This measure passed but had little effect, and Yrigoyen did not institute further changes.[33]

Inflation and hardship had also hurt the landless laborers, who became receptive to the idea of protest. The anarchists "rode the rails" through the countryside, preaching to the dispersed labor force through song, verse, speech, and pamphlet. The *braceros* (landless workers) organized unions and affiliated with the two FORAS. In December 1919 these groups carried out huge strikes which lasted for a few weeks—and quelled their employers' incipient radicalism. Fearing further disruption of production, FAA members applauded the government's heavy-handed repression of the *bracero* movement. Protests by landless laborers continued, however, as did conflicts between tenants and landowners. The peons affiliated with FORA IX and FAA farmers made a valiant effort in 1920 to overcome their differences, but their agreement fell apart. The two beleaguered groups battled each other as well as the *latifundistas*.[34]

League activity began to pick up in the countryside in response to the strikes of December 1919. Every day the press announced the formation of rural brigades or rural branches of small town brigades in Buenos Aires, Santa Fe, Córdoba, La Pampa, Río Negro, Entre Ríos, and Corrientes. In pursuit of the anarchists, the League headquartered many brigades in train stations. The brigade of San Antonio Oeste in Río Negro, for example, announced its establishment of nineteen sub-brigades in railroad stations on the line which led from its base city to the Andes.[35] Brigades began to form "commissions in defense of rural labor," or roaming squadrons, to patrol the countryside. One of the first arose in December 1919 in Tres Arroyos, Buenos Aires, where about 2,500 peons had struck. Amid increasing disorder, Carlés sent delegates to "affected areas" and notified local officials that League brigades were ready to cooperate with the authorities. The League asked police forces to prevent the distribution of posters, journals, and pamphlets threatening public order.[36] These activities continued into the first months of 1920.

The League also began to create free labor brigades in the grain zone. A worker later described this process in his home region of southern Buenos Aires province for *La Protesta*. Although anarchism had barely reached his area, the League had formed a brigade consisting of ranchers and tenant farmers. Liguistas forced their peons to join a free labor brigade and carry the League's banner in parades. They rewarded workers with free meat and wine; the correspondent wished the anarchists could afford such inducements. Two peon members admitted to him that they did not really understand what the League was. All they knew was that they were supposed to defend the fields against strikers during the harvest, and the police would not interfere with their duty. The author added that ranchers and farmers would only hire members of the free labor brigade.[37]

By the summer of 1920–21, rural protest resumed. The Catholic paper *El Pueblo* complained about the League's inability to curb the violent strikes taking place in Santa Fe, Córdoba, and Entre Ríos. Its many brigades in these areas had satisfied themselves with sending reports of rural agitation to the Central Junta, which in turn forwarded these descriptions to the newspapers. Action, not simply information, was needed.[38]

The League quickly fulfilled this demand. The brigades of Pehuajó, De Bary, Trenque Lauquen, and Rivadavia in western Buenos Aires and Bragado in the center of the province informed the central authorities of their "plan for the salvation of the harvest" in early January 1921. Special brigade commissions would meet the *braceros* in the train stations and accompany them to the fields. There, other brigade members would instruct the workers on techniques of resisting "agitators." These units reported that other brigades throughout the grain zone were taking similar steps.[39]

In early 1921 Entre Ríos became a center of labor mobilization, as militants of the Federación Obrera Comarcal (Territorial Workers' Federation), tied to FORA IX, organized seventy-four unions in the province's many ports and rich fields.[40] League operations also blossomed, and two of the League's most important clashes with labor occurred here. The first of these took place in Villaguay, a department located in the middle of the province and in the Jewish agricultural zone, which encompassed the departments of Villaguay, Gualeguay, Gualeguaychú, Colón, and Uruguay. The roots of the conflict went back at least to early

1920, when small farmers, threshing-machine owners, and businessmen in the department formed a "social defense brigade" and affiliated themselves with the League.[41] Other brigades formed in neighboring towns and departments.

In early January 1921, a union in Villa Domínguez, a Jewish settlement, presented a list of demands to farmers and owners of threshing machines. The laborers asked for better working conditions and recognition of their union, representing different categories of workers, mostly Creoles, throughout the region. When these demands were rejected, the union called a strike. The machine owners brought in scabs from Corrientes, but union members in the railroad stations refused to handle grain from farms employing nonfederated workers. Some colonists were willing to compromise with the union, but the machine owners held out for a complete victory.

Two members of the Villa Domínguez brigade, allegedly Jews, assaulted José Axentzoff, the union secretary and also a Jew.[42] Department Police Chief Galaor Cintor went to Villa Domínguez and freed the assailants, while charging their victim with breaking the Social Defense Law. He took the wounded Axentzoff into custody on February 1. The doctor assigned to the Villa Domínguez police, the Jewish vice-president of the local brigade, refused to treat the prisoner. Cintor transferred Axentzoff to the Villaguay jail, and the two men sent by the Territorial Workers' Federation to replace him also were imprisoned there. While he was in prison, Axentzoff's home in Villa Domínguez was attacked by Liguistas, including a local police deputy.

The union, the Territorial Workers' Federation, and the Socialist party center of Villaguay decided to sponsor a peaceful mass protest against the imprisonments. Fearful of vigilante action, the federation first asked the provincial minister of government to guarantee the demonstrators' safety. A member of a Radical administration, the minister replied that such guarantees were unnecessary because national law permitted demonstrations. The protest was scheduled for February 11. Rumors of Jewish and Creole "maximalists" advancing toward the department seat alarmed local citizens, and the League brigade prepared itself to greet the "horde."[43] Indeed, FORA later claimed that the brigade met in Cintor's office, as was its custom, to plan its assault on the demonstration.

On February 11 a line of protesters stretching one and a half blocks headed for the main plaza of the town. Women and children, forming a third of the group, led the march. Townspeople and police surrounded them when they reached the square. A local printer and secretary of the federation addressed the crowd, reminding them of their purpose. Suddenly, according to *La Vanguardia*, Alberto Montiel, a provincial senator, "local conservative" caudillo, and League member, attacked the speaker. Shots rang out, but it was not clear whether they came from the protesters or the surrounding crowd.

Pandemonium broke loose as mounted police and Liguistas charged through the crowd, and women and children escaped in fright. Approximately thirty were wounded, mostly workers, and as many as five were killed, including one of the horseback riders, Montiel's son. *La Vanguardia* speculated that a worker or political enemy had aimed at his father, who was nearby, and missed. Julio Serebrinsky, editor of a Socialist newspaper in Concordia, the nearest city, was slashed with a machete and thrown into jail, along with seventy-five workers. Eighteen of them, at most, were Jews, including Serebrinsky.[44] The prisoners received no medical attention and generally brutal treatment. Lawmen cut off the moustache of one worker as they took him into custody, and they dragged another to the station by his hair. Both were Jews. Armed Liguistas and policemen guarded the railway station, ready to arrest any suspicious-looking passenger. Whether it had started the shooting or not, the Villaguay bourgeoisie had been better prepared than the workers for action.

Ironically, four days after the demonstration, its organizers' plea was granted. A Judge Izaguirre arrived from Gualeguay and released Axentzoff on the fifteenth. Realizing that he would be freed, a police sergeant and a deputy, brother of a Liguista, beat him while he was still under their custody. The night of his release, Axentzoff headed for his home in Villa Domínguez. As he passed the Montiel estate, two men jumped him and hit him with the butts of their revolvers. A pro-League newspaper of Villaguay, *La Nueva Epoca*, reported that the unidentified assailants had punished Axentzoff for his "insolence." The newspaper implicitly credited the League with this "act of justice," and it explicitly warned that similar deeds might follow. True to these words, on February 18 League members attacked the Socialist center of Concordia and destroyed the printing press of Serebrinsky's paper.[45]

The Villaguay incident sparked further League activity and solidarity in the vicinity from February through April. Dr. Sixto Vela, president of the Gualeguaychú brigade, sent Montiel his condolences and offered his brigade's assistance to help maintain order. Brigades in nearby departments replaced existing juntas with more action-oriented leaders, held parades, and set up branches and free labor brigades in the countryside. This flurry of mobilization spread to Corrientes as well.[46] Interestingly enough, many of the new recruits were Jews.

The Jewish question was intertwined with the Villaguay controversy. Provincial newspaper editors, police, vigilantes, and politicians, including a Radical deputy from Entre Ríos, Eduardo Mouesca, blamed the episode on Jewish extremists such as Axentzoff and Serebrinsky. *La Nación* originally characterized the incident as a case of "Jewish revolutionaries" pitted against "orderly creoles." Two days later, however, it retracted its words, finding that there were few Jews among the agitators—but many among the farmers. Socialist Deputy Andréis agreed, noting in the Chamber of Deputies that few of the prisoners in Villaguay were Jewish. Mouesca insisted that he was mistaken; all were of that faith. He also defended the League's actions. Even if they were all Jews, retorted Andréis, what difference would it make, as they were also Argentines? The Radical deputy responded, "It matters to me since this represents a custom of those people." Labeling his words "reprehensible," Repetto denounced Mouesca for expressing racist sentiments in a country where they did not exist.[47] On the contrary, the Villaguay incident proved that some Liguistas, Radicals, and others indeed were anti-Semitic.

Eager to blame leftism on foreigners, the League and its allies found in the Jews a scapegoat. Soon, however, they conveniently "forgot" their words. Jews participated on both sides in Villaguay, yet the colonists among them outnumbered the landless peons. The majority's interests were opposed to those of workers and therefore were the same as those of Liguistas. Even some Jews who might have found the League distasteful were anxious to distance themselves from anarchism or maximalism. Such persons in the colonies of Clara and Lucienville sent a delegation to Radical Governor Celestino Marcó, informing him that the recent disturbances were not the fault of Jews.[48]

Meanwhile Jews were joining the League. M. Abramovich, a founder of the colonies in the province, visited Carlés's office to request incorporation into the League on March 2. In his petition he wrote that most residents of the colonies were "Argentines," unswayed by "Russian sects." He saw the League as the institution that would best teach his coreligionists how to cement the nationality to the economic sovereignty of society.[49] Jewish farmers also wrote the Central Junta, expressing their wish to form brigades and belong to the country that had welcomed them with such hospitality. The Villaguay brigade created a free labor chapter of Jewish workers in Clara. *La Fronda* noted that "despite rumors to the contrary," existing *entrerriano* (Entre Ríos) brigades ratified the decision of Jews to join the organization. At least twelve of the approximately thirty brigades in the Jewish settlement zone had Jewish officers, and perhaps more had Jewish members.[50]

The League continued its intimidation campaign in Villaguay. The Socialist party sent Andréis there in February to defend the imprisoned workers. Fearful of League reprisals, local Socialists did not meet him at the railroad station. The League pressured hotel owners into denying him a room, forcing Andréis to stay at a friend's house. A brigade delegation visited the house that night and asked the Socialist to leave town immediately. Andréis remained, however, and the next day he interviewed a few of the prisoners; despite a judge's ruling to the contrary, the police kept most of them incommunicado. His clients' accounts, popular fears, and his encounter with the brigade impressed Andréis with the danger of his position. When six brigades of the area held a rally in Villaguay, Andréis telegraphed the Chamber, asking it to guarantee his safety. Some of the deputies expressed their shock over the League's audacity.

The Chamber forwarded Andréis's telegram to the Radical governor of Entre Ríos, whose position throughout the incident had been ambivalent. By this time Marcó had also received a letter from Andréis, asking him to protect the prisoners, as the police had not adequately guarded those in jail or those freed. Marcó replied that police protection was sufficient and added that such repressions were inevitable, for society had to carry them out "more in order to save its honor than to assure its stability." Perhaps to remind policemen of their honor, Marcó sent them a copy of his answer to Andréis. When the Socialist deputy left town, an official police statement declared: "Happily Deputy de Andréis leaves today; if his stay had been longer . . . the guarantees that he demands needlessly would not have served to protect him. . . ." Not surprisingly, the junta of the Villaguay brigade included relatives of local policemen, and Cintor was friendly to the League. Andréis summed up the whole incident by noting that the main causal agent was the police—"at the exclusive service of . . . the Patriotic League.[51]

On March 22 Judge Izaguirre finally released the remaining prisoners, claiming that he could not prove their guilt. Angered by this decision, the local brigade might have carried out further "acts of justice" if trouble had not been brewing elsewhere in the province. The *entrerriano* brigades now turned their attention to Gualeguaychú. Intimately tied to the mobilization of port workers in Buenos Aires and the entire littoral waterway system, the capital–labor conflict in that department had sharpened over the last few years. The longshoremen's union of Gualeguaychú, affiliated with FORA IX, frequently struck during this period. The FOM workers in Buenos Aires refused to handle cargoes consigned to Gualeguaychú merchants who employed free laborers and then tried to ship their goods through the more expensive railroad–ferry network. FOM-affiliated ferrymen in Zaraté, Buenos Aires, however, foiled this method by refusing to carry merchandise destined for Gualeguaychú across the branches of the Paraná River to Entre Ríos. As a result, businessmen were forced to resort to roundabout and even more costly means of sending their goods through intermediaries.[52]

Meanwhile, the militancy of other workers in the department exacerbated the friction between capital and labor. Carters, bakers, store employees, and others resorted to strikes and almost continual boycotts against employers of nonfederated workers, as well as against businessmen who dealt with such employers, from 1919 on. In October 1920 carriers of rural cargoes created a union, affiliated with FORA IX, and immediately raised their rates. Other FORA affiliates, like the longshoremen, warehouse workers, and millers, refused to unload or process grain carried by free laborers, except those employed by small farmers with limited means. Mills suffered tremendously, having to use cereals carted in from other areas at high prices. In one incident in October 1920, two Foristas (FORA members) killed Pedro Illesca, an elderly nightwatchman for a commercial establishment that used nonfederated employees. The League seized upon his death as an instance of foreign tyrants refusing to allow native-born free laborers to work as they saw fit, although there was no evidence that the assailants were immigrants.

The FORA affiliates and employers continued to clash. On January 20, 1921, a Liguista landowner asked railroad station workers in Gilbert to unload grains transported by nonfederated carters from his property. When the workers, who belonged to FORA, refused, the League member and his armed companions forced them to do so at gunpoint. On February 9, in the Palavecino station, federated workers refused to unload grain from nonfederated carts, and an agent from the grain-exporting firm supported them. This time the Liguista landowner and his men destroyed a grain storehouse near the tracks.

Such incidents angered the local bourgeoisie. Labor militancy clearly had hurt business—yet it had not hurt all businesses uniformly. The large cereal exporters in the capital had already capitulated to labor demands, and their branches in Entre Ríos employed union men. Thus, labor boycotted only the small local merchants, who sustained the greatest losses among employers during this crisis. Their difficulties, along with the inflation of the times, caused sharp increases in retail prices. This, in turn, resulted in hardships for all consumers, particularly the non-unionized landless peons. Ranchers and farmers were determined to maintain low wages and keep the rural workers of Gualeguaychú out of unions. Significantly, small businessmen and other local employers viewed themselves as nationalists who opposed both foreign radicals and foreign capital, as represented by the export–import firms. Although most of the federated workers were Creoles, the bourgeoisie regarded them as foreign, citing the red flag, Rosa Luxembourg Library, and leftist views of the local FORA headquarters as proof. These businessmen, along with "local conservative" and dissident Radical politicians who opposed the Marcó government, created the Gualeguaychú brigade in late 1919.[53] Other brigades soon arose in the department.

The Gualeguaychú brigade set out to register all who worked in cereal houses, farms, ranches, warehouses, and other establishments owned by Liguistas. The League resolved to fire and blacklist workers who denigrated the League, the fatherland, or the principle of free labor; proposed a strike; or tried to impose disorder in their workplaces. They were enemies of the League's "liberal humanitarian principles," according to the statutes. Brigade members also agreed to lend each other support in case of strikes and boycotts.[54]

On February 3, 1921, the Gualeguaychú brigade celebrated the anniversary of the battle of Caseros of 1852, in which the *entrerriano* general, Justo José de Urquiza, defeated Rosas. To the League the date symbolized the downfall of Rosas's tyranny—and heralded the downfall of labor tyranny as well. In conformity with its program of order, liberty, and work, the brigade invited the public to a celebration manifesting the Argentines' intent to defend their flag against the new despots. It asked workers and foreigners to come and listen to "the dictates of reason and patriotism" and to rid themselves of the evil propaganda of "degenerates from the sewers (*cloacas*) of the universe."[55]

The well-orchestrated ceremony included many participants.

Among the speakers were Manuel Carlés, a Miss Veglia Arigliani of the Pro-Fatherland Society of Young Women, and Sixto Vela, who had recently been accused of fraud and barred from practicing law.[56] Also addressing the crowd were other local notables, as well as a young bricklayer named Lescano, who saluted "the sons of free labor." For his part, Carlés decried the fact that the hard-working citizens of Gualeguaychú were wedged between lazy federated laborers and usurious foreign capital. A "Parade of Free Labor," consisting of 1,400 peons on horseback and hundreds of others in horse-pulled wagons, followed Carlés's speech.

In view of the pro-Rosas views of future counterrevolutionaries, it is interesting to note that both the League and its opponents distanced themselves from the dictator and the Federalists. League spokesmen often denigrated leftists as Montoneros (Federalist guerrillas) or Mazorqueros, referring to Rosas's secret terrorist organization. *La Vanguardia* frequently called the League the Mazorca. No friend of the League, one provincial official thought that with its military structure and its abuse of the national colors in its flag and insignia, the group did indeed resemble the Montoneros.[57]

During the months following the February celebration, Vela and his brigade tried to impose free labor throughout the department. In response to their activities, unidentified individuals, probably Foristas, burned the rural home of Luis Cinto, secretary of the Gualeguaychú brigade, in early March. In the middle of that month, leaders of the Gualeguaychú and Gilbert brigades met with Carlés and discussed the provincial situation.[58] The creation of workers' brigades continued, and an armed clash between capital and labor seemed likely.

For this reason, the provincial government warned police throughout Entre Ríos, especially in the vicinity of Gualeguaychú and Villaguay, to be prepared for disorders on May 1. A few days after this warning, the Gualeguaychú League chapter announced its plans for May Day festivities. Not only did labor around the world traditionally commemorate this day; *entrerrianos* revered it as the anniversary of Urquiza's declaration against Rosas in 1851. The League planned to appropriate this symbol of the international workers' struggle and transform it into a purely national holiday of free labor, in a manner similar to the policies National Socialists would follow in Germany.[59] The government gave the League permission to celebrate "The Day of the Argentine Worker" in Gualeguaychú. It also assented to FORA's plans for May Day observances in the same city. Local and provincial authorities hoped to reduce the potential for conflict by assigning the far-removed hippodrome to the League in the morning and the central plaza to the workers in the afternoon. This stratagem did not prove successful.

On the morning of May 1, 1921, the brigades of Gualeguaychú and twelve other municipalities, including Jewish settlements, paraded into town. The landowners had failed to tell the free labor contingents the reason for their journey, and many peons wondered when the elections were going to start.[60] The arrival of Carlés, flown in by a military pilot, caused great excitement. Music and fanfare accompanied the marchers to the hippodrome, where Carlés, Vela, and others gave speeches.

When Carlés left for Buenos Aires and the large rally dispersed, some of its enthused participants walked and rode by horseback to the plaza. Other Liguistas drove vehicles loaded with revolvers and rifles to that spot. The few available policemen could not stop League members from surrounding the throng of workers. Liguistas demanded that the workers take down their red flag, which authorities had permitted them to display. When they refused, Vela advanced toward the center of the plaza and asked them to lower it to avoid an incident. An uproar drowned out his words, and he asked Police Chief I. J. Lahitte to intervene. The workers consented to Lahitte's request and carried the flag to police headquarters.

After a moment, a League member unrolled an Argentine flag and penetrated the crowd, accompanied by cohorts on horseback. Workers interpreted this as the beginning of an attack, and they may have fired some shots to repel it. Then, according to Lahitte and other witnesses, an enormous discharge of gunfire came from the buildings and mounted Liguistas circling the square. At least six persons died and twenty-eight were wounded;

few of these casualties were Liguistas. Workers fled the plaza, many retreating for safety to the police station. When the firing ended, only the League members and the fallen remained in the plaza, strongly indicating the League's culpability. Indeed, Carlés did not deny his organization's responsibility for the Gualeguaychú massacre, as it came to be known, although the brigade criticized officials for scheduling the two rallies on the same day. In a telegram to Marcó, Carlés proudly asserted that the first shot, "whoever produced it, came out of the depth of our history and was not pointed against a multitude; it was directed against an apostasy."[61]

The authorities handled this situation differently than the Villaguay episode. That it occurred after the outcry over Villaguay, that the national press amply covered these events, and that the Socialist party, the UCR's rival, was not as heavily involved as in the previous case helped account for the government's change in attitude. So, too, did the League's obvious guilt. Based on reports from Lahitte and the provincial labor office president, E. Zacarías Castelltort, Governor Marcó decided that the League was at fault. Armed Liguistas had no business heading to an area outside the League's official itinerary, he wrote Vela. Marcó added that the League's provocation of workers over the flag issue was unjustified, for Argentine law permitted the display of the red flag, and workers had not insulted the national banner. Castelltort also informed Marcó that the Gualeguaychú brigade included many opponents of his administration, who cleverly exploited League activity for partisan rather than economic motives. They had attracted the support of two town newspapers and many local citizens.[62] This perception of the League as a political rival also helped determine Marcó's position.

For these reasons, government initially responded in an even-handed fashion and then even leaned toward the workers. It permitted both sides to hold their meetings, and policemen risked their lives trying to protect workers from League gunfire. One, in fact, died as a result. The police took several Foristas and four Liguistas into custody, including President Juan Francisco Morrogh Bernard of the Gilbert brigade, a "local conservative" leader, and President Luis Salduna of the Perdices brigade, but quickly freed the workers. Amid rumors that the League was preparing to free its jailed comrades and storm FORA headquarters, Marcó reinforced the local police and the troops permanently stationed near Gualeguaychú. Vela, however, denied these allegations. At the end of May, Marcó again moved against the League by denying juridical personage to the Civic Guard of Concordia, a participant in the League's May Day festivities, claiming that it and other groups undermined governmental authority. In his July speech to the legislature, the governor added that the League's actions had adulterated its patriotism and disturbed social harmony. Moreover, the national Radical press blamed the League for the massacre.[63]

Radical attitudes then seemed to turn toward the League. Police in Buenos Aires did not permit workers to hold anti-League rallies in May and June, citing the danger of League retaliation, although they allowed the League to meet. More important, during the protracted judicial process that followed May Day, the local government extended little aid to labor. Socialists Federico Pinedo and Antonio de Tomaso and other lawyers representing the families of the slain workers accused the imprisoned Liguistas, Vela, and a Father Blasón, from whose house shots were fired, of murder. Fearing League reprisals, three judges excused themselves from trying the case, and another, a Dr. Arrigos de Elía, tried to and failed. Perhaps for similar reasons, Gualeguaychú policemen reversed their story. Having first blamed the League for the shooting, now they alternately insisted they knew nothing or implicated the workers. Their shift in viewpoint led shocked FORA delegates to question Marcó, who offered no explanation. Arrigos de Elía released the League members on June 16 on the basis of insufficient evidence, despite witnesses to the contrary. The workers appealed the judge's decision, and the case resumed.[64]

By the end of November 1921, however, the Liguistas were still free—and they had turned the tables on the victims. The departmental FORA council had proclaimed in June that unionists could not rest until the League was "exterminated," and it ended the manifesto with "Long live the social revolution!" Despite FORA's claim that it meant to fight the League by organizing unions, not by violent deeds, the League denounced FORA to the police. In consultation with provincial authorities, the police detained ten Foristas for breaking the Social Defense Law. (Congress had rescinded this law on October 29, but the measure did not take effect until 1922.)[65] Socialist lawyers secured their release after a few days, but the League appealed the decision. Through these types of maneuvers the League chipped away at workers' funds and energies.

The labor movement in Gualeguaychú had lost momentum. The League convinced some businessmen who did not belong to the group to hire half federated and half free laborers. In May 1921 the stevedores and carters struck in protest, and FORA declared a general strike. The strike spread to other departments and to Corrientes, where worker solidarity prevented the League from finding many scabs. Nevertheless, the strike ended in failure on June 30. Moreover, Tomaso admitted that the Socialist party center in Gualeguaychú was barely functioning by that time.[66] Despite unfavorable publicity on the massacre, the League emerged victorious from the Gualeguaychú episode; it had boosted the cause of free labor.

The League now advanced the free labor cause throughout the cereal zone. Rural agitation had spread to Santa Fe province, prompting farmers in Carlos Pellegrini, among other localities, to request affiliation with the League. The Central Junta sent General Eduardo Oliveros Escola to that area to organize a brigade and rural defense commissions in early 1921. In March the League reported that the brigade had imposed order in Carlos Pellegrini by apprehending and jailing labor activists. In recognition of such services, the Bolsa de Cereales (Cereal Exchange), headed by a Liguista, José Etcheverry, put the League in contact with farmers throughout the pampas and asked its agents to cooperate with the organization. The League solicited funds from private companies to continue its work in safeguarding harvests.[67]

Peons were organizing in Córdoba, and the League followed closely behind. There the organization focused much of its energy on the southeastern department of Marcos Juárez, one of the country's richest grain-producing areas. Carters and steve-dores in Leones, a railroad center, had secured wage hikes in 1919. Local threshing-machine owners, who belonged to the Leones brigade, had also raised their rental fees. Squeezed by the de-mands of these two groups and by the world agricultural crisis, the beleaguered tenant farmers petitioned the brigade, ostensibly founded "in defense of the cultivator," to intervene in December 1919. When this plea failed, one hundred tenant farmers from the entire department asked the Central Junta to solve their problems with both the machine owners and the workers. The League re-ferred the matter to the brigade of Córdoba, which was unable to mediate the dispute. Threshing operations were paralyzed, and much of the harvest was lost.[68]

A year later conflicts broke out anew between colonists and *braceros* in Isla Verde, in the same department. Affiliated with the Federación Obrera Provincial (Provincial Workers' Federation), the *braceros* demanded wage increases. When the tenant farmers refused, the federated workers tried to prevent free laborers from harvesting the crops. The resulting violence prompted the inter-vention of police, who in turn asked the Isla Verde brigade for assistance. Armed with rifles loaned by a target practice club, brigade members patrolled the fields and threatened strikers.[69]

In early 1921, organizers from the Provincial Workers' Federa-tion mobilized migrant harvest laborers near Leones and the de-partmental seat into unions. The Leones brigade responded by setting up free labor brigades, and the federated workers re-sponded with work stoppages and boycotts. In one incident in Leones, federated workers exchanged gunfire with policemen and brigade members for several hours. Some of the strikers fled to the federation office, which the brigade and official forces took by force, arresting fifty men. In solidarity with these pris-oners, 20,000 workers in the department left their jobs, and the federation called a general strike.[70]

Determined to prevent disruptions of the next harvest, the Leones brigade sponsored a meeting of departmental brigades in October 1921 to discuss defense measures. By this time the brigade had become one of the largest in the interior, with more than 800 members, including free workers. The provincial government, controlled by the PDP, had granted it juridical personage. At the meeting, Leones brigade leaders admitted that agitators remained in the area, but added that the League had "the means to repress" their abuses "in whatever form and in all aspects," thus guaranteeing order, work, and "individual rights." [71]

Despite League precautions, labor militancy resumed near the town of Marcos Juárez. Tenant farmers claimed that anarchists were interrupting work in the fields. In early December 1921, the Marcos Juárez brigade asked provincial authorities to reinforce the police. Local police, a provincial security squadron, and the brigade guarded nonfederated harvest workers and brutally repressed union members, taking some into custody. Workers' representatives denounced these excesses to the provincial government, while the Marcos Juárez brigade thanked the latter for its help. When workers threatened to free the prisoners, the brigade repelled their attack and gave them two hours to leave the department. Free labor had won the battle. [72]

At the same time, workers and the League clashed at the other edge of the pampas. Railroad station stevedores in Jacinto Arauz, in southeastern La Pampa near the Buenos Aires border, organized a union and affiliated with FORA V. After much struggle, they won some concessions from cereal firms and the Pacific Railroad, but employers continued to try to break the union. Rumors circulated in Jacinto Arauz in December 1921 that the League, at the companies' behest, was recruiting *crumiros* in Buenos Aires province to replace the federated stevedores. (No brigade existed in the town.) On December 8 a Liguista named Cataldi brought fourteen nonfederated workers to Jacinto Arauz to replace union members. Early the next morning, Foristas from the vicinity conferred and agreed to resist. When the meeting ended, the stevedores occupied the grain storehouses and refused to let the free laborers enter. Only police action prevented bloodshed. The supervisor closed the storehouses, and both sides left the station to await company action. [73]

At this point the police took over the League's work. A police officer asked the federated workers to come to the commissary, unarmed, to discuss the conflict. Suspicious, the men secretly carried arms to the patio in front of the police station, where police encircled them and started to bring them inside, one at a time. They separated two from the group and beat them. The police fired on the rest when they refused to enter the building, and the Foristas responded in kind. Surprisingly, the workers managed to shoot their way through the police and were able to flee. Four policemen and two workers died in the battle. During the ensuing manhunt, police destroyed the union office in Jacinto Arauz and workers' homes in the area. When they apprehended all but two of the wanted men, they escorted the prisoners by train to Santa Rosa, where the trial would take place. One of the slain policemen was a native of Santa Rosa, and his death outraged many residents. Capitalizing on this anger, the local brigade met the prisoners at the train station and followed them to the jail, screaming for "justice." The police barely prevented the mob from lynching the Foristas. The workers were sentenced to terms ranging from four years to several months, but police never captured the other two participants in the gunfight.

By the time of the trial, news of repression in Patagonia began to circulate in Buenos Aires, drawing the attention of the labor movement away from Jacinto Arauz. Historians have referred to the chain of events in the far south as "Tragic Patagonia." Although this social conflict reached a climax in 1921, its roots stretched back to the postwar slump. The prices of mutton and wool plummeted after 1919, yet the cost of living continued to rise, alarming *estancieros* and impoverishing rural laborers. Yrigoyen's actions only deepened the gloom. In 1918 he reinstated customs duties in the former free ports of the area, and in the following year he ordered new surveys of the southern national territories as a first step toward reasserting state control over illegally occupied public lands. Ranchers feared this second measure because they were the main culprits. An incipient labor movement then gave landowners and merchants additional cause for concern. From 1918 on, FOM and FORA IX representatives helped organize unions of railroad, packinghouse, petroleum, port, and rural workers in the territories of Santa Cruz, Chubut, and Tierra del Fuego, which affiliated with the Federación Obrera Regional (Regional Workers' Federation) of Río Gallegos.[74]

As unions arose in the south, so, too, did League brigades. Significantly, foreigners were found on both sides; the largest landowners were European immigrants or representatives of foreign landholding companies, and many workers, particularly on the ranches, were Chilean. Thus both sides were able to hurl the epithet "foreigner" against each other. Despite their nationalism, Carlés and the League did not find it illogical to support European landowners, whom they considered "beneficial foreigners" contributing to national development. In their opinion the proletariat did not share this quality. As the battle lines formed between workers and employers, including League members, Carlés became convinced that the enemy was not only a foreign ideology but the neighboring country, Chile. The huge strikes in Puerto Natales and Punta Arenas in southern Chile in 1919 must have confirmed his belief that leftism had simply penetrated Patagonia from Chile.[75] National defense was the same as defense against leftism.

The League president's concern over border security in turn aroused his interest in the Indians of the frontier zones. Carlés hoped to Argentinize the Indians and in the process strengthen Argentine defenses against Chile. That the League could pit the Indians against the workers perhaps also occurred to him. According to a League press notice, Indians in Santa Cruz, Río Negro, Chubut, Neuquén, and Los Andes (now part of Neuquén) formed eighteen brigades between July 1919 and January 1920. On January 27, 1920, Carlés met with one hundred delegates of the Indian brigades in Buenos Aires. He told them that the League would ask the government to build schools for them and to return their community lands, with ownership titles.[76] Whether the League would keep its promises remained to be seen.

In 1919 and 1920 the League resorted to its familiar tactics of disrupting union activities. At first it concentrated its free labor organizing efforts in the towns and petroleum installations along the coast, where unions were increasingly militant. After several strikes hit the national oil works in Comodoro Rivadavia in 1919, its head, Captain Felipe Fliess, asked overseers and foremen to join a free labor brigade. From then on, League members clashed with unionists. In October 1919 a Liguista oil worker who had demanded a promotion was forced to return to his old job when it became clear that he could not fulfill his new duties. Dissatisfied, he assaulted the overseer responsible for his demotion, a man who had not joined the brigade. Despite workers' protests, management did not punish the Liguista, but it suspended the overseer.[77]

In December 1919 the Federación Obrera Petrolífera (FOP, Petroleum Workers' Federation) struck after Fliess rejected its demand for a wage increase. The government sent in naval troops and immigrant scab laborers to repress the strike. Businessmen, industrialists, and landowners in Comodoro Rivadavia formed a brigade, subtitled "the League of Commercial Defense," in January 1920. Claiming that union activists did not work because they were too busy agitating, brigade members refused to employ them. When news of their decision spread, other workers joined the FOP's strike. The League established squadrons of ten members each to patrol the streets at night and helped the navy crack down on the FOP. Workers in the oil industry and surrounding countryside responded by boycotting the local branch of the national bank, whose supervisor was a League member. In the end, the government and the League succeeded in undermining the unions of Comodoro Rivadavia. Nor did the League confine itself to the Argentine oil fields. During the same year, League members crossed over the border into Punta Arenas, scene of labor unrest, burned down the oil workers' union office, and killed its leader.[78]

The pace of worker and League mobilization quickened. Approximately seventy-five League brigades arose in the ports, *estancias*, and railroad stations from the Río Negro south to Ushuaia in 1920–21. Representatives from these units traveled further into the interior and organized ranchers, managers, foremen, and "loyal" laborers into branches, and the League and Labor Association augmented these forces. These brigades maintained constant communication with the central authorities, informing them of workers' activities.[79]

There was much to tell. In November 1920, rural workers organized by the Regional Workers' Federation in Río Gallegos presented a list of moderate demands to sheep ranchers and their association, the Rural Society of Santa Cruz. Smaller landowners agreed to their plans for adequate living and working conditions, but the larger *estancieros* refused to comply. A strike began, and white guards, probably League members, began to force union members off the large ranches.

By early 1921 landowners complained that local law enforcement officials could not control the wave of disorders. Reports circulated in mid-January that strikers had burned three *estancias* and attacked another, all near Río Gallegos, and that armed bands of marauders controlled the interior. Such tales were exaggerated. Nevertheless, angry ranchers warned that if the government did not send in additional troops, they would take matters into their own hands. Manifesting this attitude, the Comodoro Rivadavia brigade sent eight volunteers on a month-long search through the interior for workers who had allegedly committed four murders. The brigade reported that the chase proved successful. At the same time, the League took similar vigilante actions in Río Negro.[80]

At the end of January 1921 the Tenth Cavalry Regiment, under the command of Lieutenant Colonel Héctor Varela, a loyal Radical, disembarked in Santa Cruz. The League maintained steady pressure on Varela and local officials, also Radicals, notifying the press that brigades in Santa Cruz were ready to cooperate with the army and supply it with arms and horses. Cacique Huangelén, head of an Indian brigade in the territory, informed the government that he and his 150 horsemen were willing to help the army pacify the "foreign" rebels. Moreover, he promised the support of other Indian brigades.[81] Within a month, however, Varela helped arbitrate a solution to the strike which fulfilled some of the union's original demands. Predictably, the agreement pleased the workers but disgruntled the ranchers.

As the economic crisis deepened, the landowners laid off personnel, particularly union members, and disavowed the truce they had signed. The union declared another strike in September, and groups of unemployed workers roamed Patagonia, causing panic among ranchers. Again, rumors of violence spread, and employers demanded firm government action. In November Yrigoyen sent Varela back to Santa Cruz; this time the Radical commander and other officials of his party treated workers differently.

Meanwhile, a seemingly trivial incident sparked conflict between workers and the League in the town of Santa Cruz. On June 12, 1921, the local branch of the Regional Workers' Federation demonstrated in protest against the Gualeguaychú massacre of the previous month. As workers marched through the streets shouting "Death to the Patriotic League" and "Long live the laborers of Gualeguaychú," Miguel Sicardi, a League member, rushed at them with a gun. A prominent lawyer and notary, Sicardi was the brother of the local brigade president. Miguel Gesenko, a Russian meatpacking worker, twisted Sicardi's arm and forced him to drop the revolver, at which point the police intervened. Sicardi accused the demonstrators of insulting the nation, but the police recognized that he was to blame. The union retaliated against Sicardi by preventing deliveries to his house. When town merchants fired the employees participating in this boycott, the Regional Workers' Federation declared a general strike.[82]

The strike persisted for several months and pushed business interests into taking strong measures. Employers and the Puerto Santa Cruz brigade solicited and received free laborers from the League and Labor Association. Sicardi and other brigade members provoked strikers—and then requested government troops to "prevent disorders." After Varela returned to Santa Cruz in November, League members and police dragged unionists out of their beds early one morning to the port, where they waited, unfed, for two days, until they were forced to board a ship for Buenos Aires. Other workers were tortured and killed, including Gesenko—at Sicardi's instigation. (Later, Sicardi was imprisoned for Gesenko's death, but the League helped secure his release.) Police and brigade members destroyed the office of the union newspaper and compelled the remaining strikers to return to work or leave the region. Cruising the streets in automobiles, armed Liguistas further terrorized the working class.[83]

At the same time, from November 1921 to January 1922, the Tenth Cavalry methodically destroyed the labor movement in Patagonia, killing as many as 1,500 strikers. Although the army bore the major share of responsibility, local Radical officials, employers, and the League supported its efforts. League brigades in the interior joined the army on patrol, and those throughout the region supplied Varela's men with fuel, vehicles, housing, and provisions. After the army and its civilian supporters crushed the unions, Liguistas forced the vanquished workers into the nonfederated ranks. Carlés's view of these events was that former union members had voluntarily petitioned to join the League, thus establishing more than 200 free labor brigades. One League official later claimed that Carlés himself and Domingo Schiaffino, a Junta member, led "volunteers" from the capital to fight in the south, but he probably referred to the arrival of free laborers. Carlés only visited Patagonia after the worst of the massacre, in January 1922.[84]

Carlés journeyed down the Patagonian coast, stopping at the major ports on the way to Ushuaia, where he founded a female brigade. Its composition could not have been as aristocratic as that of other women's chapters, for, as *La Protesta* noted, most women in that town were prostitutes. At any rate, the purposes of his trip were to investigate the situation and learn how to Argentinize the region. The results of his fact-finding mission were muddled; Carlés offered different analyses to different audiences. On one occasion he claimed that the rebels had come from Chile; then he blamed the disturbances on ex-convicts in FORA's service. He also pointed his finger at Yrigoyen's favorite union, the railroad workers, and at Radical officials of Santa Cruz, whom he accused of colluding with anarchists.[85]

One of his conclusions was faultless, however, at least from his perspective: Varela had pacified the south, and his efforts deserved praise. Accordingly, President Ibón Noya of the Río Gallegos brigade and his League comrades in the local Rural Society held a banquet for Varela on January 1922. The Sicardi brothers and the Puerto Santa Cruz brigade followed suit. In May Carlés hosted a well-publicized celebration in Buenos Aires in which the League awarded medals to Varela and his soldiers. Carlés also wrote to the Chamber, reminding deputies of the army's defense of order in the south.[86]

Not coincidentally, the League's attitude toward the army's role contrasted sharply with the administration's. The massacre tarnished Yrigoyen's image among workers, and therefore he did not draw attention to the issue or commend Varela. His silence angered the military, which once again saw itself as doing the "dirty work" of a regime that portrayed itself as prolabor. He also irritated upper-class interests, who thought he had responded too slowly to the crisis. The debate in the Chamber over the government's handling of the strikes further revealed Radical ambivalence. Although Radical Deputy Leonidas Anastasi condemned the League, he and other party members helped defeat a Socialist suggestion to create a commission to investigate the events. Moreover, Radical Deputy Valentín Vergara cited Carlés's opinion of the army's role and agreed with it.[87] These stances, however, did not succeed in mollifying the military, upper class, or workers.

League involvement in the Patagonian affair continued long after the actual massacre. The League loudly protested Kurt Gustav Wilkens's assassination of Varela in January 1923 and conspicuously attended Varela's funeral. An upper-class Liguista, Radical, and former police sergeant, Jorge Ernesto Pérez Millán Temperley, resolved to avenge the death of his distant relative Varela. A violent and probably disturbed youth, Pérez Millán became a guard in the jail where Wilkens was imprisoned, and he killed the anarchist assassin in April. It is unclear whether the League helped him carry out this act. At any rate, while the press and other members of his class distanced themselves from this repugnant murderer, Carlés visited him in prison. When, in turn, Pérez Millán was killed in jail, possibly by anarchists, League members eulogized him at his funeral.[88]

1. Monsignor Gustavo Franceschi,
June 1920 (courtesy Archivo Gráfico,
Archivo General de la Nación)

2. The Workers' Circles honor Monsignor Miguel de Andrea (caped, center front), August 1920 (courtesy Archivo Gráfico, Archivo General de la Nación)

3. Insignia and motto of the Argentine Patriotic League (from Primero 1 de Mayo Argentino: Conmemoración del Pronunciamiento de Urquiza en Entre Ríos, 1921)

La "Liga Patriótica Argentina" saluda al Gran Pueblo Argentino, uno e indivisible, con su bandera azul y blanca y su himno nacional.

4. Manuel Carlés, seated between the sisters Corina Berdier and Hortensia Berdier (president of the Junta of Señoras), at a festival for the children attending a Señoras' free school. Luis Zuberbühler, vice president of the League and a prominent industrialist, is seated at the extreme left. December 1924 (courtesy Archivo Gráfico, Archivo General de la Nación)

5. Sixo Vela, president of the brigade of Gualeguaychú, and Carlés at the celebration of the Battle of Caseros, February 3, 1922 (courtesy Archivo Gráfico, Archivo General de la Nación)

6. Senoras charged with raising money for the League's schools (courtesy Archivo Gráfico, Archivo General de la Nación)

7. Julio Irazusta as a young man (courtesy Archivo Gráfico, Archivo General de la Nación)

8. Leopoldo Lugones addressing the Teatro Opera, 1928 (courtesy Archivo Gráfico, Archivo General de la Nación)

9. The Argentine Civic Legion on
parade, probably 1931 (courtesy
Archivo Gráfico, Archivo General de
la Nación)

Now the League turned to the other question Carlés had raised in his Patagonian tour: how to integrate the south into the nation. Maintaining brigades on the *estancias* and safeguarding free labor partially answered the question. Incorporating the Indians into national culture seemingly was also appropriate. Despite Cacique Huangelén's assurances, however, not all Indians had been willing to fight the workers—and the League did not take rejection lightly. When forty Indian families on state property near Lake Buenos Aires, Santa Cruz, refused to join brigade patrols, League members stole their horses, weapons, and other goods and forced them off the land, taking it for themselves. The League announced, however, that these dispossessed Indians had formed a brigade.[89] Carlés had forgotten his promises to the Indians.

The League also addressed the topic of Argentinizing Patagonia in a meeting held in Río Gallegos in late 1922. In this euphemistically titled "Congress of Good Feeling," League members and local officials discussed economic, administrative, security, and labor problems in the area. The League hosted a similar meeting in the same city in 1927. *La Nación* praised the organization's interest in Patagonia, and it advised the government to follow the League's example and begin a "reconquest of the desert."[90]

This proposed reconquest of the south, or of any other zone, was redundant. On May Day 1921 in Gualeguaychú, Carlés had predicted that all rural Argentines would celebrate the next Day of the Argentine Worker.[91] Although he overestimated workers' enthusiasm for his cause, his forecast was correct for city and country alike: the Argentine labor movement had contracted and splintered. Comintern sympathizers left the Socialist party in 1920, forming the Communist party; Palacios, the most popular Socialist figure, had already left the party in 1915. More important, FORA IX's membership fell from 118,200 in late 1919 to 42,000 in early 1922, when it collapsed. The USA replaced it, but it only attracted 26,000 members in 1922. This syndicalist-dominated federation, in turn, fragmented, and in 1926 the Socialist-leaning Confederación Obrera Argentina (COA, Argentine Workers' Confederation) took its place. Labor militancy also declined. The number of strikes and strikers dropped from 367 and 309,000 in 1919 to an annual average of 90 and 70,000, respectively, for the years 1921 to 1928, and this average would have been lower if not for one large strike in 1924.[92]

There were several reasons for labor quiescence. One was the convergence of living cost and real wage levels after 1920. Joblessness also decreased after the war, although high unemployment continued to plague the working class.[93] Nevertheless, the employers' ability to control the labor supply and break strikes was even more responsible for quelling workers' militancy. The League played a key role in the capitalist counteroffensive, supplying scab laborers and agents provocateurs, arms, publicity, and organizational talent. Together with the Labor Association, it also helped employers by pressuring local and national levels of government. Significantly, it prodded Radical administrations into withdrawing support from labor. Even when Radical commanders or leaders initially favored the unions, as in Gualeguaychú, Las Palmas, and Patagonia, they subsequently retreated and either ignored the League's actions or, as in the south, led a brutal repression of their own. The League helped tip Yrigoyen's balancing act toward the capitalist side, although, ironically, by 1922 the president's maneuverings satisfied no one.

While League brigades around the country remained vigilant, the Congress of Good Feeling symbolized the end of the postwar labor struggle, a conflict that capital, with the League's aid, had won. This victory marked a turning point in the League's strategy. From its inception, the League had shown interest in nonviolent means of class conciliation, but female members had primarily concerned themselves with these tasks. Now the entire organization focused its attention on the peaceful cooptation of labor.

FIVE

Practical Humanitarianism: The League's Strategy of Class Conciliation

Events in Las Palmas, Entre Ríos, and Patagonia reinforced the League's brutal reputation. Yet such sober, respectable citizens as Carlés and other eminent Liguistas did not seem to fit in an organization conceived and nurtured in bloodshed. League members justified their actions by insisting that their mission to end class conflict was patriotic and Christian. Once it weakened the union movement, the League resorted to peaceful methods of achieving this goal, following in the footsteps of the Social Catholics and conservative reformers. As part of this strategy, male and female League members established charitable projects and cultivated ties with similar organizations around the world. They did not, however, explicitly identify themselves with the European counterrevolutionary tradition or with Italian Fascism. League men, in fact, prided themselves on having formulated an "Argentine" alternative to leftist doctrine. Though its ideas seemed progressive in the context of the 1920s, the League's advocacy of welfare programs to coopt the working class did not contradict its opposition to radical change. Moreover, its antileftist ideologues also criticized democracy and liberalism.

The League was not the only group to consider social welfare projects in the wake of the Tragic Week. Anxious to divert workers' attention from his administration's repressive measures, Yrigoyen flirted with reform. Examples of successful Radical social legislation during Yrigoyen's first term included rent regulation; pensions for bank employees, railroad, and other workers; maximum working hours; and the previously cited Law 11,278 requiring payment of wages in national currency, first proposed in

1919 but not passed until 1925. Congress did not, however, pass other measures such as the labor code which Radicals presented in June 1921.[1]

Yrigoyen's critics on the left and right viewed his actions as politically motivated and as "too little, too late." Yet one could accuse the old elitist forces in Congress of the same partisanship. Unwilling to let the president win the credit for reform, conservatives who supported the principle of labor legislation opposed even these mild measures—and then condemned Yrigoyen for not fulfilling labor's just demands.[2]

Catholics, however, continued to manifest interest in social reform. In 1917 Andrea and two other priests planned a new organization to replace the Argentine Social League. The new group, the Unión Popular Católica Argentina (UPCA, Argentine Catholic Popular Union) held its first meeting the end of April 1919. League members in its junta included the UPCA president, Lorenzo Anadón, Fathers Andrea and Nicolás Fasolino, Dell'Oro Maini, and O'Farrell.[3]

The UPCA's first and most important activity was the Gran Colecta Nacional (Great National Collection), held from September 22 to October 1, 1919. The proceeds of this immense fund-raising drive "for re-establishing and consolidating Argentine social peace" would be spent on social welfare projects. Andrea and Anadón administered the collection, and seven of its eleven-member financial committee were Liguistas, as were other organizers and contributors, including eighteen women. The collection's broad purpose, in Andrea's words, was "to help liberate progressive and orderly workers from the tyranny of revolution," that is, to support workers who believed in "true syndicalism" for economic ends only. To illustrate this aim, a cartoon in the collection's publication, *La paz social* (Social Peace), depicted a worker breaking his chains with funds from the drive—an ironic play on Marx's famous words. The committee, however, did not really approve of any type of syndicalism. In *La paz social*, Franceschi, a UPCA member, criticized unions as "levelers" which helped the numerous mediocre workers at the expense of the able few, who were pressured into voting with the majority on strikes and other issues they actually opposed.[4]

"Give and you will conserve" was the slogan of the collection. As one committee member, Father Gabriel Palau, noted, the necessary "social counterrevolution" would be carried out peacefully through social works. Through the collection, the forces of order marshaled more than thirteen million pesos for this purpose. The main portion was spent on housing, which most observers saw as the workers' most critical need. Four small neighborhoods of houses and apartments were eventually built.[5]

Together with a Catholic women's group, the collection also helped finance a vocational school for female laborers, which manifested Andrea's abiding interest in upgrading their skills as mothers and workers. According to Andrea, the pupils also learned how to influence the female working masses in a "healthy and salvatory" fashion, thus "contributing to social tranquility." These motives led Andrea to assume control in 1922 over the three unions created by the Blanca de Castilla Studies Center. The organization he established to administer these syndicates, FACE, directed eighteen unions by 1931. Satisfied, Andrea proclaimed that year that FACE included "seven thousand women immunized now against the virus of social revolution."[6]

Social Catholic views of class harmony and female roles inspired the League. During the collection, the League was establishing its first social works. In doing so, it tapped the philanthropic experience of its female members. Juan de Dios Gallegos, a Chilean representative to the Central Junta, explained with striking imagery that the women's mission was to emulate the "white Christ" of love, as against the "red Christ" of hate.[7] The metaphorical contrast he drew between the counterrevolutionary ideal of social justice derived from Christianity and the revolutionary precept of class conflict served an important purpose. It delineated the League's ancestry, assuring potential opponents of female activism within the League that female members would not disturb existing class and gender relations. Their function represented an extension of previous Church-related labors designed to reconcile the female proletariat with the capitalist and patriarchal structure of society. Therefore, although their programs superficially resembled those of "red" Socialist feminists, the fundamental aims of the two differed.

The Señoritas carried the "white" message to the working class mainly through education. Realizing the difficulty of wooing male workers away from radical doctrines, the Señoritas followed the example of Andrea and Franceschi and concentrated their efforts on their immigrant working-class sisters, setting up tuition-free schools for them in factories and workshops. The Señoritas founded the first factory school at the Bagley plant in July 1920. By 1927 at least nineteen such institutions existed, and as late as 1950 the League claimed that more than fifty were still in operation.[8]

The schools had several purposes. The first was moralistic: to keep female workers from engaging in immoral pursuits after working hours, such as drinking in bars, taking tango lessons, watching profane films, or flirting with men in the plazas. Another was to enhance the status of working women by teaching them basic skills. Members of the proletariat, particularly women, had little opportunity to finish school. Indeed, President Cano of the Señoritas noted in 1922 that the typical incoming student was virtually illiterate. Teaching women to read and write constituted a first and necessary step toward self-improvement. The schools also offered instruction in arithmetic, typing, shorthand, sewing, embroidery, and other manual arts. Small lending libraries were located in some of the schools. Courses in hygiene, home economics, childcare, and first aid prepared students to be "real señoras."[9]

The schools also addressed another task. "Because of their ignorance," said Elisa del Campillo, first vice-president of the Señoritas, working women were "subjected to others." Before one could accuse her of feminism, Campillo added that "subversive elements took advantage of their incapacity and discontent to produce disorder." The League hoped that a nationalistic education would end this type of female subordination and, as Gallegos put it, "transform the hatred of the working class into the friendship of the workers for their employers and benefactors."[10]

The curriculum was designed to inculcate female laborers with such "Argentine values" as nobility of work, obedience to the law, patience, duties to one's family and country, patriotism, the "virtue of happiness," punctuality, courtesy, and deference toward one's betters. Not coincidentally, these were precisely the attitudes that employers sought to inspire in their personnel. The League in fact claimed that management promoted workers who had taken courses. Heavy doses of patriotism infused the lectures on Argentine history, civics, and geography, and other lessons. Pupils learned national anthems and the significance of national holidays. In Buenos Aires, they paraded downtown to the Obelisk, a famous landmark, in the independence celebrations of 1920–22. Nélida Sayans, a pupil who worked in a sandal factory, explained that the League curriculum encouraged workers to view the Argentine flag more sympathetically than the red flag.[11]

The schools helped integrate female factory workers not only into the labor force and the nationality, but into the League's conception of Argentine womanhood. Carlés believed that the atheistic education offered in public schools fomented feminism. Furthermore, atheists lacked hope or comfort, and such despair could lead to revolutionary attitudes. In order to prevent either of these dire consequences, the factory schools proselytized women. Accordingly, as Francisca Selles recalled, League teachers prepared her and fellow students to take their first communion and fulfill their religious duties. Sayans added that pupils learned that socialism and anarchism could not match the doctrines of God and fatherland.[12] This emphasis on piety helped mold workers into the League's image of "true" women.

Although they relegated instructional duties to hired teachers, female Liguistas served as role models for the pupils. Cano believed that she and other Señoritas set examples of virtue and sisterly spirit which inspired the students. María Lea Gastón, a worker at the Gratry factory, praised the upper-class girls: "descendants of Christian homes, whose mothers, Argentine matrons of noble lineage, knew how to inculcate in their souls the lovely Christian maxim which states 'Love thy neighbor as thyself.'" *La Nación* summed up what the young Liguistas offered. By confirming "the conservative feminine feeling," the schools and Señoritas gave female workers "a social vision of the real woman, not the red lady," or Socialist feminist.[13]

The League wanted its pupils to disseminate their knowledge at home and teach their children, if not their husbands, to be "good Argentines." Whether the League was able to propagate its message in this manner is difficult to determine. One possible measure of success was the rising school enrollment. The League admitted that the Bagley school began with fifteen students and that attendance at the first schools was scanty. By 1927, however, it claimed to have taught almost 10,000 women.[14] Moreover, male workers gradually joined the student body, although in small numbers.

The Argentinization of female workers was the League's most important and heavily publicized social project. This, however, was not the only program that female Liguistas initiated and administered. Señoritas collected funds and books for needy children as well as for their factory schools. They also inaugurated other lending libraries, a home for juvenile delinquents, and fund-raising drives for male brigades.[15]

Like those of the Señoritas, most of the Señoras' charitable works were dedicated to helping working-class mothers and their children, thus strengthening the immigrant family and linking it to the nation. In this regard, each brigade of Señoras administered social projects, such as maternity clinics, day-care centers for children of working women, free medical facilities in the poorer barrios, and benefits to raise money for these endeavors, such as fashion shows and theatrical events. Working-class women who had just given birth received cradles and clothing for their infants from some brigades. Señoras donated funds to causes as diverse as the Boy Scouts and earthquake victims in Mendoza. Sometimes they provided entertainment for workers and their families—always with a nationalistic slant—such as films on Argentine themes. Señoras organized other nationalistic celebrations, including folk dances, public salutes to the flag, parades, and typical national meals in towns ranging from Buenos Aires to Villa Gobernador Gálvez, Santa Fe. Education remained a matter of special concern, as Señoras opened free neighborhood schools for children, starting in October 1919, and dispensed books, clothing, food, and medical care to the young pupils and their mothers. The "ladies" (*damas*) of the League even kept their hands busy sewing for the poor during meetings.

The most interesting and far-ranging of the Señoras' undertakings involved residents of long standing in the country, rather than immigrants. This was their annual exposition and sale of textiles woven and embroidered by Indian and Creole women in cottage industries stretching from Jujuy south to San Luis. These fairs were held from 1920 at least until the mid-1930s. President Hortensia Berdier of the Señoras described the events as tributes to the women who dedicated themselves to crafts inherited from their Argentine ancestors. She believed that the nation should encourage and protect its own industries, particularly traditional ones using local raw materials. The expositions were a first step toward this goal and also stimulated the spirit of free enterprise among native Argentines. Other purposes included raising the living standards of an impoverished and truly national group, and helping women whose participation in the labor force had not yet removed them from their homes.[16]

The textile fairs differed from the other female-sponsored projects. The factory schools, clinics, and even patriotic events emphasized the ties between womanhood, family, and nation. Most of these activities represented concrete attempts to improve the working and living conditions of laborers in limited ways, without increasing their autonomy. The expositions manifested not only these characteristics, but awareness of a more abstract problem: the need for industrialization, a long-run solution to poverty that went far beyond incremental practical reforms. Generally, however, League women left the task of theorizing about such matters to the men. Furthermore, they showed no interest in other broad issues, such as women's rights. Although the 1920s witnessed the struggle to widen the rights of married women, a victory achieved with the revision of the civil code in 1926, Liguistas never mentioned these events.[17] Paradoxically, however, the Señoras and Señoritas increased their autonomy by acquiring valuable skills as administrators, public speakers, and parliamentarians in the League.

Men joined the women in establishing social projects, especially after 1922. Yet these charitable works, often financed by women's fund-raising efforts, did not assume the same importance as those of female Liguistas. Male Liguistas also emphasized education, building new schools in Magdalá, Buenos Aires; Gualeguaychú; Reconquista, Santa Fe; and other places. Workers' brigades created their own vocational institutes. For example, the electricians of the capital offered free night classes in mathematics, design, mechanics, electricity, and the sciences to their members and organized instructional visits to industrial establishments. This brigade also set up apprenticeship programs for orphans. Beginning in 1925, the brigade of Las Flores, Buenos Aires, took schoolchildren on tours of the capital, an activity duplicated by other brigades of the interior. Like the female chapters, many male brigades had their own favorite programs, such as donating money to various causes, organizing sales of consumption items at cost, and establishing free medical and legal services in some neighborhoods. Brigade Nineteen of the Federal Capital, for example, sponsored a neighborhood medical clinic in 1927, and in 1930 it set up a free vaccination service.[18]

Publicity and lobbying efforts, however, occupied more of the men's time than social projects. This division of labor between the sexes corresponded to that which characterized the larger society. Male Liguistas delivered speeches on street corners and in plazas around the country. They put up posters, sent notices to the press, and distributed free pamphlets. Brigades published magazines—usually short-run—with such titles as *El Orden* (Order), *Patria* (Fatherland), and *Revista Nacional* (National Magazine). Brigades and the Central Junta informed provincial and national governments of security, economic, educational, and other problems and lobbied for solutions.

League men and women hoped that their practical reforms and propaganda would divert workers from class struggle. These projects manifested the ideology formulated by male Liguistas in meetings and the annual congresses. Carlés and other League spokesmen gave this ideology different names: Argentinism, practical morality, political morality, practical Christianity, "catechism of the fatherland" doctrine, "positivist philosophy of possible wellbeing," and practical humanitarianism. Through these names the League emphasized its native, anti-Marxist, Social Catholic, and positivist roots. It did not acknowledge any ties to Charles Maurras (see Chapter 6), Benito Mussolini, or other contemporary European counterrevolutionaries. Although all of the League's self-designations are suggestive, I will use only one of them—practical humanitarianism—and in describing it I will rely heavily on the words of its most eloquent and prolific exponent, Carlés.

Carlés valued cultural and national diversity and, significantly, resisted using universal generalizations to interpret Argentine society. If forced to apply one, however, he preferred the positivist theory of progress as the development of order, for this principle had accounted for Argentine economic success. In the past, he believed, the people had understood that society should conserve and perfect the fundamental bases of property, family, and authority, and that negative features of development would slowly disappear. They had accepted the fact that the key to Argentine progress was to work in peace, observing the laws that guaranteed to all the fruits of their toil.[19]

Before mass immigration, then, Argentines had accepted the given order. This, to Carlés, was only fitting, for "seeing the world as it is" was a moral belief which formed the backbone of practical humanitarianism. Practical humanitarianism meant "the science of the good and . . . the habit of the truth: the truth that teaches one to know things as they are, and the good which advises one to follow the dictates of loyalty." When one looked at real life one found that there were and always would be some human beings who were weak and others who were strong, some rich and others poor, some intelligent and others ignorant, some employers and others employees. The League would not undertake the impossible task of changing reality but only that of enhancing popular welfare through "natural means," according to what was "humanly possible." All members of society would keep the positions that were "natural" to them and take only that which rightfully was theirs. The League favored laws to curb the powerful yet also prevent the weak and ignorant—that is, the lower class—from controlling society. Jobs should be guaranteed for all workers so that they could support their families and acquire property. By striving for these goals the League could perform a legitimate and useful function.[20]

Carlés criticized the "immoral" followers of the left for visualizing the world as they wanted it to be, from an exotic theoretical perspective, and denying its actual nature. These impatient social reformers could not stand by and allow society to peacefully and slowly cleanse itself of imperfections. Instead they attacked the very foundations of the social structure by dishonoring legal authority, dismissing property as theft, spurning the natural hierarchy as unjust, and rejecting the Christian family by living in sin. They could never translate their utopian humanitarianism into reality. In contrast, practical humanitarianism consisted of the workers' legitimate desires for economic betterment, which the League had stripped of theoretical trappings. Thus the League had converted the left's "illusory liberty" to a realizable "practical equality."[21]

The League also opposed the left's view of class divisions with its view of national divisions. The real world consisted of nations which through the centuries had acquired distinct cultural and linguistic traditions. Ignoring these natural boundaries, the left divided the world into the bourgeoisie and the proletariat. This arbitrary belief in class only served to disunite the homeland and did not correspond to national reality. Classes per se did not exist in Argentina. A manifesto of the Córdoba brigade stated that here there were no privileged groups or proletariat, for all were equal under the law. The unequal distribution of wealth resulted from unequal mental capacities, not from a class structure.[22]

Carlés offered his own "Argentine" definition of labor and capital: labor was nothing more than capital that produced goods and services, and capital was accumulated labor. The fact that Marx would have agreed with his definition of capital would have disconcerted him. Unlike Marx, Carlés concluded from this that without exception, all wealthy men in Argentina had started out as workers.[23] For Carlés and the Córdoba brigade, then, the possibility of upward mobility precluded the need for conceptions of class.

Liguistas viewed the leftist definition of workers as excessively narrow. The economic affairs committee at the First Congress widened this category to include all those who helped produce economic goods that enhanced national welfare. Celestino F. Gutiérrez of the Italó, Córdoba, brigade included scholars, laborers, capitalists, and employees in his definition of workers or "producers." These views enabled Liguistas to call their first three annual meetings "Congresses of Workers," to the amusement of the leftist press, which noted the presence of "worker" delegates wearing plumes and silk hats. After 1922 the League alternated between naming its meetings "Nationalist Congresses" or "Nationalist Congresses of Workers," signaling the organization's broader shift from armed confrontation to peaceful reconciliation between classes. Dr. Alberto García Torres explained the change in title by insisting that the League was not discarding the topic of labor, but that it wanted to contemplate this issue with "an eminently Argentine form of thinking."[24]

The League sometimes admitted to some distinctions between "workers" beyond mere level of ability, morality, or thriftiness. In the Third Congress, Cano noted that there were "laborers of the mind and of the muscle," but she added that they shared the same aspiration: to maximize production so as to maximize earnings. Her phrase unwittingly resembled one the Nazis used for the same ideological purpose—workers of the "hand and brain."[25] League members also commonly distinguished landowners or tenants from peons, but they believed that the traditional network of reciprocal obligations and loyalties between these groups transcended this gulf. The radical who incited laborers against their employers, according to the League, undermined the natural unity between producers as well as national tradition.

The League offered its practical humanitarianism as an alternative to revolutionary thought and practice. It preached that the latter was false because it had originated in Europe, scene of large industries and trusts, overpopulation, and huge extremes of wealth and poverty. Given these conditions, it was perhaps understandable that an ideology of class conflict would take root there. A foreign ideology could not explain the Argentine situation, however, which varied markedly from the European. (Perhaps for this reason, Liguistas claimed no links to European fascism, although they admitted ties to such European philosophical currents as Social Catholicism and positivism.) Here no concentration of industry, virtually no native capitalism, and, of course, no class divisions existed; instead, one found food, livelihood, and great empty stretches of land for all.[26] Though it was true that there was relatively little native-owned industry, these supposed differences between Argentina and Europe reflected Carlés's idealized view of conditions in both places.

Carlés blamed the diverse "races" in Argentina for finding fault with the fatherland and imitating foreign models. A half-century of hard work, optimism, faith, and social harmony had laid the foundation for Argentine development—but then the immigrants arrived and began to chip away at these foundations. Like the cultural nationalists, Carlés overlooked the fact that immigrants had provided the labor and skills necessary for economic growth. Instead, he declared that the newcomers represented the cast-offs of a decaying continent—social delinquents, orphans, men without a fatherland—and they brought with them class hatred and other problems of their native lands. These "sons of hostile races" sought to impose their foreign atheism, skepticism, decadent pessimism, and "frenetic humanitarianism" upon a society different from the ones that had nurtured these views. Moreover, they brought a form of sensualism that weakened the Argentine family and the virility of the Creole race.[27]

Argentina had entered a transitional stage of conflict between the emulators of foreign customs and loyal nationalists. Carlés admitted that Argentines had always adopted foreign ideas when advantageous to do so, as in science and economics, but he argued that immigrants wanted Argentines to forsake all local traditions. In this stage true Argentines would have to defend themselves against foreign imitations: the economic individualism that enslaved the worker and the labor unionism that tyrannized the community for the benefit of one group. The League was the repository of Argentine optimism which opposed the pessimism and sterile utopianism of the dregs of Europe. The League also stood up against other foes: atheistic cities with their sensual, aristocratic clubs, stock exchanges with their speculators, greedy political parties, and theoretically minded congressmen.[28] Because some sensual aristocrats and speculators were found in the League, however, these villains received little more punishment than occasional tongue-lashings. The League attempted to deal with greedy politicians later in the 1920s, as will be seen.

The subject of League optimism and leftist pessimism manifested one of the many inconsistencies of practical humanitarianism. The two groups' real attitudes were the reverse. The League was, perhaps, optimistic about Argentina's future but deeply pessimistic about human nature. Counterrevolutionaries believe that human beings are irrational, selfish, and sinful, and that only traditional institutions and rituals can tame their violent instincts. Accordingly, the League stressed family, religion, education, authority, and the old ties between employer and employee. In its view, any attempt to destroy traditional hierarchical relationships and mediating institutions would lead to chaos.

In contrast, the League's opponents were critical of Argentine development and hence pessimistic, yet they held an optimistic view of human nature. Leftists believe that all persons are born with potential, but under capitalism only those with the means to do so can develop their talents. Thus, men and women are perfectible, for their class affiliation and not their inherent nature accounts for their attainments. By destroying capitalism and the class structure, one would lay the foundations for a society in which all human beings could realize their abilities.

Another flaw in practical humanitarianism was the Liguistas' identification of leftism with foreigners. Although they admitted that the lower classes were poor and perhaps had reason to protest their living conditions, they contradicted themselves by blaming outside agitators for labor unrest. One could be Argentine and object to social inequities. Moreover, one could be an immigrant or an employee of a foreign concern and belong to the League, which was hardly 100 percent Argentine. Although Carlés prided himself on never having represented a foreign company or cause,[29] other Liguistas did not share his nationalistic achievement.

Everywhere the forces of counterrevolution see the left as alien. If, with some limited justification, the League called the Argentine left foreign, the French right considered its leftist opponents to be German. Even if it is not foreign in terms of nationality, the left is foreign to the right's own idealized vision of society. The right despises and fears the left not because of its national origins but because it threatens the class structure.

The League conclusively demonstrated that protecting the status quo rather than the nation was its priority in yet another manner. Its distaste for internationalism notwithstanding, the League contacted similar groups in Europe and the Americas to coordinate campaigns against the left. These organizations included the American Legion, Chilean Military Patriotic League, Orgesch and Free Workers' Association of Bavaria, Civic League of France, National League and National Propaganda (*sic*) of Great Britain, Patriotic Association of Belgium, Patriotic League of Unity and National Defense of Bolivia, Agricultural Defense Society of Uruguay, National Unity and Brazilian Nationalist League of Brazil, unnamed nationalist groups in Peru and Denmark, and a free workers' association in Uruguay. Portuguese and Swiss organizations reportedly wanted to establish relationships with the League, but it is not clear whether they did so. Many of the groups mentioned were also bourgeois strikebreaking militias with some ties to their respective governments and military forces.[30]

The League was determined to sustain this budding "nationalist international." For example, at the invitation of National Propaganda, the League sent a representative, Máxima Calvo de Troncoso, to England in August 1920. She observed the activities of this organization, which primarily devoted itself to studying economic and labor issues.[31]

More significant was Carlés's correspondence with the U.S. government. In December 1920, Ambassador Stimson forwarded to the State Department a letter in which Carlés requested names of similar North American groups. The League wanted to cultivate ties with other nations, "for . . . if all men of order were to unite, we could nullify the turbulent propaganda" of the antipatriotic left. Several League publications describing the organization accompanied the request, as did a cover letter in which Stimson praised the group as a "decided factor for good in this country." (His opinion of the League had risen since 1919.) The State Department passed on this information in February 1921 to Attorney General A. Mitchell Palmer, well known for his suppression of domestic radicalism in the Red Scare. Only five days later, Palmer remitted a list of antiradical organizations including the American Protective League, National Civic Federation, and American Institute for the Suppression of Bolshevism.[32] The incident revealed the limits to the League's nationalism, as well as the fact that some U.S. officials, like their Argentine counterparts, were willing to cooperate with paramilitary groups.

League members, however, did not recognize the contradiction between their worldwide search for allies and their "nationalism." They persisted in claiming that Argentine development was unique and that Argentine problems required Argentine solutions like practical humanitarianism. Rather than embrace foreign radicalism, the laboring classes should seek inspiration from the national reality. This meant that the laborers should work hard in order to create prosperity for all. Immigrants should emulate the discipline, submissiveness, and contentment which, according to the League, characterized Creole workers. Finally, laborers should accept the League's ideas of evolutionary change through constitutional means and allegiance to the nation rather than those of sweeping change through revolution and ties to the international proletariat. This explained how the League theoretically supported workers who organized to improve their economic status and opposed only those laborers who wanted to overturn existing property relations. In practice, however, the League did not make such distinctions, and its local chapters did not do so even in theory, as seen in the Gualeguaychú statutes.

League authorities understood that charitable projects, propaganda, and international solidarity would not suffice to implement practical humanitarianism. Broader means were necessary to assure social peace within the capitalist system. In the congresses, committees on economic, military, legislative, naval, and constitutional affairs; hygiene; internal organization; and social assistance presented their annual reports. There, Liguistas and guest speakers also discussed national problems and the merits of such curative measures as social security, a labor code, public housing projects, and cooperatives. These discussions resembled the ones found in the bulletin of the Argentine Social Museum and the *Revista de Economía Argentina*; indeed, some of the men who delivered papers at League congresses also wrote for these journals. Yet the League exercised a stricter editorial policy than these two periodicals. It insisted that all speakers relate the topics to local circumstances and interpret them with an "Argentine criterion."[33]

Land reform was a matter of special interest for the League and a useful example of its ideas. One reason for the importance of this issue was the postwar agrarian disorders. Another was the fact that League members, like cultural nationalists, believed that the countryside was the storehouse of Argentine traditions and virtues, in contrast to the decadent, cosmopolitan cities.[34] If practical humanitarianism could not be implanted here, where could it thrive?

In formulating their opinions on this topic, some Liguistas followed Andrea's dictum that order depended not on abolishing property, but on multiplying it. José Serralunga Langhi, the spokesman for rural cooperatives and member of the Chacabuco, Buenos Aires, brigade, noted that property ownership gave one a sense of self-worth and a stake in the present order; indeed, the worst enemies of bolshevism were landholding peasants. Dividing large holdings into smaller ones and facilitating their sale to small farmers would create a large antileftist constituency. Carlés added that rural agitation had primarily broken out in areas where absentee landownership and tenant farming prevailed. To prevent the recurrence of agrarian conflict, there should be "no land without an owner, nor worker without land." In one of the rare instances in which a Liguista mentioned Mussolini, Carlés suggested that Argentina follow the example of the Italian Fascists, whose land reforms were enlarging the independent peasantry.[35]

This large issue of land reform encompassed several smaller ones, including the latifundia question. Most speakers defined latifundia as oversized estates, but they did not explain their criteria for determining what was too big. A prominent landowner and member of the Central Junta, Alberto Castex maintained that the term meant large slices of unproductive land. As the great estates in Argentina were very productive, he insisted, only the huge stretches of state-owned property fell into this category. This led Castex to conclude that "the *antilatifundista* campaign is exotic" in Argentina; "it responds to a rationalistic and imaginary concept and not to objective reality." He thought that small proprietors tended to be less knowledgeable than the large non-absentee owners and hence produced less. Therefore, to increase the number of smallholders was counterproductive.[36] Castex, however, did not support his case with evidence or explain the effects of speculation.

Other Liguistas agreed with Castex that latifundia were not necessarily a function of the property ownership system; the economic affairs committee at the First Congress declared that incompetent landlords bore the responsibility for such estates. Nevertheless, Castex's view of the problem represented an extreme even among Liguistas, although many others concurred that tenants and rural laborers were incapable. Admiral Juan Pablo Sáenz Valiente of the Central Junta, a *latifundista* of Entre Ríos, blamed the miserable state of rural dwellings on tenants' laziness and "perverse" egoism. Sáenz Valiente also admitted, however, that the landowners were at fault for not helping to correct the colonists' "defects in culture and intelligence."[37]

A member of the Posadas, Misiones, brigade, Secundino Ponce de León believed that agrarian reform was needed to relieve poverty in the northeast, which agitators had exploited to foment disorder. Although he insisted that the peons of Corrientes and Misiones were content with their station, he admitted that the debt peonage system that tied them to their labors was cruel. In his opinion, "Turkish intermediaries" were mainly responsible for this abuse, but *latifundistas* also bore some of the blame. It was essential to alleviate the peons' lot and yet insure that they would continue to work. Selling them small plots of government land on credit might be the answer, but this reform would succeed only if combined with some means of forcing the "naturally indolent" Creoles to work.[38]

Other League members echoed the theme of the evil intermediary, for it was easier to blame the anonymous corporation or foreign go-between than the Argentine landowner or agricultural production system. Serralunga Langhi considered the rural merchants and colonizing companies that rented land to farmers and sold them goods as their worst enemies. In his view, rural cooperatives would do away with this problem. He proposed that landowners rent their land directly to cooperatives for no less than five years and that farmers buy their supplies at cost through the same institutions.[39]

Serralunga Langhi, Carlés, and others stressed the need for subdividing the land among those who worked it, but few Liguistas explained how to accomplish this task. Juan Patalagoyti, president of the Balcarce, Buenos Aires, brigade, offered the most radical plan. He ruled out expropriating latifundia because the twin expenses of compensating owners and creating a bureaucracy to implement this policy would be prohibitive. Furthermore, Argentines lacked the administrative experience necessary to institute such reforms. In place of expropriation he proposed a combination of measures. One was to organize all land sales under public auction and divide the land for sale into lots large enough to support families. The government would require a deposit of one-fourth of the purchase price and finance the rest with loans. Patalagoyti also advocated limiting the inheritance of land to succeeding generations, although he favored heavily taxing such legacies as well as absentee-owned estates. He believed that the growing corporate monopoly over land presented "a constant threat of social disturbance." Foreign companies exemplified an additional danger because they drained wealth from the countryside and the nation. For these reasons he wanted the government to force national as well as foreign corporations into giving up the property they already held.[40]

Probably only a minority of League members agreed with Patalagoyti's solution to the land question, but many shared his unfavorable opinion of foreign enterprises—at least, in rhetoric. The fact that some of them were foreign-born businessmen or worked in foreign-owned concerns did not prevent Liguistas from criticizing foreign capital and influence. Carlés saw economic nationalism as inseparable from the need to protect Argentina from invaders and radical immigrants. He lamented what he perceived as the lack of adequate social and economic defense: social, because the immigration laws did not keep out undesirable foreigners, and economic, because Argentina's economy was subject to control from abroad. Just as the "extremist, universalist, anarchist and terrorist illusionism that its countries of origin exiled and evicted" freely exploited and hurt the nation, so, too, did foreign capitalism.[41] As will be seen, counterrevolutionaries of the late 1920s and 1930s drew the same connection between foreign capitalism and foreign radicalism, but they extracted more radical implications from it.

Other League spokesmen also linked the issues of national defense and industrialization. Several Liguistas noted that the nation needed to mine its iron ore, tin, and coal and to establish arms industries to insure these vital supplies in case of war. Others pointed to the dangerous level of foreign economic control over Argentina. Captain Jorge Yalour noted that the nation already owed 38 percent of its income to foreign capitalists and bankers. He warned that unless precautions were taken, Argentina could go the way of Cuba, which the United States completely dominated. To guard against this potential threat to national sovereignty, Major Francisco Torres, a Central Junta member, suggested that the government create a "national defense and foresight fund" from export, lottery, and other tax receipts. The interest generated by the fund would be used solely for cancelling external debts.[42]

Other Liguistas joined these men in pointing out the perils of foreign influence. Eduardo T. González of the Twenty-Sixth Precinct brigade of the capital announced to the Eighth Congress, "We are being left behind!" He noted that after decades of rapid growth, the Argentine economy was stagnating; the main impediment to further progress was its dependency on the economies of the great powers, in whose benefit it operated. The nation would have to follow the example of Japan, which had far fewer resources than Argentina but nevertheless had managed to pull itself out of subservience.[43]

Reasserting control over its economic life would not necessarily be difficult, according to several Liguistas, for the nation possessed many natural resources, including all the minerals needed for industrial independence. Furthermore, Argentina had substituted locally manufactured goods for foreign imports during the war. The question was how to continue this process of import substitution. Guillermo Pintos of the Central Junta insisted that the nation possessed sufficient liquid capital to meet development needs, but Argentines as well as foreigners did not invest money in industry because they looked only for opportunities to make quick profits.[44]

Pintos and other Liguistas suggested a variety of measures to promote economic nationalism, including public investment funds, tariff protection, and government controls on foreign business activities. Most agreed that industrialists should first concentrate their efforts on processing agricultural goods, such as grains and meat. Colonel Enrique Peme of the Gualeguaychú brigade, for example, advocated creating a national meatpacking company with regional branches, meat markets, warehouses at home and abroad, river boats, and eventually a transatlantic fleet. The consensus also favored limiting government participation to merely offering incentives or, at most, partially owning firms, for total control would entail inefficiencies and a huge patronage army. The statements of landowners, businessmen, lawyers, and military officers in League congresses reflected changing attitudes within the hitherto liberal agro-exporting elite. The unsettling economic conditions of the 1920s led some members of this group to envision a limited industrialization program that would not dramatically alter the socioeconomic structure.[45]

Another vital component of industrialization policy was, of course, labor. Although employers and the League had tamed the union movement, labor-related problems remained. An industrialist who belonged to the Forty-Third Precinct brigade of the capital, Florentino Martín, criticized the limited extent of Argentine industry, along with what he considered the "deficient" mentality of Argentine workers. The two problems were connected. Martín believed that profit-sharing plans would not only benefit laborers economically but teach them that industries in developing nations faced special hurdles. That strikes aggravated these problems had thus far eluded workers' understanding. Juan Oyuela of the Fifth Precinct brigade agreed that profit sharing would demonstrate to workers that their interests were identical to those of employers.[46]

Many League members found the theory of profit sharing attractive because it promised to improve workers' living conditions while integrating them into the capitalist system. The economic affairs committee officially endorsed it at the First Congress. Oyuela and Arturo Pallejá, member of the Central Junta and distinguished lawyer, further suggested that profit sharing constituted the first step toward a new, more desirable form of society, one that avoided the pitfalls of liberalism and socialism. Pallejá favored organizing all inhabitants into corporations as the best means of insuring social equilibrium. Within this context, workers' corporations would eventually take over the factories by purchasing stock with funds subtracted from laborers' salaries. The corporatist system would retain capital per se by transforming it into a mere instrument of labor, but it would eliminate the true exploiter of society and of workers— usury, or avaricious speculative capital. A workers' parliament would be responsible for economic legislation. This body, however, would be subordinate to a political parliament in which labor would have no voice. Pallejá assumed that once emancipated economically, workers would have no need or desire for political emancipation. He did not explain what would happen to the former factory owners or landholders, although one could assume that, by default, they would sit in the political parliament. Pal-

lejá's views on "productive" versus speculative capital, corporations, and labor's right to a share of the profits but not to political
power resembled European fascism.[47]

Tomás Amadeo also envisioned corporatism as the system of
the future. He saw two currents within corporatism: the reactionary, antiindividualistic type, and the type that favored organizing
all professions and job categories into free syndicates. Amadeo
placed himself within the second, more democratic current and in
later years specifically condemned the Italian Fascist type. In the
past, unions had generated class conflict, but today (that is, the
late 1920s) they primarily represented the means of creating a
corporatist society, as union cooperatives demonstrated. Syndicates could also provide the technical expertise that representative
governments so badly needed. Amadeo thought that the contemporary decay of political parties and the parliamentary system did not necessarily mean the end of democracy. The ideal
future government would consist of a combined corporatist–
representative system, in which professional syndicates would
insure efficient solutions to economic problems, while a parliament would represent individuals and the general interest.[48]

Few Liguistas other than Palleja and Amadeo were willing to
contemplate such far-reaching alterations in the existing system
in order to preserve the social hierarchy. Carlés's views on the
subject were ambivalent. On the one hand, he believed that syndicates of workers and employers were institutions extraneous to
Argentine reality.[49] On the other hand, as the decade wore on he
became more critical of liberal democracy and more receptive
to corporatism, at least as a temporary solution to Argentine
problems.

The League also addressed educational issues, particularly the
Argentinization of primary and secondary schools. As in the cultural nationalism movement, the League indicated in its statutes
its desire to intensify nationalist education in the public system,
to insure that private schools followed a uniform national curriculum and conducted classes only in Spanish, and to convince
the government to hire only Argentine citizens as educational administrators. Carlés believed that a nationalist education could

not be laical in character. The latter's critical, rationalistic bent implanted doubt within children's minds and instilled them with "sickly humanitarianisms." The emphasis on science and mathematics, and the dearth of lessons on national heroes, had created a "generation of foreignized materialists." Only the reintroduction of patriotism and religious morality into the curriculum could reverse these tendencies. Carlos Ibertis Correa, a member of the teachers' brigade and a normal school professor, suggested that only Argentines or foreigners with locally earned degrees teach the Spanish language and Argentine history. He also recommended giving priority to these two groups when awarding university chairs.[50]

Occasionally Liguistas alluded to the university reform movement. For example, Vice-President Luis Zuberbühler observed that more and more incapable individuals sought "vainglorious" university titles. This lamentable occurrence in education was mirrored in government by the increasing number of aspirants to public office.[51] Both comments were slaps at the Yrigoyen regime, which opened higher education and the political patronage system to the middle class. Generally, however, Liguistas confined their criticism of university reform to vague comments on student leftism and the loss of authority in teacher–student relations.

Another theme in discussions on education was the idea that workers turned to the left only when they lacked sufficient professional training. Partly for this reason, League spokespersons and the statutes stressed the need for vocational schools. In this context, one can better understand the motives behind the creation of the factory schools and the free workers' vocational programs. Father Juan B. Lagos, a Central Junta member, believed that through education, one could tame the rural masses who desired revolution and convince them to remain in the countryside, where life was better for them than in the city[52] (and where landowners needed their labor). The great rural-urban migration of the following decade showed that his words had little effect.

League speakers also addressed the topic of the arts. Discussing music from an "Argentine viewpoint," Ismael Gutiérrez of the Eleventh Precinct brigade decried the foreign styles followed by local musicians. He declared that to be a real nation, Argentina had to purify its culture and music of outside influences. This sentiment corresponded with contemporary movements throughout Latin America seeking to affirm independence from Europe, such as the Modern Art Week of 1922 in São Paulo. Arguing the same for the visual arts, Blanco Villalta of the Central Junta also explained their practical function within League-style counterrevolution. Instilling workers with aesthetic values would integrate them into the nation: "The mental man searches for evolution through the universal laws that are pure harmony. Rebellion never came out of artists." [53] Like education, art would serve to coopt the masses.

Cultural nationalists and members of the upper class had advocated limiting immigration as a means of removing the revolutionary specter. As previously indicated, the League statutes recommended excluding immigrants who opposed the Argentine constitution. During the height of labor mobilization, debates on immigration marked the pages of widely read journals. Several Liguistas joined this debate by contributing to a special issue of the Argentine Social Museum bulletin that came out in 1919, before the League began to hold congresses. In this issue, leftists such as the Socialist Augusto Bunge predictably defended immigration and attributed the workers' militancy to the existence of social problems, whereas counterrevolutionaries found fault with the newcomers. League member Estanislao Zeballos wanted to exclude all but agricultural workers. A future minister in the Uriburu government (1930–32), Horacio Beccar Varela echoed this theme, claiming that those who settled in the cities were the undesirable immigrants. Huge numbers of workers in congested urban areas had created "our social problem." Worst of all were the Russian immigrants; all those who were urban and literate should be excluded. The illiterate Russian, on the other hand, was "uncontaminated" and would "easily adapt himself to our environment of liberty and order." [54] Clearly Beccar Varela was distinguishing between Jewish Russians, generally of small-town background, and non-Jewish Russians, who tended to be peasants.

Two League members shared these views. Tomás Amadeo designated all who would join the proletariat, the "yellow races," Russians "of whatever class or condition," and indigents as undesirables. (In the 1930s he modified these views, urging that immigrants, including Jews, be judged on the basis of talent, not ethnicity.) According to General Proto Ordóñez, unwanted immigrants included the sick and invalid, beggars, gypsies, Egyptians, Russian Jews, members of the "black and yellow races," and "individuals of evil antecedents, rebellious against order and contrary to all principle of authority." [55] Except for the Villaguay episode, these were the only cases I could find of League members expressing anti-Jewish attitudes during the period under study. Despite League criticism of foreigners and leftists, and the brutality of the League's predecessors during the Tragic Week, anti-Semitism never found its way into practical humanitarianism. Undoubtedly many Liguistas agreed with Amadeo and Ordóñez, but the Jewish question did not play a role in the League's official ideology.

Even future counterrevolutionaries were not conspicuously anti-Semitic in the early postwar period. In late January 1919, the Jewish monthly *Vida Nuestra* asked prominent intellectuals and politicians for their opinions of the treatment of Jews. Lugones, Ibarguren, and Juan P. Ramos were among the respondents. Ibarguren tersely replied that the Jewish community could not be blamed for the events surrounding the general strike, although some Jews had participated in them. He condemned the vigilante actions against innocent persons, Jews and non-Jews. In his opinion, "Jewish immigration, laborious and honest, is useful for the country and contributed efficiently to the development of national life." [56]

Ramos's answer was favorable toward the Jews, but in a more equivocal manner. He expressed his admiration for the Jewish "race's" contributions to civilization, as well as for the idealism, courage, and tenacity it demonstrated in its long struggle against persecution. Nevertheless, Jewish immigration would suit the country only if the Jews truly incorporated themselves into the nation. [57]

Lugones delivered the most eloquent defense of the Jews—
and of a non-League style of patriotism.[58] Ever the anticlerical,
he denounced the "artificial anti-Semitism, fomented here by
foreign friars, infesting the soul of our governing class." Persecution of the Jews was a means of expressing fear of revolution. The
perpetrators of violence claimed to defend Argentinism against
the Russians, yet the list of contributors to the Commission for
the Defense of Order included many foreign bankers and merchants. On the other hand, the casualty lists of workers indicated
that the majority were not Russian but Spanish and Italian in
background, like most *porteños*. They formed the true core of
Argentinism.

The constitution was based not on "Argentine principles" but
on the international doctrine of the rights of man, and it guaranteed the freedom of all who wished to live in Argentina. Like all
immigrant groups, the Jews had a right to expect Argentine hospitality, and because of their diligence, integrity, and intellectual
talents perhaps had more right than most. According to Lugones,
they had indeed assimilated, and they proudly raised their children as Argentines.

These men and others of the right revised their attitude toward
Jews later in the decade, when political crisis and the beginnings
of the Depression led them to devise more radical explanations of
Argentine ills than the League's. Their words in 1919 indicated
that the League was not alone in its indifference to the "Jewish
question" at this time. Similarly, government made no attempt to
restrict Jewish immigration. After a World War I lull, over 70,000
Jews entered the country from 1921 to 1930. One wish of Argentine counterrevolutionaries came true, however: after 1917 Jews
could no longer leave Russia. The new emigrants came from
Poland and neighboring countries and from former Ottoman
territories.[59]

The League devoted remarkably little attention to the general
issue of immigration restriction. After the postwar crisis, a few
presentations on this topic appeared in the congresses, but they
lacked the precision and sense of urgency that characterized discussions of economic reforms. League members demonstrated

practicality by recognizing that the continuing influx of laborers would weaken unions. They seemed to be more concerned with Argentinizing and controlling immigrants than with excluding them. On the few occasions when Liguistas discussed immigration restriction, beyond citing the need to keep out leftists and urban workers, they tended to focus on saving Argentina for the "white race," as Fernando Gowland, a Central Junta member, put it.[60]

Speaking at the Ninth Congress, the essayist Lucas Ayarragaray, who did not belong to the organization, linked immigration to an old concern of the right—the family. He observed that unmarried men were more susceptible to "extremist influences" than married men. For this reason he favored the immigration of complete (and white) families rather than single men. This view harked back to the demographic imbalance in Argentina and the feared decline of the family. League members continued to voice this apprehension, sometimes by lashing out at feminism and divorce.[61] The factory school program was a more constructive approach to strengthening the family by preparing women to find better-paying jobs and raise healthier children. League spokesmen also proposed other measures to help women in the workplace yet keep them as close to their families as possible. Pascual Anselmi of the stevedores' brigade and Manuel López Cepero of the Central Junta suggested that the League convince employers to provide clean and safe environments for female workers so as not to damage their health or that of future children. They also urged maternity leaves with guaranteed jobs after childbirth, day-care centers within factories, free courses in hygiene and childbearing, and six-hour working days for mothers. One Liguista asked the organization to lobby for a municipal law to create a hygiene office in each neighborhood that would inspect sweatshops.[62]

Another group that interested the League was the middle class. C. A. Henderson of the Central Junta remarked that organized capital and organized labor both incited social dissolution by only focusing on their own interests, not those of the community. Constituting three-fourths of the population, the dis-

organized middle class found itself unprotected and insecure between these two mobilized groups. Henderson offered no clear
solution to this dilemma, nor was his percentage accurate; the
upper and middle classes combined made up somewhat over a
third of the inhabitants of the city and province of Buenos
Aires.[63] A League committee defined the middle class as consisting of office workers, salespeople, reporters, teachers, bureaucrats, and other employees. It suggested special retirement and
pension plans for these groups, financed by contributions from
employers and individual salaries.[64] This attention to the needs of
the middle class, as well as those of workers and employers,
manifested the League's desire to attract the support of all "producers" and to mediate between them. This, again, clearly resembled the aim of European fascism.

Many of the League members' proposals were indeed both
practical and humanitarian. The Socialists implicitly recognized
the similarity between some of their ideas and those of the
League when they complained that they had advocated lending
libraries, night schools, and the like long before Liguistas "discovered" these issues.[65] These programs fit into the Socialist
minimal platform, designed to improve labor's status within the
given order, but the party's maximal platform called for changing the system. Moreover, laborers and their representatives were
supposed to struggle for these changes themselves. Social programs had a different significance for the League; they constituted its "maximum" platform of saving the essentials of capitalism. Under the League's scheme, employers would control the
free workers in their nationalized "unions" and would dispense
charity to them. The government would add to private alms-
giving.

Practical humanitarianism, however, depended upon upper-
class willingness to cooperate, and such cooperation was not
forthcoming in the 1920s—or later. Wealthy Argentines and
their representatives in government saw little reason to extend
favors to a weakened labor movement. Moreover, League members did not agree on all the issues discussed in the congresses.
Finally, even if they had, it would have been difficult to push re-

forms through a national congress increasingly divided along partisan lines. For these reasons, practical humanitarianism had little impact on government in the 1920s.

The League was anxious to deny Argentines their autonomy in respects other than labor organizing. Carlés and other Liguistas defined the general rights of the people very narrowly. They recognized the constitutionally stated rights of equality before the law and "social equality," which Carlés defined as the privilege of all inhabitants—rich or poor, male or female—to belong to the Argentine people. According to his definition, social equality was perfectly consistent with social hierarchy. Argentines were also entitled to live, work, and acquire goods with the earnings from their labor.[66] These were among the few rights recognized by the League.

Notably absent from this list of human rights was liberty. Indeed, League spokesmen rarely mentioned liberty as an inherent right of Argentines, except in the same breath as order. I have already noted Carlés's opposition to intellectual curiosity in the discussion of education. Carlés complained that liberty of thought was inefficient, for it did not guarantee that people would think well. Freedom of thought also had led Argentines to forsake traditional ideas for foreign ones. Work no longer meant an effort ennobled by the hope of individual mobility; immigrant radicals had deformed this concept into one which stood for a means of avoiding honest toil. Whole new phrases had been adopted from abroad, such as "strike," "worker agitation," and even "liberty," which signified allowing "foreign bandits" to enter and stir up the populace.[67] Carlés viewed the concept of freedom as foreign.

Dr. Eufemio Muñoz of the Gualeguaychú brigade derided those he called *enfermos de utopia* (those stricken by the utopian disease) for not comprehending that some people had more than others because they were more capable and hard-working. If the utopian agitators truly wanted equality and liberty, as they insisted, they could increase their own freedom by destroying the yokes of ignorance, fanaticism, and superstition that imprisoned them. The fact that they instead fought against the established order demonstrated that they did not really want liberty—or at least not liberty within the law, a "controlled liberty."[68] As Carlés had noted, what the left sought was "illusory liberty," which the League considered an immoral quest.

One of the few types of liberty that the League viewed positively and upheld was, of course, "liberty of work." This consisted of the "right" to remain independent of unions and to work wherever and in whatever capacity one wished. The League did not explain, however, how the poor were truly free to choose their own professions and employers. Another principle of free labor stated that all men must work and no one should support oneself from the proceeds of "outside labors," defined as union activities. (Although at other times Liguistas criticized the idle rich, they did not include inheritances, stock dividends, and speculative profits in this category.) The League did not explain how unions could operate without paid leadership. Workers' associations were permissible only if they were "practical democratic" entities, which meant not only that they held secret elections but, more importantly, that they eschewed strikes and opposition to the class system. The principles of free labor again showed that despite its rhetorical support for labor organization, the League in reality denied the legitimacy of any autonomous union, revolutionary or not. Moreover, "free labor" included the right to work, but not necessarily the right to have work; many League members did not agree with Carlés's idea of guaranteeing jobs for all. Despite these limitations, a member of the Civic Guard of Concordia, Entre Ríos, a League affiliate, asserted that to defend liberty of work was "to secure the liberty of all, the maintenance of order and national security."[69] His juxtaposition of terms revealed the League's true priority.

Independent unions that did not accept the League's "liberty of work" were dangerous and unacceptable. Their search for utopia was illegitimate, for as the League statutes put it, "only those who want to perfect their fatherland can have the right to improve humanity as an ideal." Ricardo Cranwell, Central Junta member and distinguished jurist, insisted that unions affiliated with the syndicalist and anarchocommunist federations existed outside the constitution. According to Article 14, associations with useful ends were permitted, but these unions had no such purpose, because their aim was to annihilate the social order. These subversive organizations threatened the system and therefore should be destroyed.[70] Liguistas implied that as unions were outside the constitution, one need not observe the niceties of law in doing so. Indeed, League members seemed to suggest that the scrupulous practice of liberal democratic ideals played into the hands of agitators. To protect their own standing, League members denied others their constitutional rights and dishonored the principles they claimed to revere. They also set an unfortunate precedent for the future.

Despite their affinities to fascism, Liguistas did not explicitly identify themselves with the European counterrevolutionary tradition, as did the right-wing nationalists who followed them. Carlés instead considered himself a follower of Roque Sáenz Peña, for whom he had campaigned. Despite his support for this reformer and his original sympathy for Radicalism, Carlés did not believe in democracy and rarely used the term except to criticize it. He noted that the word did not appear in any important national document; instead, Argentine forefathers had established what they called a "republic." As the decade passed, Carlés reminded his listeners more and more frequently that the two were very different. A republic was a form of government that assured the welfare of all on the basis of mutual respect; in other words, one that guaranteed "Argentine social justice." It was "a social state where the peace of tranquil consciousness reigned through order and wellbeing."[71] In a democracy such as Argentina, presumably these conditions did not exist or were threatened by "demagoguery"—the regime's alliance with the mob. Carlés seemed to reach the conclusion that liberal democracy inevitably led to disorder.

Sometimes it was unclear whether Carlés disliked democracies in general or only the post-1912 Argentine type. In the First Congress, he seemingly approved of the earlier Argentine "democracy," when the will of the "tame majority" had predominated, resulting in peace. Society changed for the worse when "the few" began to assert their will over the rest: the "eminent few" with their political coteries and the "inferior few" with their terrorism. (One notes here that as early as 1920, Carlés was beginning to identify the "eminent few", or democratic Radicalism, with the left.) Then Carlés contradicted himself by praising authority as "the great leveler because it governs with ideas emerging from the environment." "Subordination to the *jefe* (chief)" had been an essential part of "our democracy," which Carlés defined as a state of justice for all.[72] Carlés did not explain why what he saw as the new authoritarianism of the Radicals or of the left did not fit Argentine tradition.

In the mid-1920s, however, Carlés complained that Argentine democracy was not genuine. The electorate excluded women, unnaturalized immigrants, and citizens who neglected their voting duties. Of ten million Argentines, only 300,000 were registered voters, and half of these, or 1.25 percent of the population, constituted the "democratic majority." Their viewpoint did not reflect a real national consensus. Therefore, an "electoralist democracy" was inevitably a "false" one.[73]

Carlés's critique was incisive but his figures were inaccurate. In 1926 there were almost 1,800,000 registered voters, half of whom equaled 8.6 percent of the population. Moreover, that year 875,033 persons voted in elections—almost three times Carlés's figure for registered voters.[74] Besides, Carlés and other Liguistas did not propose to expand the electorate to include the outsiders. Although Carlés had invited women into the League, he opposed female suffrage. Other Liguistas favored restricting the electorate and representative system even further. President Vela of the Gualeguaychú brigade wanted to prohibit naturalized foreigners from occupying congressional seats. In a more extreme proposal, Father Saravia Ferré of the Quilmes, Buenos Aires, brigade favored reducing the weight of a naturalized foreigner's vote to a mere fraction of a native-born citizen's. If the immigrant demonstrated his love for the nation by shedding blood for it or by some other means, the government could award him a whole vote.[75] Although League members recognized some of the deficiencies of Argentine political institutions, they were unwilling to make them more democratic.

Furthermore, Carlés never clarified how an ideal democracy or a republic chose its leaders. As early as 1923 he disapproved of the modern political parties which were a legacy of electoral reform: "the evil political breed that stimulates all the sensualities of the low social levels."[76] Given this critique, one would assume that he was suspicious of all leaders chosen under universal suffrage. Carlés implied that republics were governed by self-perpetuating elites, similar to the one that had ruled Argentina before 1916, and that such lealders often were morally and intellectually superior to those of democracies. His notions resembled those of the Catholic statesmen and Civistas of 1890, who wanted to purify the Argentine oligarchy rather than remove it completely from power. Subsequent right-wing nationalists, who explicitly traced their opinions back to early Radicalism, agreed with Carlés and further developed these ideas.

To oppose "demagoguery," a favorite word in the organization's lexicon, some League members supported the creation of a national conservative party. A League committee ruefully summed up the attempts to build such a group and ascribed the failure to personal ambitions and lack of self-sacrifice. In a 1920 manifesto, the Córdoba brigade stated that, at any rate, narrow political parties could not solve pressing economic and social conflicts. Argentine democracy was too partisan, personalistic, and anger-ridden to accomplish the task. The brigade hinted that a group above the party system, presumably the League, was the answer. In view of the vacuum on the right and the deficiencies of Argentine parties, Amadeo, Pallejá, and other Liguistas inched toward advocating corporatist government. Rear Admiral Lagos, for example, concluded that Argentine democracy would be stronger if it expressed the needs of the various classes or corporations that composed the society.[77]

Until the late 1920s, however, the League did not take a corporatist stance or officially enter partisan struggle. Although it attempted to influence government policy, it did not run candidates for office. The League was satisfied with the Alvear presidency, which appointed Carlés and Domecq García to high office. Indeed, as naval minister, Domecq García controlled the port area and protected "free laborers" against the unions. The former League president and the other aristocrats who staffed this government safeguarded propertied interests. By 1926, however, the League began to fear the return of Yrigoyen to power and the resurgence of "demagoguery" and labor activism. Disillusioned with the political system, Carlés urged the formation of new citizens' groups to supersede the corrupt political parties and conciliate labor and capital. These groups would elect "Argentines" to office, replacing the Radical, Conservative, and Socialist politicians, who only sought financial gain. The League would help promote this new civic attitude, as it previously had promoted nationalism.[78]

Carlés wanted to convert the League into such a group and lead it into power. On one occasion in 1928 he briefly noted that "when it assumed the government of the Nation," the League would propagate nationalistic ideals. Most Liguistas, however, ignored his call. Only two replies to his proposal were discussed publicly, and both were negative. Federico de la Villa of the Thirty-Third Precinct brigade said that the League should not be a political party, although it should continue to promote good government. Agreeing that electoral reform had failed to create organic political parties, Paulino P. Ramírez of the San Juan brigade nevertheless advised the organization to limit its action to civic education.[79]

Opposition to class struggle remained the core of the League's ideology, yet the distance between an antileftist and an antidemocratic stance narrowed with Yrigoyen's reelection. Fearing disorder, the League adopted a more active political role after 1928, although not precisely the one Carlés had advocated. New counterrevolutionary groups with acknowledged European roots proved more responsive to his political ideas than did the League. They also developed and made more explicit the antidemocratic and antiliberal tenets of practical humanitarianism. Whereas Carlés and other League spokesmen had only sketchily outlined these tenets, the latter nevertheless demonstrated that the League opposed the entire emancipatory process.

SIX

The League and the New Forces
of Counterrevolution

Looking over his organization's past, in 1935 Carlés proclaimed
that from 1919 to 1924 the League "tranquilized the public
spirit," from 1924 to 1928 it "guided the nation's social conscience," and from 1928 to 1933 it defended Argentine liberty.[1]
At the beginning of the third stage, the League's central preoccupation shifted from the leftist threat to the socioeconomic
system to the Yrigoyenist threat to the political system, although
in the League's view the two were intertwined. New groups
helped the League defend "Argentine liberty," a task that led to
the Revolution of 1930. Not long after this event, however, ideological fissures split the counterrevolutionary ranks. Despite the
differences between the League's ideas and those of the "nationalists," as Argentines and scholars have called the newer circles,
in many ways the latter represented a logical extension of the
former.

Leftism clearly threatened capitalist interests in the postwar
years; it is more difficult to understand how Yrigoyenism presented a danger. The explanation lies in the economic and political conditions of the 1920s. During the years 1922 to 1929, fluc-
tuation and uncertainty replaced the gloomy postwar economic
climate. A period of recovery lasting from mid-1922 to 1925 was
followed by a year of depression, another recovery from 1927 to
October 1929, and then the Great Depression. Largely determined by international conditions, these cycles manifested the
dependent nature of the Argentine economy.

Low investment, misgivings about the world market, and lack
of high-quality virgin land to bring into cultivation limited agri-

cultural growth. Grain production expanded somewhat but at a much slower rate than before the war. Doubts about prices were not misplaced. From 1921 to 1924 the value of grain exports increased about 50 percent; in the two subsequent years their value dropped abruptly, but prices rallied from 1927 until 1929, when they began a steady decline before reaching a nadir in 1933.[2] At the same time, chilled beef exports assumed preeminence over those of frozen and conserved beef. The prosperity of the chilled beef industry, however, did not arrest the decline of the livestock sector in general. The prices of meat other than chilled beef, wool, and other livestock products remained stable or declined, decreasing the value of exports.

The Argentine economy was in a transitional stage. Slowly it was beginning to direct more of its production toward the internal market—and to fall under U.S. domination. Government investment, the raising of tariff barriers in 1923, and the renewed importation of industrial machinery after the war helped stimulate industrial growth. So, too, did U.S. investment, which more than doubled between 1923 and 1927, compared to an increase of only 5 percent for the British. British investment in 1927 still amounted to over four times that of the North American, but the latter was concentrated in manufacturing and other new, dynamic areas of the economy.[3] Led by the metallurgical, meatpacking, and state-administered petroleum sectors, industrial production rose from 1922 to 1927. For the most part, industry continued to grow from 1927 to 1931, although at a reduced pace, particularly when the investment level fell sharply in 1929.

The labor movement was generally weak and fragmented during the period. Unopposed by a united labor federation, the Radical party made inroads into working-class barrios, offering services and patronage to their inhabitants in exchange for support. This represented a change from previous tactics; Yrigoyen and his associates had cultivated relations with unions rather than with individual workers in the days before the League had pushed the government to the right. Yet even during this period of weakness some unions were active, particularly the railroad and municipal workers, who in 1926 formed COA. The Socialist-leaning

COA and the syndicalist USA merged in 1930 to form the Confederación General de Trabajadores (CGT, General Confederation
of Workers), ushering in a new period of Argentine labor history.
The political left remained divided, however. The Independent
Socialists departed from the Socialist party in 1927, and the
fledgling Communist party remained weak. The proletariat no
longer threatened the social order as it had in 1919.

Political changes, however, threatened the former elite. These
alterations did not affect economic policy to any great extent.
The Radicals had little if any inclination to modify the agrarian
export economy. The social measures they supported were moderate in character: the income tax, the nationalization of oil, limited land reform, an industrial tariff. The opposition, which controlled the Chamber until 1920 and the Senate throughout the
period, did not allow any of these measures to pass except Alvear's tariff. Often portrayed as reactionary, in contrast to the
"progressive" Yrigoyen administrations, the Alvear presidency
broke with the Rural Society on such issues as the tariff—which,
however, Alvear may have intended more for revenue than for
protective purposes. The fact that the League and the old political elite did not oppose Alvear, despite his stands, demonstrates
that their antipathy for Yrigoyen had little to do with economic
policy differences, except over the budget, as will be seen.[4]

By no means a leftist, Yrigoyen was, however, interested in
attracting middle-class votes. One way of appealing to this group
was by providing opportunities for its advancement in the professions. Yrigoyen demonstrated his willingness to aid the middle
class in this quest for mobility by implementing the proposals of
the university reform movement. Among other consequences,
these measures helped open faculties and administrations to the
middle class.

Members of the middle class also entered the bureaucracy.
Rock reported that Yrigoyen created 10,000 to 20,000 additional
federal jobs in Buenos Aires between 1921 and 1922 alone. The
fact that the federal budget climbed 63 percent from 1916 to 1922
seemed to support this assertion,[5] although inflation accounted
for some of this increase. Deficit financing was required to fi-

nance the expansion of the bureaucracy. This, in turn, increased the foreign debt, which landowning interests opposed. They favored a balance of payments equilibrium in order to protect exports and facilitate cheap credit. Reflecting their wishes, Alvear trimmed the budget and bureaucracy in his first years in office, although he reversed these efforts by 1925.[6]

Displeased that the middle class was taking over positions that once would have gone to its own members, the upper class criticized the budget increases and what it viewed as a bloated bureaucracy. *La Fronda* and other opposition spokesmen constantly ridiculed Yrigoyen's appointees for their lack of experience, education, and proper social graces. The same upper class that had been responsible for excluding the middle class from opportunities to acquire these traits blamed the victims of its policies.

The middle class also was making inroads into the Radical party organization. After 1900 Yrigoyen had begun to recruit precinct leaders from first- and second-generation Argentines. In the internal party elections of 1918, about half of those chosen had non-Spanish names; many in the other half may have had Spanish immigrant forebears.[7] Members of the middle class also were increasingly elected to public office. Smith classified only 31 percent of the Radical deputies in the Chamber from 1916 to 1930 as aristocrats, compared with 53 percent of the PDP and 73 percent of the Conservatives. The departure of the highly aristocratic Antipersonalists from the Radical party in 1924 accounted for the low figure, which represented a significant drop from previous years.[8] Although Alvear did not join this group, his appointees were of perceptibly higher social origins than many of Yrigoyen's, especially in the latter's second presidency. At any rate, the Personalists of lower social origins were the Radicals more likely to engage in what the old elite regarded as demagogic rhetoric and corrupt patronage practices.

An example of the Personalists' "demagoguery" was their economic nationalism, which was related to their attitude toward the middle class. This faction implicitly realized that the government could not enlarge the budget and the bureaucracy indefinitely without new sources of revenue. The creation of federal economic monopolies such as the oil industry could help stimulate government revenues and provide patronage jobs.[9]

The *régimen* in 1912 had intended to limit middle-class political participation to voting, thus preserving the elite's control over the political system. Increased middle-class access to education, the bureaucracy, the political parties, and public office, however, threatened the old political order—and it seemed likely that the Personalists would grant such access to the native-born lower class in the near future. Perhaps more important, by 1928 the old political elite feared that it would never return to office. In his first presidency, Yrigoyen had expelled *régimen* cliques from provincial governments through repeated interventions. This policy helped his party win congressional elections in those areas, thus gradually increasing Radical power in the legislative branch. By 1928, the opposition controlled only the Senate, and the wily Radical caudillo had found ways of getting around it and ruling through decree. Moreover, Yrigoyen's enormous presidential victory in 1928 seemed to confirm the Radical stranglehold on national government. The 1912 electoral reform had backfired on the old political elite; democracy seemed to mean Personalist domination.[10]

The loss of political power embittered the *régimen* and its descendants. It meant forfeiting the economic spoils that had always depended on political ties, as well as what the elite regarded as its birthright. Many sons of landowning families thought that their rank and intellectual training entitled them to public office, as would have been true in the past. The postwar agrarian crisis and then the Depression aggravated their fears of displacement. As the export economy neared collapse, they identified their sinking fate with that of their homeland.

From the viewpoint of the *régimen* and its scions, democracy was prohibitively costly. A system that perpetuated the rule of one party—and its middle-class faction at that—was deficient. The old elite conveniently forgot that it had monopolized power before 1916 without the people's consent. The popular mandate for Radicalism showed the masses' greed and stupidity in electing "mediocrities" and "demagogues." Democracy inevitably led to dictatorship: the ruthless domination of the party that promised the most to the electorate, and the domination of one man over that party and the entire political system. Moreover, in its demagoguery this dictatorship resembled bolshevism and could, perhaps, lead to it. Younger, angrier, and more insecure than the Liguistas of 1919, the spokesmen for these beliefs, the "nationalists," lashed out at the mass democracy responsible for their declining fortunes. To a much greater extent than the League, they identified some of Argentina's ills with the liberal-conservative bourgeoisie which had presided over electoral reform and which in many ways they despised.

Lugones was the first to voice these counterrevolutionary sentiments. The fact that the League cosponsored his initial talks on this theme in July 1923 symbolized the continuity between the new viewpoint and the old.[11] The eclectic poet declared that he was the enemy of those immigrants who had brought discord from overseas, disturbing the peace and harmony that had reigned in the country. Significantly, the events of early 1919, in which workers had fought for revolutionary rather than purely economic ends, had shown him this danger. War had to be declared against these rebels; it would not be a civil war but a national war of Argentines against aliens.

Lugones saw foreign leftism as half of a double threat against national unity, the lack of Argentine military preparedness constituting the other half. He admitted that the war had demonstrated the absurdity of his former antimilitarism. To defend the nation against external foes, ideological or territorial, the people would have to assert their love for the fatherland and rally behind the armed forces. This meant supporting increases in military strength and uniting in spirit with the military. Then the well-paid bureaucrat went on to criticize democracy, denouncing the electoralism, bloated public budget and bureaucracy, and corruption which he believed characterized the system. *La Protesta* summed up the talk by noting that Lugones, desirous of recognition, had converted to Carlés's "rabid patriotism."[12] The postwar labor upsurge had influenced his change of sentiments.

Lugones's militarism and opposition to democracy, however,

surpassed Carlés's. In a well-known speech in December 1924, he depicted force as the basic reality underlying society and as the only sure means of preventing social dissolution. Force meant authority, which in turn implied social, political, and cultural hierarchy and the enforcement of strict discipline. Only the army could maintain these values; hence the "hour of the sword" had arrived.[13]

Lugones continued to lambast electoral democracy in *La organización de la paz* (1925). Democracies treated all persons identically according to the abstract theory of equality; hence, they considered the votes of all citizens to be the same. This was absurd, for citizens differed according to ability and other traits, a point with which Carlés would have agreed. Then Lugones noted that as the weaker outnumbered the stronger individuals, democracy favored the former: "satisfying . . . the paradoxical piety that pursues the triumph of the most inept in life. . . . that piety is the fundamental virtue of Christianity."[14]

This piety assumed an ecumenical character that negated all possibility of "durable aggregation," motivated by geography, race, history, or nationalism. The two most common manifestations of this ecumenicism were Christianity and democracy; others were the concepts of God, humanity, and the international proletariat. Lugones explained his distaste for Christianity by noting its internationalist, communist, and antipatriotic roots. Both Christianity and democracy aspired toward universal brotherhood, the former through faith and the latter through reason. Life, however, was not susceptible to reason or faith. Its evolution was mysterious and instinctive, and no one was capable of discerning its purpose, if, indeed, it had any at all. Force and nationalism had triumphed over democracy, humanity, and ecumenicism in the war, demonstrating the failure of rationalists and religious believers to order life according to metaphysical concepts. Men could not rule over life but could only exist within it.[15]

Lugones hoped for a revival of paganism, which would subordinate piety to power. Men would once more accept life the way it was in reality, not the way they conceptualized it. They would end democratic rule, which simply allowed the incompetents to subjugate the able. One might feel sorry for the former, but one could not organize life on the basis of charity and compassion, only on the basis of force and hierarchy.[16]

Here, Lugones injected Argentine nationalism with the vitalism missing since the Youth Committee. He also denounced Western civilization in a manner similar to that of European fascists. He brutally rejected "ecumenicism," or the universal emancipatory process. God, morality, brotherhood, peace, and other transcendent values had no place in his system. His conception of life was a narrow biological one in which power, the struggle for survival, and racial or geographical particularisms were the sole realities. Although Carlés also rejected abstractions and internationalism, he never carried these negations to their ultimate conclusion. Carlés would have abhorred Lugones's atheism, paganism, and vitalism. The League's promilitary stance did not translate into favoring military rule. Furthermore, although the League "Argentinized" religion, morality, and charity, its members never explicitly denied the universality of these values.

The strong Catholic influence on other nationalists also led them to repudiate some of Lugones's ideas, although they admired him as a teacher. One can trace the religious roots of their beliefs back to the same Social Catholicism (and Catholic antileftism) that nourished the League. In response to the university reform movement, the Federación de Estudiantes Católicos (Federation of Catholic Students) was formed in Córdoba in 1917. The federation claimed to support the Catholic and patriotic Argentine tradition against the anticlericalism and leftism of the reformers. It believed that university reform threatened the pillars of tradition, authority, and hierarchy that bolstered society. The reformers' intention to open the universities to Marxist-tainted ideas also endangered Catholic values and the present order. The organization could not prevent the reforms, and its statements presaged those of nationalist groups to come.[17]

One of the aims of the 1919 Great National Collection had been to finance youth organizations devoted to social peace and Catholic education. A result was the Cursos de Cultura Católica

(Catholic Culture Courses), founded in 1922 by the Catholic scholar César Pico, Dell'Oro Maini, and others. Participants in the courses included Mario Amadeo, Federico Ibarguren, Marcelo Sánchez Sorondo, Nimio de Anquín, Julio Meinvielle, Samuel Medrano, Guillermo Gallardo, and other future nationalists. The founders and students of the courses disassociated themselves from established Catholic circles, which they saw as arid and bourgeois. They considered themselves dissenters from this establishment, despite their traditionalist and rightist leanings. Baluarte, another training ground in Catholic ideas for young nationalists, arose out of the courses in late 1928. This group was more political in orientation than the latter. Mario Amadeo, one of its founders, later described it as "profoundly traditionalist" though not yet consciously nationalist. Baluarte proclaimed itself Hispanist, corporatist, Thomist, and completely antiliberal and antidemocratic.[18]

One of the modern writers these groups discussed was Charles Maurras, who exerted the single strongest foreign influence on Argentine nationalists. They particularly admired what they considered the Frenchman's patriotism.[19] Maurras venerated his fatherland, which to him was a concrete entity made up of blood, soil, and history with a life of its own and a right to protect its existence and freedom of movement. Citizens owed their allegiance to the fatherland regardless of its shortcomings. Maurras exhibited this belief in his fight against the Dreyfusards. French security and strength mattered far more than Dreyfus's innocence or guilt; because the Dreyfusards' accusations were weakening the military and the state, their cause was unjust and harmful.

Maurras thought that France reached its zenith under the Old Regime. The hereditary system of estates, families, guilds, the Church, the monarchy, and other mediating institutions tempered the destructive individualism of human beings and thus promoted harmony in society. Vital in the maintenance of order was the Church, which through its Romanized version of Christianity had introduced classicism to Europe. The product of Judaism, Jewish (non-Romanized) Christianity, German Protestantism, and German tribalism, the French Revolution which began in 1789 destroyed the system responsible for French glory. Maurras believed that these five forces shared a barbaric and an-archical stress on individual liberty and monotheism, which rep-resented two heads of a single danger. Establishing direct rela-tions with the Absolute diminished one's obedience to earthly masters.[20] Thus monotheism and individual rights were equally subversive because both undermined authority.

Christianity itself, or at least the non-Catholic version, formed part of the emancipatory process that was freeing some human beings from domination by others. Accordingly, Maurras, an atheist, found "non-Romanized" religion suspect. The doctrines of political liberty, equality, fraternity, and the essential goodness of humanity, which also pertained to the emancipatory process, were anathema to him, as, of course, was Marxism. Maurras be-lieved that liberalism and Marxism were linked in the same gen-eral revolutionary succession and that one led inexorably to the other. As liberal democratic republicanism had, in his opinion, damaged the nation more than Marxism, Maurras reserved most of his criticism for the former.

The revolution was responsible for French decay. Lifeless uto-pian abstractions such as liberty and democracy assumed prece-dence over family, tradition, and the historical reality of the land. In contrast to the pre-1789 monarchy, democratic society was ruled by demagoguery, money, greed, and anarchic public opin-ion. A government composed of the best minds and scions of the oldest families offered the only guarantee of good administra-tion. Unlike democratic plutocrats, the elite would govern in the best interests of the people. The fact that the most glorious pe-riod of French history had occurred under the Old Regime justi-fied a return to that system.

Maurras believed that only outside enemies prevented France from reembracing its "natural" form of rule. Indeed, the whole emancipatory process was foreign, essentially German and Jew-ish. Maurras did not use these terms to refer to specific groups, but rather to forces that he believed threatened the unity and strength of France, such as Marxism, international finance, mo-nopoly capitalism, anticlericalism, and antimilitarism.

In 1926 the pope condemned Maurras for subordinating religion to politics and converting the former into the latter's servant. For this reason Argentine Catholic nationalists were obliged to formally reject Maurras's teachings. Still, they applauded his impassioned defense of the nation's interests against liberals, democrats, foreigners, plutocrats, and Jews. It is not difficult to understand his appeal for the young intelligentsia of old lineage whose talents were rejected by Yrigoyenist democracy. They continued to voice Maurrasian sentiments and to identify themselves with the European, particularly French, counterrevolutionary tradition. They also expressed admiration for Mussolini, an admiration reinforced by the Duce's good relations with the Church.[21]

The condemnation of Maurras also led nationalists to look to Spain for inspiration. The works of cultural nationalists such as Gálvez helped assuage the old *porteño* distaste for its own Spanish heritage. The visits in 1928 of José Ortega y Gasset and Ramiro de Maeztu aroused further interest in Spanish thought. Maeztu frequently met with participants in the Catholic Culture Courses and with Julio and Rodolfo Irazusta, who at the time were involved in the nationalist press (discussed later). Many of the ideas expressed in his famous *Defensa de la hispanidad* (1934) may have emerged from these sessions.[22] Members of Baluarte claimed Spaniards as their philosophical forefathers: in particular, Juan Donoso Cortés, a nineteenth-century conservative, and Juan Vásquez de Mella, who tried to reconcile the ultrareactionary Carlists with modern times.

These Hispanist, Catholic, elitist, and Maurrasian ideas found expression in such journals as *La Voz Nacional* (1925), *Criterio* (1928–), *Número* (1930–31), and *La Nueva República* (1927–28, 1930–31).[23] The Irazusta brothers and their friends founded the last of these, which became the most influential nationalist organ of the period. The prominent Irazusta family of Entre Ríos lost much of its land and fortune in the postwar agrarian crisis. The brothers' ancestors included liberals and supporters of Rosas alike, and their father was an early Radical and follower of Alem. Their uncle Julián had been an officer of the League's Gualeguaychú brigade. The Irazustas' circle included, among others, the former syndicalists Ernesto Palacio and Juan Carulla, the Catholic traditionalist Pico, and Alfonso de Laferrère, a PDP member. Some of these men would eventually leave the group for ideological reasons. Despite their diverse affiliations, all agreed that demagoguery threatened national institutions. Most of them despised liberalism and parliamentarism and advocated a strong government that would maintain discipline, hierarchy, religion, and the social order. This government would take the shape of a "functional democracy," or corporatist system, based on the vital forces of society instead of the corrupt parties. These beliefs, along with a growing consciousness of imperialism and a vigorous opposition to socialism, immigration, and university reform, constituted what they called nationalism. To this definition, Palacio added that as the term implied reverence for "an existent historical formation," it was "an essentially conservative phenomenon."[24]

The founders of *La Nueva República* maintained close ties with the editors of *La Fronda*. A strong supporter of the League in the postwar era, *La Fronda* agreed with the nationalists on many issues, including the need to abolish the current electoral system. The newspaper's chief editor was Francisco Uriburu, former member of the Youth Committee and the League. He, the Laferrère brothers, and other nationalists such as Ibarguren and José F. Uriburu had been PDP members. Many nationalists traced their origins further back to Alem and early Radicalism, which they characterized as Creole, intransigent, and austere, in contrast to Yrigoyenism, which had become a "vehicle for the New Argentines."[25]

La Nueva República focused on interpreting current political events from a nonpartisan nationalistic viewpoint. The influence of Maurras continued to be strong, but staff members were firmly republican in keeping with Argentine tradition—hence the title. In its first issue, December 1, 1927, Julio and Rodolfo Irazusta defined the Argentine dilemma. Forty years of "spiritual disorientation" had produced ideological confusion within the ruling classes. Liberalism had served adequately during the period of national organization, but its time had passed. The electoral reform had encouraged the rise of political parties which pandered to the masses and exploited the country. The object of life was not to produce but to work for the government; Argentina had become a country of functionaries.

The authors protested other shortcomings: government corruption and mishandling of finances, anticlericalism, excessive presidential interference in politics, lack of genuine political representation, violations of the constitution and of Argentine republican traditions. "Exaggeratedly egalitarian" inheritance laws and the threat of divorce legislation imperiled family solidarity. Poorly adapted to national conditions, the economic system was in extreme disarray, and the mother industries suffered under the enormous burden of foreign capital. The old financial structure did not adequately protect agrarian production, and the exodus of rural population to the cities and the lack of incentive further weakened this mainstay of the economy. The authors warned that Argentina's wealth and prosperity were shallow and exhaustible.

The solution to this crisis was to overturn the ruling liberal democratic ideologues and substitute a nonpartisan elite guided by principles opposed to those of the French Revolution. As Palacio exclaimed in the same issue, "Organicemos la contrarrevolución" (Let's organize the counterrevolution). Indeed, though they usually called themselves nationalists, the editors also referred to their ideas as counterrevolutionary and reactionary.[26]

Palacio distinguished the periodical's nationalism from that of democrats. True nationalists desired nothing more than what was best for the nation. They believed that individual interests must be subordinated to the interests of the community, and individual rights to the rights of the state. In contrast, democratic ideologues overlooked the common welfare and substituted in its place abstract principles—popular sovereignty, liberty, equality, victory of the proletariat—as the proper goals of government. With their concern for abstract principles and individual rights, rather than the nation's rights, democrats were the enemies of order and national welfare. Democrats were agents of dissolution because organized society would never fit the ideal model that they carried in their imaginations. Nationalists would always accept society as given and try to work within it. Thus the two could never be compatible. Moreover, the Argentine constitution and republican tradition precluded democracy because they stood for rule of law rather than of the masses, provincial autonomy rather than centralist dictatorship, and representation of the vital forces rather than representation of the machine. Restoring republicanism would strengthen Argentina, but this task would entail fighting democracy, liberalism, and romantic humanitarianism.[27] This was one of many articles pointing out that the constitution did not contain democratic ideas. It was also one of many selections that manifested the editors' priority for order over purely "national" concerns.

The periodical's sentiments strikingly resembled those of its local predecessor, the League. Like the Irazustas, Carlés criticized liberalism and party politics, and he favored rule by a nonpartisan, austere, well-educated elite. Carlés would have agreed with Palacio on the need for authority, republicanism, unity, and "seeing the world as it is." Carlés also subordinated abstract freedoms to civic duty and national prerogative. Although in the early 1920s, Carlés cast leftists alone in the role of "agents of dissolution," by the end of the decade he, like Palacio, also included democrats in that category. Finally, both Carlés and many nationalists admired Alem's current of Radicalism and fancied themselves as its successors.

The editors of *La Nueva República* acknowledged the overlap between their ideas and those of Carlés. Rodolfo Irazusta recalled that Carlés had differentiated republics from democracies years ago. He cited a speech in which Carlés defined a republic in terms virtually identical to the periodical's definition: "a social state where discipline, the principle of authority, individual security in work, and civil peace reign."[28] The newspaper frequently described Carlés's speeches and League activities in glowing terms.

Nevertheless, despite the paper's sympathy for its precursor, the ideas and social bases of the League and early nationalism differed in some ways. The nationalists' corporatism and their em-brace of irrationalism, youth, and vitalism, characteristics of the Youth Committee that had not carried over into the League, set them apart from the latter. Their denial of individual rights only represented a difference of degree from Carlés's viewpoint, but it was nonetheless significant. They even opposed one of the few means of mass mobility ratified by Carlés (and Argentine liber-alism)—universal education—on the grounds that literacy did not mean moral perfection and that it increased the people's sus-ceptibility to demagoguery.[29] (Nationalist opposition to the laical character of and alleged bolshevik inroads into public education, however, resembled League sentiments.) These differences re-flected social changes since the League's heyday and European in-fluences on nationalism. The mere fact that the young activists claimed foreign sources of inspiration—in apparent contradic-tion with their nationalism—set them apart from the League.

Another glaring distinction was the nationalists' disdain, at least in the 1920s, for a female or middle-class following. They had no interest in appealing to the class that threatened their position. As for women, most nationalists believed that females were only conservative when they remained in the home. When they engaged in political or other activities outside the domestic sphere, they were more likely than men to succumb to anarchy and moral disorder.[30] Nationalists were less willing than Liguis-tas to run the risk of increasing female autonomy. Furthermore, nationalists primarily devoted themselves to intellectual, propa-ganda, and, later on, violent activities which bore no relationship to women's charitable roles within society or the League. The ab-sence of women from nationalist ranks also indicated the group's lack of interest in the proletariat. These and other divergences between the League and the nationalists became more apparent after the Revolution of 1930.

Even before Yrigoyen's reelection, nationalists decided that the reign of democracy had to be ended by force, if necessary. At the end of 1927, Rodolfo Irazusta and Juan Carulla asked General Uriburu to lead an uprising. Uriburu had also moved from anti-leftism to antiliberalism. One of the few subscribers to *La Voz*

Nacional, Uriburu refused, but he maintained contact with nationalists and read *La Nueva República.* In early 1929, Rodolfo Irazusta and Roberto de Laferrère, Alfonso's brother, told Uriburu about their plans to form a youth militia to combat Argentina's "internal enemies" and carry out a revolution. The general reminded them that he was on active duty and could not participate at this stage. He tacitly approved of their intention, however, by saying that the task of action corresponded to the youth, as it had to him and others in 1890—again tying nationalism to the old UCR. Later that year, nationalists established the Liga Republicana (Republican League), and by 1930 they convinced Uriburu to head a revolution.[31]

By this time Yrigoyen had returned to office and the Great Depression had begun. Many believed that the Radical leader, well into his seventies, was senile. Whether this was true or not, Yrigoyen's inability to delegate authority and act decisively prevented him from effectively managing the economic crisis. Moreover, many of his associates were corrupt and inefficient, and they warred with each other rather than devise solutions to mounting national problems. Congressmen meanwhile were arguing bitterly over provincial election results, lending credence to the counterrevolutionary view that they were more concerned with partisan politics than with the national situation. Under these circumstances, it was not surprising that the right-wing critique of democracy found an audience, particularly among disaffected sectors of the old elite. Yrigoyen's past relations with the military, his continuing interference in its affairs, and the sense of impending political and economic chaos also convinced many officers of the need for a coup—and perhaps for a new political system.[32]

At the same time that youths associated with *La Nueva República* and *La Fronda* were forming the Republican League, Carlés became the first prominent figure to call for Yrigoyen's overthrow. At the Señoras' annual textile exposition on July 12, 1929, he complained that the government had failed to address critical national issues and to observe the constitution. The moment was approaching, he warned, when Argentines would have to obey their duty and rebel to protect their country's institutions. The Argentine Patriotic League had another good reason to support a revolution, or rather counterrevolution: Radicalism, in its view, had become an agent of dissolution. Carlés reported on several occasions that Personalists had made a pact with anarchists, an action "proven" by Yrigoyen's indecisive response to strikes in Rosario in 1928. *La Nueva República* agreed with him.[33] Liguista spokesmen complained frequently that Yrigoyen was not combating bolshevism vigorously enough, although there were few other indications of labor militancy. The Argentine Patriotic League had not forgotten Yrigoyen's *obrerismo* during his first administration, and it was not leaving anything to chance.

In mid-1929 the U.S. embassy took note of the political crisis. At the end of July, Carlés informed Ambassador Robert Woods Bliss that ultimately Yrigoyen would be ousted, but he assured the diplomat that the revolution would be bloodless. An army officer told the U.S. military attaché that high-ranking army and naval officials, in close contact with Liguistas, had agreed on what to do at the first signs of internal disturbance. Bliss noted that the Argentine Patriotic League still commanded much prestige and a large following, particularly among military men and the upper classes, and had conserved its brigades throughout Argentina. Thus it remained the main bulwark against communism. He dismissed the widespread fears that government weakness had encouraged the spread of bolshevism. Nevertheless, he noted that many Argentines thought they needed a strong leader to arrest this threat. Bliss believed that Carlés intended to be this man, and the thought pleased him. He concluded, however, that the League would spark a revolution only if a general strike broke out. Otherwise, the ouster probably would come from within Yrigoyen's own party.[34]

An official campaign against Carlés began in mid-July 1929. Radicals denounced his call for rebellion as seditious—which indeed it was. A Radical public prosecutor, Manuel Ortiz Pereyra, asked a federal judge to investigate the records of the League and the Labor Association to find out their actual intentions. The judge eventually ruled that Carlés's actions did not warrant an in-

vestigation, and the League president continued his antiadmin-
istration speeches. The government's decision manifested its regard for civil liberties (and, perhaps, its indecisiveness), but the
right continued to view it as despotic. In early October the
Liguistas put up posters proclaiming that the "hour of ven-
geance" had arrived, in which Argentines had to choose between
the fatherland and a government that disobeyed the law. Police
tore down the posters and detained some of the Liguistas who
had distributed them. Carlés declared that despite persecution,
the Argentine Patriotic League would continue to support "Fatherland and Order" against dictators, as it had done in the past
against extremists.[35]

Public opinion and the press turned against the administration
after a Radical, presumably at Yrigoyen's behest, assassinated
Carlos Washington Lencinas, the anti-Yrigoyenist boss of Mendoza, in early November. The Argentine Patriotic League and
the Republican League, among others, condemned the killing at
large protest meetings in the capital. In response, young Yrigoy-
enists took their cause into the streets, forming what opponents
called the "Radical Klan." The Republicans followed closely behind, engaging in battle with the Radical Klan, leftist students,
and police. To stimulate and unite popular opposition to the administration, the Republicans also appeared at virtually every opposition rally, organized public meetings, disseminated posters,
and sent delegations to the provinces. One participant claimed
that by the end of 1929, there were 2,800 Republicans. The organization's hard core, however, numbered only several hundred.[36]

In the Republican League's declaration of aims, Roberto de
Laferrère wrote that the group resisted not only the government
in power but the actual system of government. The militia's main
organizer, Laferrère personally went much further and declared
his opposition to those who "put humanity before the fatherland." The Republicans coordinated their actions with other opposition groups such as the staff of *La Nueva República*, Conservative party members, PDP members, Independent Socialists, the
Argentine Patriotic League, and, on the eve of the revolution, the
Legión de Mayo (May Legion). At times, however, the Republi-

cans' ideals and methods antagonized their allies. The PDP, for example, criticized the militia's violence. Republicans responded in *La Nueva República* that the moribund PDP was trying to revive the corpse of democracy, whereas they supported a vigorous government of order. Once led by brilliant men, the PDP had decayed and turned leftist.[37]

Despite the groups' shared ideals and personnel, differences arose between the Republican League and *La Nueva República*. Although both opposed political parties, Carulla and Roberto de Laferrère supported the Independent Socialists in the 1930 congressional elections; Rodolfo Irazusta wanted to join a coalition that would offer its own list of candidates, headed by Carlés. The first plan prevailed, and Irazusta resigned from the Republicans.[38] The rift notwithstanding, the newspaper reported approvingly on the militia's activities.

The ideology and membership of the May Legion, founded in August 1930, also overlapped those of the Republicans and the newspaper staff. Named in honor of the May Revolution, the May Legion invited Argentine youths to defend their democratic heritage and arrest the slide into anarchy that had occurred since the passage of the Sáenz Peña Law. The May Legion's statement of aims lauded the democratic system established between 1810 and 1912. *La Nueva República* praised the Legion's intentions but reproved its leaders for characterizing the heroes of May as democrats.[39] Its manifesto indicated, however, that the May Legion's version of democracy bore more resemblance to the Argentine Patriotic League's than to Yrigoyen's.

Meanwhile counterrevolutionaries once again raised the specter of communism. In October 1929 the firemen of Buenos Aires demanded concessions from the city government, including the removal of their chief officers. Many frightened *porteños* viewed this militancy as a sign that leftism was spreading even within the forces of order. Ambassador Bliss believed that the officers' ill treatment of the firemen, however, was to blame. Backed up by the federal administration, the municipality agreed to the demands, lending credence to the opposition's view that leftists were taking advantage of the precarious economic and political situation. In December 1929, Uriburu claimed to have learned of a communist-inspired plot of firemen and policemen. Later, after the coup, the general insisted that if events had continued in the same path, there would have been a social revolution. "Anarchism was the specter which appeared to us at the end of the road." [40]

To the nationalists and the Liguistas, a leftist upheaval seemed the logical consequence of Yrigoyenist demagoguery. At the League's Eleventh Congress in May 1930, Carlés once again insisted that the government had allied itself with anarchism. The university reform movement had opened the educational system to bolshevik influence, and such ideas had affected even professors and students of the aristocracy. In August 1930, brigades in the capital met to express their solidarity with Carlés and discuss means of defending their neighborhoods against communists and anarchists. [41]

These were the final days before the coup. While Carlés continued to speak out against the government with little police interference, the government struck at other members of the opposition. When the police killed an anti-Yrigoyenist youth in a demonstration in early September, Liguistas put up posters and loudly protested. The combined Republican and May Legion forces, numbering about 1,000, now readied themselves for action under the command of Alberto Viñas, a Conservative party deputy. Armed Republicans guarded Uriburu as the police chased him from one hiding place to another on the eve of the revolution. In the early hours of September 6, small groups of Republicans and May Legionnaires headed toward the plaza of Flores, where they expected to join the rebelling soldiers. Instead they encountered the police, who dispersed and jailed some of the civilian revolutionaries. Others managed to escape and find the troops on their way from the Campo de Mayo barracks, and they accompanied them on their victorious march to the center of the capital. [42]

The coup succeeded with relative ease because the once-popular Yrigoyen had lost his mass following. The upper rungs of society and the military had long since found him wanting.

Government austerity measures prompted by the Depression alienated his supporters in the popular sectors, as did the regime's image of disunity, corruption, and inertia. Many Argentines may not have favored the military revolution, yet few actively opposed it. They hoped that the new government would solve critical economic problems and speedily restore constitutional rule.

Uriburu and his nationalist friends, however, interpreted popular acceptance of the coup to mean widespread agreement on the need for a government above politics and above classes, one that would implant discipline, hierarchy, and unity. They believed that the people had given the new government a mandate for doing away with the old, corrupt political parties, which represented little more than the machinations of oligarchs or demagogic caudillos. Uriburu wanted to create a corporatist system of "organic" parties, or "permanent homogeneous forces" with concrete programs that truly represented the nation's interest groups and social values. Argentina needed a governing system based on national experience, not on vague democratic theories. Uriburu agreed with Aristotle's definition of democracy as government of the majority exercised by the best; the problem was to insure that the best did indeed rule. This was a difficult task in a country where 60 percent of the population was illiterate, according to the general. Before the coup this 60 percent had ruled, for they were the majority. (In reality, only one-third of the populace was illiterate even in 1914.) Only rule by an intelligent minority, however, could guarantee order and prosperity. Moreover, it made no sense for lawyers and medical doctors to sit in Congress and represent a nation of "agriculturalists and landowners." When workers, ranchers, farmers, and industrialists served as the people's delegates, democracy would become something more than just a "pretty word." Indeed, like Carlés and *La Nueva República*, Uriburu preferred the word "republic" to democracy.[43]

European counterrevolutionary thought influenced his pronouncements. Also evident was the continuity between his ideas and those of Carlés. Nevertheless, Uriburu's reforms entailed annulling the Sáenz Peña Law, amending the constitution, and creating a corporatist system which Carlés had regarded as foreign. Whether the general's proposals would appeal to all of the coup's allies was questionable. Certainly the nationalist assessment of the popular mood for change was inaccurate.

Initially the Argentine Patriotic League was pleased with the result of its anti-Yrigoyenist campaign. Uriburu asked Carlés to deliver a speech praising the overthrow on the afternoon of the coup, and the latter gladly complied. The president intended to award Carlés with a post in the San Juan intervention, but Carlés denied any interest in government service, insisting that he preferred his patriotic tasks in the nonpartisan Argentine Patriotic League. Carlés indicated that the League had never been happier with the state of government; members of Brigade Nineteen of the Federal Capital referred to the "glorious events" of September 6 in a meeting that month. Uriburu met with League delegates eleven days after the coup, manifesting his desire to retain the organization's support.[44]

The Liguistas seemed to agree with Uriburu and the nationalists on the need for change. The League's committee on social affairs planned a series of conferences throughout the capital to explain that the real revolution was just beginning: namely, the struggle to rid Argentina of political parties and to lift national interests above partisan ends. The Central Junta declared that the League would use any means to help sustain the republican form of government. Government should be exercised with the people's consent, but not directly by the people themselves. The League would mobilize its urban defense commissions to protect the revolution against the hordes, if necessary.[45]

The issues of *La Nueva República* and *Criterio* that immediately followed the revolution reflected the nationalists' satisfaction with the coup. They generally approved of Uriburu's advisors, who included Carlos Ibarguren (senior), Carulla, and Lugones. To staff the cabinet and head the provincial interventions designed to reduce the power of the UCR, Uriburu mostly chose persons tied to the *régimen*. The nationalists suspected these appointees of lingering electoralist and liberal sentiments, but were encouraged when Conservatives Matías Sánchez Sorondo, Minister of the Interior, and Carlos Meyer Pellegrini, Interventor of Buenos Aires province, publicly criticized the old political system. They watched with interest as Ibarguren laid the groundwork for a "functional democracy" during his intervention in Córdoba province. Uriburu also appointed nationalists and Catholic spokesmen to federal and provincial positions, and he facilitated their access to other, lower-level posts. Palacio and four other editors of *La Nueva República* received sinecures, as did at least fourteen Republicans and eleven May Legionnaires.[46] The revolution had reversed Yrigoyen's democratic recruitment policy; the elite was governing again.

To further incorporate young nationalists into the revolution and prevent Radical subversion, Uriburu supported the continuation of the two militias that had participated in the coup. The May Legion, which had dissolved in September 1930, reconstituted itself in February 1931. Aided by military advisors, the May Legion began to establish brigades, principally in the capital and Buenos Aires province. Many members of these new brigades carried Italian names and came from industrial neighborhoods, indicating the emerging mass character of nationalism. Like its comrade-in-arms, the Republican League also perpetuated itself after the coup, forming brigades under military leadership.[47]

Early in 1931 a new group, the Legión Cívica Argentina (Argentine Civic Legion), arose under the command of Dr. Floro Lavalle, a prominent landowner and Liguista. It assumed control over the May Legion's and Republican League's brigades and created new ones of its own. The aims of the Civic Legion were to help the authorities promote order, Argentinism, and social and moral unity. It would also provide citizens with military training. The Civic Legion supported the government's program of constitutional reform and functional democracy. It believed that only native-born Argentines should occupy official posts and that immigration should be strictly regulated. Concern for laborers was among its preoccupations; it wanted to help all workers to improve their skills and acquire property. The government quickly granted it juridical personage. On May 20, the administration officially recognized the Civic Legion as its partner in the task of "institutional reconstruction."[48]

As *La Vanguardia* noted, there were many similarities between the Civic Legion and the Argentine Patriotic League of 1919. One of the most important resemblances was that both were paramilitary organizations, yet the Civic Legion was even more militarized than its predecessor. The Ministry of War issued uniforms and arms to its members, and the army assigned regular officers to assist the group. Officers trained Civic Legionnaires to march and use arms, and frequently they commanded Civic Legion brigades. Military training assumed precedence over ideological indoctrination, which was limited to the repetition of slogans emphasizing the defense of order, God, family, and country. The military also participated at higher levels of the Civic Legion; of its original fourteen-member Consejo Superior (Superior Council), four were officers.[49]

The Civic Legion's first public appearance, in late April 1931, was a parade in Uriburu's honor. A squadron of twenty-four planes piloted by civilian members escorted it, in a manner reminiscent of the Argentine Patriotic League's aeronautic brigade. In contrast to the League's parades, however, the participants marched in military formation. *La Fronda* estimated the number of marchers at 15,000, *La Vanguardia* at half that figure.[50] According to the sympathetic *La Fronda*, the Civic Legion marshaled about 27,000 and 35,000 members for its parades of May 25 and July 9, respectively, while the Socialist paper counted only 8,000 participants on May 25.[51] After these occasions, Civic Legionnaires wore gray uniforms and carried rifles in public. Brigade members were even classified according to their readiness for battle, as combatants, replacements, and auxiliaries.[52]

At the April parade, Uriburu congratulated the group for establishing a link between the people and the military. On May 25 he defined the organization as a "civic force" that represented order, discipline, and abnegation and defended a fatherland threatened by anarchy and demagoguery. In another speech he added that the Civic Legion, an apolitical force instructed and disciplined by officers, constituted a reserve army. The reason for its semiofficial status was that the state could not afford a large military draft.[53]

The Civic Legion began to attract many recruits. By mid-1931, there were between 10,000 and 30,000 brigade members in the capital, eleven provinces, and one territory. Floro Lavalle proudly called attention to the primary school and university student brigades, and to the female brigades in the larger cities. Critics of the organization, including nationalists, pointed out that it recruited common criminals, Conservative party hacks, and other lumpen figures. These remarks, as well as the fact that a lower percentage of female Civic Legionnaires than female Liguistas was upper-class (79 percent versus close to 100 percent, respectively), demonstrated the widening appeal of Argentine nationalism.[54] Nevertheless, in contrast to the League's strength throughout the republic, the Civic Legion's base remained metropolitan Buenos Aires and the provinces of Buenos Aires and Córdoba. Nor did female Civic Legionnaires ever attain the importance of their League counterparts, for the legion's main target was not the left.

Many observers questioned whether the Civic Legion was indeed apolitical and whether the state needed a large paramilitary organization to defend itself, although several Radical uprisings took place. They suspected that the government viewed the group as its weapon to use against potential opponents. The Civic Legionnaires' main "defense activities" of domestic spying and repressing students, Radicals, and union members confirmed their fears. Legionnaires reportedly forced government employees to join the group or at least attend its parades. High-level Uriburu appointees used their positions to publicize the Civic Legion within the national and provincial bureaucracies. Opponents of the group cited not only its ties with the military but the other forms of assistance it received from the government, such as permission to hold meetings in public buildings and to use the post office's printing press at no charge. Despite its supposed nonpartisanship, the Civic Legion worked together with the Conservative party of Buenos Aires and local conservatives in at least one other province. Many persons feared that Uriburu planned to use the Civic Legion to perpetuate his rule or to bring the Conservative party into power.[55]

Even the establishment press which had supported the League found the Civic Legion unacceptable. *La Prensa* criticized the latter's "political character" and its official status. It also strongly opposed the participation of women and children in the Civic Legion, although it had never opposed their activities in the League. An editorial objected to Civic Legionnaire army instructors training young students to march and use weapons, questioning whether this kind of "patriotism" was needed. Civic education and the celebration of national holidays were sufficient, in its opinion.[56] Why it considered female brigades undesirable was not clear, considering that Civic Legion women were supposed to dedicate themselves to social projects like those of female Liguistas. Perhaps the editors believed that association with a partisan and militarized organization would truly remove women from their sphere, which the League had not done.

The establishment's objections to the Civic Legion, but not to the League, hinted at the differences between the two groups. The League had also supported the unity of military and fatherland, its members had engaged in armed activities, and military officers had occupied an even more prominent role in the League's organizational structure than in the Civic Legion's. The Civic Legion on occasion repressed workers, yet its main purpose was not to pacify labor but to defend the regime, primarily against democratic opponents. The Civic Legion also possessed extensive formal ties to the national government and a party far beyond those enjoyed by the League, despite its *régimen* and Antipersonalist contacts.

For these reasons, some military officers opposed the Civic Legion. Although they or their predecessors had supported the League's nonpartisan forays against the left, they viewed the Civic Legion's militarization of society as usurping their authority. In contrast to the League, the Civic Legion also was too overtly fascistic to appeal to this faction, which defined itself as liberal democratic. These officers saw their role in the revolution as one of returning Argentina quickly to constitutional rule, and they disapproved of military participation in a partisan organization designed to prop up a government whose corporatist designs they rejected. Collaborating with the Civic Legion would only entangle officers further in politics, which in turn would corrupt the military as an institution. General Agustín P. Justo's election to the presidency in November 1931 symbolized the eventual victory of this anti–Civic Legion, anticorporatist faction. (Its use of electoral fraud, however, demonstrated the limits of its "liberal-democratic" sentiments.) Nevertheless, the Civic Legion continued to exist and to receive support from other sectors of the military after 1931.[57]

Justo and his faction, however, were not the only opponents of corporatism within the governing sectors, although they were the most influential. The old Conservative party of Buenos Aires, well represented among Uriburu's appointees, had increasingly assumed influence in the provisional government. It was far more interested in power than in counterrevolutionary principles. A combination of poor health, disillusionment, and susceptibility to friends' influence led Uriburu to delegate more and more responsibilities to Sánchez Sorondo. Uriburu also allowed him to maneuver his party back into office. Over nationalist protest, the government scheduled elections in Buenos Aires province for April 1931, which it confidently expected the Conservatives to win. When the UCR won instead, the shocked and dismayed regime nullified the returns.

Under the state-of-siege and martial law decrees that had existed since the coup, the Uriburu government had already detained and deported both Radicals and labor activists. The election results and another pro-Radical uprising in July, led by the same Pomar who had intervened in Las Palmas, sparked more repression. The regime closed down Radical offices and publications, exiled leading figures such as Alvear, and proscribed many party members from running for office in the upcoming November presidential election. The Radical party decided to abstain completely from these elections, leaving a PDP–Socialist alliance as the only opposition. The obviously fraudulent victory of the Justo ticket, backed by the government, military, and a Conservative-led alliance, surprised no one. The revolution against Yrigoyenist "dictatorship" had installed its own dictatorship.

By this time, Uriburu had alienated his early supporter and old friend—Carlés. Carlés wrote Uriburu on the eve of the April election, asking him to change his administration's policies. Although he did not object to the crackdown on labor, Carlés believed that the state of siege, press censorship, and Uriburu's equivocal statements on democracy had proved counterproductive. Instead of destroying Personalism once and for all, the government had actually increased the people's sympathy for the party by making martyrs of its leaders. He reminded Uriburu that he owed his office to the people, yet his administration had shown no interest in the people's wishes. Uriburu did not answer the well-publicized letter.[58]

When Uriburu announced in May that general elections would take place six months later, Carlés pointed out that a free election campaign could not take place under a state of siege. The government would at least have to assure the people that martial law would end after the election. Otherwise the voters would think that they were electing nothing more than officials who would obey the orders of the provisional government. Stung, Uriburu prohibited Carlés from speaking in churches at Sunday mass. Carlés bitterly rejoined that Uriburu's ban only increased the people's respect for him as a victim of persecution. He added that Uriburu was a vengeful man who used force to get his way—and force was all he had left. Carlés accused his old friend of hurting the country and destroying the citizenry's former admiration for the military. Uriburu also had dashed popular hopes for freedom and peaceful reorganization. The League president denounced the regime for filling jails with political prisoners and assigning officers to train "phalanges" of public employees to repress those who disagreed with the government, referring to the Civic Legion. Surprisingly, he insisted that Argentina was not the "militaristic" country the regime wanted it to be. The regime and the Civic Legion were too extreme even for Carlés.

In his final act of defiance against the government, Carlés paradoxically defended the Radical party. During his class on civic morality in the National High School of Buenos Aires, Carlés denounced Uriburu's decree excluding certain citizens from the November election as one which had no legal or moral basis. He called it a "Creole-style bolshevik parody." He then declared that he would not continue to teach constitutional law under a government that shut down papers, exiled and arrested citizens opposed to dictatorship, and took away suffrage and other rights: a government, in other words, that made the very subject matter of his courses irrelevant. In July 1931, Carlés resigned the chair that he had held for forty years. Even the League's leftist opponents applauded his actions, which demonstrated the gulf between the League's views and the nationalists'. Underscoring this difference, Carlés lashed out at extremists of the left and right in succeeding speeches, praising instead the "liberalism" of the constitution.[59]

Carlés had once favored the formation of a party and a government "above politics," but he could not accept the level of repression against the middle and upper classes needed to implement this ideal. He fled from the consequences of his thought, back to simple antileftism and to his Civista roots. During the 1930s he denounced electoral fraud and supported Alvear's attempts to unite and strengthen Radical forces. If he used the terms "democracy" and "liberty" more frequently than in the 1920s, he defined them as narrowly as before.[60]

Meanwhile, Uriburu had also alienated some of his former nationalist allies. As early as October 1930, Rodolfo Irazusta began to find fault with the regime. In a letter to his brother, he criticized its ties to the old political elite and the Jockey Club. A few weeks later in *La Nueva República*, he decried the lack of genuine change and concluded that "things are not going very well." Much nationalist dissatisfaction focused on the Civic Legion. Roberto de Laferrère opposed the incorporation of the Republican League into the Civic Legion, which he saw as opportunistic, oversized, and undisciplined, in contrast to the former's selectivity and disinterested spirit. Laferrère manifested the resistance of elitist nationalists to popularizing the movement. The

Civic Legion's ties to the Conservative party alienated *La Nueva República*, which deplored the government's abandonment of its original antielectoral ideals.[61] Repelled by Civic Legionnaire corruption and officialism, many nationalists who had joined the group soon thereafter left it.

Unlike Carlés, the Irazustas and their circle did not object to the lack of civil liberties; after all, they blamed liberal democracy for the nation's problems. The reversion to electoralism, however, dashed their hopes for the revolution, which was supposed to have changed the political system. Instead, as Palacio noted, Uriburu had called in the "valetudinarian" figures of the *régimen* to end demagoguery by destroying Radicalism. This plan failed, for, as the April election had demonstrated, the people preferred the UCR to the inept oligarchy, which had long since outlived its usefulness to the nation. Palacio praised the Radical party for having weakened the "conservative" forces. The revolution should have completed this chore and demolished Radicalism rather than revive it, thus opening the way for new leadership and the reabsorption of the Radical masses into a renovated political system. Uriburu, however, had opted for the worst of both worlds, as Julio Irazusta pointed out, by setting up a dictatorship that had accomplished little beyond alarming the public, and by tacitly subverting the constitution without genuinely amending it.[62]

The newspaper's analysis of the reasons for the failure of the Uriburu experiment increasingly intertwined with its economic reasoning. As lawyers and representatives for foreign firms, members of the *régimen* were tied to the liberal economic and political system which favored outside interests to the detriment of the local. Thus, according to Palacio, the liberal-conservative "mummies" had obstructed change because it would have hurt their pocketbooks.[63] One of the League's favorite themes, the issue of economic dependency and its implications had also been found in nationalist writings. After the coup, however, it gradually became the nationalists' overriding concern, preempting discussions of the most desirable form of government.

Like earlier League spokesmen, the nationalists wanted Argentina to consolidate its internal market and industrialize to insure the well-being of its inhabitants, the strength of its defenses, and its liberation from colonial status. Lugones was their most outspoken advocate for establishing basic industries, creating infrastructure, and erecting protective tariffs. Acción Republicana (Republican Action), a short-lived group formed in 1931 by Lugones, the Irazustas, Palacio, Pico, and others also proposed economic defense measures against foreign exploitation, particularly for the agrarian sector. It wanted the government to supervise the meatpackers' price-setting operations, grant incentives for building native-owned grain elevators and meatpacking plants, and seek Latin American markets for Argentine products. The government should also set grain prices, shipping charges, rates of exchange, and land rents and further aid farmers by providing easy access to credit. Republican Action favored protecting industries, particularly those based on national raw materials, nationalizing electric power, limiting the public debt, organizing nonideological labor unions, and establishing an economic union between the Platine countries.[64]

The nationalists still retained some aspects of economic liberalism in their programs. Though they opposed the concept of the state as mere watchdog, Lugones and *La Nueva República* agreed with the Liguistas that government was a poor administrator. Nevertheless, the periodical advocated constant state vigilance over foreign capitalist activities. Laissez-faire liberalism also influenced the nationalists' view of the masses and the labor movement. Julio Irazusta characterized the eight-hour day and the minimum wage as unnecessary limits on production and on the size of the labor force, respectively. (On another occasion, however, he praised Mussolini's labor policies, including the institution of the eight-hour day.) Lugones criticized labor unions on the grounds that they supported these measures.[65]

In general, Lugones and the newspaper staff supported the "trickle-down" theory of wealth; workers would profit more from government stimulation of production than from demagogic prolabor policies, such as those of Yrigoyen. Nationalists did not coincide in their views on workers, however, nor were their ideas well developed on this topic. Manuel Gálvez and Civic Legion spokesmen paid more attention to the social question than did *La Nueva República*, and the former's attitudes were more paternalistic than the latter's.[66] The proletariat's fate was less important to many nationalists than it was to the League.

The Depression and nationalistic ideas motivated the Uriburu administration into reversing the long-dominant liberal policies. It imposed a 10 percent surcharge on the tariff and additional duties on some commodities. An exchange control commission set priorities on imports and the use of hard currency. The administration also studied such matters as economic diversification and the establishment of new industries, and it initiated road building and other massive public works programs.[67]

Nationalists and the League had reason to be pleased with such measures. *La Nueva República*, however, was more concerned with agriculture and agrarian-based industry than with other economic sectors, and in this regard it found the government's performance wanting. Perhaps the main contributing factor to the Irazusta brothers' economic consciousness was the plight of the meatpacking plant in their hometown of Gualeguaychú. Uriburu's indifference to the financial problems of the plant, one of the few owned and operated by Argentines (including Julián Irazusta), convinced the Irazustas of government apathy and even hostility toward national capital. They reached this conclusion during the Uriburu administration, before the Roca–Runciman Pact of 1933, which historians have usually seen as the catalyst of nationalist antiimperialism.[68]

Given the usual composition of Argentine governments, this lack of official concern was hardly surprising, according to Rodolfo Irazusta. He divided Argentine society into two classes: the administrators and the producers. The nation's greatest problem was that the administrative class of merchants, professionals, financiers, and bureaucrats governed it, not the productive class of landowners, small farmers, industrialists, peons, and urban workers. The administrators were part of the "foreignizing" (*extranjerizante*) civilization of commerce, linked to cosmopolitan urban life, immigrants, foreign capitalism, and democracy. Indeed, democracy represented the domination of the administrators over the producers, of persons who created nothing over those who created the national wealth. In their haste to reap profits from speculation and from the "political industry," parasitic administrators neglected or actively harmed the rural industries which formed the backbone of the local economy. High taxes levied on landowners and the lack of credit and infrastructure were some examples of government disfavor. So, too, was the fact that governments had not sufficiently regulated foreign-owned railroads or obtained better prices from foreign exporters. The type of corporatist system that Uriburu had originally proposed would have put government in the hands of producers and alleviated these ills. The general's inability to carry out this reform, therefore, doubly angered and disillusioned the Irazustas and other nationalists.[69]

Yet past governments, particularly before 1916, had supposedly represented agrarian producers. Why had these regimes actually hurt their interests? The reason, according to the Irazustas, was that the administrators who ruled in the landowners' name were not tied to this group or to the nation, but to foreign interests. Those administrators who owned land had acquired it through political or professional influence, or they had spent all the income from their property to obtain their political positions. Those who did not fall into these categories were lackeys, content with bribes received from foreign capitalists. In any case, one could hardly consider them representatives of the landowners. The Irazustas called these administrators the professional, conservative, or liberal oligarchy or, increasingly borrowing the Radicals' old term, the *régimen*.[70]

The *régimen*, according to Fausto de Tezanos Pinto, journalist and theater critic, had willfully erected obstacles to industrialization. It had extended unlimited credit from national banks to foreign speculators, enabling them to buy local crops at low prices and make huge profits at the expense of Argentine proprietors, tenants, and peons. The oligarchy acted at the behest of its foreign masters under a liberal constitution that gave more rights to non-Argentines than to native sons. This document had also stimulated immigration, resulting in the entrance of numerous undesirables. Thus liberal democracy meant "renunciation, social dissolution, and total delivery to the foreigner." Liberalism, like its oligarchical spokesmen, was a tool of foreign domination.[71]

The foreigners who controlled national destiny, according to nationalists, were not only British but Jewish. Many nationalists saw the Jews as part of or synonymous with the international threat against Argentina and its rural producers. Lugones, for example, had transformed himself from defender of the Jews into their critic. Alienated from agrarian life and lacking a fatherland, the Jew would play no role in the upcoming era of "national reconstruction," according to the poet. The farmer, soldier, and artist would rule in place of the banker and parliamentarian. The incarnation of the last two figures, the Jew was "systemizing and tenacious; astute and skeptical; an intellectual and a twister of words; adaptable and absorbent." In his opinion, "international finance" was "a Hebrew organization, and international socialism a genuine Jewish sect." Claiming that he was not anti-Semitic, Lugones characterized his observation as purely objective.[72] It was true that he did not hate Jewish individuals. The word "Jew" in the nationalists' vocabulary, as in Maurras's, no longer signified a member of a particular ethnic group or practitioner of a certain religion. Instead it stood for disparate and antithetical modern forces that the nationalists found threatening: leftism, democracy, international capital, liberalism, urbanism, materialism, and atheism.

Augusto Gozalbo, a writer for *La Nueva República*, explored the common "Hebrew origin" of socialism, internationalism, and anti-Catholicism. The simple fact that Marx was Jewish indicated the nature of socialism, for his parents' conversion to Christianity could not change his background. Socialism owed its international nature to the rootlessness of Jews, who for centuries had taken advantage of the "privileged circumstance of being foreigners in every country." Gozalbo did not show how this constituted an advantage, yet he thought it explained Jewish hatred for all nations, a hatred that had transformed itself into the antipatriotic internationalism of the socialists. Similarly, Jewish hatred for Catholicism lay underneath the socialists' anticlerical-ism and atheism.[73]

Jewish internationalism and infiltration into socialism served as that "race's" tools for world domination. To increase the wealth and power of Israel, Jewish bankers had internationalized finance, and the members of the Zwi Migdal, an organization of Jewish white slavers, had internationalized the prostitution trade. The latest evidence of Jewish inroads into leftism was the mar-riage of Jewish women to Socialist leaders. Here Gozalbo referred to Enrique Dickmann (himself a Jew), Justo's first marriage, and Nicolás Repetto. He did not explain, however, why Jews needed to penetrate a movement that was already Jewish.

Other discussions in *La Nueva República* of the multifaceted international threat treated the connections between socialism and capitalism—the two heads of a single international movement de-signed to enslave Argentina. An anonymous author tied these strands together in an article entitled "The Enemy." Nineteenth-century liberalism had created the proper conditions for the de-velopment of capitalism, which in turn had injected utilitarian-ism and materialism into all aspects of human existence. These dominant philosophies, along with the political system of de-mocracy and the ideal of social equality, were responsible for the reign of money over present-day society. In this environment certain groups flourished, especially the Jews, for Jewish interna-tional capitalism ruled over the entire world. One of its means for control was regulating credit; governments had mortgaged the future of their nations to the exclusive benefit of this interna-tional power. Either in pursuit of their own interests or under outside pressure, the press, the political parties, and the govern-ment had united to maintain the established materialistic order. The conservatives and the bourgeois parasites of international capitalism had given part of their wealth to the people to help preserve the status quo. Despite this largess, they were accused of being responsible for capitalism and had lost influence. Mean-while international capitalism had struck a bargain with social-ism. The latter would support internationalism, free trade, and democracy and oppose truly radical, nationalistic innovations, while the former would create the petite bourgeoisie, a socialist constituency (in Argentina, at any rate).[74]

Two forces had arisen to fight Jewish capitalism—fascism and Russian communism. Communism, which the author did not identify with socialism or Judaism, had erred by attacking money as a means of exchange. Instead, the capitalist view of money as an end in itself was evil. The true solution was to create a national capitalist system completely independent of Jewish finance. This was the fascist program. This writer himself erred, however, in believing that communists concentrated their attack on money. The left opposed the whole system of capitalism, whereas European fascists and Argentine nationalists opposed only a small portion of it—finance and international capital.

This conspiracy theory was more extreme than any held by League spokesmen, although Carlés had drawn some connections between foreign capitalism and foreign leftism. Liguistas had criticized professional politicians, foreign enterprise, capitalist excesses, economic liberalism, and, of course, leftism, but they had not seen these forces as part of a single conspiracy against the nation, nor had they identified them with Judaism. Mostly secure, middle-aged, and influential, League leaders of the early 1920s had rarely castigated Jews or the bourgeoisie as a whole, and never in such a harsh fashion. In contrast, extreme anti-Semites like the nationalists have usually experienced a sense of powerlessness and a decline in status. Although anti-Semitism was not the central feature of their doctrine, it nevertheless was integrally tied to the nationalists' world view. It intersected many issues that concerned them. As such, their anti-Semitism was ideological, and it varied markedly from the traditional anti-Semitism of some Liguistas. This difference was also a critical measure of nationalist extremism, vis-à-vis the conservatism of bourgeois Liguistas.

The League and the nationalists shared the same ultimate fear of social dissolution, yet the latter's preoccupations were broader. The League had criticized liberalism and foreign capitalism but primarily had blamed leftists and workers for economic and political difficulties. It had offered an "Argentine alternative" to

Marxism and anarchism in order to stave off revolution. The Irazustas and their followers, whom Zuleta Alvarez called "republican nationalists,"[75] believed that an entire system was at fault: not the system of property relations tied to the world capitalist framework, but the ties themselves, the nexus of foreign domination. The League had denied class differences and insisted that all Argentines were "workers," except for the diehard leftists who did not belong in the country. Taking this idea much further, republican nationalists divided Argentines into two groups. These were not the bourgeoisie and the proletariat, but rather all who worked for foreign interests, be they socialist laborers, lawyers employed by foreign companies, or liberal ideologues, versus those producers who reserved their allegiance for the nation.

The nationalists went beyond the League's criticism of liberalism; they considered it the principal cause of Argentine economic and political retardation. Furthermore, its adherents were not simply wrong or misguided, but traitors who had sold out to Argentina's enemies. An international conspiracy against the nation was afoot and only the strongest countermeasures could arrest it: the complete overhaul of the political system, the expulsion of all foreign lackeys (*entreguistas*) from positions of influence, and an end to economic imperialism. Although not genuinely anticapitalistic, these measures were certainly extreme; if carried out, they would have completely altered the status quo. The League did not favor this radical change. With its reversion to electoralism and its ties to foreign companies, it, too, was part of the *régimen*.

Yet in the waning months of the Uriburu government, Carlés and the Irazusta group trod the same path back to the UCR. Their reasons were very different. Carlés denounced Uriburu's persecution of Radicalism. In contrast, the Revolution of 1930 taught republican nationalists that they could not easily impose their program from above. Instead, such beliefs had to come from below, from the people—and that meant from within the Radical party. Despite what they viewed as its defects, Radicalism was the only nationalistic force with popular support in the country. Moreover, it was blessedly free of doctrine. Still wary of mass suffrage, the Irazustas were nevertheless willing to accept it as a means of reaching their end: the creation of a strong antiliberal and antiimperialistic government. Furthermore, they and other nationalists began to realize that the great caudillo Yrigoyen had not always followed liberal sirens. In the Irazustas' own province, the Radicals had promoted economic nationalism, in the form of the Gualeguaychú meatpacking plant, far more than the old elitist parties. For these reasons, the Irazusta group returned to its Radical roots, and in the 1930s it influenced other economic nationalists within the UCR, such as Raúl Scalabrini Ortiz.[76] Other nationalists remained loyal to Uriburu, even after his death in 1932, and continued to favor corporatist or militaristic regimes.

The counterrevolutionary forces that had supported the 1930 coup splintered, and they have never reunited since. Nourished by foreign inspiration and popular bitterness over economic stagnation, political fraud, and subservience to Great Britain, nationalist groups proliferated in succeeding decades. The League declined in face of the antiliberal nationalist upsurge, and women's roles in the right faded. When the leftist threat reemerged in the 1940s and 1970s, however, politicians and military leaders rediscovered League-style alternatives to revolution.

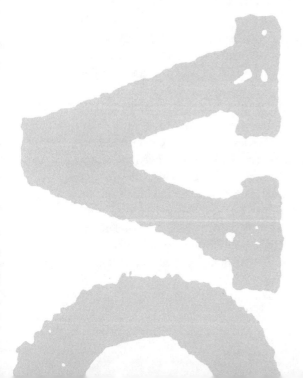

SEVEN

The League in Comparative Perspective

The Argentine Patriotic League, the first important counterrevolutionary group of the twentieth century in that country, was primarily a bourgeois response to the largely immigrant left, and only secondarily an upper-class response to middle-class democracy. It grew out of efforts to destroy unionism, identify foreigners with the left, and bring labor under the wing of the Church. It also was a reaction against Yrigoyenism, but it mainly opposed what it regarded as the Radical president's sympathy for workers and inability to maintain order in the face of their demands. The organization exercised a broader appeal than historians have usually attributed to the right, attracting women, members of the middle sectors, and adherents across the nation. Finally, this inward-oriented group, relatively free of foreign inspiration, influenced the "nationalist" currents of the late 1920s. Scholars have usually overlooked the League's impact on nationalism, emphasizing instead the latter's European roots.

To argue that the League was homegrown is not to deny the possibility of comparing it with other contemporary movements. The League resembled groups that arose in the United States, Latin America, and Europe during the same years, groups that historians have characterized as fascist or protofascist. Many scholars and Latin Americans, however, are reluctant to employ the term *fascist* and to compare Latin America and Europe. The variations between groups defined as fascist have led Gilbert Allardyce to insist that no such generic phenomenon exists. As Anthony James Joes pointed out, however, the same diversity characterizes both communist and representative democratic systems, yet few would question the validity of these terms.[1]

Members of the Latin American left and "national left" raise a more pertinent objection: that the economic and social conditions which produced fascism in Europe differed markedly from those in the dependent economies of Latin America. Fascism, then, characterizes advanced industrial powers, not colonial or semicolonial nations.[2] This view, in my opinion, is unwarranted. National leftists also have pointed out that nineteenth-century Latin American liberalism was false and artificial, because its standard bearers did not fill the role of a true national bourgeoisie; its policies promoted dependence rather than autonomous economic development, in contrast to the European case. Although the objective conditions that produced liberalism in Latin America differed from those in Europe, these scholars do not hesitate to call Latin Americans of this political orientation liberals. Why, then, the aversion to the word fascism?

Some writers betray ignorance of Europe and of European fascism. Europe is not a homogeneous area, for parts of it are underdeveloped. Romania, Hungary, Slovakia, and Spain in the interwar period were poor, agrarian societies, and yet they had prominent fascist movements. National Socialism was born in Bavaria, one of the least industrialized areas of Germany. Even where the objective conditions differed greatly from those in Latin America, the subjective conditions were often similar. The Nazis and their predecessors in the late nineteenth and early twentieth centuries complained about the monopolizing tendency of British capitalism and how it impeded native efforts, despite the fact that by this time Germany had become a great industrial power.[3] This attitude clearly resembles that of many Latin American nationalists of the left and the right. Furthermore, the European countries that spawned the most important fascist parties, such as Germany, Italy, and the successor states of the Hapsburg empire, shared with Argentina such significant traits as recent nationhood or newly forged unity (for Argentina, 1880), and an insecure national identity.

A few scholars have referred to the post-1929 Argentine right as fascist, but they have been the exceptions. Most have accepted the counterrevolutionaries' own disclaimers with little additional scrutiny. They may be correct, yet the arguments they have marshaled to refute fascist tendencies are unconvincing. In the introduction I disposed of the notion that Argentine counterrevolutionaries were not "cruel" enough to be fascists, although by this criterion the League, with its defense commissions, fits the fascist label. Some have claimed that the social origins of potential Argentine counterrevolutionaries (déclassé aristocrats, for the groups of the 1930s; proletarian, for Peronism) differed greatly from those of fascists, yet recent studies have shown that members of the lower and upper classes were found in European fascism, particularly in nonindustrialized areas, and in Brazilian Integralism.[4]

In her study, Navarro gave several reasons why the nationalists were not fascists. She claimed that the right's Catholicism prevented it from being fascist, but the Belgian Rex combined fascism with staunch Catholicism, and the Romanian Iron Guard was devoutly religious, if not Catholic. She also stated that fascism provided the Argentine right of the 1930s and 1940s with a political model and an example that justified its conduct. Nevertheless, most of its members were not true fascists because they did not consistently practice what they preached. How a group can follow a fascist model, albeit erratically, and yet not be fascist is unclear. Furthermore, many scholars have pointed to Hitler's and Mussolini's pragmatism, concluding that inconsistency is a trait of fascism—at least, of those movements that came to power. Finally, Navarro did not define fascism, but in this respect she is accompanied by most Argentinists who have written on counterrevolutionary groups.[5]

Manuel Gálvez—significantly, a self-proclaimed fascist sympathizer—came close to the mark when he concluded that the post-1929 Argentine right in general, including nationalists and conservatives, was not fascist because of its French counterrevolutionary intellectual roots, its upper-class character, and, in particular, its lack of social conscience. Although some scholars view French counterrevolutionary currents as fascist, these criteria are nonetheless more comprehensive than those offered by Argentine specialists.[6] And yet, by Gálvez's standards, the League

was indeed fascist; it had a middle-class contingent, a social conscience, and little foreign inspiration.

One must carefully define fascism before one can decide
whether the League or any other group fits under its rubric. The
task of definition has inspired a body of literature too vast to cite.
The examination of several definitions, however, will reveal certain commonalities.

Among the many definitions, Ernst Nolte's stands out for its
sophistication and profundity. He offered a three-tiered explanation of the term. At its first level, fascism opposes Marxism by
developing a radically different yet related ideology and using
"almost identical and yet typically modified methods, always,
however, within the unyielding framework of national self-
assertion and autonomy."[7]

The League opposed Marxism and sought to destroy the labor
movement through violent actions and the formulation of an
ideological alternative to leftism, one that substituted nationalism for class struggle, and social justice within the private enterprise system for overturning that system. The League advocated
an economic system between pure free-market capitalism and
communism that would retain the individual pursuit of profits
yet introduce social welfare reforms. This middle road, or "third
way," was a goal common to all fascist movements and governments; for this reason, Stanislav Andreski called fascism the "cen-
trism of extremists." The League's purpose strikingly resembled
the political function of the Nazi seizure of power, which demolished working-class organizations in order to protect "the essentials of the existing power structure" and stabilize "an economic
system in crisis."[8]

Yet the League's ideology and methods were not linked to
those of the left in the way that those of, say, the Italian Fascists
or Hungarian Arrow Cross were. Its leaders were too bourgeois,
middle-aged, sedate, and republican to infuse their message with
enough dynamism to appeal to disaffected segments of the
masses. Although the League recruited from the middle sectors,
it appealed primarily to those who had gained prestige and economic independence through the development process, rather

than those who had lost these traits, like many European fascists.[9] This was not necessarily the League's intention; it hoped that the workers' brigades would attract the masses to the "national" cause. This task, however, was accomplished later by Juan and Eva Perón, who enjoyed much greater rapport with the people.

This staid quality which set the League apart from fascism is also apparent when one considers Nolte's second level of definition. Here he noted that fascism represented the "life-and-death struggle of the sovereign, martial, inwardly antagonistic group" referring primarily to the Social Darwinist, racist, and militaristic tendencies of fascism. Carlés lauded what he saw as the virile and martial traits of Argentine manhood before immigration.[10] The League sponsored Lugones's militaristic lectures in 1923, and it also sought to increase popular admiration for the armed forces. Nevertheless, the organization was unwilling to militarize society, as it demonstrated through its opposition to the Civic Legion and its preference for parliamentary government. Racism and anti-Semitism barely figured in the League's ideology, nor did Social Darwinism, beyond the belief in lower-class inferiority and the idea that defense of the borders was related to defense against leftism. The League was not as "inwardly antagonistic" as many fascists; it was satisfied to smash unions without attempting to kill or neutralize all leftist and democratic opponents.

Thus far the League does not seem fascist, but Nolte's third level of definition, his deepest and broadest, gives one pause. Here he characterized fascism as "resistance to transcendence." According to Nolte, the desire for freedom from the confines of class, religion, family, ethnicity, locality, nation, and other traditional bonds has formed a major theme in the history of Western civilization. The twin bourgeois and Industrial Revolutions eliminated many of these ties, a step toward what Nolte called "practical transcendence." Some limitations on human freedom, such as class exploitation and division of labor, however, still existed, and Marxists intended to destroy these remaining shackles.

Fascists fear the dissolution of traditional allegiances and hierarchies, or what I earlier termed the emancipatory process, and thus oppose practical transcendence. They also resist "theoretical transcendence," which Nolte described as surpassing the bounds of concrete reality through abstract and universalist thought. Theoretical transcendence includes the belief that life should conform to certain ideals and that it can be restructured to do so. In contrast, fascists insist on "seeing the world as it is" and not judging it by "outside" criteria. They consider both forms of transcendence unnatural and foreign: unnatural, because particularistic ties are, in their view, essential for the maintenance of order; and foreign, because the criteria do not emerge directly out of local experience. (Leftists would insist that the criteria do indeed emerge from the conditions under which laborers work and struggle.) Their vision of "reality," however, is based on an idealized view of the past and therefore, like the leftist utopia they perceive and criticize, is an abstraction.

Nolte's third level of definition offers much insight into the League. The League opposed freedom from many traditional bonds and the formulation of universalist abstractions, both of which it regarded as foreign tendencies. Carlés insisted on "viewing the world as it is" and used religion, a universalist creed, as an Argentinizing force. Therefore, according to Nolte, the League was fascist. Yet one could say that all the counter-revolutionary factions—Mayer's conservatives, reactionaries, and counterrevolutionaries (or fascists)—have resisted features of rationalism, liberalism, industrialism, and Marxism, and thus they have opposed both forms of transcendence. Nolte's third level of definition seems to characterize all of the right, not just the fascists. Of the counterrevolutionary triad, fascists mounted the most extreme assault on the emancipatory process, but the other two groups frequently were their allies. Two questions remain: What distinguishes fascists from other members of the right, and where did the League fit in the ranks of counterrevolution?

The difficulties of defining generic fascism have led some scholars to compile an inventory of the features common to all fascist movements, rather than a comprehensive statement of its nature. In his "fascist minimum," Stanley G. Payne first identified the fascist negations.[11] Fascists oppose liberalism, communism, and to some extent conservatism, with whose adherents, however, they cooperate at times. By these criteria the League falls short; sometimes it identified itself with conservatism, and by 1931 it unequivocally favored a parliamentary regime that recognized some civil liberties.

Fascist ideological goals, according to Payne, include the creation of an authoritarian nationalist state departing from the traditional dictatorships of the past. Though some League spokesmen may have favored this goal under Radicalism, they changed their minds under Uriburu. Furthermore, the older model of the *régimen* exerted more sway than the new corporatist model, which appealed to nationalists. Fascists also advocate the creation of a corporatist economic structure capable of controlling workers. Some Liguistas agreed, although most favored mere social welfare reforms and the establishment of free labor brigades. The latter, however, represented a type of national syndicalism not alien to fascism. Fascists seek to establish empires or at least boost their nation's standing in the world. Specific territorial goals received little attention in League congresses (although they interested Carlés),[12] but reversing economic dependency did. Formulating an idealistic national culture, usually secular in nature, is another fascist aim. League members manifested a similar concern, although the type of culture they favored was less youth-oriented and irrational, and more religious and traditional in inspiration, than the fascist model.

Payne then identified the elements of fascist style and organization. The League shared with fascism an emphasis on male dominance and the masculine principle, accompanied by a view of society as an organic whole. The fascist preference for an authoritarian, personal, and charismatic type of leadership was mirrored only to a limited extent in the League, whose admittedly long-lasting president was not a führer or caudillo figure. Though willing to battle its enemies, the League did not exalt violence as an overriding principle, nor did the primarily middle-aged organization laud youth. The League used symbols and new technologies (for example, Carlés's use of the airplane), and it choreographed some of its functions, as in Gualeguaychú, but it never exploited crowd psychology, national myths, and the aesthetics of mass meetings to the extent fascists did. Finally, as stated earlier, the League did not systematically attempt to mobilize the masses, much less through its militias, whose primary purpose was to attack unions.

Nolte's and Payne's explanations of fascism differ, yet they overlap in one important regard: Despite their contempt for democracy and the people, fascists embrace mass politics. The League, on the other hand, was uncomfortable with reaching out to the masses. Its unwillingness or inability to achieve rapport with the people places it in the more moderate, traditional sectors of the right. This is the main difference between the League and fascism which emerges from the application of Nolte's and Payne's ideas. Significantly, however, the comparison also reveals many similarities between the League and its more radical cousins.

If the League was not fascist, what was it? To situate it in the counterrevolutionary spectrum, it is useful to return to Mayer's classification. He noted that conservatives are those who benefit from the existing order and strive to maintain it. Normally they are economically, politically, and socially secure, and their subdued, accommodating political style reflects their self-confidence. Their pessimistic view of human nature and of the need for hierarchy in social relations remains implicit except in times of crisis, when their beliefs harden and become ideological. At these moments their usual spirit of compromise vanishes, leaving a willingness to resort to violent means of defending the status quo.

Reactionaries are wedded to a preexisting order—and often to the land or church—and are dedicated to reviving it. They intend to restore traditional institutions and their own positions in society, which modernization has undermined. Normally they despise conservatives, who profit from and defend the status quo, as well as counterrevolutionaries, who issue demagogic appeals to the masses. Indeed, reactionaries would prefer to take the masses out of the political arena. To secure their goals and prevent revolutionary change, however, they sometimes unite with the other two groups.

Counterrevolutionaries, the archetypical fascists, usually draw adherents from poor landholders, the lower and new middle classes, and from "job-, income-, and status-seeking degree holders"; other groups, however, may also supply recruits. Even in normal times they are insecure and fearful of radical change. In crisis situations, leaders can easily manipulate "their resentment of those above them, their fear of those below them, and their estrangement from the real world about them."[13] As their name suggests, counterrevolutionaries provide the main impetus toward counterrevolution.

Mayer's typology is ambiguous in the sense that he used the same term to refer to both the entire movement and one of its components. At first glance this appears to be a weakness in his model, but it is actually a strength. When social and economic problems are sufficiently grave, and when revolution seems to threaten the status quo, otherwise staid conservatives and reactionaries assume the same extreme and violent posture that normally characterizes only counterrevolutionaries. In other words, in crisis situations the differences between the three groups disappear. Eugen Weber also noted the propensity of solidly conservative citizens to move toward more radical alternatives when threatened.[14] This explains how sober, bourgeois Liguistas, who easily fit the conservative category, perpetrated acts of violence against workers.

If the League was conservative, its nationalist allies in the Revolution of 1930 combined counterrevolutionary and reactionary traits. As already noted, they used both terms to describe themselves. Their desire for a corporatist state, their attacks on bourgeois thought and behavior, their youth, and their stress on virility and action place them within the counterrevolutionary category, as did the declining fortunes and intellectual backgrounds of many nationalists. Many of them belonged to a group displaced by political modernization from decision-making roles. They despised the groups below them: the workers and particularly the immigrant middle class. They identified their interests with those of the landed class, yet they also denigrated the latter's materialism, staleness, and spirit of *entreguismo*. Like Mayer's reactionaries, however, many of them wanted to reestablish a rigidly hierarchical society buttressed by such medieval institutions as landed estates and the Church, and, except for the Civic Legion, they were unwilling to form a popular base during the period under study.[15]

Returning to the League, the European organizations it most resembled were the same civil guards with which it established contact. In fact, the leftist Argentine press was well aware of this similarity.[16] These groups generally included ex-officers, landowners, bureaucrats, professionals, shop owners, and hired thugs, who patrolled the cities and countryside to protect private property against laborers and revolutionaries. Governments and regular military units often sponsored these civil guards, only to withdraw their support when the leftist danger receded and their handpicked guardians of order appeared to challenge official power. Militia leaders frequently claimed that they were above politics, but their nonpartisanship did not prevent them from carrying out a "civic education" mission designed to unify all classes against national enemies. Some organizations carried out cooptative social welfare programs and formulated an ideology that resembled the League's.[17]

The similarities between the League and one of these militias, the German Organisation Escherisch, or Orgesch, were especially striking. Founded by members of the upper-middle class and aristocrats displaced from government by the establishment of the Weimar Republic, the Orgesch also drew middle-class adherents and women into its ranks. Its female members were supposed to indoctrinate their children and counterbalance working-class women's organizations. The Orgesch opposed class struggle, internationalism, and political corruption. Like the League, it reflected upper- and middle-class fear of Marxism, as well as upper-class resentment against democracy.[18]

Some civil guards, such as the German Freikorps, were anti-bourgeois and fascist. Like the Orgesch, however, most were "bourgeois-conservative" in nature, lacking the chiliastic ideology and vitalism that characterized fascism. Nevertheless, they manifested some fascist ideas and practices, and they prepared the way for fascist rule in Germany and Austria by pushing the previously law-abiding bourgeoisie into the streets.[19] They as well as the League fit into the conservative component of counter-revolution. Yet at the same time, both led to more extreme counterrevolutionary trends: in Central Europe, Nazism, and in Argentina, nationalism—and perhaps Peronism.

Nationalists after 1932 split into many factions. Scholars have lumped the various tendencies into groups, but their classifications obscure rather than clarify some features of nationalism. Zuleta Alvarez divided nationalism into "republican" and "doctrinaire" wings. Republican nationalists favored ideas and governmental forms suited to Argentine tradition, and doctrinaire nationalists were unswervingly corporatist, Thomist, and militaristic despite changing local conditions. Zuleta Alvarez placed the Irazustas (and himself) in the first wing. Although he applied this distinction only to the movement after 1932, by his criteria the League also fit the republican nationalist designation. The fact that the author did not take differences in socioeconomic background and outlook into account limits the explanatory power of his model; indeed, he explicitly rejected such an approach. The model also obscures the common origin of the two wings, as well as their Catholicism and other shared features. Furthermore, he did not include leftist nationalism or Peronism in either of the two wings.[20]

Members of the national left, as previously indicated, differentiate "oligarchical" from "popular" nationalism. Oligarchical nationalists, including the Irazusta group, Civic Legion, and Republican League, were ultramontane upper-class intellectuals who opposed the masses and their political choice, Yrigoyen. They were reactionaries who wanted to restore the Old Regime rather than true nationalists. Beginning with the Radical youth organization Fuerza de Orientación Radical de la Joven Argentina (FORJA, Radical Orientation Force of Young Argentina), and continuing with Peronism, popular nationalists opposed foreign economic domination and supported democracy in the form of popular caudillos such as Rosas and Yrigoyen.[21]

This model again overlooks the bonds between the two. Certain oligarchical nationalists such as the Irazustas and Palacio sympathized with Radicalism after 1932, initiated historical revisionism and the cult of Rosas, and criticized imperialism and dependency. These thinkers influenced FORJA, which in turn contributed to Peronism. Oligarchical nationalists and FORJA members were bourgeois, antiliberal, and anti-Marxist; mainstream Peronists shared the last two traits. A more important objection from the viewpoint of this study is the difficulty of placing the League in either wing. In fact, Arturo Jauretche did not consider the League nationalistic at all, but rather a species of "liberal reaction."[22] Perhaps, then, he would have included it among the oligarchical nationalists, who also were not "truly nationalist" in his opinion, and were of exalted social background. Although the League contributed its republican elitism to oligarchical nationalism, its views on economic dependency, the abuses of capitalism and communism, the Argentinization of labor, Catholic social justice, and the mobilization of women bear an undeniable similarity to Peronism.

Scholars generally have characterized Peronism as an amalgam of diverse ingredients. Among such components they list nationalism (all types), Catholicism, corporatism, Perón's military training, his anticommunism combined with a concern for labor, his experience in Fascist Italy, and his pragmatic responses to Argentine conditions. Yet all of these ingredients, except perhaps the last, are related to counterrevolution and/or the League. To my knowledge, Perón never belonged to the League, and it is difficult to establish a direct connection between the two. It is probable, however, that Perón knew some of the many Liguistas in the officer corps and military schools, or became familiar with the organization's ideas through the military conferences regularly sponsored by the League.

Although widely discussed in influential sectors such as the military, the League's views had little impact on national government during the 1920s and 1930s. This was particularly true of the ideas relating to labor, for the union movement was relatively quiescent after 1922, and the upper class, including the nationalists, saw little need to entertain social welfare reforms. Partly for this reason, most nationalist groups after the League's heyday did not actively recruit women, whose main task in the League had been to strengthen social stability through charitable projects among immigrant workers. By the late 1930s, however, conditions changed. Migration from the interior to the littoral cities increased the size of the working class, the visibility of urban poverty, and the demographic imbalance, although unlike in the past the female newcomers outnumbered the male. At the same time, the labor movement renewed its militancy, and Communist unions grew in strength, alarming the upper classes and the armed forces. The situation was ripe for a renewal of League-style "nationalism." Thus a former Liguista and a fascist sympathizer, Governor Manuel Fresco of Buenos Aires province (1936–40), asserted control over unions and elections and implanted Catholic education in the public schools. Again, it is difficult to establish a direct link between the two men, but Perón must have observed Fresco's experience.[23]

At this juncture Perón came to power, offering the masses an alternative to Marxism which promised to improve their living standards within the context of national capitalist development. Instead of calling his program "practical humanitarianism," he referred to it as one of "social justice," a term not absent from the League's rhetoric or that of the League's Social Catholic predecessors. He also called his socioeconomic program the "Third Way" between communism and unfettered capitalism, again reminiscent of the League's statements. Eva Perón and other women were responsible for directing numerous social projects for the poor and organizing female workers, another similarity with the League. One cannot doubt Perón's sincere desire to help the masses; his administration significantly redistributed income in their favor. Yet Perón was undeniably hostile to leftism and unwilling to socialize the means of production and increase the autonomy of the masses. If under Peronism the number and size of unions grew dramatically, so, too, did the regime's control over their leadership and actions. His "nationalization of the working class," as one Peronist unionist put it,[24] truly fulfilled the League's theoretical aims, outstripping by far the achievement of the workers' brigades.

This is not to deny the fundamental differences between Peronism and the League. Unlike the elitist-led League, which was wary of popular movements, Peronists genuinely appealed to the masses. Juan and Eva Perón were charismatic leaders with highly personal and authoritarian styles of rule, in contrast to Carlés. Peronist policies decreased the economic, political, and social power of the upper class and helped increase the confidence of the workers, neither of which was intended by the League. Peronists also favored suffrage and a far greater degree of political partici- pation for women than the League had, although both move- ments were antifeminist and viewed women's public activities as extensions of their roles within the home. The passage of women's suffrage in 1947, however, was the result of a feminist struggle that had long predated Peronism. Perhaps Peronists sim- ply recognized that the time had come for women to enter the political arena; after all, Peronism arose twenty-five years after the League. Moreover, they may have wanted to steal the plat- form of feminists, most of whom were strongly anti-Peronist. Finally, Eva's image repelled the upper-class women who had formed the League's female constituency, and her social endeav- ors lacked the spirit of noblesse oblige that characterized elitist charities of the past.[25] For these reasons, Peronists would not identify the League as a precursor.

The unique feature of Peronism that emerges from this com- parison is the movement's ability to infuse vitality and egalitari- anism into what was originally an upper-class, antirevolutionary ideology, thus making it appealing to the masses. This is a key characteristic of fascism, as is Peronism's contradictory radical yet anti-Marxist nature. Decades of governmental indifference to the proletariat's needs also helped make a conservative program seem revolutionary when put into practice.

This comparison of the League and Peronism should enable researchers to view Peronism in a new light. Scholars usually characterize the latter as populist, which José Luis Romero de- fined as "politically right" and "socioeconomically left," because populist movements have defended the interests of the masses under elite auspices. Yet Peronist socioeconomic planks were in- herited from the League, Social Catholicism, and the Irazusta group, not from the left.[26] The Argentine left had been weak since the early 1920s and, moreover, had not uniformly sup- ported economic independence. This heritage, combined with Peronist hierarchical social relations and political style, indicates that Peronism was essentially counterrevolutionary. What made it counterrevolutionary rather than conservative, according to Mayer's typology, was its embrace of the masses.

Viewing Peronism as counterrevolutionary or fascist also clarifies other, hitherto puzzling features of the movement. Its ability to attract support in urban working-class and poor rural districts, according to Peter Smith and Manuel Mora y Araújo, makes Peronism difficult to categorize. Yet a prominent specialist in European fascism, Eugen Weber, noted that this same appeal characterized Hungarian and Romanian fascism. He also found other similarities between these movements and Peronism: they all advocated nationalist and radical change in industrializing, urbanizing countries dominated by foreign capital, and they mobilized poorer sectors and idealistic intellectuals. Weber concluded that in such areas, where the radical left is weak and nationalism is a vital ingredient of progress, right-wing extremism is perhaps the only possible, and, in some respects, healthy response to poverty and stagnation.[27]

The subject of this work is the League and its place in history, not Peronism per se, although the study sheds some light on the latter, at least on its pre-1955 manifestation. The movement fits Payne's criteria except possibly for the fascist glorification of violence, although even this point is debatable. It does not, however, fit Mayer's description of counterrevolutionaries. Nevertheless, by referring to detailed studies on European fascism, one can seriously question the criteria used by Latin Americanists to deny Perón's fascist tendencies. Moreover, the working-class component of many fascist movements and fascist interest in popular welfare demonstrate that one need not interpret the masses' attraction to Perón as irrational, as some scholars who originally viewed Peronism as fascist had believed. This discussion at the very least illustrates the need for careful analyses of Peronism in an explicitly comparative context.[28]

Yet the League's influence has persisted in other forms besides mainstream Peronism. The League's ideas and practices resemble those of the recent military regime (1976–83), although its leaders did not claim the League as an ancestor. Certainly there were other factors that influenced the dictatorship: Juan Carlos Onganía's rule (1966–70), neighboring bureaucratic-authoritarian governments, and internal economic and political conditions. Still, as Thomas Skidmore has pointed out for the entire Southern Cone, elite responses to labor protest in the post–World War I years set a precedent that has affected labor relations and governance down to the present.[29]

The situation the military inherited in 1976 did, however, differ from the one faced by the League in 1919. The 1976 coup followed a period of economic chaos and decades of intense political factionalism, more pervasive than that of the early twentieth century. Although many of the guerrillas active in the 1960s and 1970s were not as unreservedly leftist as the workers of the earlier period, they presented a graver threat to both the social order and the military as an institution. Furthermore, the tactics and composition of the death squads varied from those of the League brigades. Whereas the League recruited military and police officers as well as civilians, it is doubtful that the dictatorship's death squads included the latter. The League assaulted its opponents and sometimes delivered them to the police for imprisonment, but it did not make them "disappear." Finally, the Radical government's relationship with the League was more complex than that of the military regime with its own personnel, for the military did indeed control the "dirty war."[30]

Nevertheless, the ideological similarities between the recent dictatorship and the League are striking. The League defended the "constitution" and the class system against what it considered to be a multifaceted subversive threat. After the height of the repression, President Jorge Videla declared that international subversives had attacked Argentina, "not only in a material sense but, what is worse, on the level of ideas, since this aggression aimed at subverting our system of life." In the face of this threat to national security, Argentina had defended the "human rights" of its own society. Indeed, Culture and Education Minister Juan José Catalán in 1977 boasted of Argentina's "almost religious" respect for human rights.[31] To Videla and Catalán, human rights did not mean much beyond free individual pursuit of profits, nor did they for the League during its prominence. Freedom from assault, kidnapping, and torture was not included, nor was freedom of thought and political expression. Even between 1955 and 1973, the military had only permitted those who opposed "demagoguery" (that is, Peronism, rather than Radicalism) to participate politically, when it had allowed any participation at all. Furthermore, human rights decidedly did not include the right to form independent unions and to strike; "liberty of work" was still a desirable goal for military leaders, although one that ultimately eluded them.

The military regime's views on democracy were as restrictive as those of the League. Roberto Viola in 1981 claimed that under his presidency Argentina had returned to democracy. He admitted that some factors were still missing or conditional, "like the expression of the people's will" and certain aspects of union and political activity. Despite these critical omissions, he asserted that the fundamental democratic values of "freedom and justice" were present.[32] If one substitutes Carlés's "republic" for democracy, Viola's statement becomes comprehensible. Carlés's state of discipline, authority, work, and order, where liberty is "controlled" and the ruling minority eschews "demagoguery" in the name of liberal principles, closely resembled the military's desired polity.

In order to protect the class hierarchy and its own privileges, the armed forces, like the League, denied those "outside the system" the rights it claimed to uphold. Brigadier General Fernando Humberto Santiago noted that for the subversives, the end justified the means.[33] The same was true for both the League and the Argentine military in the wars they waged on human rights in their self-styled defense of the constitution.

The Argentine Patriotic League still exists; as of 1977 its office was located in the heart of Buenos Aires. Other groups have long since assumed the roles of the League, which is now but a mere shadow of its former powerful self. Although Argentina returned to constitutional democracy in 1983, grave political and economic crises plague the nation. As long as these conditions persist, the League's successors may once again foment counterrevolution.

Notes

Biographical information
in the text comes from the
biographical sources listed in
Part IV of the bibliography,
unless otherwise indicated.

Introduction

1 I prefer using the term *counterrevolution* rather than *right*, although I
consider them synonymous. Arno J. Mayer described counterrevolution in *Dynamics of Counterrevolution in Europe, 1870–1956: An
Analytic Framework* (New York, 1971). For a critique, see Eugen
Weber, "Revolution? Counterrevolution? What Revolution?" in Walter Laqueur, ed., *Fascism, a Reader's Guide: Analyses, Interpretations,
Bibliography* (Berkeley, Calif., 1976), pp. 435–67.

2 Enrique Zuleta Alvarez, in *El nacionalismo argentino*, 2 vols. (Buenos
Aires, 1975), 1: 11; and Arthur P. Whitaker and David C. Jordan, in
Nationalism in Contemporary Latin America (New York, 1966), p. 53,
agreed on the importance of the Argentine right.

3 Charles W. Bergquist contrasts leftist and rightist nationalism in
*Workers in Modern Latin American History: Capitalist Development and
Labor Movement Formation in Chile, Argentina, Venezuela, and Colom-
bia* (Stanford, Calif., forthcoming).

4 See, for example, Marysa Navarro Gerassi, *Los nacionalistas*, trans.
Alberto Ciria (Buenos Aires, 1968), p. 92. Examples of works that
concentrate on the post-1929 years are Navarro, *Los nacionalistas*;
Juan José Hernández Arregui, *La formación de la consciencia nacional
(1930–1960)* (Buenos Aires, 1960); David Crichton Jordan, "Argentina's Nationalist Movements and the Political Parties (1930–1963):
A Study of Conflict" (Ph.D. Diss., Univ. of Pennsylvania, 1964);
Marvin Goldwert, *Democracy, Militarism, and Nationalism in Argentina, 1930–1966: An Interpretation* (Austin, Tex., 1972). Exceptions
are Zuleta, *El Nacionalismo*; María Inés Barbero and Fernando
Devoto, *Los nacionalistas (1910–1932)* (Buenos Aires, 1983); and
David Rock's discussion of the League in *Politics in Argentina,
1890–1930: The Rise and Fall of Radicalism* (London, 1975), pp. 180–

202, passim. On the historiography of the right, see Zuleta, *El nacionalismo*, 2: 565–811; and Alistair Hennessy, "Fascism and Populism in Latin America," in Laqueur, ed., *Fascism*, pp. 272–80.

5 See Navarro, *Los nacionalistas*; Hernández, *La formación*. The only exceptions are Ronald Dolkart, "Manuel A. Fresco, Governor of the Province of Buenos Aires, 1936–1940: A Study of the Argentine Right and Its Response to Economic and Social Change" (Ph.D. Diss., Univ. of California, Los Angeles, 1969); and Rock's examination of the League in *Politics in Argentina*.

6 Jorge Abelardo Ramos, *Revolución y contrarrevolución en la Argentina: Las masas en nuestra historia* (Buenos Aires, 1957), pp. 386–96. Also see Jorge Enea Spilimbergo, *Nacionalismo oligárquico y nacionalismo revolucionario* (Buenos Aires, 1958).

7 On the League see Navarro, *Los nacionalistas*, pp. 39–40, 64; Rock, *Politics in Argentina*, pp. 180–202, passim; Osvaldo Bayer, "1921: La masacre de Jacinto Arauz," *Todo Es Historia* no. 45 (Jan. 1971): 40–55; and scattered references in Osvaldo Bayer, *Los vengadores de la Patagonia trágica*, 3 vols. (Buenos Aires, 1972–74); Sandra F. McGee, "The Visible and Invisible Liga Patriótica Argentina, 1919–1928: Gender Roles and the Right Wing," *Hispanic American Historical Review* 64, no. 2 (May 1984): 233–58 (hereinafter, HAHR); Alain Rouquié, *Poder militar y sociedad política en la Argentina*, trans. Arturo Iglesias Echegaray (Buenos Aires, 1981), pp. 144–51, passim; Barbero and Devoto, *Los nacionalistas*, pp. 40–42.

8 See, for example, Arturo Jauretche, "Los movimientos nacionales," *Polémica* no. 69 (1971): 233–34.

9 Jorge Abelardo Ramos, *Revolución y contrarrevolución en la Argentina*, 2 vols., 3d ed. (Buenos Aires, 1965), 2: 241.

10 Navarro, *Los nacionalistas*, pp. 104–5; Alberto Ciria, *Perón y el justicialismo* (Buenos Aires, 1971), p. 94. Navarro noted, however, that nationalists exalted violence as a principle.

11 Zuleta, *El nacionalismo*, 1: 23, 45.

12 Mayer, *Dynamics of Counterrevolution*, p. 46.

13 George L. Mosse, "The Genesis of Fascism," *Journal of Contemporary History* 1 (1966): 14–26; Mayer, *Dynamics of Counterrevolution*, pp. 39, 48–55.

Chapter 1

1 On the ideology of the oligarchy, see Thomas F. McGann, *Argentina, the United States, and the Interamerican System, 1880–1914* (Cam-

bridge, Mass., 1957), esp. pp. 43–45; and Natalio Botana, *El orden conservador: La política argentina entre 1880 y 1916* (Buenos Aires, 1977).

2 Carlos Ibarguren, *La historia que he vivido*, 2d ed. (Buenos Aires, 1969), pp. 56–57; and José Manuel Estrada, "Discursos sobre el liberalismo," in José Luis Romero and Luis Alberto Romero, eds., *Pensamiento conservador (1815–1898)* (Caracas, 1978), pp. 254–72.

3 Gino Germani, *Política y sociedad en una época de transición: De la sociedad tradicional a la sociedad de masas* (Buenos Aires, 1962), pp. 180–81.

4 Ibid., pp. 179, 188; Argentina, Dirección Nacional del Servício Estadístico, *Cuarto censo general de la Nación*, 3 vols. (Buenos Aires, 1947–52), 1: lxii, 1.

5 U.S. Department of Commerce, Bureau of Foreign and Domestic Commerce, *Statistical Abstract of the United States, 1915* (Washington, D.C., 1916), p. 712.

6 Adolfo Dorfman, *Historia de la industria argentina*, 2d ed. (Buenos Aires, 1970), p. 285.

7 James R. Scobie, *Buenos Aires: Plaza to Suburb, 1870–1910* (New York, 1974), p. 273.

8 This demographic imbalance was by no means typical of other immigration centers or export economies. See Argentina, Comisión Nacional del Censo, *Tercer censo nacional, levantado el primero de junio de 1914*, 10 vols. (Buenos Aires, 1916–19), 1: 130–31, 188; Mexico, Dirección General de Estadística, *Quinto censo de población, 15 de mayo de 1930*, 8 vols. (Mexico City, 1932–36), vol. 8, Part 32: xix, 50.

9 Argentina, Dirección General de Estadística, *La población y el movimiento demográfico en el período 1910–1925* (Buenos Aires, 1926), p. 29. The illegitimacy rate in the provinces was much higher than in the capital. According to Charles C. Cumberland, *Mexico: The Struggle for Modernity* (New York, 1968), p. 193, 45 percent of Mexican children born in the early twentieth century were illegitimate. Some of these, however, were the offspring of couples married in religious rather than civil ceremonies.

10 Katherine S. Dreier, *Five Months in the Argentine from a Woman's Point of View, 1918–1919* (New York, 1920), pp. 18–20, 168; *Revista Militar* 9 (Feb. 1919): 386; Manuel Gálvez, *La trata de blancas* (Buenos Aires, 1904); *La Prensa*, May 18, 1919; Enrique Ruiz Guiñazú, "Las fuerzas perdidas en la economía nacional," *Instituto Popular de Conferencias* 3 (Aug. 10, 1917): 178 (hereinafter, IPC);

Robert Edward Shipley, "On the Outside Looking In: A Social History of the 'Porteño' Worker during the 'Golden Age' of Argentine Development, 1914–1930" (Ph.D. Diss., Rutgers Univ., 1977), pp. 112–14; Julia Kirk Blackwelder and Lyman L. Johnson, "Changing Criminal Patterns in Buenos Aires, 1890 to 1914," *Journal of Latin American Studies* 14, no. 2 (Nov. 1982): 371 (hereinafter, JLAS).

11 Scobie, *Buenos Aires*; Carl Solberg, *Immigration and Nationalism: Argentina and Chile, 1890–1914* (Austin, Tex., 1970), pp. 93–102; Shipley, "A Social History," pp. 101–3, 108–10; Blackwelder and Johnson, "Criminal Patterns."

12 Roberto Cortés Conde, *El progreso argentino, 1880–1914* (Buenos Aires, 1979), pp. 236–39; Scobie, *Buenos Aires*, pp. 137–42; Shipley, "A Social History," pp. 75, 82–83, 95–96 nn. 1–2.

13 Shipley, "A Social History," pp. 49–52, 89–92, 198–99; Argentina, Comisión Nacional del Censo, *Tercer censo*, 1: 252; Lily Sosa de Newton, *Las argentinas, de ayer a hoy* (Buenos Aires, 1967), pp. 185, 216; Carolina Muzzilli, "El trabajo femenino," *Boletín Mensual del Museo Social Argentino* 2, nos. 15–16 (Mar.–Apr. 1913): 65–90 (hereinafter, BMSA).

14 Sources on labor history include Hobart A. Spalding, Jr., *La clase trabajadora argentina (documentos para su historia—1890/1912)* (Buenos Aires, 1970), pp. 17–95; Sebastián Marotta, *El movimiento sindical argentino: Su génesis y desarrollo*, 3 vols. (Buenos Aires, 1960–61, 1970); Richard J. Walter, *The Socialist Party of Argentina, 1890–1930* (Austin, Tex., 1977); Richard Alan Yoast, "The Development of Argentine Anarchism: A Socio-Ideological Analysis" (Ph.D. Diss., Univ. of Wisconsin, Madison, 1975); Rubén Iscaro, *Historia del movimiento sindical argentino*, 2 vols. (Buenos Aires, 1973); Samuel L. Baily, *Labor, Nationalism and Politics in Argentina* (New Brunswick, N.J., 1967); Dardo Cúneo, *Juan B. Justo y las luchas sociales en la Argentina* (Buenos Aires, 1943); S. Fanny Simon, "Anarchism and Anarcho-Syndicalism in South America," HAHR 26, no. 1 (Feb. 1946): 38–59.

15 Walter, *The Socialist Party*, p. 63; and Peter H. Smith, *Argentina and the Failure of Democracy: Conflict among Political Elites, 1904–1955* (Madison, Wis., 1974), p. 31.

16 Dreier, *Five Months*, p. 207; Nancy Caro Hollander, "Women in the Political Economy of Argentina" (Ph.D. Diss., Univ. of California, Los Angeles, 1974), pp. 192–94; Yoast, "Argentine Anarchism,"

pp. 299–300; Juana Rouco Buela, *Historia de un ideal vivido por una mujer* (Buenos Aires, 1964), p. 15. On the tenant strike see Spalding, *La clase trabajadora*, pp. 449–96; and Scobie, *Buenos Aires*, pp. 156–58.

17 Dreier, *Five Months*, pp. 46, 200–201; Yoast, "Argentine Anarchism," p. 300; Rouco, *Historia de un ideal*; María del Carmen Feijoó, "Las luchas feministas," *Todo Es Historia* no. 28 (Jan. 1978): 7–23; Marifran Carlson, "Feminism and Reform: A History of the Argentine Feminist Movement to 1926" (Ph.D. Diss., Univ. of Chicago, 1983).

18 Dreier, *Five Months*, p. 40. Also see the following memoirs by upper-class women: Julia Valentina Bunge, *Vida, época maravillosa, 1903–1911* (Buenos Aires, 1965); Celina de Arenaza, *Sin memoria* (Buenos Aires, 1980); Carmen Peers de Perkins, *Eramos jóvenes el siglo y yo* (Buenos Aires, 1969).

19 Peers, *Eramos jóvenes*, p. 37; Frederic Jesup Stimson, *My United States* (New York, 1931), p. 310. Also see Cynthia Jeffress Little, "The Society of Beneficence in Buenos Aires, 1823–1900" (Ph.D. Diss., Temple Univ., 1980).

20 Upper-class female institutions are named in Miguel J. Font, ed., *La mujer. Encuesta feminista argentina. Hacia la formación de una Liga Feminista Sudamericana* (Buenos Aires, 1921), pp. 217–20; Adolfo Sciurano Casteñeda, ed., *Album de oro de la mujer argentina* (Buenos Aires, 1930). I borrow the term "social housekeeping" from Mary P. Ryan, *Womanhood in America: From Colonial Times to the Present*, 2d ed. (New York, 1979), pp. 136–50.

21 Cecilia Grierson, *Decadencia del Consejo Nacional de Mujeres de la República Argentina* (Buenos Aires, 1910); Hollander, "Political Economy," pp. 179–186; Carlson, "Feminism," pp. 61–101.

22 "Consejo Nacional de Mujeres," BMSA 1, no. 6 (1912): 163.

23 Hollander, "Political Economy," p. 225.

24 Ambassador Frederic J. Stimson to Secretary of State, Jan. 25, 1919, Dispatch no. 737, U.S. Department of State, National Archives Microfilm Copy M514, 835.00/164. On rural workers also see Spalding, *La clase trabajadora*, pp. 242–45; Carl Solberg, "Farm Workers and the Myth of Export-Led Development in Argentina," *The Americas* 31, no. 2 (Oct. 1974): 121–38.

25 Yoast, "Argentine Anarchism," pp. 209–10; Walter, *The Socialist Party*, pp. 127–28; Carl Solberg, "Rural Unrest and Agrarian Policy in Argentina, 1912–1930," *Journal of Inter-American Studies and*

World Affairs 13 (Jan. 1971): 18–27; Silvio Spangemberg, "El conflicto agrario del sud de Santa Fe," BMSA 1, nos. 11–12 (1912): 522–31.

26 Walter, *The Socialist Party*, p. 56.

27 Spalding, *La clase trabajadora*, p. 51.

28 Ibarguren, *La historia*, p. 68. On the Revolution of 1890, the Radical Civic Union, and its leaders, see Julio Godio, ed., *La revolución del 90* (Buenos Aires, 1974); Peter G. Snow, *Argentine Radicalism: The History and Doctrine of the Radical Civic Union* (Iowa City, Iowa, 1965); Rock, *Politics in Argentina*; Manuel Gálvez, *Vida de Hipólito Yrigoyen—el hombre del misterio*, 2d ed. (Buenos Aires, 1939); Félix Luna, *Yrigoyen, el templario de la libertad* (Buenos Aires, 1954).

29 Ezequiel Gallo (h.) and Silvia Sigal, "La formación de los partidos políticos contemporáneos: La U.C.R. (1890–1916)," in Torcuato S. Di Tella, Gino Germani, and Jorge Graciarena, eds., *Argentina, sociedad de masas*, 2d ed. (Buenos Aires, 1965), pp. 162–69. I use *régimen* to refer to the old political elite, rather than translating it into "regime," in order to avoid confusion.

30 José Luis Romero, *A History of Argentine Political Thought*, trans. Thomas F. McGann, 2d ed. (Stanford, Calif.), p. 218.

31 Ibarguren, *La historia*, pp. 26, 279–94; Botana, *El orden conservador*, pp. 315–36; Oscar Cornblit, "La opción conservadora en la política argentina," *Desarrollo Económico* 14 (Jan.–Mar. 1975): 624–28; Lisandro de la Torre, *Obras*, Vol. 5: *Campañas presidenciales*, ed. Raúl Larra (Buenos Aires, 1952), pp. 89, 102–3, 107–9. Note the difference between the Conservative party of Buenos Aires, the "local conservative" parties (provincial groups formerly allied with the PAN), and conservatives (true exponents of conservative thought).

32 Oscar Cornblit described the Liga del Sur in "Inmigrantes y empresarios en la política argentina," *Desarrollo Económico* 6 (Jan.–May 1967): 641–91.

33 *La Prensa*, Sept. 12, 1915; Partido Demócrata Progresista, *Programas y plataformas electorales* (Buenos Aires, 1930), pp. 3–16; Ezequiel Gallo (h.) and Roberto Cortés Conde, *Argentina, la república conservadora* (Buenos Aires, 1972), p. 230.

34 *Buenos Aires Herald*, April 10, 1977. Also see Oscar Cornblit, *El fracaso del conservadorismo en la política argentina*, Instituto Torcuato Di Tella Trabajo Interno no. 14 (Buenos Aires, 1973), p. 51.

Chapter 2

1 Jerónimo Remorino, ed., *Anales de legislación argentina*, 4 vols. (Buenos Aires, 1953–55), 3: 560; Solberg, *Immigration and Nationalism*, p. 109.

2 Eduardo Gilimón, *Un anarquista en Buenos Aires (1890–1910)* (Buenos Aires, 1971), p. 99; Osvaldo Bayer, "Simón Radowitzky, Mártir o asesino?" *Todo Es Historia* no. 4 (Aug. 1967): 60–62; Marotta, *Movimiento sindical*, 2: 25–35, 41.

3 *La Prensa*, Nov. 15, 1909; Marotta, *Movimiento sindical*, 2: 39; Bayer, "Radowitzky," 64–65; Solberg, *Immigration and Nationalism*, p. 112; *Caras y Caretas* no. 581 (Nov. 20, 1909).

4 Carlés and Rojas in *La Nación*, Nov. 17, 1909; *Caras y Caretas* no. 581 (Nov. 20, 1909).

5 *La Protesta*, Jan. 19 and 26, 1910.

6 G. H. Sherill to Secretary of State, May 15, 1910, Dispatch no. 371 and May 21, 1910, Dispatch no. 381, U.S. Dept. of State, 835.00/77–78; *Caras y Caretas* no. 606 (May 14, 1910); Gilimón, *Un anarquista*, p. 106; Marotta, *Movimiento sindical*, 2: 72 n. 1.

7 Charles Warren Currier, *Lands of the Southern Cross: A Visit to South America*, pp. 105–7; Sherill to Secretary of State, May 21, 1910, Dispatch no. 381, U.S. Dept. of State, 835.00/78.

8 Daughters of Mary manifesto, quoted in Celia La Palma de Emery, *Discursos y conferencias: Acción pública y privada en favor de la mujer y del niño en la República Argentina* (Buenos Aires, 1910), pp. 247–49; Bunge, *Vida*, pp. 138, 214, and passim; Ambrosio Romero Carranza, *Itinerario de Monseñor de Andrea* (Buenos Aires, 1957), pp. 69–70; *El Pueblo*, May 2–3, 12, 22, 1910.

9 José R. Romariz, *La semana trágica: Relato de los hechos sangrientos del año 1919* (Buenos Aires, 1952), p. 170; Marotta, *Movimiento sindical*, 2: 73–77; Gilimón, *Un anarquista*, p. 107; Enrique Dickmann, *Recuerdos de un militante socialista* (Buenos Aires, 1949), pp. 185–88; Walter, *The Socialist Party*, p. 52.

10 Currier, *Southern Cross*, p. 129. Also see Leonardo Senkman, "Crónica documentada del problema judío en la Argentina. Primer hito: De 'La Bolsa' a la Semana Trágica," *Nueva Presencia*, July 9, 1977.

11 Marotta, *Movimiento sindical*, 2: 77, 81; Solberg, *Immigration and Nationalism*, p. 114; Remorino, *Anales*, 3: 787–89; Simon, "Anarchism," 44; Dickmann, *Recuerdos*, pp. 188–89; Sherill to Secretary of State, June 27, 1910, Dispatch no. 446, and June 29, 1910, Dispatch no. 450, U.S. Dept. of State, 835.00/92–93.

12 Simon, "Anarchism," 46; Spalding, *La clase trabajadora*, p. 88.

13 In *Immigration and Nationalism*, Solberg demonstrated that these identifications were uniquely Argentine by comparing Argentine and Chilean nationalism. In contrast to Argentina, in Chile the working and middle classes were largely native-born, and they were the advocates of nationalism. As a result, their nationalism was more leftist in character than the Argentine variety.

14 *La Prensa*, Dec. 10, 1901. Also see *La Prensa*, Dec. 1901–Jan. 1902; *Caras y Caretas*, no. 167 (Dec. 14, 1901), no. 168 (Dec. 21, 1901), no. 169 (Dec. 28, 1901), and no. 172 (Jan. 18, 1902).

15 *La Prensa*, Dec. 17, 19–20, 1901, and Jan. 14, 1902; Scobie, *Buenos Aires*, p. 240.

16 José F. Uriburu, "Socialismo y defensa nacional," *Anales de la Facultad de Derecho y Ciencias Sociales* 4 (1914): 268–90.

17 Clifton B. Kroeber, "Rosas and the Revision of Argentine History, 1880–1955," *Revista Interamericana de Bibliografía* 10 (Jan.–Mar. 1960): 5–7.

18 Julio Irazusta, *Genio y figura de Leopoldo Lugones* (Buenos Aires, 1961), pp. 7–8, 23–25; Alfredo Canedo, *Aspectos del pensamiento político de Leopoldo Lugones* (Buenos Aires, 1974), pp. 13–24, 34; and esp. Carlos Manuel Payá and Eduardo José Cárdenas, "Manuel Gálvez y Ricardo Rojas, protonacionalistas," *Todo Es Historia* no. 107 (Apr. 1976): 32–48.

19 Manuel Gálvez, *El diario de Gabriel Quiroga* (Buenos Aires, 1910), pp. 101–3; Manuel Gálvez, *El solar de la raza*, 2d ed. (Buenos Aires, 1920), pp. 13–21, 52–60.

20 Whitaker and Jordan, *Nationalism*, p. 55; Germani, *Política y sociedad*, p. 200; Solberg, *Immigration and Nationalism*, pp. 154–56; Canedo, *Lugones*, pp. 104–6.

21 Juan Carlos Tedesco, *Educación y sociedad en la Argentina (1880–1900)* (Buenos Aires, 1970), pp. 159–60; Solberg, *Immigration and Nationalism*, p. 170; Hobart A. Spalding, Jr., "Education in Argentina, 1890–1914: The Limits of Oligarchical Reform," *Journal of Interdisciplinary History* 3 (Summer 1972): 42–45. The visitor's comment was cited by Spalding, "Education," 43.

22 Sarmiento cited in Juan José Sebreli, *La cuestión judía en la Argentina* (Buenos Aires, 1968), pp. 50–51, 226; Ricardo Rojas, *La restauración nacionalista: Crítica de la educación argentina y bases para una reforma en el estudio de las humanidades modernas*, 3d ed. (Buenos Aires, 1974), p. 254 and passim.

23 Rojas, *La restauración*, pp. 140–41.

24 Ira Rosenwaike, "Jewish Population of Argentina: Census and Estimates, 1887–1947," *Jewish Social Studies* 22 (Oct. 1960): 197. On the Jews of Argentina also see Robert Weisbrot, *The Jews of Argentina: From the Inquisition to Perón* (Philadelphia, 1979); Boleslao Lewin, *Cómo fue la inmigración judía a la Argentina* (Buenos Aires, 1971); Judith Laikin Elkin, *Jews of the Latin American Republics* (Chapel Hill, N.C., 1980); Eugene F. Sofer, *From Pale to Pampa: A Social History of the Jews of Buenos Aires* (New York, 1982).

25 Lewin, *La inmigración judía*, pp. 100–102; Victor A. Mirelman, "Jewish Settlement in Argentina, 1881–1892," *Jewish Social Studies* 33 (Jan. 1971): 8.

26 Julián Martel (José María Miró), *La bolsa* (Buenos Aires, 1891), pp. 111–32; Gladys S. Onega, *La inmigración en la literatura argentina, 1880–1910* (Buenos Aires, 1969), pp. 109–23. As of 1981, *La bolsa* was widely sold in newsstands and bookstores.

27 Gino Germani, "Antisemitismo ideológico y antisemitismo tradicional," *Comentario* 34 (1962): 55–63. A historical explanation of ideological anti-Semitism, albeit in a different context, is found in Peter G. J. Pulzer, *The Rise of Political Anti-Semitism in Germany and Austria* (New York, 1974).

28 Weisbrot, *The Jews of Argentina*, p. 60. Also see Weisbrot, pp. 59–66; Boleslao Lewin, *La colectividad judía en la Argentina* (Buenos Aires, 1974), pp. 150–54; Nora Glickman, "The Jewish White Slave Trade in Latin American Writings," *American Jewish Archives* 34 (Nov. 1982): 182.

29 Ysabel F. Rennie, *The Argentine Republic* (New York, 1945), pp. 330–33; Harry O. Sandberg, "The Jews of Latin America," *American Jewish Yearbook 1917–18* (Philadelphia, 1917), p. 46.

30 Leonardo Senkman, "El nacionalismo y los judíos: 1909–1932," *Nueva Presencia*, July 23, 1977; *La Prensa*, Nov. 25, Dec. 26 and 28, 1908. Rojas's praise for Martel is mentioned in Vicente Osvaldo Cutolo, *Nuevo diccionario biográfico argentino (1750–1930)*, 5 vols. (Buenos Aires, 1968–78), 4: 570.

31 Rojas, *La restauración*, pp. 124–28.

32 "Argentina," *Encyclopedia Judaica*, 16 vols. (New York, 1971–72), 3: 426; Jedida Efrón, "La obra escolar en las colonias judías," in Delegación de Asociaciones Israelitas Argentinas, *Cincuenta años de colonización judía en la Argentina* (Buenos Aires, 1939), pp. 241–48; Solberg, *Immigration and Nationalism*, p. 149.

33 Rojas cited in Payá and Cárdenas, "Gálvez y Rojas," 45; Earl T. Glauert, "Ricardo Rojas and the Emergence of Argentine Cultural Nationalism," HAHR 43, no. 1 (Feb. 1963): 7–12.

34 Sebreli, *La cuestión judía*, pp. 86–90, 107.

35 Cited by Senkman, "El nacionalismo."

36 On Social Catholicism see Richard L. Camp, *The Papal Ideology of Social Reform. A Study in Historical Development, 1878–1967* (Leiden, 1969); Joseph N. Moody, ed., *Church and Society: Catholic Social and Political Thought and Movements, 1789–1950* (New York, 1953); David J. O'Brien and Thomas A. Shannon, eds., *Renewing the Earth. Catholic Documents on Peace, Justice and Liberation* (New York, 1977), pp. 11–37.

37 Spalding, *La clase trabajadora*, p. 509; Alfredo Sánchez Gamarra, *Vida del padre Grote. Redentorista* (Buenos Aires, 1949), pp. 168–69, 193–94.

38 José Pagés, "Los ensayos sindicales de inspiración católica en la Republica Argentina," *Anales de la Comisión de Estudios y Conferencias de la Corporación de Ingenieros Católicos* (1944): 82–83; Ambrosio Romero Carranza, Alberto Rodríguez Varela, and Eduardo Ventura Flores Pirán, *Historia política de la Argentina*, Vol. 3: *Desde 1862 hasta 1928* (Buenos Aires, 1974), p. 449; Guillermo Furlong, "El catolicismo argentino entre 1860 y 1930," in Academia Nacional de la Historia, *Historia argentina contemporánea, 1862–1930* (Buenos Aires, 1964), 2: 274.

39 Romero, Rodríguez, and Ventura, *Historia política*, pp. 445–48, 453; Néstor Tomás Auza, *Los católicos argentinos: Su experiencia política y social* (Buenos Aires, 1962), pp. 100–107; Scobie, *Buenos Aires*, p. 145.

40 Pagés, "Los ensayos," 98–116; Spalding, *La clase trabajadora*, pp. 502–4; Auza, *Los católicos argentinos*, pp. 78–84.

41 Auza, *Los católicos argentinos*, pp. 87–88, 92–98; Furlong, "El catolicismo," 280; José Luis de Imaz, "Alejandro E. Bunge, economista y sociólogo (1880–1943)," *Desarrollo Económico* 14 (Oct.–Dec. 1974): 545–67.

42 Spalding, *La clase trabajadora*, pp. 548–49.

43 J. Serralunga Langhi, "Las cajas rurales en la República Argentina," *Estudios* 1 (Oct. 1911): 341–51.

44 La Palma, *Discursos*, pp. 20, 240–42. The idealization of womanhood was a common theme in Western thought in the nineteenth and early twentieth centuries. See, for example, Barbara Welter, "The Cult of True Womanhood: 1820–1860," *American Quarterly* 18

(Summer 1966): 151–74. For diverse Argentine viewpoints on womanhood and female labor, see Font, *La mujer; Primer Congreso Femenino Internacional de la República Argentina* (Buenos Aires, 1910); and Catalina H. Wainerman and Marysa Navarro, *El trabajo de la mujer en la Argentina: Un análisis preliminar de las ideas dominantes en las primeras décadas del siglo XX*, Cuadernos del Centro de Estudios de Población no. 7 (Buenos Aires, 1979). Also see Camp, *The Papal Ideology*, pp. 52–56.

45 Miguel de Andrea, "Orientaciones sociales," IPC 3 (June 22, 1917): 82.

46 Miguel de Andrea, *La perturbación social contemporánea* (Buenos Aires, 1944), p. 111; Andrea, "Orientaciones sociales," 85.

47 Andrea, *La perturbación*, pp. 113–14; Gustavo Franceschi, "Sobre feminismo católico," *El Pueblo*, June 17, 1920.

48 La Palma, *Discursos*, pp. 34, 181; Hollander, "Political Economy," pp. 195–96; José Elías Niklison, "Acción social católica obrera," *Boletín del Departamento Nacional del Trabajo* 46 (March 1920): 73, 89, 94.

49 Niklison, "Acción social," 274–77.

50 Ibid., 18, 112; Pagés, "Los ensayos," 107; *El Pueblo*, Feb. 26, 1920; Bayer, *Los vengadores*, 1: 48–50, with note.

51 Arenaza, *Sin memoria*, pp. 24–25; Niklison, "Acción social," 266–69; and periodic coverage on the center in *El Pueblo*.

52 Arenaza, *Sin memoria*, p. 25.

53 Miguel de Andrea, *Pensamiento cristiano y democrático de Monseñor de Andrea: Homenaje del Congreso Nacional* (Buenos Aires, 1963), pp. 83–84.

54 Ibid., pp. 59–60.

55 Shipley, "A Social History," pp. 83–106.

56 Tomás Amadeo, *La función social* (Buenos Aires, 1929), p. 240; see pp. 25, 219–25, 240–41, 370–75, 475–79, 548–55 for information on the museum. See also "Orígenes y desenvolvimiento del Museo Social Argentino," BMSA 1, no. 1 (1912): 5–12.

57 Ibarguren, *La historia*, pp. 102–4.

58 Ibid., pp. 229–30. For a similar statement, also see Estanislao S. Zeballos, "Discurso inaugural," IPC 1 (July 8, 1915): 17.

59 Shipley, "A Social History," p. 233; Ibarguren, *La historia*, pp. 234–37.

60 On the conference see "Congreso de la Mutualidad," BMSA 7 (1918): 5–379; *La Prensa*, Mar. 24–27, 1918.

61 Spalding, *La clase trabajadora*, pp. 224–25; *La Protesta*, Nov. 9, 1919.

62 Spalding, *La clase trabajadora*, pp. 332, 354–62; Shipley, "A Social History," pp. 285–87.

63 *La Nación*, May 23 and July 13, 1918; *La Vanguardia*, May 15, 1919.

Chapter 3

1 Vicente Vásquez-Presedo, *Estadísticas históricas argentinas (comparadas)*, Vol. 2: *Segunda parte 1914–1939* (Buenos Aires, 1976), p. 46. On the economic history of this period, see Guido Di Tella and Manuel Zymelman, *Los ciclos económicos argentinos* (Buenos Aires, 1973), pp. 129–86; Joseph S. Tulchin, "The Argentine Economy during the First World War," *Review of the River Plate*, June 19 and 30, and July 10, 1970; Darío Cantón, José L. Moreno, and Alberto Ciria, *Argentina, la democracia constitucional y su crisis* (Buenos Aires, 1972), pp. 21–50.

2 Shipley, "A Social History," p. 75.

3 Rock, *Politics in Argentina*, pp. 190–91.

4 Vásquez-Presedo, *Estadísticas*, 2: 47. On organized labor in this period, see Rock, *Politics in Argentina*, pp. 125–56; Shipley, "A Social History"; and Heidi Goldberg, "Railroad Unionization in Argentina, 1912–1929: The Limitations of Working Class Alliance" (Ph.D. Diss., Yale Univ., 1979).

5 Gálvez, *Yrigoyen*, pp. 242–43; *La Fronda*, Oct. 24, 1919; Walter, *The Socialist Party*, pp. 140–57; Luna, *Yrigoyen*, pp. 256–59; Rock, *Politics in Argentina*, pp. 125–56; Carl Solberg, "The Tariff and Politics in Argentina, 1916–1930," HAHR 53, no. 2 (May 1973): 260–84.

6 Warren D. Robbins to Secretary of State, Aug. 26, 1918, Dispatch no. 652, U.S. Dept. of State, 835.00/155.

7 Stimson to Secretary of State, Jan. 25, 1919, Dispatch no. 737, U.S. Dept. of State, 835.00/164.

8 *El Diario*, Oct. 31, Nov. 1–2 and 14–15, 1918; *Caras y Caretas*, nos. 1051–52 (Nov. 23 and 30, 1918); Juan E. Carulla, *Al filo del medio siglo* (Parana, 1951), p. 150. Two future counterrevolutionaries, José F. Uriburu and Juan P. Ramos, however, supported the German side in the war. See Glauert, "Ricardo Rojas," p. 5.

9 Stimson to Secretary of State, Nov. 13, 1918, Telegrams, U.S. Dept. of State, 835.00/156–57.

10 Ibarguren, *La historia*, p. 165; Carulla, *Al filo*, pp. 72–73; H. Stuart Hughes, *Consciousness and Society: The Reconstruction of European Social Thought, 1890–1930* (New York, 1958).

11 Carulla, *Al filo*, pp. 145–49. On Maurras see Chapter 6 of this book.

12 *La Vanguardia*, Jan. 5, 1919; *Caras y Caretas* no. 1058 (Jan. 11, 1919); *La Prensa*, Jan. 2–3, 1919; *La Nación*, Jan. 9, 1919.

13 *La Fronda*, Oct. 2, 1919 and Feb. 21, 1920.

14 My account of the Tragic Week is based on the following sources: David Rock, "Lucha civil en la Argentina. La Semana Trágica de enero de 1919," *Desarrollo Económico* 11 (Mar. 1972): 165–215; Hugo del Campo, "La Semana Trágica," *Polémica* no. 53 (1971): 63–84; Nicolás Babini, "La Semana Trágica. Pesadilla de una siesta de verano," *Todo Es Historia* no. 5 (Sept. 1967): 8–20; Julio Godio, *La Semana Trágica de enero de 1919* (Buenos Aires, 1972); "La Semana Tragica," *La Nación*, Jan. 9–19, 1969.

15 Babini, in "Pesadilla," 16, and Rock, in *Politics in Argentina*, p. 178, concluded that Dellepiane took the initiative. Rouquié in *Poder militar*, pp. 142–44, took the other viewpoint and noted the plans for a coup.

16 Lewin, *La colectividad*, p. 128. Also see Nahum Solominsky, *La semana trágica en la Argentina* (Buenos Aires, 1971), pp. 17–21. My account of the civilian-led repression and formation of militias, Jan. 10–14, is based on the sources named in note 14, above, and the following: *La Prensa*, Jan. 12–15, 1919; *La Nación*, Jan. 11–15, 1919; *La Epoca*, Jan. 10–12, 1919; *Caras y Caretas* no. 1059 (Jan. 18, 1919); Carulla, *Al filo*, pp. 159–60; Romariz, *La semana trágica*. Rock, in "Lucha civil," 180, estimated that the Tragic Week resulted in 200 deaths.

17 Octavio A. Piñero, *Los orígenes y la trágica semana de enero de 1919* (Buenos Aires, 1956), p. 68.

18 Romariz, *La semana trágica*, p. 170; also see Sofer, *From Pale to Pampa*, p. 44.

19 Rouquié, *Poder militar*, pp. 141, 150. On the soviets, see Robert A. Potash, *The Army and Politics in Argentina, 1928–1945. Yrigoyen to Perón* (Stanford, Calif., 1969), p. 12.

20 *Revista Militar* 19 (Jan. 1919): 198.

21 Lewin, *La colectividad*, p. 142. The figure of 150,000 Jews was probably an overestimate. In 1917 there were between 110,000 and 113,000 Jews in the country according to Elkin, *Jews*, p. 72. Also see *La Nación*, Jan. 14, 1919; Solominsky, *La semana trágica*, pp. 27–28.

22 *La Prensa*, Jan. 25–26, 1919; Leonardo Senkman, "De 'La Bolsa' a la Semana Trágica," *Nueva Presencia*, July 16, 1977.

23 *La Prensa*, Jan. 26, 1919.

24 *La Vanguardia*, Jan. 23, 1919; *La Prensa*, Jan. 26, 1919.

25 *La Vanguardia*, Feb. 7, 1919; *La Prensa*, Jan. 21, 1919; *La Razón*, Jan. 13, 1919; *La Epoca*, Jan. 16–17, 26, 1919; *La Nación*, Jan. 14, 1919.

26 *La Epoca*, Jan. 22, 1919; *La Vanguardia*, Feb. 7, 1919.

27 *Revista Militar* 19 (Jan. 1919): 199–202; *La Razón*, Jan. 17, 1919; *La Prensa*, Jan. 21, 1919.

28 On this meeting and the statement of purpose that follows, see *La Epoca*, Jan. 21, 1919; *La Prensa*, Jan. 20–21, 1919.

29 Argentina, Policía de la Capital Federal, *Orden del día* 34 (1920): 832–34; Liga Patriótica Argentina, *Solemne homenaje de la Liga Patriótica Militar de Chile a la Liga Patriótica Argentina* (Santiago, Chile, 1922), p. 16.

30 Victor A. Mirelman, "The Semana Trágica of 1919 and the Jews in Argentina," *Jewish Social Studies* 37 (Jan. 1975): 72–73.

31 Clodomiro Araújo Salvadores, Secretary-General of the Liga Patriótica Argentina, interview, Nov. 3, 1977; *La Fronda*, Jan. 12 and Mar. 24, 1920; *La Protesta*, Jan. 20, 1920. Examples of brigade formation are found throughout the press.

32 *La Prensa*, Jan. 30; Feb. 2, 4, and 28; Mar. 31, 1919.

33 Liga Patriótica Argentina, *Estatutos* (Buenos Aires, 1919), pp. 11, 18–23.

34 Ibid., pp. 23–29.

35 *La Vanguardia*, May 17, 1919; James M. Diehl, *Paramilitary Politics in Weimar Germany* (Bloomington, Ind., 1977), p. 57.

36 "Estatutos de la Liga Patriótica Argentina, Gualeguaychú," manuscript, n.d., Julio Irazusta Papers, Notebook 1 (Las Casuarinas, Entre Ríos).

37 *La Prensa*, Feb. 2 and Apr. 6, 1919; Sumner Welles to Jordan H. Stabler, Apr. 25, 1919, Daily Diary, U.S. Dept. of State, 835.00/185.

38 On Carlés see *La Prensa*, Oct. 26, 1946; Pedro P. Maglione Jaimes, "Una figura señera—Manuel Carlés," *La Nación*, Jan. 12, 1969; Newspaper clippings, Archivo de *La Prensa*, File 20137.

39 *La Prensa*, Feb. 4, 1919. The following agreed on Carlés's Radical affiliation: Rouquié, *Poder militar*, p. 144; Zuleta, *El nacionalismo*, 1: 193; Robbins to Secretary of State, Aug. 6, 1918, Dispatch 641, U.S. Dept. of State, 835.00/154. Rock concluded that Carlés's origins were "conservative" but that he was sympathetic to the UCR, in *Politics in Argentina*, p. 183. His obituary in *La Prensa*, Oct. 26, 1946, specifically indicated that Carlés did not belong to any party after 1912. *La Voz del Interior* (Córdoba), Dec. 12, 1919, and *La*

Protesta, Jan. 13, 1920, noted Carlés's connections to the Conservative party and *régimen*.

40 Liga Patriótica Argentina, *Discurso pronunciado por el Dr. Manuel Carlés ante la honorable Sociedad de Beneficencia el 26 de mayo de 1919 en el acto de la distribución de los Premios a la Virtud* (Buenos Aires, 1919), pp. 3–9. Carlés's later statements are in Liga Patriótica Argentina, *Catecismo de la doctrina patria* (Buenos Aires, 1921), p. 14; Liga Patriótica Argentina, Comisión de Bellas Artes, Brigadas de Señoras de la Liga Patriótica Argentina, *Discursos pronunciados en el acto inaugural y veredicto del Jurado de la Tercera Exposición Nacional de Tejidos y Bordados 1–15 julio 1922* (Buenos Aires, 1922), p. 7.

41 Liga Patriótica Argentina, *Octavo Congreso Nacionalista organizado por la Liga Patriótica Argentina* (Buenos Aires, 1927), pp. 52–53; Liga Patriótica Argentina, *Sexto Congreso Nacionalista de Trabajadores organizado por la Liga Patriótica Argentina* (Buenos Aires, 1925), p. 44.

42 Font, *La mujer*, p. 163; Liga, *Octavo Congreso*, p. 57.

43 Liga, *Estatutos*, p. 11; Liga Patriótica Argentina, *Declaración de principios, organización y propósitos de los Soviets Argentinos: Con introducción y notas marginales del sentido común por la Liga Patriótica Argentina* (Buenos Aires, 1920), p. 16.

44 *La Prensa*, Apr. 15, May 13 and 25, 1919. The daily press reported extensively on League communications with such groups, brigade formation, and activities.

45 *El Pueblo*, June 30–July 1, July 21–22, 1919; *La Fronda*, Oct. 8, Nov. 1, 1919; *La Nación*, Nov. 4, 1919.

46 *La Voz del Interior*, Oct. 23, 1919.

47 Liga Patriótica Argentina, *Tercer Congreso de Trabajadores de la Liga Patriótica Argentina* (Buenos Aires, 1922), pp. 327–28.

48 *La Fronda*, Aug. 10, 1920; *El Pueblo*, Aug. 10, 1919.

49 *El Pueblo*, Aug. 15, 1919; Hobart A. Spalding, Jr., *Organized Labor in Latin America: Historical Case Studies of Workers in Dependent Societies* (New York, 1977), p. 65. League men and women are compared extensively in McGee, "Gender Roles."

50 *La Prensa*, Jan. 12 and 31, 1920; *La Nación*, Aug. 13, 1920; *La Capital* (Rosario), Jan. 26, 1921.

51 The Teachers' statutes were mentioned in *La Prensa*, Jan. 8, 1920. I found no mention of statutes for brigades of Señoras or Señoritas, unlike male brigades.

52 *La Protesta*, Oct. 29, 1919.

53 *La Prensa*, Apr. 18, 1919.

54 Stimson to Secretary of State, May 8, 1919, Dispatch no. 810, U.S. Dept. of State, 835.00/171.

55 *Caras y Caretas* no. 1077 (May 25, 1919).

56 *Review of the River Plate*, May 30, 1919; *La Prensa*, May 25, 1919; Rock, *Politics in Argentina*, pp. 195–96.

57 *La Fronda*, Nov. 2 and 28, 1919.

58 *La Fronda*, Dec. 28, 1920; Liga Patriótica Argentina, *Primero de Mayo Argentino: Conmemoración del Pronunciamiento de Urquiza en Entre Ríos* (Buenos Aires, 1921), p. 76 (for 1921); Liga, *Solemne homenaje*, p. 18 (1922); Liga, *Sexto Congreso*, p. 35 (1925); Liga, *Octavo Congreso*, p. 409 (1927). Population figures were found in Vásquez-Presedo, *Estadísticas*, 2: 19.

59 Liga Patriótica Argentina, Brigada 19 de la Capital Federal, Libro de Actas, 1926–30 (Liga Patriótica office, Buenos Aires), did not mention the number of brigade members, but its entry for May 18, 1927, listed fifteen officers. According to *La Voz del Interior*, Oct. 23–26, 1919, the Córdoba brigades of men and women had 275 and 550 members, respectively, but it is not clear whether these brigades were typical. Press notices on League activities only listed brigade officers, not members.

60 Donna J. Guy, "The Rural Working Class in Nineteenth-Century Argentina: Forced Plantation Labor in Tucumán," *Latin American Research Review* 13 (1978): 135–57; William J. Fleming, "The Cultural Determinants of Entrepreneurship and Economic Development: A Case Study of Mendoza Province, Argentina, 1861–1914," *Journal of Economic History* 39 (Mar. 1979): 211–24.

61 Walter, *The Socialist Party*, p. 173.

62 Nevertheless, Rouquié erred when he cited Rojas's Radical affiliation as evidence of the "undeniable" link between the Youth Committee (and the League) and the ruling party, in *Poder militar*, p. 145. As already noted, Rojas did not join the party until the 1930s. I agree with Héctor J. Iñigo Carrera, who noted in *La experiencia radical, 1916–1922*, 2 vols. (Buenos Aires, 1980), 1: 213, that on the surface the relationship between the League and Radicalism was generally not conflictive but sometimes became tense.

63 Liga Patriótica Argentina, Brigada 19 y 20, *La verdad de la Liga Patriótica Argentina* (Buenos Aires, 1950), pp. 6–7.

64 Romariz, *La semana trágica*, p. 171; Rock, *Politics in Argentina*, p. 183; Rouquié, *Poder militar*, p. 146. The major newspapers also referred to these meetings daily.

65 Welles to Stabler, Apr. 25, 1919, Daily Diary, U.S. Dept. of State,

835.00/185; *La Vanguardia*, June 11, 1919; *La Protesta*, Jan. 13, 1920; Costa in Argentina, Congreso Nacional, *Diario de sesiones de la Cámara de Diputados* (Buenos Aires, 1919–32), 6 (Feb. 23, 1921; in 1920 series): 389 (hereinafter, *Diputados*).

66 Agote in *Diputados* 1 (June 10, 1919): 442; Liga, *La verdad*, p. 7.

67 *La Prensa*, May 24, 1919.

68 *Diputados* 1 (June 10, 1919): 429–43. Nicolás Repetto, in *Mi paso por la política*, 2 vols. (Buenos Aires, 1956–57), 1: 213, incorrectly recalled the year as 1918; Navarro, in *Los nacionalistas*, p. 39, also erred in citing the year as 1916. Other Radicals such as Valentín Vergara also supported the League in Congress; see next chapter.

69 *Review of the River Plate*, July 25, 1919; also cited in Rock, *Politics in Argentina*, p. 193.

70 *La Vanguardia*, Mar. 2, 1919 and June 11, 1919.

71 Rock, *Politics in Argentina*, pp. 183, 198; Romariz, *La semana trágica*, p. 171; *El Pueblo*, July 21–22, 24, 1919.

72 On military grievances see Rouquié, *Poder militar*, pp. 151–57; Potash, *The Army*, pp. 9–12. Juan V. Orona did not, however, mention the League in *La Logia Militar que enfrentó a Hipólito Yrigoyen* (Buenos Aires, 1965). Nor did the members of the San Martín Lodge, the first explicitly anti-Yrigoyenist military group named by Orona, belong to the League.

73 Liga, *La verdad*, p. 8. On the League's effect and Yrigoyen's shift to the right, see Rock, *Politics in Argentina*, pp. 197–98; Walter, *The Socialist Party*, pp. 157, 160; Ambassador J. W. Riddle to Secretary of State, May 10, 1922, Dispatch no. 44, U.S. Dept. of State, 835.00/298; *Review of the River Plate*, June 13, 1919.

74 The year 1920 marked the first annual congress, while after 1928 the congresses declined in importance, and their proceedings are not available for each year. I thank Néstor Tomás Auza and José Luis de Imaz for checking my list of League members and confirming their class backgrounds, formulated from Part IV of the bibliography.

75 Smith, *Argentina and the Failure of Democracy*, p. 31.

76 Darío Cantón, *El parlamento argentino en épocas de cambio: 1890, 1916, y 1946* (Buenos Aires, 1966), p. 47.

77 *La Vanguardia*, May 24, 1924.

78 Liga, *Primero de Mayo*, p. 75.

79 *La Fronda*, Feb. 9, 1920.

80 *La Vanguardia*, Apr. 1, 1919; San Salvador brigade officers in *La Fronda*, Nov. 16, 1920. Indications of brigade members' professions are also found in *La Fronda*, Apr. 11, 1920; Araújo, interview; Liga,

Primero de Mayo, p. 75; *La Nación*, Mar. 20, 1921. Brigade members' names were not listed in the press or congresses.

81 *La Protesta*, Jan. 31 and Apr. 24, 1920; *La Fronda*, July 1, 1920; *Primer Congreso de Trabajadores de la Liga Patriótica Argentina* (Buenos Aires, 1920), pp. 221–22; Juan J. Linz, "Some Notes Toward a Comparative Study of Fascism in Sociological Historical Perspective," in Laqueur, *Fascism*, pp. 63, 68.

82 *La Fronda*, Nov. 1, 1919; *La Voz del Interior*, Oct. 24, 1919. Bayer, in *Los vengadores*, 1: 48, claimed that the female brigades consisted of upper-class officers and lower-class members, but he did not document this assertion.

83 The best sources for family relationships were the social registers and Carlos Calvo, *Nobiliario del Antiguo Virreynato del Río de la Plata*, 6 vols. (Buenos Aires, 1936–43). "Close relationships" include those of the nuclear family, aunts and uncles, nieces and nephews, grandparents and grandchildren, first cousins, and brothers- and sisters-in-law.

84 Liga, *Tercer Congreso*, p. 327.

85 Liga Patriótica Argentina, *Cuarto Congreso Nacionalista de la Liga Patriótica Argentina* (Buenos Aires, 1923), p. 470.

Chapter 4

1 Stimson to Secretary of State, May 8, 1919, Dispatch no. 810, U.S. Dept. of State, 835.00/171; *La Vanguardia*, May 5, 1921.

2 *Los Principios* (Córdoba), Nov. 1, 1921.

3 Ibid., May 23, 25, 27, 1920; *La Voz del Interior*, May 25 and 27, 1920.

4 *La Vanguardia*, Nov. 6, 1921.

5 *La Fronda*, Nov. 24, 1919, and Jan. 1, 1920; *La Prensa*, Jan. 15–25, 27–28, 1920; *Review of the River Plate*, Jan. 23, 1920; *La Protesta*, Jan. 21–22, 1920.

6 *La Vanguardia*, Oct. 31, 1920 and Dec. 25, 1921.

7 Ibid., May 17, 1921.

8 For examples of these actions and proposals, see Argentina, Policía de la Capital Federal, *Memoria. Antecedentes y datos estadísticos correspondientes al año 1921* (Buenos Aires, 1922), pp. 79–80; *La Fronda*, Dec. 5 and 22, 1919, and Oct. 17, 1920; Liga Patriótica Argentina, *Homenaje a la Prefectura General de Puertos: Distribución de 'Medallos al Mérito.' Discurso pronunciado por el Señor Jefe de Puertos Don José Riobón* (Buenos Aires, 1923).

9 *La Fronda*, Nov. 21 and 25, Dec. 11, 1919; *La Prensa*, Mar. 22, 1920.

10 *La Fronda*, Mar. 22–23, Apr. 12, May 7, 1921.

11 For examples of student anti-League sentiments, see *La Vanguardia*, Aug. 14, 1921; Gabriel del Mazo, ed., *La reforma universitaria*, 6 vols. (Buenos Aires, 1926–27), 5: 80–83, 155–62. On League opposition to student organizations, see *Los Principios*, May 31, 1919; *La Nación*, Nov. 22, 1919; *La Voz del Interior*, Dec. 17, 1921.

12 For example, see *Review of the River Plate*, July 30, 1920.

13 *La Fronda*, Mar. 15, 1920; Liga, *Tercer Congreso*, pp. 153–54; *La Prensa*, Jan. 15, 1920. For examples of "job placement," see *La Vanguardia*, Dec. 15, 1921; *La Protesta*, June 14, 1923.

14 *La Prensa*, Jan. 25, 1920; *Boletín de Servicios de la Asociación del Trabajo* 1, no. 1 (Feb. 5, 1920): 1 (hereinafter, BSAT); *La Vanguardia*, May 16, 1919.

15 Riddle to Secretary of State, Apr. 10, 1922, Dispatch no. 25, U.S. Dept. of State, 835.5043/1; Shipley, "A Social History," pp. 293–97, 317–18; Asociación del Trabajo, *¿Qué es la Asociación del Trabajo?* (Buenos Aires, 1921); *La Vanguardia*, May 15, 1919; *La Protesta*, Apr. 29, 1922; Liga, *La verdad*, pp. 5–6.

16 *La Prensa*, Feb. 15–16, 1920; *La Fronda*, Jan. 6–7, 1921; *Review of the River Plate*, June 3, 1921.

17 Unless otherwise stated, my reconstruction of the two strikes and surrounding events from May 25 to June 7 is based on the following: *La Vanguardia*, May 26–30, June 2–4, 6–7, 1921 (for the most detailed version); *Review of the River Plate*, June 3, 1921; *La Fronda*, May 27–30, 1921; BSAT 2, no. 33 (June 5, 1921): 290, 292–93, 295–97; Rock, *Politics in Argentina*, pp. 184–87, 209–15; Shipley, "A Social History," pp. 298–301; Chargé D'Affaires Ad Interim Donald White to Secretary of State, June 1, 1921, Dispatch no. 1567, U.S. Dept. of State, 835.00/237.

18 *La Vanguardia*, June 9, 1921.

19 Marotta, *Movimiento sindical*, 2: 259–63; BSAT 2, no. 31 (May 5, 1921): 198, and no. 32 (May 20, 1921): 357; Asociación del Trabajo, *Memoria y Balance de la Asociación del Trabajo, correspondiente al ejercicio de 1920–1921* (Buenos Aires, 1921), p. 19.

20 Unsigned, "Argentina," Feb. 23, 1921, U.S. Dept. of State, 835.00/326.

21 Asociación, *Memoria y Balance*, pp. 20–21; Bayer, *Los vengadores*, 2: 85.

22 *La Vanguardia*, July 13 and 16, 1921.

23 Ibid., Aug. 14 and 26, 1921.

24 Ibid., Aug. 26 and Dec. 29, 1921.

25 Ibid., Feb. 16 and May 5, 1921; *La Protesta*, Apr. 29, 1922; Agustín

S. Muzio in *Diputados* 4 (Aug. 31, 1920): 652; Shipley, "A Social History," p. 317.

26 On La Forestal and labor mobilization in the Argentine northeast, see Gaston Gori, *La Forestal (La tragedia del quebracho colorado)*, 2d ed. (Buenos Aires, 1974). Rock noted in *Politics in Argentina*, p. 214, that before 1921 the League primarily opposed peripheral groups such as Jews and maximalists; only after that point did it become more and more explicitly antiunion. The League's involvement in the northeast and in the grain zone, however, invalidates his conclusion, as do League antilabor remarks in *Primer Congreso*.

27 Unless otherwise noted, information on conditions in Las Palmas and events there through August 1920 comes from: Crisanto Domínguez, *Rebelión en la selva* (Buenos Aires, 1948), pp. 27–30, 42–64; Crisanto Domínguez, *Tanino (Memorias de un hachero)* (Buenos Aires, 1956), pp. 111–12; *La Nación*, Aug. 10 and 12, 1920; and esp. *La Vanguardia*, Aug. 12, 14, 17, 19, 24, 26, 30, 1920. Also see Ramón Tissera, "Revolución social en la selva," *Todo Es Historia* no. 12 (Apr. 1968): 64–75. Company directors are named in W. H. Morton Cameron, ed., *Enciclopedia Comercial (Encyclopedia Commercial): Unico órgano oficial, anual o bienal, de la British and Latin American Chamber of Commerce. Argentina, Brasil, Chile, Perú, Uruguay, Suplemento Británico* (London, 1922), p. 305.

28 *La Fronda*, May 9, 1920.

29 *La Vanguardia*, Aug. 19 and 30, 1920; Fernando de Andréis in *Diputados* 4 (Aug. 31, 1920): 648.

30 *La Nación*, Aug. 26, 1920; Mario Bravo in *Diputados* 4 (Aug. 25, 1920): 488–89.

31 On these events and the strike's conclusion see Tissera, "Revolución," 74–75; *La Vanguardia*, Sept. 2, 10, 12, 1920, and Jan. 17, 1921; *La Nación*, Aug. 21, 1920; Gori, *La Forestal*, pp. 175–93.

32 José García Pulido, *El Gran Chaco y su imperio Las Palmas* (Buenos Aires, 1951), pp. 134–44; Juan Antonio Solari, *Parias argentinas: Explotación y miseria de los trabajadores en el norte del país* (Buenos Aires, 1940), pp. 13–17, 54–61.

33 On agrarian protest and the administration, 1917–21, see Solberg, "Rural Unrest," pp. 29–44.

34 Solberg, "Rural Unrest," pp. 40–43; Solberg, "Farm Workers," pp. 134–35; G. Cuadrado Hernández, "La rebelión de los braceros," *Todo Es Historia* no. 185 (Oct. 1982): 80–82; Marotta, *Movimiento sindical*, 2: 284–87.

35 *La Prensa*, Jan. 26 and Feb. 19, 1920.

36 Cuadrado, "La rebelión," pp. 82–86; *La Fronda*, Feb. 3 and Apr. 11, 1920; *Review of the River Plate*, Jan. 23, 1920.

37 *La Protesta*, June 14, 1922. Also see Serafín Fernández, *Recuerdos de la vida pampera (La semana trágica de enero de 1919)* (Paris, 1962), pp. 21–22.

38 *El Pueblo*, Dec. 3, 1920.

39 *La Fronda*, Jan. 10, 1921.

40 Gori, *La Forestal*, p. 242. Also see Cuadrado, "La rebelión," p. 82; Marotta, *Movimiento sindical*, 2: 262–63.

41 The Villaguay brigade was represented in the First Congress of May 1920.

42 On the events involving Axentzoff, see *La Fronda*, Feb. 27, 1921; *La Vanguardia*, Feb. 18, 1921. Unless otherwise stated, the information on Villaguay comes from the detailed account in *La Vanguardia*, Feb. 15–21, 24–28, 1921.

43 *La Fronda*, Feb. 27, 1921.

44 Andréis in *Diputados* 6 (Feb. 23, 1921; in 1920 series): 360.

45 *La Fronda*, Feb. 27, 1921.

46 *La Nación*, Feb. 14, Mar. 6 and 27, Apr. 12 and 16, 1921.

47 *La Nación*, Feb. 17 and 19, 1921; *Diputados* 6 (Feb. 23, 1921; in 1920 series): 358–63. The entire debate on the episode is found in *Diputados* 6 (Feb. 18 and 23, 1921; in 1920 series): 311–16, 355–92.

48 *La Nación*, Mar. 11, 1921.

49 *La Fronda*, Mar. 3, 1921.

50 Ibid., Mar. 14, 1921; *La Nación*, Mar. 2 and 14, 1921; Héctor González Iramaín, in *Diputados* 6 (Feb. 23, 1921; in 1920 series): 370. Members of brigade juntas were listed in the press and in Liga, *Primero de Mayo*.

51 *La Vanguardia*, Feb. 20–21, 1921.

52 On the background to events in Gualeguaychú, see *La Nación*, Mar. 23 and 31, 1921; Liga, *Primero de Mayo*, pp. 61–67; President of the Provincial Labor Office, Dr. E. Zacarías Castelltort, to Minister of Government, Professor Richard Poitevin, May 16, 1921, in Provincia de Entre Ríos, *Memoria de los Ministerios de Gobierno, Hacienda, Justicia e Instrucción Pública, 1918–1922*, 3 vols. (Parana, 1922), 2: 519–22.

53 *La Fronda* mentioned the Gualeguaychú brigade as early as Nov. 15 and Dec. 14, 1919.

54 "Estatutos de Gualeguaychú," pp. 1–2.

55 On this celebration and preparations for it, see Liga Patriótica Argentina, *Humanitarismo práctico: La Liga Patriótica Argentina en Gualeguaychú* (Buenos Aires, 1921).

56 On Sixto Vela see *La Vanguardia*, May 16, 1921.

57 Castelltort to Poitevin, in Entre Ríos, *Memoria*, 2: 521.

58 *La Nación*, Mar. 10 and 26, 1921; *La Fronda*, Mar. 19, 1921.

59 *La Nación*, Apr. 19, 1921. On the details of the ceremony and the League's view of May Day, see Liga, *Primero de Mayo*, esp. pp. 57–60.

60 *La Vanguardia*, May 10, 1921. On the following May Day events, see *La Vanguardia*, May 2–4, 6, and July 12, 1921; *La Fronda*, May 4, 1921; Gualeguaychú Police Chief I. J. Lahitte, to Poitevin, May 2 and 4, 1921, in Entre Ríos, *Memoria*, 3: 1026–27; *La Prensa*, May 2–3, 1921; (eyewitness) Antonio A. Giménez, interview, June 1977.

61 Liga, *Primero de Mayo*, pp. 85–86.

62 Governor Celestino Marcó to Sixto Vela, May 10, 1921, in Entre Ríos, *Memoria*, 3: 1029–30; and Castelltort to Poitevin, in *Memoria*, 2: 521, 523–34.

63 Vela to Marcó, May 5, 1921, and Marcó's statements, in ibid., 3: 1029, 1031–33, 1035–36; *La Vanguardia*, May 2–3, 8, 1921; *La Fronda*, May 3, 1921.

64 *La Vanguardia*, May 8, 10, 16, 27; June 15, 18, 22, 24, 29; July 6, 12, 18; Nov. 26, 1921; Marotta, *Movimiento sindical*, 3: 39.

65 *Diputados* 5 (Oct. 29, 1921): 281.

66 *La Vanguardia*, June 15 and 24, July 6, 1921.

67 *La Nación*, Mar. 9 and Apr. 25, 1921; *La Vanguardia*, Aug. 1, 1921.

68 Cuadrado, "La rebelión," 94; *La Voz del Interior*, Dec. 27, 1919; *Los Principios*, Jan. 1, 1920.

69 *La Voz del Interior*, Dec. 5, 1920. The federation was probably affiliated with one of the FORAS.

70 *El Pueblo*, Feb. 19 and 21–22, Mar. 3–4, 1921; *Los Principios*, Nov. 11, 1921.

71 *Los Principios*, Nov. 10 and 16, 1921.

72 Ibid., Dec. 2–3, 1921; *La Prensa*, Dec. 3 and 6, 1921; Bayer, *Los vengadores*, 1: 50–51.

73 For information on this episode I depended on Bayer, "Jacinto Arauz." Also see *La Vanguardia*, Dec. 23, 1921; *La Prensa*, Dec. 10–11, 13, 1921.

74 Iscaro, *Movimiento sindical*, 2: 189–91; Vásquez-Presedo, *Estadísticas*, 2: 196, 203–5; Susana Fiorito, "Un drama olvidado: Las huelgas patagónicas de 1920–1921," *Polémica* no. 54 (1971): 92–96; Liga Pa-

triótica Argentina, *El culto de la Patagonia: Sucesos de Santa Cruz* (Buenos Aires, 1922), pp. 14–16.

75 José María Borrero, *La patagonia trágica*, 2d ed. (Buenos Aires, 1957), pp. 63–65; Carlés in Liga, *Sucesos*, p. 27.

76 *La Prensa*, Jan. 28, 1920.

77 *La Vanguardia*, Oct. 23, 1919; Carl Solberg, *Oil and Nationalism in Argentina: A History* (Stanford, Calif., 1979), pp. 66–67.

78 Iscaro, *Movimiento sindical*, 2: 189; *La Vanguardia*, Feb. 27, 1920; *La Prensa*, Jan. 27, 1920; Solberg, *Oil and Nationalism*, p. 68.

79 Liga, *Sucesos*, pp. 9, 25; *La Fronda*, Mar. 30, 1921; Bayer, *Los vengadores*, 2: 84–85, passim, on free labor.

80 Stimson to Secretary of State, Feb. 2, 1921, Dispatch no. 1455, U.S. Dept. of State, 835.00/219; Bayer, *Los vengadores*, 2: 142; *La Fronda*, Mar. 30, 1921; *Review of the River Plate*, Mar. 18, 1921.

81 *La Fronda*, Feb. 8 and 23, 1921.

82 Bayer, *Los vengadores*, 2: 72–76; *La Vanguardia*, Dec. 7, 1921.

83 Bayer, *Los vengadores*, 3: 231–40, 244–49.

84 Liga, *Solemne homenaje*, p. 20; *La Vanguardia*, Nov. 23, 1921; Iscaro, *Movimiento sindical*, 2: 193–94; Liga, *Sucesos*, pp. 29–30, 45.

85 *La Protesta*, June 14, 1922; Bayer, *Los vengadores*, 3: 43–47; White to Secretary of State, Jan. 16, 1922, Dispatch no. 1812, U.S. Dept. of State, 835.00/273; Rouquié, *Poder militar*, p. 149.

86 Bayer, *Los vengadores*, 2: 350–52, 3: 87–88, 143–50; Liga, *Sucesos*, p. 42; Liga Patriótica Argentina, *Campaña de Santa Cruz. Homenaje al Ejército y Armada* (Buenos Aires, 1922). These banquets were portrayed in the film *La patagonia rebelde* (Rebellion in Patagonia, 1974), by Héctor Olivera, distributed in the United States by Unifilm, New York.

87 Rouquié, *Poder militar*, p. 149; debate in *Diputados* 5 (Feb. 1, 1922; in 1921 series): 54–110.

88 Osvaldo Bayer, "Los vengadores de la Patagonia trágica," *Todo Es Historia* no. 15 (July 1968): 69–85.

89 *La Protesta*, Feb. 15, 1923, and Feb. 6, 1924.

90 Liga, *Sucesos*, p. 30; *La Protesta*, Jan. 3, 1923; *La Nación*, Feb. 4, 1922; Liga Patriotica Argentina, *Congreso General de Territorios Nacionales* (Buenos Aires, 1927).

91 Liga, *Primero de Mayo*, p. 75.

92 Vásquez-Presedo, *Estadísticas*, 2: 47; Rock, *Politics in Argentina*, pp. 190, 214; Shipley, "A Social History," pp. 292, 302–5.

93 Vásquez-Presedo, *Estadísticas*, 2: 46; Shipley, "A Social History," p. 75.

Chapter 5

1 Walter, *The Socialist Party*, pp. 159–60, 168; Luna, *Yrigoyen*, pp. 259–60.

2 *La Fronda*, Oct. 12, 1919.

3 Andrea, *Pensamiento cristiano*, pp. 84–87, 98–99; Juan Carlos Zurretti, *Nueva historia eclesiástica argentina. Del Concilio de Trento al Vaticano Segundo* (Buenos Aires, 1972), p. 393; *Caras y Caretas* no. 1073 (Apr. 26, 1919).

4 Andrea, *Pensamiento cristiano*, pp. 81–91, 105–8, 135; *La Fronda*, Oct.–Nov. 1919; Comité Ejecutivo de la Gran Colecta Nacional, *La paz social* (Buenos Aires, 1919).

5 Comité, *La paz social*; *La Fronda*, Oct. 2, 1919; Andrea, *La perturbación*, p. 81.

6 Andrea, *La perturbación*, pp. 111–13, 165; Elisa Esposito, "La Federación de Asociaciones Católicas de Empleadas," *Boletín de la Acción Católica Argentina* (Apr. 1951): 109–12; Archivo de *La Prensa*, File 46948.

7 Liga, *Solemne homenaje*, p. 35.

8 *La Fronda*, July 2, 1920. I found nineteen schools mentioned in League publications and the press; Liga, *La verdad*, p. 11, offered the figure of fifty schools in 1950, which I could not verify. Pictures of the schools found in the press and the Archivo Gráfico de la Nación, and my interview with María Luján Baylac de Eizaguirre, former chief of social services, Grafa Factory, July 6, 1981, however, confirmed the continuation of these projects long after the period under study.

9 Liga Patriótica Argentina, Comisión de Señoritas de la Liga Patriótica Argentina, *Sus escuelas de obreras en las fábricas* (Buenos Aires, 1922), pp. 1–2, 7, 13; *La Fronda*, Jan. 27, 1921; Liga Patriótica Argentina, Comisión Central de Señoritas, *Memoria de diez escuelas obreras, 1924-mayo-1925* (Buenos Aires, 1925), p. 9.

10 Campillo in Liga, *Sus escuelas*, p. 4; Gallegos in Liga, *Solemne homenaje*, p. 18.

11 Sayans in Liga Patriótica Argentina, *Quinto Congreso Nacionalista de Trabajadores organizado por la Liga Patriótica Argentina* (Buenos Aires, 1924), pp. 458–59; Liga, *Memoria 1924–1925*, pp. 45–46, 50; Liga, *La verdad*, pp. 11–12, 14.

12 Carlés in Liga, *Octavo Congreso*, p. 57; Liga, *La verdad*, pp. 12–13; Selles in Liga Patriótica Argentina, *Noveno Congreso Nacionalista*

organizado por la Liga Patriótica Argentina (Buenos Aires, 1928),
pp. 553–54; Sayans in Liga, *Quinto Congreso,* p. 459.

13 Liga, *Sus escuelas,* pp. 12, 20; *La Nación,* July 5, 1920.

14 Liga Patriótica Argentina, Comisión Central de Señoritas, *Memoria, 1927-mayo-1928* (Buenos Aires, 1928), p. 5.

15 The Señoritas' and Señoras' projects were described in the daily press and League publications. Also see Brigada 19, Libro de Actas, Sept. 28, 1927 and Apr. 16, 1928; *La Capital,* Dec. 9, 1919; Liga Patriótica Argentina, *Acción civilizadora de las escuelas de la Liga Patriótica Argentina* (Buenos Aires, 1921). Women of the Spanish Falange conducted very similar projects, according to María Teresa Gallegos Méndez, *Mujer, Falange y Franquismo* (Madrid, 1983).

16 *La Fronda,* July 25, 1920; Liga, *Tercera Exposición,* pp. 1–5; Liga Patriótica Argentina, *Discursos pronunciados en el acto inaugural y veredicto del Jurado de la Cuarta Exposición Nacional de Tejidos y Bordados, 4–20 agosto 1923* (Buenos Aires, 1923), p. 2.

17 On the feminist struggle to revise the civil code, see Carlson, "Feminism and Reform," pp. 294–96.

18 On male activities see, in addition to the daily press, Liga, *La verdad,* p. 15; *La Fronda,* Oct. 20, 1919, Feb. 12 and Dec. 14, 1920; Liga Patriótica Argentina, *Acción civilizadora de las escuelas de la Liga Patriótica Argentina, 23 abril 1922* (Buenos Aires, 1922); Brigada 19, Libro de Actas, May 18, 1927 and April 1, 1930.

19 Liga, *Tercera Exposición,* p. 6; Liga, *Humanitarismo práctico,* p. 18; Liga, *Primer Congreso,* pp. 43–44.

20 Liga, *Tercer Congreso,* pp. 23, 29; Liga, *Catecismo,* pp. 15–16; Liga Patriótica Argentina, *Definición de la Liga Patriótica Argentina (guía del buen sentido social)* (Buenos Aires, 1921), pp. 20–21.

21 Liga, *Catecismo,* pp. 14–17; *Tercer Congreso,* p. 29.

22 *Los Principios,* May 8, 1920.

23 Liga Patriótica Argentina, *Séptimo Congreso Nacionalista de la Liga Patriótica Argentina* (Buenos Aires, 1926), pp. 60–61.

24 Liga, *Primer Congreso,* pp. 41, 197–98; Gutiérrez in Liga, *Octavo Congreso,* p. 291; *La Protesta,* May 24, 1924; García Torres in Liga, *Cuarto Congreso,* p. 36. I provide biographical information on individual League spokesmen when it is available.

25 Cano in Liga, *Tercer Congreso,* p. 35; Max H. Kele, *Nazis and Workers. National Socialist Appeals to German Labor, 1919–1933* (Chapel Hill, N.C., 1972), pp. 10, 43–44.

26 Carlés in Liga, *Primero de Mayo,* p. 37.

27 Liga, *Tercer Congreso*, p. 26; Liga Patriótica Argentina, *Restauración de la Moral Argentina, 22 May 1930* (Buenos Aires, 1930), pp. 9–10; Liga, *Humanitarismo práctico*, pp. 19, 31.

28 Liga, *Quinto Congreso*, pp. 35–36; Liga, *Primer Congreso*, pp. 38–40.

29 Maglione, "Una figura señera."

30 The League named these foreign organizations in daily press notices, 1919–21. Also see White to Secretary of State, May 2, 1921, Dispatch no. 1547, U.S. Dept. of State, 835.00/226. The nontranslated names are as follows, respectively: Liga Patriótica Militar, Freie Vereinigung der Arbeiter, Ligue Civique, Asociacion Patriotique, Liga Patriótica de Unidad y Defensa Nacional, Sociedad Defensa Agricola, União Nacional, Liga Nacionalista Brasileira. Civil guards are discussed in Diehl, *Paramilitary Politics*; and David Large, "The Politics of Law and Order: Counterrevolutionary Self-Defense Organizations in Central Europe, 1918–1923" (Ph.D. Diss., Univ. of California, Berkeley, 1976).

31 *La Nación*, Aug. 7, 1920.

32 Stimson to Acting Secretary of State, Dec. 21, 1920, Dispatch no. 1422; Attorney General A. Mitchell Palmer to Secretary of State, Feb. 16, 1921; Alvey A. Adler to Stimson, Mar. 3, 1921, U.S. Dept. of State, 835.00/L62–L62/1. On Palmer and the Red Scare, see Robert K. Murray, *Red Scare. A Study in National Hysteria, 1919–1920* (New York, 1964).

33 Liga, *Octavo Congreso*, p. 19.

34 M. L. Lagos in Liga Patriótica Argentina, *El programa de la Liga Patriótica Argentina y la educación por el ejemplo. (Como una consagración del concepto Patria)* (Buenos Aires, 1923), p. 11.

35 Andrea, *La perturbación*, p. 215; Serralunga Langhi in Liga, *Primer Congreso*, pp. 166, 172; Felipe Haynes in Liga, *Cuarto Congreso*, pp. 65–66; Carlés in Liga, *Territorios Nacionales*, p. 41, and in Liga, *Quinto Congreso*, pp. 39–40.

36 Liga, *Primer Congreso*, pp. 201–3.

37 Ibid., pp. 48, 205–6.

38 Liga, *Cuarto Congreso*, pp. 355–67.

39 Liga, *Primer Congreso*, pp. 166–68.

40 Liga, *Séptimo Congreso*, pp. 177–90.

41 Liga, *Noveno Congreso*, p. 79.

42 Yalour in Liga, *Cuarto Congreso*, p. 472; Torres in Liga, *Cuarto Congreso*, pp. 440–45; also see Lagos in Liga, *El programa*, p. 12.

43 Liga, *Octavo Congreso*, pp. 203–6. Also see M. F. Dirube in Liga, *Territorios Nacionales*, p. 115.

44 Pintos in Liga, *Cuarto Congreso*, pp. 330–34. Also see C. A. Henderson in Liga, *Territorios Nacionales*, p. 95; Alberto García Torres in Liga, *Tercer Congreso*, p. 116; Alberto Castex, *Cuarto Congreso*, p. 131.

45 Peme in Liga, *Tercer Congreso*, pp. 109–13. On the changing attitudes of the agro-exporting elite, see Miguel Murmis and Juan Carlos Portantiero, *Estudios sobre los orígenes del peronismo* (Buenos Aires, 1971); Eduardo F. Jorge, *Industria y concentración económica (desde principios de siglo hasta el peronismo)* (Buenos Aires, 1971).

46 Martín in Liga, *Primer Congreso*, pp. 173–74; Oyuela in Liga, *Cuarto Congreso*, pp. 268–71.

47 Liga, *Primer Congreso*, p. 198; Pallejá in Liga, *Cuarto Congreso*, pp. 82–107; Oyuela in *Cuarto Congreso*, pp. 268–71. On corporatism see, among many other works, Laqueur, *Fascism*; Charles S. Maier, *Recasting Bourgeois Europe. Stabilization in France, Germany, and Italy in the Decade after World War I* (Princeton, N.J., 1975); Paul W. Drake, "Corporatism and Functionalism in Modern Chilean Politics," JLAS 10, no. 1 (May 1978): 83–116.

48 Amadeo, *La función social*, pp. 112–23, 143. Tomás Amadeo condemned Fascism in *El falso dilema: Fascismo o Bolcheviquismo* (Buenos Aires, 1939).

49 Liga, *Séptimo Congreso*, p. 61.

50 Liga, *Estatutos*, pp. 19–21; Carlés in Liga, *Noveno Congreso*, pp. 92–93; Ibertis Correa in Liga, *Primer Congreso*, pp. 73–74.

51 Liga, *Primer Congreso*, p. 194.

52 Lagos in Liga, *Sexto Congreso*, pp. 133–37. Also see Isabel Esther Bunge in Liga, *Quinto Congreso*, pp. 117–19; Andrés Barbadillo in Liga, *Primer Congreso*, p. 256.

53 Gutiérrez in Liga, *Sexto Congreso*, pp. 149–51; E. Bradford Burns, *Nationalism in Brazil: A Historical Survey* (New York, 1968), pp. 61–63; Villalta in Liga, *Primer Congreso*, pp. 133–36.

54 Estanislao Zeballos, Augusto Bunge, and Horacio Beccar Varela in "La inmigración después de la guerra," BMSA 8, nos. 85–90 (Jan.–June 1919): 29, 31–35, and 36–37, respectively.

55 Tomás Amadeo and Proto Ordóñez in ibid.: 54 and 84, respectively; Amadeo, *El falso dilema*, pp. 121–22, 135.

56 Carlos Ibarguren in "Encuesta de Vida Nuestra sobre la situación de los judíos en la Argentina," *Vida Nuestra* 7 (Jan. 1919): 173.

57 Juan P. Ramos in ibid.: 177–78.

58 Leopoldo Lugones in ibid.: 145–48.

59 Elkin, *Jews*, pp. 56, 76–77.

60 Liga, *Octavo Congreso*, pp. 84–88.

61 Ayarragaray in Liga, *Noveno Congreso*, p. 475. Also see Carlés in Liga, *Noveno Congreso*, p. 90; Y. Izquierdo Brown in Liga, *Octavo Congreso*, p. 410.

62 Anselmi in Liga, *Primer Congreso*, pp. 189–90; López Cepero in Liga, *Primer Congreso*, pp. 233–35; Luis P. R. Fernández in Liga, *Tercer Congreso*, pp. 186–89.

63 Henderson in Liga, *Primer Congreso*, p. 95; estimates of class sizes in Rock, *Politics in Argentina*, p. 276, and in Richard J. Walter, "Politics, Parties, and Elections in Argentina's Province of Buenos Aires, 1912–42," HAHR 64, no. 4 (Nov. 1984): 712.

64 Liga, *Primer Congreso*, pp. 221–23.

65 *La Vanguardia*, June 15, 1924.

66 Liga, *Catecismo*, pp. 8, 12–13.

67 Liga, *Primer Congreso*, pp. 38–41.

68 Liga, *Primero de Mayo*, pp. 43–45.

69 Ibid., pp. 51 and 109; Carlés in Liga, *Territorios Nacionales*, p. 42; Celestino F. Gutiérrez in Liga, *Octavo Congreso*, pp. 292–96.

70 Liga, *Estatutos*, p. 10; Cranwell in Liga, *Primer Congreso*, p. 66; Juan de Dios Gallegos in Liga, *Solemne homenaje*, p. 8.

71 Liga Patriótica Argentina, *Discurso pronunciado por el presidente de la Liga Patriótica Argentina, Dr. Manuel Carlés en la reunión celebrada por la honorable Junta de Gobierno en honor de los delegados de la Asociación de Empleados de Comercio de Río de Janeiro* (Buenos Aires, 1924). Also see Liga, *Sexto Congreso*, p. 39; *El Pueblo*, Feb. 19, 1921; Liga Patriótica Argentina, *Misión y doctrina de la Liga Patriótica Argentina* (Buenos Aires, 1956), p. 1.

72 Liga, *Primer Congreso*, pp. 40–41.

73 Liga, *Sexto Congreso*, pp. 40–42; Liga, *Séptimo Congreso*, p. 69.

74 Vásquez-Presedo, *Estadísticas*, 2: 19; Darío Cantón, *Materiales para el estudio de la sociología política en la Argentina*, 2 vols. (Buenos Aires, 1968), 1: 98.

75 Vela in Liga, *Primero de Mayo*, p. 41; Saravia Ferré in Liga, *Cuarto Congreso*, pp. 178–79.

76 Liga, *Cuarto Congreso*, p. 32.

77 Liga, *Primer Congreso*, p. 210; *Los Principios*, May 8, 1920; Lagos in Liga, *El programa*, p. 22.

78 Rock, *Politics in Argentina*, pp. 221, 227; Carlés in Liga, *Séptimo Congreso*, pp. 61, 72.

79 Carlés in Liga Patriótica Argentina, *Organización de la soberanía o Escuela de Bienestar* (Buenos Aires, 1928), p. 6; De la Villa

and Ramírez in Liga, *Séptimo Congreso*, pp. 219–20 and 225, respectively.

Chapter 6

1 Liga Patriótica Argentina, *Congreso Nacionalista de Economía Rural organizado por la Liga Patriótica Argentina* (Buenos Aires, 1935), p. 41. This chapter concentrates on the relationship between the League and early "oligarchical" nationalism, and the participation of both groups in the Revolution of 1930. For detailed histories of nationalism, see Zuleta, *El nacionalismo*; Navarro, *Los nacionalistas*.

2 Vásquez-Presedo, *Estadísticas*, 2: 189. On the economy in the 1920s, also see Vásquez-Presedo, 2: 194–95, 203, 210–13; Di Tella and Zymelman, *Los ciclos*, pp. 186–242.

3 Vernon L. Phelps, *The International Economic Position of Argentina* (Philadelphia, 1938), p. 108.

4 Solberg, "The Tariff and Politics," pp. 252–74; Rock, *Politics in Argentina*, pp. 225–26. A tariff had been passed in 1917, but it was not as significant as the one in 1923.

5 Rock, *Politics in Argentina*, pp. 223–24; Vásquez-Presedo, *Estadísticas*, 2: 286.

6 David Rock, "Radical Populism and the Conservative Elite, 1912–1930," in David Rock, ed., *Argentina in the Twentieth Century* (Pittsburgh, 1975), pp. 66–87. Also see Vásquez-Presedo, *Estadísticas*, 2: 286.

7 David Rock, "The Rise of the Argentine Radical Party (the Unión Cívica Radical), 1891–1916," University of Cambridge, Center of Latin American Studies, Working Papers no. 7 (Cambridge, England n.d.), pp. 39–40.

8 Smith, *Argentina and the Failure of Democracy*, pp. 30–31; Cantón, Moreno, and Ciria, *La democracia constitucional*, pp. 55–56.

9 Rock, *Politics in Argentina*, p. 236. Solberg also discussed this point in *Oil and Nationalism*, pp. 113, 117–18.

10 Anne L. Potter, "The Failure of Democracy in Argentina, 1916–1930," JLAS 13, no. 1 (May 1981): 83–109, esp. 101–2.

11 Leopoldo Lugones cited in Onega, *La inmigración*, pp. 216–19, and in Irazusta, *Lugones*, pp. 98–100.

12 *La Protesta*, July 17, 1923.

13 Zuleta, *El nacionalismo*, 1: 126.

14 Leopoldo Lugones, *La organización de la paz* (Buenos Aires, 1925), p. 60.

15 Ibid., pp. 11, 61–64.

16 Lugones, article in *Revista de la Facultad de Derecho y Ciencias Sociales* (July–Sept. 1927), cited by Irazusta, *Lugones,* pp. 112–13.

17 Richard J. Walter, *Student Politics in Argentina: The University Reform and Its Effects, 1918–1964* (New York, 1968), pp. 34–35.

18 Furlong, "El catolicismo argentino," p. 285; Mario Amadeo, "El grupo 'Baluarte' y los Cursos de Cultura Católica," Alberto Espezel Berro, "Un fragmento," and Bernadino Montejano (h.), "Un hogar intelectual," *Universitas* 9 (July–Sept. 1975): 23–25, 46–48, and 51–54, respectively; Comisión de Estudios de la Sociedad Argentina de Defensa de la Tradición, Familia, y Propiedad, *El nacionalismo: Una incógnita en constante evolución* (Buenos Aires, 1970), pp. 38–40. Other Catholic groups influenced nationalism (see Navarro, *Los nacionalistas,* pp. 107–11), but the ones treated here were the most important.

19 Julio Irazusta to Enrique Pérez Mariluz, Dec. 3, 1925, Letter, Irazusta Papers, Notebook 1. Many books have been written on Maurras; I have relied here on the collection of his writings found in J. S. McClelland, ed., *The French Right (from De Maistre to Maurras),* trans. John Frears (London, 1970), pp. 213–304. A concise work by an Argentine nationalist is Enrique Zuleta Alvarez, *Introducción a Maurras* (Buenos Aires, 1965).

20 Charles Maurras, *Oevres Capitales,* 2: 88, quoted by Ernst Nolte, *Three Faces of Fascism: Action Française, Italian Fascism, National Socialism,* trans. Leila Vennewitz (New York, 1964), p. 185. Nolte's discussion on pp. 185–89 also inspired the following paragraph.

21 For example, see Guillermo Sáenz, "El Vaticano, el fascismo, y L'Action Française'," *Criterio* no. 57 (Apr. 4, 1929): 436–38.

22 Julio Irazusta, interview, July 22, 1977; *La Nueva República* no. 7 (Mar. 1, 1928) (hereinafter, LNR).

23 There were differences between these periodicals, and their nature changed over time. *La Voz Nacional* and LNR were less Catholic-oriented than *Número* and *Criterio. Criterio* was less nationalistic after 1930 than before; in that year, Franceschi became its editor and instituted some changes. See Carulla, *Al filo,* pp. 228–31; Manuel Gálvez, *Entre la novela y la historia,* rev. ed. (Buenos Aires, 1962), pp. 15–17.

24 Ernesto Palacio, in *La Nación,* Jan. 29, 1928, in Irazusta Papers, Notebook 2; Julio Irazusta, *Memorias (historia de un historiador a la fuerza)* (Buenos Aires, 1975), pp. 176–78, 181, and "Historia de La

Nueva República," manuscript, Irazusta Papers, Notebook 2; Carulla, *Al filo*, pp. 241–43.

25 Roberto de Laferrère quoted by Carlos Ibarguren (h.), *Roberto de Laferrère (periodismo-política-historia)* (Buenos Aires, 1970), p. 21. Also see p. 24; LNR no. 12 (Apr. 28, 1928); Ernesto Palacio, *Historia de la Argentina, 1515–1957*, 2 vols., 2d ed. (Buenos Aires, 1957), 2: 365.

26 The term "reactionary" is used in LNR no. 42 (Nov. 24, 1928), and no. 49 (June 13, 1930). LNR constantly asked its readers to help carry out the "necessary counterrevolution" by subscribing to the paper.

27 Palacio in LNR no. 13 (May 5, 1928) and no. 43 (Dec. 1, 1928).

28 Rodolfo Irazusta in LNR no. 29 (Aug. 25, 1928).

29 Palacio in LNR no. 9 (Apr. 1, 1928).

30 Juan Carulla in LNR no. 12 (Apr. 28, 1928). Uriburu's views on female suffrage are discussed in J. Beresford Crawkes, *533 días de la historia argentina; 6 de septiembre de 1930–20 de febrero de 1932* (Buenos Aires, 1932), p. 122; and Marifran Carlson, *Feminismo: The Women's Movement in Argentina from Its Beginnings to Evita Perón* (Chicago, 1986), Chapter 8.

31 Carulla, *Al filo*, pp. 247–53; Gontrán de Güemes, "El año 27 Uriburu se negó a intervenir en una revolución," *Hechos en el Mundo*, Feb. 4, 1957; Luis Alberto Romero, "Entrevista con Julio Irazusta, 28 de mayo 1971," Transcript, Proyecto de Historia Oral del Instituto Torcuato Di Tella (Buenos Aires, 1971), pp. 15–16; LNR no. 44 (Dec. 8, 1928); Carlos Ibarguren (h.), *Respuestas a un cuestionario acerca del nacionalismo, 1930–1945* (Buenos Aires, 1971), p. 9.

32 Roberto Etchepareborda, "Aspectos políticos de la crisis de 1930," *Revista de Historia* no. 3 (1958): 7–40, and Roberto Etchepareborda, "Breves anotaciones sobre la revolución del 6 de septiembre de 1930," *Investigaciones y Ensayos* no. 8 (Jan.–June 1970): 55–103; Rouquié, *Poder militar*, pp. 190–207; Goldwert, *Democracy*, pp. 16–29; Potash, *The Army*, pp. 29–54.

33 Carlés quoted by V. Gutiérrez de Miguel, *La revolución argentina: Relato de un testigo presencial* (Madrid, 1930), pp. 91–92; also see Liga Patriótica Argentina, *La Liga Patriótica y la Revolución del 6 de septiembre de 1930* (Buenos Aires, 1930), pp. 7–8, 16; LNR no. 29 (Aug. 25, 1928).

34 Ambassador Robert Woods Bliss to Secretary of State, July 31,

1929, Dispatch no. 617, U.S. Dept. of State, 835.00/436, and Sept. 4, 1929, Dispatch no. 658, no number given.

35 Liga, *Liga y la Revolución*, pp. 9–28; Liga, Brigada 19, Libro de Actas, Oct. 10, 1929; Julio A. Quesada, *Orígenes de la revolución del 6 de septiembre de 1930 (Rosas e Yrigoyen)* (Buenos Aires, 1930), pp. 57–59.

36 C. Ibarguren, *Laferrère*, p. 43. I followed these events in *La Fronda*; Liga, *Liga y la Revolución*, p. 33; Naval Attaché "A," Office of Naval Intelligence, Navy Department, Nov. 12, 1929, Serial no. 276, Nov. 20, 1929 and Serial no. 287, File 103–100, U.S. Dept. of State, 835.00/447, 450, respectively.

37 Laferrère quoted by C. Ibarguren, *Laferrère*, p. 19; League's statement of aims in Quesada, *Orígenes*, pp. 74–78; LNR no. 60 (Aug. 30, 1930); Federico Ibarguren, *Orígenes del nacionalismo argentino* (Buenos Aires, 1969), pp. 37–39.

38 Rodolfo Irazusta to Julio Irazusta, Sept. 3, 1929, Letter, Irazusta Papers, Notebook 2. Also see Irazusta, *Memorias*, pp. 190–91; *La Fronda*, Apr. 5, 1930.

39 LNR no. 60 (Aug. 30, 1930); Quesada, *Orígenes*, p. 80; José M. Sarobe, *Memorias sobre la revolución del 6 de septiembre de 1930* (Buenos Aires, 1957), p. 59.

40 Bliss to Secretary of State, Oct. 30, 1929, Dispatch no. 701, U.S. Dept. of State, 835.00/442; Uriburu quoted by Beresford, *533 días*, p. 106; C. Ibarguren, *Laferrère*, p. 48.

41 Carlés in Liga, *Restauración*, p. 6; Brigada 19, Libro de Actas, Aug. 18 and 25, 1930.

42 Gutiérrez, *Relato*, p. 129; Quesada, *Orígenes*, pp. 57–60; C. Ibarguren, *Respuestas*, pp. 10–12; F. Ibarguren, *Orígenes*, pp. 47–49; Carulla, *Al filo*, pp. 273–74; *La revolución del 6 de septiembre de 1930: Su motivo, sus hombres, su gobierno. Apuntes para un capítulo de la Historia Nacional* (Buenos Aires, 1931).

43 José F. Uriburu, *La palabra del general Uriburu: Discursos, manifiestos, declaraciones y cartas publicadas durante su gobierno* (Buenos Aires, 1933), pp. 51, 116, 146, 166–68; *La Prensa*, Oct. 1, 1930. On literacy, see Scobie, *Argentina*, p. 155.

44 Liga, Brigada 19, Libro de Actas, Sept. 16, 1930; *Los Principios*, Sept. 14, 1930; *Caras y Caretas* no. 1667 (Sept. 13, 1930).

45 *La Fronda*, Sept. 14, 1930; LNR no. 63 (Sept. 27, 1930), no. 64 (Oct. 4, 1930), and no. 66 (Oct. 18, 1930).

46 See Meyer Pellegrini in *Caras y Caretas* no. 1669 (Sept. 27, 1930);

Ibarguren, *La historia*, pp. 383–84; Gálvez's comments on young
aristocrats receiving government employment in *Hombres en soledad*.
Information on Uriburu's recruitment of nationalists was found
in the press and in the biographical sources.

47 *Caras y Caretas* no. 1670 (Oct. 4, 1930) and no. 1675 (Nov. 8,
1930); *La Fronda*, Oct. 22 and 31, 1930, Oct. 19, 1931; *La Vanguardia*, Feb. 16, 1931.

48 Carulla, *Al filo*, pp. 291–92; *La Vanguardia*, Feb. 16 and May 17,
1931; *La Fronda*, Mar. 26 and May 17, 1931; Juan Antonio Solari
in *Diputados* 2 (May 11, 1932): 253, 257; "Declaración de principios
de la Legión," manuscript, photocopy, n.d.

49 *La Vanguardia*, June 19, 1931; *La Fronda*, Mar. 26, 1931; Potash,
The Army, p. 68; Ray Josephs, *Argentine Diary* (London, 1945),
pp. 266–67.

50 *La Vanguardia*, Apr. 27, 1931; *La Fronda*, Apr. 27, 1931.

51 *La Vanguardia*, May 26, 1931; *La Fronda*, May 27, June 18,
July 11, 1931.

52 *La Fronda*, Apr. 28 and July 7, 1931.

53 Ibid., July 7, 1931; Uriburu, *La palabra*, pp. 93–94.

54 On male Civic Legionnaires, see Lavalle in *Il Mattino D'Italia*, n.d.,
in Archivo de *La Prensa*, File 37727; Sarobe, *Memorias*, p. 206;
C. Ibarguren, *Laferrère*, p. 54; Romariz, *La semana trágica*, p. 172;
Luis L. Boffi, *Juventud, universidad y patria. Bajo la tiranía del sable*
(Buenos Aires, 1933), p. 249. On female members, see Sandra F.
McGee, "Female Right-Wing Activists in Buenos Aires,
1900–1932," in Barbara J. Harris and Jo Ann McNamara, eds.,
Women and the Structure of Society (Durham, N.C., 1984), p. 95; *La
Nación*, June 3, 1931. Only two of the seventy-one original female
Civic Legionnaires had belonged to the League.

55 Potash, *The Army*, pp. 58, 69–71; Atilio Cattáneo, *Plan 1932: Las
conspiraciones radicales contra el general Justo* (Buenos Aires, 1959),
pp. 57–61; Solari in *Diputados* 2 (May 11, 1932): 254–56; Boffi, *Ju-
ventud*, p. 250; Romariz, *La semana trágica*, p. 172; Walter, *Student
Politics*, p. 104; *La Prensa*, June 17, 1931; *La Vanguardia*, Apr. 27,
May 20, June 19 and 24, July 15, 1931; Minister of Government,
Justice and Public Instruction of Tucumán, Dr. Delfín Medina, to
Provisional President, José Félix Uriburu, June 8, 1931, Letter, José
Félix Uriburu, Private Letters, Notebook 4, Donated Documents
Collection, Archivo General de la Nación.

56 *La Prensa*, May 19, June 17, 1931.

57 *La Vanguardia*, June 15, 1932; Sarobe, *Memorias*, pp. 206–8.

58 This letter and information in the following paragraphs come from Boffi, *Juventud*, pp. 251–56.

59 Ibid., pp. 256–57; *La Prensa*, Oct. 26, 1946; *El Mundo*, Oct. 26, 1946; Carlés in *El Pueblo*, June 13–14, 1932.

60 See Carlés's correspondence with Alvear in 1934, quoted in Félix Luna, *Alvear*, pp. 132–33; Manuel Carlés, "Exégesis sobre la personalidad y la política del Dr. Marcelo T. de Alvear," Introduction to Marcelo T. de Alvear, *Democracia* (Buenos Aires, 1936), pp. 9–25.

61 Rodolfo Irazusta in LNR no. 67 (Oct. 25, 1930); "Carta a Julio Irazusta de Rodolfo Irazusta (1-10-30)," in Julio Irazusta, ed., *El pensamiento político nacionalista*, Vol. 2: *La revolución de 1930*, 111; C. Ibarguren, *Laferrère*, pp. 54–55; LNR no. 100 (Oct. 20, 1931).

62 Palacio in LNR nos. 90 (Oct. 8, 1931) and 91 (Oct. 9, 1931); Julio Irazusta in LNR nos. 71 (Nov. 22, 1930) and 92 (Oct. 10, 1931).

63 LNR no. 105 (Oct. 26, 1931).

64 Leopoldo Lugones, *La grande Argentina*, 2d ed. (Buenos Aires, 1962), pp. 134–37; Acción Republicana, *Preámbulo y programa* (Buenos Aires, 1931), pp. 9–13.

65 Irazusta in LNR nos. 13 (May 5, 1928) and 20 (June 23, 1928); Lugones, *La grande Argentina*, pp. 88–89.

66 Gálvez in LNR no. 20 (June 23, 1928); Guillermo Gallardo, "Programa de la L.C.A.," *Bandera Argentina*, Aug. 26, 1932. Gálvez and the nationalists differed on some issues, but scholars have usually placed him within that current.

67 *La Nación*, Feb. 26, 1931; Alejandro E. Bunge, "La República Argentina define su política económica nacional," *Revista de Economía Argentina* 18, no. 163 (1932): 3–4; Mensaje del Presidente Provisional de la Nación, Teniente General José F. Uriburu, al Pueblo de la República, *La obra de gobierno y de administración del 6 de septiembre de 1930 al 6 de septiembre de 1931* (Buenos Aires, 1931), pp. 40–52.

68 Irazusta, *Memorias*, pp. 205–7, 219–20. Briefly, the Roca–Runciman Pact guaranteed Argentina a stable but reduced share of the British beef, wool, and grain markets, yet forced Argentina into granting concessions to British manufacturers and other interests. Nationalists (and many other Argentines) thought that the pact helped Great Britain and the large *estancieros* at the expense of the Argentine people.

69 Rodolfo Irazusta in LNR nos. 3 (Jan. 1, 1928); 52 (July 5, 1930);

57 (Aug. 9, 1930); 85 (Mar. 7, 1931); Acción Republicana, *Preámbulo*, p. 7.

70 These terms are found in LNR nos. 67 (Oct. 25, 1930); 73 (Dec. 6, 1930); 109 (Oct. 30, 1931). Also see Julio Irazusta, "La oligarquía conservadora y los estancieros," in Irazusta, *El pensamiento*, 2: 166–68.

71 LNR nos. 74 (Dec. 13, 1930) and 75 (Dec. 20, 1930). Also see Rodolfo Irazusta in LNR no. 70 (Nov. 15, 1930).

72 Leopoldo Lugones, *El estado equitativo (ensayo sobre la realidad argentina)* (Buenos Aires, 1932), p. 31. The nationalists did not leave traditional anti-Semitism completely behind, however; examples can be found in *Criterio* and LNR during the late 1920s and early 1930s.

73 LNR no. 60 (Aug. 30, 1930).

74 LNR no. 88 (Oct. 6, 1931); "The Enemy," LNR no. 92 (Oct. 10, 1931).

75 Zuleta, *El nacionalismo*, 1: 263–64.

76 Rodolfo Irazusta in LNR no. 107 (Oct. 28, 1931); Rodolfo Irazusta and Ernesto Palacio in LNR no. 108 (Oct. 29, 1931); Romero, "Entrevista con Irazusta," pp. 14, 23; Zuleta, *El nacionalismo*, 1: 336–39; Mark Falcoff, "Raúl Scalabrini Ortiz: The Making of an Argentine Nationalist," HAHR 52, no. 1 (Feb. 1972): 74–101. Gálvez expressed sympathy for the UCR in *Yrigoyen*.

Chapter 7

1 Gilbert Allardyce, "What Fascism Is Not: Thoughts on the Deflation of a Concept," *American Historical Review* 85 (Apr. 1979): 367–88; Anthony James Joes, *Fascism in the Contemporary World: Ideology, Evolution, Resurgence* (Boulder, Colo., 1978), pp. 5–6.

2 For example, see Alberto J. Pla, *Ideología y método en la historiografía argentina* (Buenos Aires, 1972), p. 160; Hennessy, "Fascism and Populism," pp. 260–61.

3 Such views are described in Klemens von Kemperer, "Towards a Fourth Reich? The History of National Bolshevism in Germany," *Review of Politics* 13 (Apr. 1951): 194; Leonore O'Boyle, "Theories of Socialist Imperialism," *Foreign Affairs* 28 (Jan. 1950): 290–98. On fascist regimes as development dictatorships, see Henry Ashby Turner, Jr., "Fascism and Modernization," *World Politics* 24 (July 1972): 547–64.

4 Rennie, *Argentine Republic*, pp. 268–73, and Romero, *Argentine Po-*

litical Thought, pp. 228–31, called certain Argentine activists fascist; Barbero and Devoto, *Los nacionalistas*, referred to the Civic Legion, May Legion, and to some extent the League as "philofascist." Rennie, however, distinguished between fascist and nonfascist members of the right, and Romero changed his views later (see note 26, below). None of these authors defined fascism. Paul H. Lewis, however, both defined fascism and used the term to refer to Perón in "Was Perón a Fascist? An Inquiry into the Nature of Fascism," *The Journal of Politics* 42 (1980): 242–56. The diversity of fascist appeals is explored at great length in Stein Ugelvik Larsen, Bernt Hagtvet, Jan Petter Myklebust, eds., *Who Were the Fascists? Social Roots of European Fascism* (Oslo, Norway, 1980). On Brazilian Integralists see Hélgio Trindade, *Integralismo (O fascismo brasileiro na década de 30)* (São Paulo, 1974), pp. 144–46. Also see note 28, below.

5 Navarro, *Los nacionalistas*, pp. 104–5.

6 Manuel Gálvez, *Este pueblo necesita* (Buenos Aires, 1934), pp. 104, 120, 128. Nolte considered Maurras a fascist and discussed previous French counterrevolutionaries as precursors of fascism in *Three Faces of Fascism*.

7 Nolte, *Three Faces of Fascism*, p. 40. My explanation of Nolte's work cannot do justice to the complexity of his ideas. Other scholars, however, have criticized his approach. See, for example, Karl Friedrich, "Fascism Versus Totalitarianism," *Central European History* 4 (Sept. 1971): 271–84.

8 Stanislav Andreski, "Fascists as Moderates," and Bernt Hagtvet, "The Theory of Mass Society and the Collapse of the Weimar Republic: A Re-Examination," in Larsen, et al., *Who Were the Fascists?*, pp. 52–55 and 104, respectively.

9 On fascism as the "revolt of the losers," see Wolfgang Sauer, "National Socialism: Totalitarianism or Fascism?" *American Historical Review* 73 (Dec. 1967): 408–22.

10 Nolte, *Three Faces of Fascism*, p. 537; Liga, *Restauración*, p. 10. The following discussion of Nolte is based on *Three Faces of Fascism*, pp. 537–67.

11 Stanley G. Payne, "The Concept of Fascism," in Larsen, et al., *Who Were the Fascists?*, pp. 20–21.

12 Manuel Carlés, *Diplomacia y estrategia: Conferencia dada en el Colegio Militar de la Nación por el Dr. Manuel Carlés, junio de 1915. Suplemento al no. 270 de la Revista Militar* (Buenos Aires, 1915); Roberto Etchepareborda, "La generación argentina del destino manifiesto:

Un intento hacia la concreción de la Patria Grande," *Investigaciones y Ensayos* no. 16 (Jan.–June 1974): 132.

13 Mayer, *Dynamics of Counterrevolution*, pp. 48–85; last quote from pp. 60–61.

14 Eugen Weber, "The Right: An Introduction," in Hans Rogger and Eugen Weber, eds., *The European Right: A Historical Profile* (Berkeley, Calif., 1965), pp. 19–20.

15 Navarro characterized the nationalists as reactionaries in *Los nacionalistas*, p. 17.

16 *La Protesta*, Nov. 6, 1919.

17 On the civil guards see Diehl, *Paramilitary Politics*; Large, "The Politics of Law and Order"; Bruce F. Pauley, "Nazi and Heimwehr Fascists: The Struggle for Supremacy in Austria, 1918–1938," in Larsen, et al., *Who Were the Fascists?*, pp. 226–38.

18 Diehl, *Paramilitary Politics*, pp. 79–93.

19 The term "bourgeois-conservative" is used in ibid. Also see Large, "The Politics of Law and Order," pp. 397–99.

20 Zuleta, *El nacionalismo*, 1: 262–68. Comisión de Estudios de la Sociedad Argentina de Defensa de la Tradición, Familia y Propiedad, *El nacionalismo*, p. 23, passim, essentially agreed with this distinction, labeling the two wings as "political" and "Catholic" nationalism.

21 Ramos, *Las masas*, pp. 386–96; Spilimbergo, *Nacionalismo*; Jauretche, "Movimientos nacionales."

22 Jauretche, "Movimientos nacionales," pp. 233–34. Zuleta, *El nacionalismo*, 2: 629–33; and Ismael Viñas, "La reacción nacionalista," *Polémica* no. 56 (1971): 145–46, both challenged this distinction by stressing the ties between oligarchical and popular nationalisms.

23 Argentina, *Cuarto censo*, 1: xxxiii–xxxvi; on Fresco as a precursor to Perón, see Dolkart, "Fresco." Fresco was listed as a member of the Merlo, Buenos Aires, brigade in *La Fronda*, Apr. 25, 1919.

24 Juan Carlos D'Abate, "Trade Unions and Peronism," in Frederick C. Turner and José Enrique Miguens, eds., *Juan Perón and the Reshaping of Argentina* (Pittsburgh, 1983), p. 56. D'Abate claimed that workers increased their control over their own lives under Peronism, but he did not explain how this *autogestión* related to control over working conditions. Daniel James disagreed with D'Abate in "Rationalisation and Working-Class Response: The Context and Limits of Factory Floor Activity in Argentina," JLAS 13, no. 2 (Nov. 1981): 375–402.

25 See Nicolas Fraser and Marysa Navarro, *Eva Perón* (New York, 1980).

26 José Luis Romero, *El pensamiento político de la derecha latinoamericana* (Buenos Aires, 1970), p. 146; also see pp. 145 and 177. This represented a change from Romero's earlier view of Peronism as a fascist movement. José Enrique Miguens agreed on Peronism's Catholic nationalist roots, in "The Presidential Elections of 1973 and the End of an Ideology," in Turner and Miguens, *Juan Perón*, pp. 147–48. Miguens, however, characterized this ancestry as very different from fascism.

27 Peter H. Smith and Manuel Mora y Araújo, "Peronism and Economic Development: The 1973 Elections," in Turner and Miguens, *Juan Perón*, pp. 174, 185–86; Weber, "The Right," pp. 11, 15.

28 Lewis's "Was Perón a Fascist?" is such a study. On violence, see Lewis, p. 255. Ciria concluded that Peronism was not fascist because of its lower-class base, unsophisticated techniques of repression, support for labor (versus capital), leadership style drawn largely from military experience rather than fascist models, and because it placed less emphasis on militarism, totalitarianism, economic controls, and expansionism than European fascist regimes. See Ciria, *Perón y el justicialismo*, pp. 89–98, to compare these criteria with Payne's. In "The Function of the Little Known Case in Theory Formation or What Peronism Wasn't," *Comparative Politics* 6 (Oct. 1973): 17–45, Eldon Kenworthy ably criticized the arguments of some scholars who had maintained that Peronism was fascist. Neither he nor Ciria, however, defined fascism, although Ciria identified certain characteristics of such movements. Joseph A. Page described some of the similarities between Peronism and fascism in *Perón: A Biography* (New York, 1983), esp. pp. 88–91, 220–21, but he essentially viewed Perón as a pragmatic politician rather than as a fascist.

29 Thomas E. Skidmore, "Workers and Soldiers: Urban Labor Movements and Elite Responses in Twentieth-Century Latin America," in Virginia Bernhard, ed., *Elites, Masses, and Modernization in Latin America, 1850–1930* (Austin, Tex., 1979), p. 88.

30 General Ramón J. A. Camps cited in *Latin American Weekly Report*, Feb. 4, 1983.

31 Videla and Catalán in *Buenos Aires Herald*, Dec. 18 and July 17, 1977, respectively.

32 *Time*, July 20, 1981, p. 18.

33 *Buenos Aires Herald*, Mar. 20, 1977.

Bibliography

I. Government Documents

A. MEXICO

Dirección General de Estadística. *Quinto censo de población, 15 de mayo de 1930.* 8 vols. Mexico City, 1932–36.

B. ARGENTINA

Comisión Directiva del Censo. *Segundo censo de la República Argentina, mayo 10 de 1895.* 3 vols. Buenos Aires, 1898.

Comisión Nacional del Censo. *Tercer censo nacional, levantado el primero de junio de 1914.* 10 vols. Buenos Aires, 1916–19.

Congreso Nacional. *Diario de sesiones de la Cámara de Diputados.* Buenos Aires, 1919–32.

Dirección General de Estadística. *La población y el movimiento demográfico en el período 1910–1925.* Buenos Aires, 1926.

Dirección Nacional del Servício Estadístico. *Cuarto censo general de la Nación.* 3 vols. Buenos Aires, 1947–52.

Mensaje del Presidente Provisional de la Nación, Teniente General José F. Uriburu, al Pueblo de la República. *La obra de gobierno y de administración del 6 de septiembre de 1930 al 6 de septiembre de 1931.* Buenos Aires, 1931.

Policía de la Capital Federal. *Memoria. Antecedentes y datos estadísticos correspondientes al año 1921.* Buenos Aires, 1922.

———. *Orden del día* 34 (1920): 832–34.

Provincia de Entre Ríos. *Memoria de los Ministerios de Gobierno, Hacienda, Justicia e Instrucción Pública, 1918–1922.* 3 vols. Paraná, 1922.

C. UNITED STATES

Department of Commerce. Bureau of Foreign and Domestic Commerce. *Statistical Abstract of the United States, 1915.* Washington, D.C., 1916.

Department of State. Records of the Department of State Relating to the Internal Affairs of Argentina, 1910–29. General Records, Decimal File, National Archives Microfilm Copy M514.

II. Newspapers and Periodicals
(of Buenos Aires, unless otherwise stated)

Boletín de Servicios de la Asociación del Trabajo (1920–24)
Boletín Mensual del Museo Social Argentino (1912–21)
Buenos Aires Herald (1977)
La Capital (Rosario, 1919–24)
Caras y Caretas (1901–31)
Criterío (1928–32)
El Día (La Plata, 1921)
El Diario (1918)
La Epoca (1919)
La Fronda (1919–31)
Latin American Weekly Report (London, 1983)
El Mundo (1946)
La Nación (1909–31)
La Nueva República (1927–31)
Número (1930–31)
La Prensa (1901–31, 1946)
Los Principios (Córdoba, 1919–21, 1930)
La Protesta (1910–24)
El Pueblo (1910–32)
La Razón (1919)
Review of the River Plate (1919–22, 1970)
Revista Militar (1919)
Time (New York, 1981)
La Vanguardia (1919–32)
La Voz del Interior (Córdoba, 1919–21)

III. Liga Patriótica Argentina

Acción civilizadora de las escuelas de la Liga Patriótica Argentina. Buenos Aires, 1921.
Acción civilizadora de las escuelas de la Liga Patriótica Argentina, 23 abril 1922. Buenos Aires, 1922.
Brigada 19 de la Capital Federal. Libro de Actas, 1926–30. Liga Patriótica Argentina office, Buenos Aires.

Brigada 19 y 21. *La verdad de la Liga Patriótica Argentina*. Buenos Aires, 1950.

Campaña de Santa Cruz. *Homenaje al Ejército y Armada*. Buenos Aires, 1922.

Catecismo de la doctrina patria. Buenos Aires, 1921.

Comisión Central de Señoritas. *Memoria de diez escuelas obreras, 1924–mayo–1925*. Buenos Aires, 1925.

———. *Memoria, 1927–mayo–1928*. Buenos Aires, 1928.

Comisión de Bellas Artes. Brigadas de Señoras de la Liga Patriótica Argentina. *Discursos pronunciados en el acto inaugural y veredicto del Jurado de la Tercera Exposición Nacional de Tejidos y Bordados, 1–15 julio 1922*. Buenos Aires, 1922.

Comisión de Señoritas de la Liga Patriótica Argentina. *Sus escuelas de obreras en las fábricas*. Buenos Aires, 1922.

Congreso General de Territorios Nacionales. Buenos Aires, 1927.

Congreso Nacionalista de Economía Rural organizado por la Liga Patriótica Argentina. Buenos Aires, 1935.

Cuarto Congreso Nacionalista de la Liga Patriótica Argentina. Buenos Aires, 1923.

El culto de la Patagonia: Sucesos de Santa Cruz. Buenos Aires, 1922.

Declaración de principios, organización y propósitos de los Soviets argentinos: Con introducción y notas marginales del sentido común por la Liga Patriótica Argentina. Buenos Aires, 1920.

Definición de la Liga Patriótica Argentina (guía del buen sentido social), Buenos Aires, 1921.

Discurso pronunciado por el Dr. Manuel Carlés ante la honorable Sociedad de Beneficencia el 26 mayo de 1919 en el acto de distribución de los Premios a la Virtud. Buenos Aires, 1919.

Discurso pronunciado por el presidente de la Liga Patriótica Argentina, Dr. Manuel Carlés en la reunión celebrada por la honorable Junta de Gobierno en honor de los delegados de la Asociación de Empleados de Comercio de Río de Janeiro. Buenos Aires, 1924.

Discursos pronunciados en el acto inaugural y veredicto del Jurado de la Cuarto Exposición Nacional de Tejidos y Bordados, 4–20 agosto 1923. Buenos Aires, 1923.

Estatutos. Buenos Aires, 1919.

Homenaje a la Prefectura General de Puertos: Distribución de 'Medallas al Mérito.' Discurso pronunciado por el Señor Jefe de Puertos Don José Riobón. Buenos Aires, 1923.

Humanitarismo práctico: La Liga Patriótica Argentina en Gualeguaychú. Buenos Aires, 1921.

La Liga Patriótica y la Revolución del 6 de septiembre de 1930. Buenos Aires, 1930.

Misión y doctrina de la Liga Patriótica Argentina. Buenos Aires, 1956.

Noveno Congreso Nacionalista organizado por la Liga Patriótica Argentina. Buenos Aires, 1928.

Octavo Congreso Nacionalista organizado por la Liga Patriótica Argentina. Buenos Aires, 1927.

Organización de la soberanía o Escuela de Bienestar. Buenos Aires, 1928.

Primer Congreso de Trabajadores de la Liga Patriótica Argentina. Buenos Aires, 1920.

Primero de Mayo Argentino: Conmemoración del pronunciamiento de Urquiza en Entre Ríos. Buenos Aires, 1921.

El programa de la Liga Patriótica Argentina y la educación por el ejemplo (como una consagración del concepto Patria). Buenos Aires, 1923.

Quinto Congreso Nacionalista de Trabajadores, organizado por la Liga Patriótica Argentina. Buenos Aires, 1924.

Restauración de la Moral Argentina, 22 Mayo 1930. Buenos Aires, 1930.

Séptimo Congreso Nacionalista de la Liga Patriótica Argentina. Buenos Aires, 1926.

Sexto Congreso Nacionalista de Trabajadores organizado por la Liga Patriótica Argentina. Buenos Aires, 1925.

Solemne homenaje de la Liga Patriótica Militar de Chile a la Liga Patriótica Argentina. Santiago, Chile, 1922.

Tercer Congreso de Trabajadores de la Liga Patriótica Argentina. Buenos Aires, 1922.

IV. Biographical Sources

Abad de Santillán, Diego, ed. *Gran enciclopedia argentina.* 9 vols. Buenos Aires, 1956–63.

Archivo de *La Prensa.* Buenos Aires.

Asociación Argentina de Criadores de Shorthorn. *Guía de criadores de shorthorn.* Buenos Aires, 1934.

Calvo, Carlos. *Nobiliario del Antiguo Virreynato del Río de la Plata,* 6 vols. Buenos Aires, 1936–43.

Cameron, W. H. Morton, ed. *Enciclopedia Comercial (Encyclopedia Commercial): Unico órgano oficial, anual o bienal, de la British and Latin American Chamber of Commerce. Argentina, Brasil, Chile, Perú, Uruguay, Suplemento Británico.* London, 1922.

Carbajo Alberto, Ernesto, and Gabriel R. Lecuna. *Guía ganadera argentina, 1919.* Buenos Aires, 1919.

Castellano Sáenz Cavia, Rafael M. *Familias de traslasierra. Jurisdicción de Córdoba.* Buenos Aires, 1969.

Corbella Figini, Roberto. *Guía del ganadero: Tomo bovinos.* Buenos Aires, 1946.

Correa Luna, Carlos. *Historia de la Sociedad de Beneficencia.* 2 vols. Buenos Aires, 1923–25.

Cutolo, Vicente Osvaldo. *Historiadores argentinos y americanos.* Buenos Aires, 1966.

———. *Nuevo diccionario biográfico argentino (1750–1930).* 5 vols. Buenos Aires, 1968–78.

Del Arca de Del Campo, Sofía. *Sociedad Damas de la Misericordia: Su historia, su obra, y su organización actual.* Buenos Aires, 1946.

El Diario. Libro social. Buenos Aires, 1929.

Diccionario biográfico de hombres de negocios: Biografías contemporáneas. Buenos Aires, 1945.

Edelberg, Gregorio, ed. *Anuario Edelberg: Guía de propietarios de campos, Provincia de Buenos Aires.* Buenos Aires, 1923.

Estudio de Ingeniería de Gregorio Edelberg. *Planos catastrales de los partidos de la Provincia de Buenos Aires.* Buenos Aires, 1939.

Gajardo Cruzat, Enrique, ed. *Diccionario médico argentino.* Buenos Aires, 1932.

Guía agropecuaria argentina, 1966–1967. 2d ed. Buenos Aires, 1967.

Guía de sociedades anónimas. Buenos Aires, 1923, 1932, 1950.

Guía Lumen: Reseña geográfica y económica de todas las estaciones de F.F.C.C. de la República Argentina. Buenos Aires, 1920.

Guía Social Palma. Buenos Aires, 1929.

Guillermo Kraft Ltda. *Quién es quién en la Argentina.* Buenos Aires, 1943, 1950.

Hernando Ling, Diana. "Linajes y política." *Todo Es Historia* no. 107 (Apr. 1976): 50–69.

Imaz, José Luis de. *La clase alta de Buenos Aires.* Buenos Aires, 1962.

Instituto de Estudios Biográficos. *Los directores de la República Argentina.* Buenos Aires, 1945.

Jockey Club. *Nómina de los socios.* Buenos Aires, 1926, 1943.

Libro de oro. Buenos Aires, 1911, 1923, 1932, 1936, 1944.

Maciel, Carlos Néstor. *Las grandes estancias argentinas.* Buenos Aires, 1939–41.

Maglione Jaimes, Pedro P. "Una figura señera—Manuel Carlés." *La Nación,* Jan. 12, 1969.

Newton, Jorge. *Diccionario biográfico del campo argentino.* Buenos Aires, 1972.

Newton, Ronald. *German Buenos Aires, 1900–1933: Social Change and Cultural Crisis.* Austin, Tex., 1977.

"Nómina de socios." *Anales de la Sociedad Rural Argentina* 52 (Feb. 1918): 116–34.

Oddone, Jacinto. *La burguesía terrateniente argentina.* 3d ed. Buenos Aires, 1956.

Parker, William Belmont, ed. *Argentines of Today.* 2 vols. Buenos Aires, 1920.

Petriella, Dionisio, and Sara Sosa Miatello. *Diccionario biográfico italo-argentino.* Buenos Aires, 1976.

Piccirilli, Ricardo, and Leoncio Gianello. *Biografías navales (cuarenta y cinco semblanzas de marinos).* Buenos Aires, 1963.

Piccirilli, Ricardo, Francisco L. Romay, and Leoncio Gianello. *Diccionario histórico argentino.* 6 vols. Buenos Aires, 1953–54.

Piñeiro, Armando Alonso. *Vidas de grandes argentinos.* 3 vols. Buenos Aires, 1963.

República Argentina. Congreso Nacional. Cámara de Diputados de la Nación. *El parlamento argentino, 1854–1947.* Buenos Aires, 1948.

Régar. *Guía social argentina "Régar."* Buenos Aires, 1928.

Sciurano Casteñeda, Adolfo, ed. *Album de oro de la mujer argentina.* Buenos Aires, 1930.

Sebreli, Juan José. *Buenos Aires, vida cotidiana y alienación.* Buenos Aires, 1966.

Sociedad Conferencias de Señoras de San Vicente de Paúl—República Argentina (reseña histórica) 1864–1942. Buenos Aires, 1942.

Sociedad de Beneficencia de la Capital. *Reseña sobre su organización y su obra, 1823–1942.* Buenos Aires, 1942.

Sociedad Inteligencia Sudamericana. *Hombres del dia 1917, el diccionario biográfico argentino.* Buenos Aires, 1917.

Sociedad Rural Argentina. *Nómina de socios.* Buenos Aires, 1938, 1948, 1956, 1962.

Sosa de Newton, Lily. *Diccionario biográfico de mujeres argentinas.* 1st and 2d eds. Buenos Aires, 1972, 1980.

Udaondo, Enrique. *Diccionario biográfico argentino.* Buenos Aires, 1938.

Yaben, Jacinto R. *Biografías argentinas y sudamericanas.* 4 vols. 2d ed. Buenos Aires, 1952.

V. Other Sources

Abad de Santillán, Diego. *La F.O.R.A.: ideología y trayectoria del movimiento obrero revolucionario en la Argentina.* Buenos Aires, 1933.

Acción Republicana. *Preámbulo y programa*. Buenos Aires, 1931.

Allardyce, Gilbert. "What Fascism Is Not: Thoughts on the Deflation of a Concept." *American Historical Review* 85 (Apr. 1979): 367–88.

Amadeo, Mario, "El grupo 'Baluarte' y los Cursos de Cultura Católica." *Universitas* 9 (July–Sept. 1975): 23–25.

Amadeo, Tomás. *El falso dilema: Fascismo o Bolsheviquismo*. Buenos Aires, 1939.

———. *La función social*. Buenos Aires, 1929.

Andrea, Miguel de. "Orientaciones sociales." *Instituto Popular de Conferencias* 3 (June 22, 1917): 78–90.

———. *Pensamiento cristiano y democrático de Monseñor de Andrea*. *Homenaje del Congreso Nacional*. Buenos Aires, 1963.

———. *La perturbación social contemporánea*. Buenos Aires, 1944.

Andreski, Stanislav. "Fascists as Moderates." In Stein Ugelvik Larsen, Bernt Hagtvet, Jan Petter Myklebust, eds., *Who Were The Fascists? Social Roots of European Fascism*. Oslo, Norway, 1980, pp. 52–55.

Araújo Salvadores, Clodomiro. Secretary-General of the Liga Patriótica Argentina. Interview with author. Nov. 3, 1977. Buenos Aires.

Arenaza, Celina de. *Sin memoria*. Buenos Aires, 1980.

Asociación del Trabajo. *Estatutos de la Asociación del Trabajo*. Buenos Aires, 1921.

———. *Memoria y Balance de la Asociación del Trabajo correspondiente al ejercicio de 1920–1921*. Buenos Aires, 1921.

———. *¿Qué es la Asociación del Trabajo?* Buenos Aires, 1921.

Auza, Néstor Tomás. *Los católicos argentinos: Su experiencia política y social*. Buenos Aires, 1962.

Babini, Nicolás. "La Semana Trágica. Pesadilla de una siesta de verano." *Todo Es Historia* no. 5 (Sept., 1967): 8–20.

Baily, Samuel L. *Labor, Nationalism, and Politics in Argentina*. New Brunswick, N.J., 1967.

Barbero, María Inés, and Fernando Devoto. *Los nacionalistas (1910–1932)*. Buenos Aires, 1983.

Bayer, Osvaldo. "1921: La masacre de Jacinto Arauz." *Todo Es Historia* no. 45 (Jan. 1971): 40–55.

———. "Simón Radowitzky, Mártir o asesino?" *Todo Es Historia* no. 4 (Aug. 1967): 58–79.

———. *Los vengadores de la Patagonia trágica*. 3 vols. Buenos Aires, 1972–74.

———. "Los vengadores de la Patagonia trágica." *Todo Es Historia* no. 15 (July 1968): 69–85.

Baylac de Eizaguirre, María Luján. Former chief of social services, Grafa factory. Interview with author. July 6, 1981. Buenos Aires.

Beresford Crawkes, J. *533 días de la historia argentina; 6 de septiembre de 1930–20 de febrero de 1932.* Buenos Aires, 1932.

Bergquist, Charles W. *Workers in Modern Latin American History: Capitalist Development and Labor Movement Formation in Chile, Argentina, Venezuela, and Colombia.* Stanford, Calif., forthcoming.

Blackwelder, Julia Kirk, and Lyman L. Johnson. "Changing Criminal Patterns in Buenos Aires, 1890 to 1914." *Journal of Latin American Studies* 14, no. 2 (Nov. 1982): 359–80.

Boffi, Luis L. *Juventud, universidad y patria: Bajo la tiranía del sable.* Buenos Aires, 1933.

Borrero, José María. *La Patagonia trágica.* 2d ed. Buenos Aires, 1957.

Botana, Natalio R. *El orden conservador: La política argentina entre 1880 y 1916.* Buenos Aires, 1977.

Bunge, Alejandro E. "La República Argentina define su política económica nacional." *Revista de Economía Argentina* 18, no. 163 (1932): 3–4.

Bunge, Julia Valentina. *Vida, época maravillosa, 1903–1911.* Buenos Aires, 1965.

Burns, E. Bradford. *Nationalism in Brazil: A Historical Survey.* New York, 1968.

Camp, Richard L. *The Papal Ideology of Social Reform: A Study in Historical Development, 1878–1967.* Leiden, 1969.

Campo, Hugo del. "La Semana Trágica." *Polémica* no. 53 (1971): 63–84.

Canedo, Alfredo. *Aspectos del pensamiento político de Leopoldo Lugones.* Buenos Aires, 1974.

Cantón, Darío. *Materiales para el estudio de la sociología política en la Argentina.* 2 vols. Buenos Aires, 1968.

————. *El parlamento argentino en épocas de cambio: 1890, 1916 y 1946.* Buenos Aires, 1966.

Cantón, Darío, José L. Moreno, and Alberto Ciria. *Argentina: la democracia constitucional y su crisis.* Buenos Aires, 1972.

Carlés, Manuel. *Diplomacia y estrategia: Conferencia dada en el Colegio Militar de la Nación por el Dr. Manuel Carlés, junio de 1915. Suplemento al no. 270 de la Revista Militar.* Buenos Aires, 1915.

————. "Exégesis sobre la personalidad y la política de Marcelo T. de Alvear." Introduction to Marcelo T. de Alvear, *Democracia,* pp. 9–25. Buenos Aires, 1936.

Carlson, Marifran. "Feminism and Reform: A History of the Argentine Feminist Movement to 1926." Ph.D. Dissertation, University of Chicago, 1983.

———. *Feminismo: The Women's Movement in Argentina from Its Beginnings to Evita Perón.* Chicago, 1986.

Carulla, Juan E. *Al filo del medio siglo.* Paraná, 1951.

Cattáneo, Atilio. *Plan 1932: Las conspiraciones radicales contra el general Justo.* Buenos Aires, 1959.

Ciria, Alberto. *Perón y el justicialismo.* Buenos Aires, 1971.

Comisión de Estudios de la Sociedad Argentina de Defensa de la Tradición, Familia y Propiedad. *El nacionalismo: Una incógnita en constante evolución.* Buenos Aires, 1970.

Comité Ejecutivo de la Gran Colecta Nacional. *La paz social.* Buenos Aires, 1919.

"Congreso de la Mutualidad." *Boletín Mensual del Museo Social Argentino* 7 (1918): 5–379.

"Consejo Nacional de Mujeres." *Boletín Mensual del Museo Social Argentino* 1, no. 6 (1912): 161–67.

Cornblit, Oscar. *El fracaso del conservadorismo en la política argentina.* Instituto Torcuato Di Tella Trabajo Interno no. 14. Buenos Aires, 1973.

———. "Inmigrantes y empresarios en la política argentina." *Desarrollo Económico* 6 (Jan.–Mar. 1967): 641–91.

———. "La opción conservadora en la política argentina." *Desarrollo Económico* 14 (Jan.–Mar. 1975): 599–639.

Cortés Conde, Roberto. *El progreso argentino, 1880–1914.* Buenos Aires, 1979.

Cuadrado Hernández, G. "La rebelión de los braceros." *Todo Es Historia* no. 185 (Oct. 1982): 78–96.

Cumberland, Charles C. *Mexico: The Struggle for Modernity.* New York, 1968.

Cúneo, Dardo. *Juan B. Justo y las luchas sociales en la Argentina.* Buenos Aires, 1943.

Currier, Charles Warren. *Lands of the Southern Cross. A Visit to South America.* Washington, D.C., 1911.

D'Abate, Juan Carlos. "Trade Unions and Peronism." In Frederick Turner and José Enrique Miguens, eds., *Juan Perón and the Reshaping of Argentina,* pp. 55–78. Pittsburgh, 1983.

"Declaración de principios de la Legión." Manuscript, photocopy, n.d.

Díaz Alejandro, Carlos F. *Essays on the Economic History of the Argentine*

Republic. New Haven, Conn., 1970.

Dickmann, Enrique. *Recuerdos de un militante socialista.* Buenos Aires, 1949.

Diehl, James M. *Paramilitary Politics in Weimar Germany.* Bloomington, Ind., 1977.

Di Tella, Guido, and Manuel Zymelman. *Los ciclos económicos argentinos.* Buenos Aires, 1973.

Dolkart, Ronald. "Manuel A. Fresco, Governor of the Province of Buenos Aires, 1936–1940: A Study of the Argentine Right and Its Response to Economic and Social Change." Ph.D. Dissertation, University of California, Los Angeles, 1969.

Domínguez, Crisanto. *Rebelión en la selva.* Buenos Aires, 1948.

———. *Tanino (Memorias de un hachero).* Buenos Aires, 1956.

Dorfman, Adolfo. *Historia de la industria argentina.* 2d ed. Buenos Aires, 1970.

Drake, Paul W. "Corporatism and Functionalism in Modern Chilean Politics." *Journal of Latin American Studies* 10, no. 1 (May 1978): 83–116.

Dreier, Katherine S. *Five Months in the Argentine from a Woman's Point of View. 1918–1919.* New York, 1920.

Efron, Jedida. "La obra escolar en las colonias judías." In Delegación de Asociaciones Israelitas Argentinas, *Cincuenta años de colonización judía en la Argentina,* pp. 241–52. Buenos Aires, 1939.

Elkin, Judith Laikin. *Jews of the Latin American Republics.* Chapel Hill, N.C., 1980.

"Encuesta de Vida Nuestra sobre la situación de los judíos en la Argentina." *Vida Nuestra* 7 (Jan. 1919): 145–86.

Encyclopedia Judaica. 16 vols. New York, 1971–72.

Espezel Berro, Alberto. "Un fragmento." *Universitas* 9 (July–Sept. 1975): 46–48.

Esposito, Elisa. "La Federación de Asociaciones Católicas de Empleadas." *Boletín de la Acción Católica Argentina* (Apr. 1951): 109–12.

Estrada, José Manuel. "Discursos sobre el liberalismo." In José Luis Romero and Luis Alberto Romero, eds., *Pensamiento conservador (1815–1898),* pp. 254–72. Caracas, 1978.

Etchepareborda, Roberto. "Aspectos políticos de la crisis de 1930." *Revista de Historia* no. 3 (1958): 7–40.

———. "Breves anotaciones sobre la revolución del 6 de septiembre de 1930." *Investigaciones y Ensayos* no. 8 (Jan.–June 1970): 55–103.

———. "La generación argentina del destino manifiesto: Un intento hacia la concreción de la Patria Grande." *Investigaciones y Ensayos* no. 16 (Jan.–June 1974): 111–37.

Falcoff, Mark. "Raúl Scalabrini Ortiz: The Making of an Argentine Nationalist." *Hispanic American Historical Review* 52, no. 1 (Feb. 1972): 74–101.

Feijoó, María del Carmen. "Las luchas feministas." *Todo Es Historia* no. 28 (Jan. 1978): 7–23.

Fernández, Serafín. *Recuerdos de la vida pampera (La semana trágica de enero de 1919)*. Paris, 1962.

Fiorito, Susana. "Un drama olvidado: Las huelgas patagónicas de 1920–1921." *Polémica* no. 54 (1971): 89–112.

Fleming, William J. "The Cultural Determinants of Entrepreneurship and Economic Development: A Case Study of Mendoza Province, Argentina, 1861–1914." *Journal of Economic History* 39 (Mar. 1979): 211–24.

Font, Miguel J., ed. *La mujer: Encuesta feminista argentina. Hacia la formación de una Liga Feminista Sudamericana*. Buenos Aires, 1921.

Franceschi, Gustavo. "Sobre feminismo católico." *El Pueblo*, June 17, 1920.

Fraser, Nicholas, and Marysa Navarro. *Eva Perón*. New York, 1980.

Friedrich, Karl. "Fascism versus Totalitarianism." *Central European History* 4 (Sept. 1971): 271–84.

Furlong, Guillermo. "El catolicismo argentino entre 1860 y 1930." In Academia Nacional de la Historia, *Historia argentina contemporánea, 1862–1930*, 2: 251–92. Buenos Aires, 1964.

Gallardo, Guillermo. "Programa de la L.C.A." *Bandera Argentina*, Aug. 26, 1932.

Gallegos Méndez, María Teresa. *Mujer, Falange y Franquismo*. Madrid, 1983.

Gallo, Ezequiel (h.), and Roberto Cortés Conde. *Argentina, la república conservadora*. Buenos Aires, 1972.

Gallo, Ezequiel (h.), and Silvia Sigal. "La formación de los partidos políticos contemporáneos: La U.C.R. (1890–1916)." In Torcuato S. Di Tella, Gino Germani, Jorge Graciarena, eds., *Argentina, sociedad de masas*, 2d ed., pp. 124–76. Buenos Aires, 1965.

Gálvez, Manuel. *El diario de Gabriel Quiroga*. Buenos Aires, 1910.

———. *Entre la novela y la historia*. Rev. ed. Buenos Aires, 1962.

———. *Este pueblo necesita*. Buenos Aires, 1934.

———. *Hombres en soledad*. Rev. ed. Buenos Aires, 1957.

———. *El solar de la raza*. 2d ed. Buenos Aires, 1920.

————. *La trata de blancas.* Buenos Aires, 1904.

————. *Vida de Hipólito Yrigoyen—el hombre del misterio.* 2d ed. Buenos Aires, 1939.

Germani, Gino. "Antisemitismo ideológico y antisemitismo tradicional." *Comentario* 34 (1962): 55–63.

————. *Política y sociedad en una época de transición: De la sociedad tradicional a la sociedad de masas.* Buenos Aires, 1962.

Gilimón, Eduardo. *Un anarquista en Buenos Aires (1890–1910).* Buenos Aires, 1971.

Giménez, Antonio A. Interview with author. June 1977. Buenos Aires.

Glauert, Earl T. "Ricardo Rojas and the Emergence of Argentine Cultural Nationalism." *Hispanic American Historical Review* 43, no. 1 (Feb. 1963): 1–13.

Glickman, Nora. "The Jewish White Slave Trade in Latin American Writings." *American Jewish Archives* 34 (Nov. 1982): 178–89.

Godio, Julio, ed. *La revolución del 90.* Buenos Aires, 1974.

————. *La Semana Trágica de enero de 1919.* Buenos Aires, 1972.

Goldberg, Heidi. "Railroad Unionization in Argentina, 1912–1929: The Limitations of Working Class Alliance." Ph.D. Dissertation, Yale University, 1979.

Goldwert, Marvin. *Democracy, Militarism, and Nationalism in Argentina, 1930–1966: An Interpretation.* Austin, Tex., 1972.

Gori, Gaston. *La Forestal (La tragedia del quebracho colorado).* 2d ed. Buenos Aires, 1974.

Grierson, Cecilia. *Decadencia del Consejo Nacional de Mujeres de la República Argentina.* Buenos Aires, 1910.

Güemes, Gontrán de. "El año 27 Uriburu se negó a intervenir en una revolución." *Hechos en el Mundo,* Feb. 4, 1957.

Gutiérrez de Miguel, V. *La revolución argentina: Relato de un testigo presencial.* Madrid, 1930.

Guy, Donna J. "The Rural Working Class in Nineteenth-Century Argentina: Forced Plantation Labor in Tucumán." *Latin American Research Review* 13 (1978): 135–57.

Hagtvet, Bernt. "The Theory of Mass Society and the Collapse of the Weimar Republic: A Re-Examination." In Stein Ugelvik Larsen, Bernt Hagtvet, and Jan Petter Myklebust, eds., *Who Were the Fascists? Social Roots of European Fascism,* pp. 66–117. Oslo, Norway, 1980.

Hennessy, Alistair. "Fascism and Populism in Latin America." In Walter Laqueur, ed., *Fascism, a Reader's Guide: Analyses, Interpreta-*

tions, Bibliography, pp. 255–94. Berkeley, Calif., 1976.

Hernández Arregui, Juan José. *La formación de la conciencia nacional (1930–1960)*. Buenos Aires, 1960.

Hodges, Donald G. *Argentina, 1943–1976: The National Revolution and Resistance*. Albuquerque, N.M., 1976.

Hollander, Nancy Caro. "Women in the Political Economy of Argentina." Ph.D. Dissertation, University of California, Los Angeles, 1974.

Hughes, H. Stuart. *Consciousness and Society: The Reconstruction of European Social Thought, 1890–1930*. New York, 1958.

Ibarguren, Carlos. *La historia que he vivido*. 2d ed. Buenos Aires, 1969.

Ibarguren, Carlos (h.). *Respuestas a un cuestionario acerca del nacionalismo, 1930–1945*. Buenos Aires, 1971.

———. *Roberto de Laferrère (periodismo-política-historia)*. Buenos Aires, 1970.

Ibarguren, Federico. *Orígenes del nacionalismo argentino*. Buenos Aires, 1969.

Imaz, José Luis de. "Alejandro E. Bunge, economista y sociólogo (1880–1943)." *Desarrollo Económico* 14 (Oct.–Dec. 1974): 545–67.

"La inmigración después de la guerra." *Boletín Mensual del Museo Social Argentino* 8, nos. 85–90 (Jan.–June 1919): v–283.

Iñigo Carrera, Héctor J. *La experiencia radical, 1916–1922*. 2 vols. Buenos Aires, 1980.

Irazusta, Julio. *Genio y figura de Leopoldo Lugones*. Buenos Aires, 1961.

———. *Memorias (historia de un historiador a la fuerza)*. Buenos Aires, 1975.

———. Papers. 2 Notebooks. Las Casuarinas, Entre Ríos.

———, ed. *El pensamiento político nacionalista*. Vol. 2: *La revolución de 1930*. Buenos Aires, 1975.

———. Interview with author. July 22, 1977. Las Casuarinas, Entre Ríos.

Iscaro, Rubén. *Historia del movimiento sindical argentino*. 2 vols. Buenos Aires, 1973.

James, Daniel. "Rationalisation and Working-Class Response: The Context and Limits of Factory Floor Activity in Argentina." *Journal of Latin American Studies* 13, no. 2 (Nov. 1981): 375–402.

Jauretche, Arturo. "Los movimientos nacionales." *Polémica* no. 69 (1971): 230–52.

Joes, Anthony James. *Fascism in the Contemporary World: Ideology, Evolution, Resurgence*. Boulder, Colo., 1978.

Jordan, David Crichton. "Argentina's Nationalist Movements and the

Political Parties (1930–1963): A Study of Conflict." Ph.D. Dissertation, University of Pennsylvania, 1964.

Jorge, Eduardo F. *Industria y concentración económica (desde principios de siglo hasta el peronismo)*. Buenos Aires, 1971.

Josephs, Ray. *Argentine Diary*. London, 1945.

Kele, Max H. *Nazis and Workers: National Socialist Appeals to German Labor, 1919–1933*. Chapel Hill, N.C., 1972.

Kemperer, Klemens von. "Towards a Fourth Reich? The History of National Bolshevism in Germany." *Review of Politics* 13 (Apr. 1951): 191–210.

Kenworthy, Eldon. "The Function of the Little Known Case in Theory Formation or What Peronism Wasn't." *Comparative Politics* 6 (Oct. 1973): 17–45.

Kroeber, Clifton B. "Rosas and the Revision of Argentine History, 1880–1955." *Revista Interamericana de Bibliografía* 10 (Jan.–Mar. 1960): 3–25.

La Palma de Emery, Celia. *Discursos y conferencias: Acción pública y privada en favor de la mujer y del niño en la República Argentina*. Buenos Aires, 1910.

Laqueur, Walter, ed. *Fascism, a Reader's Guide: Analysis, Interpretations, Bibliography*. Berkeley, Calif., 1976.

Large, David. "The Politics of Law and Order: Counterrevolutionary Self-Defense Organizations in Central Europe, 1918–1923." Ph.D. Dissertation, University of California, Berkeley, 1974.

Larsen, Stein Ugelvik, Bernt Hagtvet, and Jan Petter Myklebust, eds. *Who Were the Fascists? Social Roots of European Fascism*. Oslo, Norway, 1980.

Lewin, Boleslao. *La colectividad judía en la Argentina*. Buenos Aires, 1974.

———. *Cómo fue la inmigración judía a la Argentina*. Buenos Aires, 1971.

Lewis, Paul H. "Was Perón a Fascist? An Inquiry into the Nature of Fascism." *The Journal of Politics* 42 (1980): 242–56.

Linz, Juan J. "Some Notes Toward a Comparative Study of Fascism in Sociological Historical Perspective." In Walter Laqueur, ed., *Fascism, A Reader's Guide: Analyses, Interpretations, Bibliography*, pp. 3–121. Berkeley, Calif., 1976.

Little, Cynthia Jeffress. "The Society of Beneficence in Buenos Aires, 1823–1900." Ph.D. Dissertation, Temple University, 1980.

Lugones, Leopoldo. *El estado equitativo (ensayo sobre la realidad argentina)*. Buenos Aires, 1932.

———. *La grande Argentina.* 2d ed. Buenos Aires, 1962.

———. *La organización de la paz.* Buenos Aires, 1925.

———. *El payador.* 2d ed. Buenos Aires, 1944.

Luna, Félix. *Alvear.* Buenos Aires, 1958.

———. *Yrigoyen, el templario de la libertad.* Buenos Aires, 1954.

McClelland, J. S., ed. *The French Right (from De Maistre to Maurras).* Trans. John Frears. London, 1970.

McGann, Thomas F. *Argentina, the United States and the Interamerican System, 1880–1914.* Cambridge, Mass., 1957.

McGee, Sandra F. "Female Right-Wing Activists in Buenos Aires, 1900–1932." In Barbara J. Harris and Jo Ann K. McNamara, eds., *Women and the Structure of Society,* pp. 85–97. Durham, N.C., 1984.

———. "The Visible and Invisible Liga Patriótica Argentina, 1919–1928: Gender Roles and the Right Wing." *Hispanic American Historical Review* 64, no. 2 (May 1984): 233–58.

Maier, Charles S. *Recasting Bourgeois Europe: Stabilization in France, Germany, and Italy in the Decade after World War I.* Princeton, N.J., 1975.

Marotta, Sebastián. *El movimiento sindical argentino: Su génesis y desarrollo.* 3 vols. Buenos Aires, 1960–61, 1970.

Martel, Julián (José María Miró). *La bolsa.* Buenos Aires, 1891.

Mayer, Arno J. *Dynamics of Counterrevolution in Europe, 1870–1956: An Analytic Framework.* New York, 1971.

Mazo, Gabriel del, ed. *La reforma universitaria.* 6 vols. Buenos Aires, 1926–27.

Miguens, José Enrique. "The Presidential Elections of 1973 and the End of an Ideology." In Frederick Turner and José Enrique Miguens, eds. *Juan Perón and the Reshaping of Argentina,* pp. 147–70. Pittsburgh, 1983.

Mirelman, Victor A. "Jewish Settlement in Argentina, 1881–1892." *Jewish Social Studies* 33 (Jan. 1971): 3–12.

———. "The Semana Trágica of 1919 and the Jews in Argentina." *Jewish Social Studies* 37 (Jan. 1975): 61–73.

Montejano, Bernardino (h.). "Un hogar intelectual." *Universitas* 9 (July–Sept. 1975): 51–54.

Moody, Joseph N., ed. *Church and Society: Catholic Social and Political Thought and Movements, 1789–1950.* New York, 1953.

Mosse, George L. "The Genesis of Fascism." *Journal of Contemporary History* 1 (1966): 14–26.

Mujica, Adolfo. "La agitación obrera y el estado." *Instituto Popular de Conferencias* 5 (July 18, 1919): 101–10.

Murmis, Miguel, and Juan Carlos Portantiero. *Estudios sobre los orígenes del peronismo*. Buenos Aires, 1971.

Murray, Robert K. *Red Scare: A Study in National Hysteria, 1919–1920*. New York, 1964.

Muzzilli, Carolina. "El trabajo femenino." *Boletín Mensual del Museo Social Argentino* 2, nos. 15–16 (Mar.–Apr. 1913): 65–90.

Navarro Gerassi, Marysa. *Los nacionalistas*. Trans. Alberto Ciria. Buenos Aires, 1968.

Niklison, José Elías. "Acción social católica obrera." *Boletín del Departamento Nacional del Trabajo* 46 (Mar. 1920): 15–286.

Nolte, Ernst. *Three Faces of Fascism: Action Française, Italian Fascism, National Socialism*. Trans. Leila Vennewitz. New York, 1966.

O'Boyle, Leonore. "Theories of Socialist Imperialism." *Foreign Affairs* 28 (Jan. 1950): 290–98.

O'Brien, David J., and Thomas A. Shannon, eds. *Renewing the Earth: Catholic Documents on Peace, Justice, and Liberation*. New York, 1977.

Onega, Gladys S. *La inmigración en la literatura argentina, 1880–1910*. Buenos Aires, 1969.

"Orígenes y desenvolvimiento del Museo Social Argentino." *Boletín Mensual del Museo Social Argentino* 1, no. 1 (1912): 5–12.

Orona, Juan V. *La logia militar que enfrentó a Hipólito Yrigoyen*. Buenos Aires, 1965.

Page, Joseph A. *Perón: A Biography*. New York, 1983.

Pagés, José. "Los ensayos sindicales de inspiración católica en la República Argentina." *Anales de la Comisión de Estudios y Conferencias de la Corporación de Ingenieros Católicos* (1944): 73–118.

Palacio, Ernesto. *Historia de la Argentina, 1515–1957*. 2 vols. 2d ed. Buenos Aires, 1957.

Partido Demócrata Progresista. *Programas y plataformas electorales*. Buenos Aires, 1930.

Pauley, Bruce F. "Nazi and Heimwehr Fascists: The Struggle for Supremacy in Austria, 1918–1938." In Stein Ugelvik Larsen, Bernt Hagtvet, and Jan Petter Myklebust, eds. *Who Were the Fascists? Social Roots of European Fascism*, pp. 226–38. Oslo, Norway, 1980.

Payá, Carlos Manuel, and Eduardo José Cárdenas. "Manuel Gálvez y Ricardo Rojas, protonacionalistas." *Todo Es Historia* no. 107 (Apr. 1976): 32–48.

Payne, Stanley G. "The Concept of Fascism." In Stein Ugelvik Larsen, Bernt Hagtvet, and Jan Petter Myklebust, eds. *Who Were the Fascists? Social Roots of European Fascism*, pp. 14–25. Oslo, Norway, 1980.

Peers de Perkins, Carmen. *Eramos jóvenes el siglo y yo*. Buenos Aires, 1969.

Phelps, Vernon L. *The International Economic Position of Argentina*. Philadelphia, 1938.

Piñero, Octavio A. *Los orígenes y la trágica semana de enero de 1919*. Buenos Aires, 1956.

Pla, Alberto J. *Ideología y método en la historiografía argentina*. Buenos Aires, 1972.

Potash, Robert A. *The Army and Politics in Argentina, 1928–1945: Yrigoyen to Perón*. Stanford, Calif., 1969.

Potter, Anne L. "The Failure of Democracy in Argentina, 1916–1930." *Journal of Latin American Studies* 13, no. 1 (May 1981): 83–109.

Primer Congreso Femenino Internacional de la República Argentina. Buenos Aires, 1910.

"Progreso urbano y rural." *Boletín Mensual del Museo Social Argentino* 1, no. 6 (1912): 173–81.

Pulido, José García. *El Gran Chaco y su imperio Las Palmas*. Buenos Aires, 1951.

Pulzer, Peter G. J. *The Rise of Political Anti-Semitism in Germany and Austria*. New York, 1964.

Quesada, Julio A. *Orígenes de la revolución del 6 de septiembre de 1930 (Rosas e Yrigoyen)*. Buenos Aires, 1930.

Ramos, Jorge Abelardo. *Revolución y contrarrevolución en la Argentina: Las masas en nuestra historia*. Buenos Aires, 1957.

———. *Revolución y contrarrevolución en la Argentina*. 2 vols. 3d ed. Buenos Aires, 1965.

Remorino, Jerónimo, ed. *Anales de legislación argentina*. 4 vols. Buenos Aires, 1953–55.

Rennie, Ysabel F. *The Argentine Republic*. New York, 1945.

Repetto, Nicolás. *Mi paso por la política*. 2 vols. Buenos Aires, 1956–57.

La revolución del 6 de septiembre de 1930: Su motivo, sus hombres, su gobierno. Apuntes para un capítulo de la Historia Nacional. Buenos Aires, 1931.

Rock, David. "Lucha civil en la Argentina. La Semana Trágica de enero de 1919." *Desarrollo Económico* 11 (Mar. 1972): 165–215.

———. *Politics in Argentina, 1890–1930: The Rise and Fall of Radicalism*. London, 1975.

———. "Radical Populism and the Conservative Elite, 1912–1930." In

David Rock, ed. *Argentina in the Twentieth Century*, pp. 66–87. Pittsburgh, 1975.

———. "The Rise of the Argentine Radical Party (the Unión Cívica Radical), 1891–1916." University of Cambridge, Center of Latin American Studies, Working Papers no. 7. Cambridge, England, n.d.

Rogger, Hans, and Eugen Weber, eds. *The European Right: A Historical Profile*. Berkeley, Calif., 1965.

Rojas, Ricardo. *La restauración nacionalista: Crítica de la educación argentina y bases para una reforma en el estudio de las humanidades modernas.* 3d ed. Buenos Aires, 1971.

Romariz, José R. *La semana trágica: Relato de los hechos sangrientos del año 1919.* Buenos Aires, 1952.

Romero, José Luis. *A History of Argentine Political Thought*. Trans. Thomas F. McGann. 2d ed. Stanford, Calif., 1968.

———. *El pensamiento político de la derecha latinoamericana.* Buenos Aires, 1970.

Romero, Luis Alberto. "Entrevista con Julio Irazusta, 28 de mayo 1971." Transcript. Proyecto de Historia Oral del Instituto Torcuato Di Tella. Buenos Aires, 1971.

Romero Carranza, Ambrosio. *Itinerario de Monseñor de Andrea.* Buenos Aires, 1957.

———, Alberto Rodríguez Varela, and Eduardo Ventura Flores Pirán. *Historia política de la Argentina.* Vol. 3: *Desde 1862 hasta 1928.* Buenos Aires, 1975.

Rosenwaike, Ira. "Jewish Population of Argentina: Census and Estimates, 1887–1947." *Jewish Social Studies* 22 (Oct. 1960): 195–214.

Rouco Buela, Juana. *Historia de un ideal vivido por una mujer.* Buenos Aires, 1964.

Rouquié, Alain. *Poder militar y sociedad política en la Argentina.* Trans. Arturo Iglesias Echegaray. Buenos Aires, 1981.

Ruiz Guiñazú, Enrique. "La fuerzas perdidas en la economía nacional." *Instituto Popular de Conferencias* 3 (Aug. 10, 1917): 168–93.

Ryan, Mary P. *Womanhood in America: From Colonial Times to the Present.* 2d ed. New York, 1979.

Sáenz, Guillermo. "El Vaticano, el fascismo y 'L'Action Française'." *Criterio* no. 57 (Apr. 4, 1929): 436–38.

Sánchez Gamarra, Alfredo. *Vida del padre Grote: Redentorista.* Buenos Aires, 1949.

Sandberg, Harry O. "The Jews of Latin America." *American Jewish Yearbook 1917–1918*, pp. 35–105. Philadelphia, 1917.

Sarmiento, Domingo Faustino. *El pensamiento vivo de Sarmiento.* Ed. Ricardo Rojas. 2d ed. Buenos Aires, 1964.

Sarobe, José M. *Memorias sobre la revolución del 6 de septiembre de 1930.* Buenos Aires, 1957.

Sauer, Wolfgang. "National Socialism: Totalitarianism or Fascism?" *American Historical Review* 73 (Dec. 1967): 408–22.

Scobie, James R. *Argentina: A City and a Nation.* New York, 1964.

———. *Buenos Aires: Plaza to Suburb, 1870–1910.* New York, 1974.

Sebreli, Juan José. *La cuestión judía en la Argentina.* Buenos Aires, 1968.

"La Semana Trágica." *La Nación,* Jan. 9–19, 1969.

Senkman, Leonardo. "Crónica documentada del problema judío en la Argentina. Primer hito: De 'La Bolsa' a la Semana Trágica." *Nueva Presencia,* July 9, 1977.

———. "De 'La Bolsa' a la Semana Trágica." *Nueva Presencia,* July 16, 1977.

———. "El nacionalismo y los judíos: 1909–1932." *Nueva Presencia,* July 23, 1977.

Serralunga Langhi, J. "Las cajas rurales en la República Argentina." *Estudios* 1 (Oct. 1911): 341–51.

Shipley, Robert Edward. "On the Outside Looking In: A Social History of the 'Porteño' Worker during the 'Golden Age' of Argentine Development, 1914–1930." Ph.D. Dissertation, Rutgers University, 1977.

Simon, S. Fanny. "Anarchism and Anarcho-Syndicalism in South America." *Hispanic American Historical Review* 26, no. 1 (Feb. 1946): 38–59.

Skidmore, Thomas E. "Workers and Soldiers: Urban Labor Movements and Elite Responses in Twentieth-Century Latin America." In Virginia Bernhard, ed. *Elites, Masses, and Modernization in Latin America, 1850–1930,* pp. 79–126. Austin, Tex., 1979.

Smith, Peter H. *Argentina and the Failure of Democracy. Conflict among Political Elites, 1904–1955.* Madison, Wis., 1974.

Smith, Peter H., and Manuel Mora y Araújo. "Peronism and Economic Development: The 1973 Elections." In Frederick Turner and José Enrique Miguens, eds. *Juan Perón and the Reshaping of Argentina,* pp. 171–88. Pittsburgh, 1983.

Snow, Peter G. *Argentine Radicalism: The History and Doctrine of the Radical Civic Union.* Iowa City, Iowa, 1965.

Sofer, Eugene F. *From Pale to Pampa: A Social History of the Jews of Buenos Aires.* New York, 1982.

Solari, Juan Antonio. *Parias argentinas: Explotación y miseria de los trabajadores en el norte del país*. Buenos Aires, 1940.

Solberg, Carl. "Farm Workers and the Myth of Export-Led Development in Argentina." *The Americas* 31, no. 2 (Oct. 1974): 121–38.

———. *Immigration and Nationalism: Argentina and Chile, 1890–1914*. Austin, Tex., 1970.

———. *Oil and Nationalism in Argentina: A History*. Stanford, Calif., 1979.

———. "Rural Unrest and Agrarian Policy in Argentina, 1912–1930." *Journal of Inter-American Studies and World Affairs* 13 (Jan. 1971): 18–27.

———. "The Tariff and Politics in Argentina, 1916–1930." *Hispanic American Historical Review* 53, no. 2 (May 1973): 260–84.

Solominsky, Nahum. *La semana trágica en la Argentina*. Buenos Aires, 1971.

Sosa de Newton, Lily. *Las argentinas, de ayer a hoy*. Buenos Aires, 1967.

Spalding, Hobart A., Jr. *La clase trabajadora argentina (documentos para su historia—1890/1912)*. Buenos Aires, 1970.

———. "Education in Argentina, 1890–1914: The Limits of Oligarchical Reform." *Journal of Interdisciplinary History* 3 (Summer 1972): 31–61.

———. *Organized Labor in Latin America: Historical Case Studies of Workers in Dependent Societies*. New York, 1977.

Spangemberg, Silvio. "El conflicto agrario del sud de Santa Fe." *Boletín del Museo Social Argentino* 1, nos. 11–12 (1912): 522–31.

Spilimbergo, Jorge Enea. *Nacionalismo oligárquico y nacionalismo revolucionario*. Buenos Aires, 1958.

Stimson, Frederic Jesup. *My United States*. New York, 1931.

Tedesco, Juan Carlos. *Educación y sociedad en la Argentina (1800–1900)*. Buenos Aires, 1970.

Tissera, Ramón. "Revolución social en la selva." *Todo Es Historia* no. 12 (Apr. 1968): 64–75.

Torre, Lisandro de la. *Obras*. Vol. 5: *Campañas presidenciales*. Ed. Raúl Larra. Buenos Aires, 1952.

Trindade, Helgio. *Integralismo (O fascismo brasileiro na década de 30)*. São Paulo, 1974.

Troncoso, Oscar A. *Los nacionalistas argentinos*. Buenos Aires, 1957.

Tulchin, Joseph S. "The Argentine Economy during the First World War." *Review of the River Plate*, June 19 and 30, July 10, 1970.

Turner, Henry Ashby, Jr. "Fascism and Modernization." *World Politics* 24 (July 1972): 547–64.

Uriburu, José F. *La palabra del general Uriburu: Discursos, manifiestos, declaraciones y cartas publicadas durante su gobierno.* Buenos Aires, 1933.

———. Private letters. 4 Notebooks. Donated Documents Collection. Archivo General de la Nación. Buenos Aires.

———. "Socialismo y defensa nacional." *Anales de la Facultad de Derecho y Ciencias Sociales* 4 (1914): 268–90.

Vásquez-Presedo, Vicente. *Estadísticas históricas argentinas (comparadas).* Vol. 2: *Segunda parte 1914–1939.* Buenos Aires, 1976.

Viñas, Ismael. *Orden y progreso.* Buenos Aires, 1960.

———. "La reacción nacionalista." *Polémica* no. 56 (1971): 145–68.

Wainerman, Catalina H., and Marysa Navarro. *El trabajo de la mujer en la Argentina: Un análisis preliminar de las ideas dominantes en las primeras décadas del siglo XX.* Cuadernos del Centro de Estudios de Población no. 7. Buenos Aires, 1979.

Walter, Richard J. "Politics, Parties, and Elections in Argentina's Province of Buenos Aires, 1912–42." *Hispanic American Historical Review* 64, no. 4 (Nov. 1984): 707–36.

———. *The Socialist Party of Argentina, 1890–1930.* Austin, Tex., 1977.

———. *Student Politics in Argentina: The University Reform and Its Effects, 1918–1964.* New York, 1968.

Weber, Eugen. "Revolution? Counterrevolution? What Revolution?" In Walter Laqueur, ed., *Fascism, a Reader's Guide: Analyses, Interpretations, Bibliography,* pp. 435–67. Berkeley, Calif., 1976.

———. "The Right: An Introduction." In Hans Rogger and Eugen Weber, eds. *The European Right: A Historical Profile,* pp. 1–28. Berkeley, Calif., 1965.

———. *Varieties of Fascism.* Princeton, N.J., 1964.

Weisbrot, Robert. *The Jews of Argentina: From the Inquisition to Perón.* Philadelphia, 1979.

Welter, Barbara. "The Cult of True Womanhood: 1820–1860." *American Quarterly* 18 (Summer 1966): 151–74.

Whitaker, Arthur P., and David C. Jordan. *Nationalism in Contemporary Latin America.* New York, 1966.

Yoast, Richard Alan. "The Development of Argentine Anarchism: A Socio-Ideological Analysis." Ph.D. Dissertation, University of Wisconsin, Madison, 1975.

Zeballos, Estanislao S. "Cuestiones y legislación del trabajo." *Instituto Popular de Conferencias* 5 (June 27, 1919): 17–88.

———. "Discurso inaugural." *Instituto Popular de Conferencias* 1 (July 8, 1915): 11–24.

Zuleta Alvarez, Enrique. *Introducción a Maurras.* Buenos Aires, 1965.

———. *El nacionalismo argentino.* 2 vols. Buenos Aires, 1975.

Zurretti, Juan Carlos. *Nueva historia eclesiástica argentina: Del Concilio de Trento al Vaticano Segundo.* Buenos Aires, 1972.

Index

Abramovich, M., 133
Acción Republicana (Republican Action), 217
Agote, Luis, 99, 100
Agricultural Defense Society of Uruguay, 166
Aldao, Ricardo, 117
Alegría, Pedro, 124, 125
Alem, Leandro N., 27, 28, 31, 197, 200
Allardyce, Gilbert, 225
Allies, World War I, 71, 76
Alvear, Marcelo T. de, 86, 99, 101, 185, 189, 190, 213, 215
Amadeo, Mario, 185, 195
Amadeo, Tomás, 60, 174, 177
American Institute for the Suppression of Bolshevism, 167
American Legion, 67, 166
American Protective League, 67, 167
Anadón, Lorenzo, 123, 154
Anarchism, 7, 18, 19, 21, 25, 26, 35, 38, 40, 51, 52, 55, 64, 71, 81, 128, 129, 133, 143, 149, 205, 206, 210. See also Federación Obrera Regional Argentina V; Protesta, La
Anastasi, Leonidas, 150
Anchorena, Joaquín de, 60, 79, 117, 120
Andrea, Miguel de, 36, 51, 53, 54, 55, 58, 59, 61, 81, 82, 87, 101, 154, 155, 156, 168

Andréis, Fernando de, 126, 132, 133, 134
Andreski, Stanislav, 228
Anquín, Nimio de, 195
Anselmi, Pascual, 179
Antipersonalists. See Unión Cívica Radical
Anti-Semitism, 37, 38, 44, 45, 46, 48, 49, 50, 74, 75, 78, 132, 177, 178, 220, 221, 222, 229; 277n.72. See also Jews; Racism
Anti-Yrigoyenism, 72, 99, 101, 197, 206, 208
Araya, Rogelio, 100
Argentine Agrarian Federation. See Federación Agraria Argentina
Argentine Civic Legion. See Legión Cívica Argentina
Argentine Industrial Union (Unión Industrial Argentina), 65, 79
Argentine Regional Workers' Federation. See Federación Obrera Regional Argentina
Argentine Patriotic League. See Liga Patriótica Argentina
Argentine Regional Workers' Confederation. See Confederación Obrera Regional Argentina
Argentine Rural Society (Sociedad Rural Argentina), 65, 102

Argentine Social League. *See*
Liga Social Argentina
Argentine Social Museum. *See*
Museo Social Argentina
Argentine Workers' Confedera-
tion (Confederación Obrera
Argentina), 151
Argentine Workers' Federation
(Federación Obrera Argen-
tina), 17
Arpellito, Lorenzo, 126
Arrigos de Elía, Dr., 140
Arrow Cross of Hungary, 228
Asociación de Damas Patricias
(Association of Patrician
Ladies), 81, 87, 89, 91
Asociación del Trabajo (Labor
Association), 65, 69, 73, 80,
112, 117, 119, 120, 121, 122,
124, 126, 148, 152, 203. *See
also Boletín de Servicios de la
Asociación del Trabajo*
Asociación de Universitarias Ar-
gentinas (Association of Ar-
gentine University Women),
23
Asociación Nacional Pro-Patria
de Señoritas (National Pro-
Fatherland Association of
Señoritas), 88–89, 137
Aubone, Carlos, 37, 82
Avellaneda, 56, 57
Axentzoff, José, 129, 130, 131,
132
Ayarragaray, Lucas, 179
Ayrolo, Bartolomé, 56

Bahía Blanca, 64, 114, 115
Balestra, Juan, 35, 37
Baluarte, 195, 197
Barth, Santiago, 56
Bavastro, Francisco, 103
Beccar Varela, Horacio, 176

Becú, Carlos T., 123, 124, 126
Beneficent Society. *See* Sociedad
de Beneficencia
Berdier, Hortensia, 89, 159
Bernstein, Eduard, 16
"Blanca de Castilla" Studies
Center (Centro de Estudios
"Blanca de Castilla"), 57,
155
Bliss, Robert Woods, 203, 205
*Boletín de Servicios de la Asociación
del Trabajo*, 117. *See also*
Asociación del Trabajo
Bolsa de Cereales (Cereal Exchange), 141
Brigades (Liga Patriótica Argentina), 82, 83, 84, 93, 94, 96,
98, 101, 106, 108, 111, 113,
114, 115, 119, 123, 128, 129,
132, 133, 138, 141, 145, 146,
151, 152, 229, 240; automobile
workers, 118, 121; delegates,
102; female, 90, 97 table 3, 91,
92, 112, 149, 160, 212; free labor, 82, 106, 116, 128, 129,
132, 142, 146, 231; Indian,
145, 147, 151; male, 95 table
1, 96 table 2, 103 table 4, 104
table 5, 112, 157, 160; poster-
fasteners, 113; professional,
91; provinces, 237; rural, 94,
107, 129; stevedores, 120, 179;
teachers' (*magisterio*), 90, 91,
175
—regional: Andean, 94; Balcarce,
Buenos Aires, 170; Banfield,
Buenos Aires, 113; Bragado,
Buenos Aires, 129; Brigade
Nineteen, 160; Chacabuco,
Buenos Aires, 168; Colón,
Buenos Aires, 115; Cór-
doba, 89, 142, 162, 163;
De Bary, Buenos Aires, 129;

Eleventh Precinct, 176; Entre
Ríos (*entrerriano*), 133, 134;
Fifth Precinct, 173; Forty-
third Precinct, 173; Gilbert,
Entre Ríos, 127, 139; Guale-
guaychú, Entre Ríos, 132,
136, 141, 172, 198; Isla Verde,
Córdoba, 142; Las Flores,
Buenos Aires, 160; Las Pal-
mas, El Chaco, 124; League of
Commercial Defense (Como-
doro Rivadavia, Chubut), 146,
147; Leones, Córdoba, 142,
143; Marcos Juárez, Córdoba,
143; Mendoza, 92, 116; Mis-
iones, 127; Pehuajó, Buenos
Aires, 129; Perdices, Entre
Ríos, 140; Puerto Santa Cruz,
Santa Cruz, 148, 150; Posadas,
Misiones, 169; Río Gallegos,
Santa Cruz, 150; Rivadavia,
Buenos Aires, 129; San Antonio Oeste, Río Negro, 128;
Santa Fe province (north-
ern), 127; Trenque Lauquen,
Buenos Aires, 129; Twenty-
sixth Precinct, 171; Villa
Guillermina, Santa Fe, 123;
Villa Ocampo, Santa Fe, 123;
Villaguay, Entre Ríos, 133
Brunet, Luis, 124
Buenos Aires: city, 7, 9, 13, 14,
16, 17, 20, 22, 23, 27, 34, 36,
37, 41, 43, 45, 46, 49, 57, 62,
64, 67, 73, 78, 80, 84, 85, 90,
91, 93, 94, 97, 113, 122, 125,
126, 134, 138, 140, 145, 148,
157, 158, 180, 189, 205, 211,
241; city council, 100; port,
120; province, 32, 45, 73, 94,
97, 105, 128, 129, 143, 180,
209, 211, 213
Buenos Aires Herald, 32

Bunge, Alejandro E., 53
Bunge, Augusto, 176

Cafferata, Juan F., 59
Calvo, Nicolás A., 80, 82
Campillo, Elisa del, 156
Cano, Jorgelina, 89, 90, 110, 156,
163
Cantilo, José Luis, 119
Carlés, Carlos, 37
Carlés, Manuel, 27, 35, 37, 75,
82, 85–89, 91, 92, 99, 107,
110, 114, 116, 117, 120, 128,
133, 137–39, 145, 149–51,
153, 157, 160–62, 164, 166,
168, 170, 171, 174, 181–87,
192, 194, 200, 203–7, 214–16,
222, 223, 229, 230, 231, 238,
241, 256n.39
Carlists, 197
Carulla, Juan, 71, 198, 201, 205, 208
Castelltort, E. Zacarías, 139
Castex, Alberto, 169
Catalán, Juan José, 240
Catholic Church and Catholicism, 10, 11, 51, 52, 90, 154,
155, 209, 211, 227, 234, 235,
236; "Catholic syndicates" (female laborers), 57; education,
194, 237; influence on nationalists, 194–97; journals, 154,
197, 208; meetings of 1906,
1907, 1908, 56; National Congress of 1884, 51; organizations of, 35, 36, 51–53, 54,
56, 57, 58, 60, 80, 105, 108,
154, 155, 194, 195, 197; statesmen, 185; Social Catholic
movement, 51, 53–56, 58, 59,
105, 108, 153, 161, 164, 194,
236, 237, 238. *See also* Andrea,
Miguel de; Franceschi, Gustavo J.

Centennial of Argentine Independence (1910), 35
Centro de Estudios "Blanca de Castilla" ("Blanca de Castilla" Studies Center), 57, 155
Centro de Navegación Transatlántica (Transatlantic Navigation Center), 64
Centro Naval (Naval Center), 76, 77, 80, 92, 98
Cereal Exchange (Bolsa de Cereales), 141
Chilean Military Patriotic League, 166
Christophersen, Pedro, 65, 73, 79. See also Asociación del Trabajo
Chubut, 145
Cinto, Luis, 137
Cintor, Galaor, 130, 134
Círculo de Armas (Circle of Arms), 81, 102
Círculo Militar (Military Circle), 77, 81
Círculos de Obreros (Workers' Circles), 35, 51–53, 56, 57, 60, 80, 105
Civic Guard of Concordia, Entre Ríos, 140, 182
Civic League of France, 166
Civic Legion. See Legión Cívica Argentina
Civic Union. See Unión Cívica
Civil code: women under, 24; revision of 1926, 159
Civil guard movement, 97, 234. See also Militias
Clara, Entre Ríos, 133
Colón, Entre Ríos, 129
Comisión Pro-Defensa del Orden (Commission for the Defense of Order), 79, 80, 82, 178
Comité Nacional de la Juventud

(National Youth Committee), 70, 71, 75, 76, 77, 80, 97, 194, 198, 201
Comité Oficial Israelita (Official Jewish Committee), 78, 79
Comité Pro Aliados (Pro-Allies Committee), 70
Comité Pro Argentinidad (Pro-Argentinism Committee), 79
Communism, 75, 189, 203, 205, 206, 222, 225, 228, 236, 237
Comodoro Rivadavia, Chubut, 146
Concordia, Entre Ríos, 131, 132
Confederación General de Trabajadores (CGT) (General Confederation of Workers), 189
Confederación Obrera Argentina (COA) (Argentine Workers' Confederation), 151, 188
Confederación Obrera Regional Argentina (CORA) (Argentine Regional Workers Confederation), 19, 34, 36
Congregation of the Daughters of Mary, 36, 56
Congress, 59, 70, 86, 127, 202; Chamber of Deputies, 17, 32, 78, 100, 102, 126, 132, 133, 150, 189, 190; Senate, 32, 189, 191
Congress of Good Feeling, 151, 152
Consejo Nacional de Mujeres (National Council of Women), 22, 88
Conservatism: ideology of, 8, 10, 30, 32, 59–63, 70, 98, 152, 185, 198, 227, 230, 231, 232, 238, 248n.31; League as conservative, 222, 233, 234; "local conservatives," 30, 102, 113, 131, 136, 139, 211. See also Partido Conservador

Conservative Coalition of Buenos
Aires, 86
Constitution, Argentine, 178,
200, 202, 207, 215, 216, 219,
240
Contreras Feliú, María, 91
CORA. *See* Confederación Obrera
Regional Argentina
Córdoba: city, 3, 16, 112–13,
116, 194; province, 41, 73, 94,
96, 128, 129, 141, 209, 211
Corporatism, 198, 207, 208, 213,
219, 233, 236
Correa, Justo P., 91, 92
Corrientes, 125, 126, 128, 129,
132, 141, 169
Costa, Julio A., 99
Counterrevolution and counter-
revolutionaries, 1, 4–9, 27,
33–65, 72, 77, 78, 99, 165,
166, 171, 176, 178, 186, 187,
192, 199, 202, 205, 224–27,
230, 232, 233, 235, 236, 239,
241, 243 n.1; European, 207;
French, 197. *See also* Conservatism; Fascism; Practical humanitarianism; Reactionaries
Cranwell, Ricardo, 182
Criterio, 197, 208
Crotto, José Camilo, 103
Cursos de Cultura Católica
(Catholic Culture Courses),
194, 195

Danzey, Alberto, 124, 126
Dellepiane, Luis, 36, 73, 74, 75,
77, 78, 80, 98
Dell'Oro Maini, Atilio, 117, 154,
195
Demarchi, Antonio (Italian
baron), 37
Democracy, 192, 193, 199–202,
205, 207, 214, 215, 218–19,

225, 232, 234, 235, 241; func-
tional, 198, 209; League cri-
tique of, 183, 184, 185, 186;
nationalist opposition to, 191–
93, 197, 198–200, 207, 220,
221
Democratic Christian League
(Liga Demócrata Cristiana),
52, 56
Depression, 191; of 1926, 187;
of 1929, 187, 202, 207, 218;
of World War I, 67–68
Diana, Justo E., 80, 81, 82
Dickmann, Enrique, 221
Dictatorship of 1976–83, 239–41
Domecq García, Manuel, 76, 77,
79, 80, 81, 82, 85, 86, 185
Donoso Cortés, Juan, 197
Drumont, Edouard, 45. *See also*
Anti-Semitism

Economic nationalism. *See*
Nationalism
Education, 43, 44, 100, 107, 115,
158, 160, 174, 175, 212
El Chaco, 123, 127. *See also*
Las Palmas
Elections, 16, 237; of 1916, 72; of
1931, 213, 215; electoral fraud,
215; electoral reform, 199; reform of 1912, 191, 192
Elías, José, 120
Elite (oligarchy), the, 9, 10, 11,
13, 26, 27, 29, 30, 31, 32, 61,
70, 81, 185, 189, 191, 196,
209, 215, 216, 219, 224, 237,
238; ideology of, 244 n.1
Employer groups: union-breaking
efforts of, 64. *See also* Asociación del Trabajo; Centro de
Navegación Transatlántica;
Liga Propietarios de Automóviles Particulares; Sociedad

Employer groups (*continued*)
Obrera Marítima Protectora
del Trabajo Libre; Sociedad
Unión Protectora de Trabajo
Libre
Entre Ríos, 45, 47, 48, 103, 107,
128, 129, 132, 134, 135, 137,
153, 169, 197
Epoca, La, 98
Estrada, Celina de, 89
Estrada, José Manuel, 10, 11, 27,
51, 59, 89
Etchepare, Pedro, 81
Etcheverry, José, 141

FAA. *See* Federación Agraria
Argentina
Factory schools, League, 90, 156,
157, 158, 159, 175, 179. *See
also* Liga Patriótica de
Señoritas
Falcón, Ramón L., 34, 36, 115
Farmers: *chacareros*, 107, 129, 132,
141, 142, 143; conflicts with
landowners, 128, 142; proposed aid for, 217; protests by,
127; strikes by, 20, 54, 55; tenants, 24, 25, 67. *See also* Land
Fascism, 1, 4, 5, 68, 212, 222,
225, 227, 228, 229, 230, 231,
232, 234, 238, 239; 277–
78 n.4; Austrian, 234; European, 164, 180, 194, 226, 227,
229, 239; German, 234; Hungarian, 239; Italian, 169, 174,
228, 236; Latin American, 226;
Romanian, 239. *See also*
Counterrevolution
Fasolino, Monsignor, 154
Federación Agraria Argentina
(FAA) (Argentine Agrarian
Federation), 26, 54, 127, 128
Federación de Asociaciones

Católicas de Empleadas (FACE)
(Federation of Catholic Asso-
ciations of Female Employees),
58, 155
Federación de Estudiantes
Católicos (Federation of
Catholic Students), 194
Federación Obrera Argentina
(FOA) (Argentine Workers'
Federation), 17
Federación Obrera Comarcal
(Territorial Workers' Federa-
tion), 129
Federación Obrera Marítima
(FOM) (Maritime Worker Fed-
eration), 64, 119, 120, 121,
122, 123, 124, 126, 134, 144
Federación Obrera Provincial
(Provincial Workers' Federa-
tion), 142
Federación Obrera Regional (Re-
gional Workers' Federation),
145
Federación Obrera Regional Ar-
gentina (FORA) (Argentine Re-
gional Workers' Federation),
18, 19, 26, 34, 38, 73, 124,
125, 126, 128, 131, 135, 136,
137, 139, 140, 141, 148, 149;
FORA V, 120, 143; FORA IX, 68,
74, 119, 120, 123, 124, 128,
129, 134, 144, 151
Federal Capital. *See* Buenos Aires
(city)
Federation of Workers' Circles.
See Círculos de Obreros
Feminism and feminists, 22, 23,
24, 26, 55, 58, 60, 88, 90, 156,
157; antifeminism, 1, 23, 88,
155, 157, 238; women's movement, 21–23
Figueroa Alcorta, José, 86
First Workers' International, 16

Fliess, Felipe, 146
FOA. *See* Federación Obrera Argentina
FORA. *See* Federación Obrera Regional Argentina
Foreign interests in Argentina, 225, 230, 240; capital, 199, 217; capitalism, 63; enterprises, 170, 171, 172; foreign investments, 188, 223, 239; foreignizing (*extranjerizante*), 218; foreign lackeys (*entreguistas*), 223; landowners, 145; nationalist opposition to, 197, 220; railroads, 219. *See also* Nationalism
FORJA. *See* Fuerza de Orientación Radical de la Joven Argentina
Formosa, 123
Franceschi, Gustavo J., 53, 55, 57, 87, 154, 156
Free labor, 117, 138, 142, 143, 148, 180; brigades, 82, 128, 129, 132, 142, 146; principles, 182; societies, 64, 127; vocational programs, 175; workers, 180, 186
Free Workers' Association of Bavaria, 166
Freikorps of Germany, 234
Fresco, Manuel, 237
Fronda, La, 133, 190, 198
Fuerza de Orientación Radical de la Joven Argentina (FORJA) (Radical Orientation Force of Young Argentina), 235

Gallardo, Guillermo, 195
Gallegos, Juan Carlos, 35
Gallegos, Juan de Dios, 155, 156
Gallo, Vicente, 79, 80
Gálvez, Manuel, 41, 42, 63, 68, 197, 218, 227

García Torres, Alberto, 163
Gastón, María Lea, 157
Gauchos, 43, 49; customs of, 44; *Los Gauchos Judíos* (The Jewish Gauchos), 48
General Confederation of Workers (Confederación General de Trabajadores), 189
Generation of Eighty, 9, 11, 12, 61
Gerchunoff, Alberto, 48, 70, 72
Gesenko, Miguel, 148, 149
Gilbert, Entre Ríos, 135; brigade, 137, 139
Golondrinas, 14, 24
Gómez, Ramón, 98
González, Eduardo T., 171
González, Elpidio, 77, 119
González, Joaquín V., 52
Goyena, Pedro, 10, 27, 51
Goyeneche, Arturo, 80
Gozalbo, Augusto, 220, 221
Gran Colecta Nacional (Great National Collection), 154, 155
Grierson, Cecilia, 22
Grote, Federico, 51, 52
Gualeguay, Entre Ríos, 129, 131
Gualeguaychú, Entre Ríos, 85, 129, 134, 136, 137, 140, 151, 152, 160, 167, 218, 224, 232; brigade, 132, 136–41, 172, 198; massacre of May 1, 1921, 138, 139, 141, 147; Socialist Center, 141
Gutiérrez, Celestino F., 163
Gutiérrez, Ismael, 175

Henderson, C. A., 179
Hernández Arregui, Juan José, 3
Hitler, Adolf, 227
Hogar y Asociación de Domésticas (Home and Association of Domestics), 56

Huanca, Jesús, 121
Huangelén (Indian cacique), 147,
   151

Ibarguren, Carlos (Senior), 31,
   60, 61, 62, 63, 177, 208, 209
Ibarguren, Federico, 195, 198
Ibertis Correa, Carlos, 175
Illesca, Pedro, 135
Immigration, 12, 13, 16, 18, 25,
   27, 33, 34, 38, 39, 40, 41, 43,
   45, 48, 60, 62, 63, 87, 135,
   145, 161, 176, 177, 179, 184,
   198, 199, 209, 220, 229; Jewish, 79, 178; restriction of,
   33–34, 38, 178–79
Indians, 125, 145, 151, 159; brigades, 145, 147, 151; conquest
   of, 12
Industrial development. *See* Economic nationalism
Integralists of Brazil, 2, 107, 227
Irazusta, Julián, 197, 218
Irazusta brothers, 200, 216–19,
   223, 224, 235, 238; Julio, 197,
   198, 216, 217; Rodolfo, 198,
   200, 201, 205, 215, 218
Iron Guard of Romania, 5, 227
Izaguirre, Judge, 131, 134

Jacinto Arauz, La Pampa, 143,
   144
Jauretche, Arturo, 236
Jews, 34, 44, 46, 48, 49, 78, 79,
   82, 131, 132, 133, 138, 177,
   178, 195, 196, 220, 221, 222;
   agricultural zone, 129; farmers, 133; free labor workers,
   133; *Los Gauchos Judíos* (The
   Jewish Gauchos), 48; Jewish
   Colonization Association
   (JCA), 45, 47, 79; "Jewish question," 50, 132; League and,
   130–33, 176–77; leftists, 78;

Liga Israelita Pro Argentinidad
   (Jewish Pro-Argentinism
   League), 82; nationalists and,
   177–78, 195, 197; population,
   255n.21; Russian, 37, 45, 176;
   schools, 47, 48, 50. *See also*
   Anti-Semitism; Comité
   Oficial Israelita; Semana
   Trágica
Jockey Club, 60, 81, 102, 215
Joes, Anthony James, 225
Juareguiberry, Luis, 103
Juarès, Jean, 16
Juárez Celman, Miguel, 27, 28
Jujuy, 159
Junín, Buenos Aires, 114
Justo, Agustín P., 213, 221
Justo, Juan B., 16, 27, 49
Juventud Autonomista. *See* Par-
   tido Autonomista Nacional

Ku Klux Klan, 2

Labor and laborers, 25, 85, 100,
   101, 106, 107, 116, 148, 150,
   163, 180, 192, 201, 212, 213,
   222, 236; boycotts, 135, 142,
   148; braceros, 128, 129; child,
   52, 57; Chilean, 145; communist unions, 237; eight-
   hour work day, 217; female
   workers, 52, 57, 155–59, 179,
   237, 252n.44; history, 246n.14;
   legislation, 31, 154; nonfederated workers, 135; Petroleum
   Workers' Union (FOP), 146;
   railroad workers, 149; regulations for female and child, 16,
   59; rural, 67, 94, 136; stevedores, 120, 143; strike support, 135; taxi drivers, 117,
   118; union movement, 15, 16,
   17, 18, 24, 26, 33, 34, 38, 50,
   52, 63, 64, 65, 68, 69, 73, 84,

112, 118, 121, 123, 127, 129, 135, 141, 142, 144, 145, 147, 148, 149, 151, 153, 155, 174, 180, 182, 183, 188, 211, 217, 225, 228, 229, 236, 237, 241; urban, 67; workers' congresses, 163; working conditions, 15, 279n.24. *See also* Employer groups; Federación Obrera Regional Argentina; Free labor; Strikes

Labor Association. *See* Asociación del Trabajo

Laferrère brothers, 198; Alfonso de, 70, 71, 72, 198, 202; Roberto de, 202, 204, 215

La Forestal company, 123, 127

Lagos, Juan B., 175

Lagos, Rear Admiral, 185

Lamarca, Emilio, 35, 51, 53, 60

Land: availability of, 12; distribution of, 12; latifundia, 128, 170; nationalist views on, 199, 217, 218–20, 234; reform, 169, 170, 189; owners, 107, 144, 151, 219, 232

La Palma de Emery, Celia, 54, 56

La Pampa, 45, 128

La Plata, 37

Las Palmas, El Chaco, 124, 125, 126, 152, 153, 213; Las Palmas del Chaco Austral Company, 123–27

Lavalle, Floro, 209, 210

Law of Social Defense (1910), 38, 101, 130, 141

League. *See* Liga Patriótica Argentina

League of Argentine Catholic Ladies. *See* Liga de Damas Católicas Argentinas

League of the South (Liga del Sur), 31, 42

Left, the, 187, 189, 192, 194, 205, 206, 215, 222, 224, 228, 229, 230, 237, 238; Latin American, 226; League alternatives to, 138, 222, 224; Marxism, 6, 7, 16, 154, 162, 196, 223, 228, 229, 230, 234, 237; national left, 5, 226; socialism, 7, 11, 37, 51, 71, 75, 198, 221. *See also* Anarchism; Communism; Partido Socialista; Syndicalism

Legión Cívica Argentina (Argentine Civic Legion), 209, 210, 214, 215, 218, 229, 234; brigades of, 211, 212; children in, 212; women in, 211, 212

Legión de Mayo (May Legion), 204, 205, 206, 209

Lencinas, Carlos Washington, 204

Leo XIII, 51, 54

Liberalism and liberals, 9, 10, 11, 12, 43, 196, 198, 200, 201, 217, 222, 223, 230; Latin-American, 226; liberal-conservatism, 10, 72, 216; liberal democracy, 49, 212, 216, 220; nationalist opposition to, 192, 197, 201, 216, 220, 221, 222, 223, 224

Liga de Damas Católicas Argentinas (League of Argentine Catholic Ladies), 36, 56

Liga del Sur (League of the South), 31, 42

Liga Demócrata Cristiana (Democratic Christian League), 52, 56

Liga Israelita Pro Argentinidad (Jewish Pro-Argentinism League), 82

Liga Patriótica Argentina (Argentine Patriotic League), 3, 4, 7, 8, 9, 27, 53, 60, 65, 66–111, 113–26, 128; annual congresses, 84, 102, 163, 169,

Liga Patriótica (*continued*)
172, 173, 183, 259n.74; Central Junta, 82, 83, 89, 91, 100, 102, 105, 114, 115, 116, 208; characterization of, 228–33; Congress of Good Feeling, 151, 152; delegates, 105; Dirección de Gremios (Union Governing Board), 117; Directive Commission, 91; election of April 5, 1919, 85; Executive Council, 83, 84, 102, 105; female members, 89, 90, 105, 107, 108, 109 table 6, 110 table 7, 111, 211; functions, 111; headquarters, 92; ideological legacy, 200, 207, 210, 235–41; male members, 103–5; membership figures, 92–94; military members, 100; repression of labor, 117–52; in Revolution of 1930, 202–4, 206, 208, 214–15; statutes (goals), 82, 83; workers' roles in, 106. *See also* Brigades; Carlés, Manuel; Liga Patriótica de Señoras; Liga Patriótica de Señoritas; Practical humanitarianism
Liga Patriótica de Señoras (Patriotic League of Señoras) (Señoras), 89, 108, 110, 113, 158, 159; annual textile fair, 159, 202; day-care centers, 158; entertainment, 158; Executive Junta, 92, 108; home for juvenile delinquents, 158; libraries, 158; maternity clinics, 158; medical facilities, 158
Liga Patriótica de Señoritas (Patriotic League of Señoritas) (Señoritas), 89, 90, 156, 157, 159; Central Commission, 92, 93, 108, 110. *See also* Factory

schools; Liga Patriótica Argentina
Liga Patriótica Nacional (National Patriotic League), 39, 40, 141
Liga Pro-Patria (Pro-Fatherland League), 80
Liga Propietarios de Automóviles Particulares (League of Private Automobile Owners), 117, 120
Liga Republicana (Republican League), 202, 204, 205, 206, 209, 215
Liga Social Argentina (Argentine Social League), 52, 53, 54, 154
Lobos, Eleodoro, 60
López Cepero, Manuel, 179
Los Andes, 145
Lucienville, Entre Ríos, 133
Lugones, Leopoldo, 41, 43, 49, 50, 70, 71, 177, 178, 192, 193, 194, 208, 217, 220, 229
Luro, Pedro, 37

Maeztu, Ramiro de, 197
Magdalá, Buenos Aires, 160
Marcó, Celestino, 133, 134, 136, 139, 140
Marcos Juárez, Córdoba, 142, 143; brigade, 143
Martel, Julían, 45, 46, 47, 49, 63
Martín, Florentino, 173
Martínez de Hoz, Julia Elena A. de, 89
Martínez Zuviría, Gustavo, 60
Marxism. *See* Left, the
Maurras, Charles, 72, 161, 195–98, 220
May Day: of 1909, 34; of 1921, 137–39, 140, 151
May Legion. *See* Legión de Mayo
Mayer, Arno J., 8, 230, 232, 233, 239

Mazorca, 137
Meatpacking industry, 217, 218, 224
Medina, Rodolfo, 81
Medrano, Samuel, 195
Meinvielle, Julio, 195
Melo, Leopoldo, 79, 103
Mendoza, 73, 90, 91, 94, 158, 204; brigade, 92, 116
Meyer Pellegrini, Carlos, 209
Middle class, 17, 29, 68, 106, 107, 108, 111, 175, 189, 190, 191, 201, 215, 225, 228, 232, 234; immigrant, 233; women, 89
Mihanovich shipping firm, 64
Military, 40, 76, 87, 97, 100, 101, 105, 106, 113, 121, 150, 166, 192, 196, 203, 206, 209, 210, 212, 214, 224, 229, 234, 236, 239, 240, 241; antimilitarism, 196; army, 16, 36, 76; draft, 211; navy, 76
Military Circle, 77, 81
Militias, 38, 82, 97, 98, 204, 209; thirteenth precinct, 75. *See also* Civil guard movement
Misiones, 123, 169
Mitre, Bartolomé, 45
Modern Art Week (1922), São Paulo, 176
Montes de Oca, Manuel A., 60
Montiel, Alberto, 131, 132
Montoneros (Federalist guerrillas), 137
Mora y Araújo, Manuel, 239
Moreno, Rodolfo, 100
Morrogh Bernard, Juan Francisco, 139
Mosse, George, 8
Mouesca, Eduardo, 132
Munilla, Eduardo, 82
Muñoz, Eufemio, 181

Museo Social Argentina (Argentine Social Museum), 60, 62, 168; bulletin of, 176
Mussolini, Benito, 7, 161, 168, 197, 217, 227
Mutualism, 60, 62; conference of March 1918, 62

Nación, La, 45, 47, 132, 151, 157
National Civic Federation, 167
National Council of Women (Consejo Nacional de Mujeres), 22, 88
Nationalism, 3, 4, 5, 6, 7, 44, 71, 136, 145, 164; cultural, 41, 42, 43, 44, 50, 174, 176; doctrinaire, 235; economic, 49, 63, 159, 171, 172, 189, 190, 217–24; Latin American, 226; left-wing (national left), 5, 6, 235; oligarchical, 3–6, 235, 236; popular, 3, 5, 235; practical humanitarianism, 161–82, 186, 237; republican, 223, 235; right-wing, 5, 6, 185; rise of after mid-1920s, 191–224
Nationalist League of Brazil, 166
National League of Great Britain, 166
National Patriotic League. *See* Liga Patriótica Nacional
National Pro-Fatherland Association of Señoritas. *See* Asociación Nacional Pro-Patria de Señoritas
National Propaganda of Great Britain, 166
National Socialism (Nazism), 5, 7, 8, 138, 163, 226, 228
National Socialist party of Chile, 2
National Unity of Brazil, 166

National Youth Committee. *See* Comité Nacional de la Juventud
Naval Center. *See* Centro Naval
Navarro Gerassi, Marysa, 3, 227
Nazism. *See* National Socialism
Neuquén, 145
Noel, Carlos, 103
Nolte, Ernst, 228, 229, 230, 232
Noya, Ibón, 150
Número, 197

O'Farrell, Santiago, 53, 117, 154
Official Jewish Committee. *See* Comité Oficial Israelita
Oil industry, 190; nationalization of, 189
Oligarchy. *See* Elite, the
Oliveros Escola, Eduardo, 141
Onganía, Juan Carlos, 239–40
Ordóñez, Proto, 60, 177
Organisation Escherisch (Orgesch) of Germany, 166, 234
Organización de la Paz, La (1925), 193
Orgesch. *See* Organisation Escherisch
Ortega y Gasset, José, 197
Ortiz Pereyra, Manuel, 203
Oyuela, Juan, 173

Palacio, Ernesto, 198, 199, 200, 209, 216, 217, 235
Palacios, Alfredo J., 17, 57, 70, 72
Palau, Gabriel, 155
Palavecino station, Entre Ríos, 135
Pallejá, Arturo, 173, 174, 185
Palmer, A. Mitchell, 167
PAN. *See* Partido Autonomista Nacional
Partido Autonomista Nacional (PAN) (National Autonomist Party), 27, 28, 30, 32, 34; Youth (Juventud Autonomista), 34
Partido Conservador (Conservative Party), 32, 99, 100, 103, 186, 190, 204, 206, 211, 212, 213, 214, 216, 248n.31. *See also Régimen, el*
Partido Demócrata Progresista (PDP) (Progressive Democrat Party), 30, 31, 60, 62, 71, 73, 96, 99, 127, 143, 190, 197, 204; PDP-Socialist alliance, 213
Partido Feminista Nacional (National Feminist Party), 23. *See also* Feminism and feminists
Partido Socialista (Socialist Party), 16–17, 18, 19, 21, 23, 25, 26, 30, 31, 34, 40, 42, 54, 55, 59, 69, 70, 72, 96, 98, 99, 100, 101, 112, 114, 115, 120, 123, 126, 127, 130, 131, 132, 133, 134, 139, 140, 141, 150, 151, 176, 180, 186, 188, 189, 221; Independent Socialists, 204; PDP-Socialist Alliance, 213; women among, 21, 23, 155, 157. *See also Vanguardia, La*
Partido Socialista Obrero Internacional (International Socialist Workers' Party), 16
Patagonia, 67, 112, 143, 145, 148, 149, 151, 152, 153; League membership in, 94; massacre, 149, 150
Patalagoyti, Juan, 170, 171
Patriotic Association of Belgium, 166
Patriotic League of Señoras. *See* Liga Patriótica de Señoras
Patriotic League of Señoritas. *See* Liga Patriótica de Señoritas
Patriotic League of Unity and

National Defense of Bolivia, 166

Payne, Stanley G., 230, 231, 232, 239

Paz Social, La (Social Peace), 154

PDP. *See* Partido Demócrata Progresista

Pellegrini, Carlos, 86

Peme, Enrique, 172

Pérez Millán Temperley, Jorge Ernesto, 150

Perón, Eva, 229, 237, 238

Perón, Juan Domingo, 2–4, 229, 236, 239

Peronism, 4, 227, 235, 236, 238, 239, 241; and fascism, 280n.28; anti-Peronism, 238

Personalists. *See* Unión Cívica Radical

Piaggio, Monsignor, 81

Pico, César, 195, 198, 217

Pinedo, Federico, 14

Pintos, Guillermo, 172

Pius XI, 197

Plaza, Victorino de la, 30, 32

Police, 115, 128, 134, 138, 139, 140, 142, 143; federal, 76, 118; and the League, 101, 126, 130–31, 134

Policía Civil Auxiliar (Auxiliary Civil Police), 37

Pomar, Gregorio, 126, 213

Ponce de León, Secundino, 169

Positivism, 10, 164

Practical humanitarianism, 161–82, 186, 237. *See also* Counterrevolution; Liga Patriótica Argentina; Nationalism

Principios, Los, 113

Pro-Allies Committee. *See* Comité Pro Aliados

Pro-Argentinism Committee. *See* Comité Pro Argentinidad

Pro-Fatherland League (Liga Pro-Patria), 80

Progressive Democrat Party. *See* Partido Demócrata Progresista

Prostitution: Jews and, 46; white slave trade, 14, 221

Protesta, La, 18, 19, 34, 35, 36, 92, 107, 119, 128, 149, 192

Puerto Natales, Chile, 145

Pujato Crespo, Mercedes, 89

Punta Arenas, Chile, 145, 146

Quesada, Ernesto, 41

Quesada, Julio, 117

Racism, 63, 179, 229. *See also* Anti-Semitism

Radical Orientation Force of Young Argentina. *See* Fuerza de Orientación Radical de la Joven Argentina (FORJA)

Radicalism Party. *See* Unión Cívica Radical

Radowitzky, Simón, 34, 37

Ramírez, Paulino P., 186

Ramos, Jorge Abelardo, 3, 4

Ramos, Juan P., 177

Reactionaries, 199, 230, 232, 233

Reconquista, Santa Fe, 160

Red Scare, U.S., 67

Régimen, el (regime), 28, 30, 31, 32, 61, 62, 70, 79, 99, 103, 191, 208, 212, 216, 219, 223, 231, 248n.29

Regional Workers' Federation (Federación Obrera Regional), 145

Repetto, Nicolás, 99, 100, 101, 132, 221

Republican Action (Acción Republicana), 217

Republican League. *See* Liga Republicana

Rerum Novarum (1891 papal encyclical), 51
Residence Law of 1902, 33, 35, 101
Resistencia, El Chaco, 126
Revista de Economía Argentina (Review of Argentine Economy), 53, 168. *See also* Bunge, Alejandro E.
Revolution, 1, 18, 223, 238; French, 199; of May 1810, 7, 38; of 1893, 86, 205; of 1905, 29; of 1910, 79; of 1930, 2, 3, 187, 201, 202, 204, 206, 207, 208, 209, 213, 216, 223, 233; Russian, 68
Rex of Belgium, 227
Right, the, 4, 5, 7, 225, 230, 238; Argentine, 225, 226. *See also* Counterrevolution; Fascism; Nationalism
Río Gallegos, Santa Cruz, 145, 147, 151; brigade, 150
Río Negro, 128, 145, 146, 147
Rivadavia, Bernardino, 12
Roca, Julio, 27, 37, 52, 61, 70
Roca-Runciman treaty of, 1933, 218, 276n.68
Rojas, Julio A., 35
Rojas, Ricardo, 41, 42, 44, 47, 48, 49, 63, 70, 72, 258n.62; *La Restauración Nacionalista* (The Nationalist Restoration), 44, 47, 48, 49
Romero, José Luis, 238
Rosario, 37, 64, 85, 87, 92, 106, 116, 203
Rosas, Juan Manuel de, 10, 41, 136, 137, 197, 235; followers of (*rosismo*), 27
Rouco Buela, Juana, 20

Sáenz Peña, Roque, 30, 31, 86, 183; death of, 62; electoral reform law of, 17, 30, 72, 205, 207
Sáenz Valiente, Juan Pablo, 169
Sáenz Valiente, Justo P., 82
Salduna, Luis, 140
Salta, 61, 86
San Fernando, Buenos Aires, 121
San Juan, 86; intervention of 1930 in, 208
San Luis, 159
San Martín, José de, 36
Sánchez Sorondo, Marcelo, 195
Sánchez Sorondo, Matías, 100, 208, 213
Santa Cruz, 145, 147, 148, 149, 151
Santa Fe: city, 78; province, 25, 31, 42, 45, 73, 78, 96, 123, 128, 129, 141
Santa Rosa, La Pampa, 143
Santiago, Fernando Humberto, 241
Santiago del Estero, 42
Saravia Ferré, Father, 184
Sarmiento, Domingo Faustino, 41, 42, 43, 85
Sayans, Nélida, 157
Scalabrini Ortiz, Raúl, 224
Schiaffino, Domingo, 149
Schiavino, Eduardo, 122
Segismundo Masferrer, R. P., 56
Selles, Francisca, 157
Semana Trágica (Tragic Week), 9, 73–78, 82, 97, 106, 112, 153, 177
Señoras. *See* Liga Patriótica de Señoras
Señoritas. *See* Liga Patriótica de Señoritas
Serebrinsky, Julio, 131, 132
Serralunga Langhi, José, 53, 168, 170
Sicardi brothers, 150; Miguel, 148

Silva, Eleodoro, 122
Sinarquistas of Mexico, 2
Skidmore, Thomas, 240
Smith, Peter, 102, 190, 239
Social Darwinism, 11, 229
"Social housekeepers," 22, 23, 24
Socialism (ideology). *See* Left, the
Socialist Party. *See* Partido Socialista
Sociedad de Beneficencia (Beneficent Society), 22, 36, 87, 89
Sociedad "La Cruz" de Obreras Fosforeras ("The Cross" Society of Female Match Workers), 56
Sociedad Obrera Marítima Protectora del Trabajo Libre (Protective Maritime Worker Society of Free Labor), 64
Sociedad Rural Argentina (Argentine Rural Society), 65, 102, 110, 189; Sociedad Rural de Santa Cruz, 147
Sociedad Sportiva Argentina (Argentine Sport Society), 36
Sociedad Unión Protectora de Trabajo Libre (Protective Union Society of Free Labor), 64
Sorel, Georges, 72
Stimson, Frederic J., 22, 24, 70, 112, 166, 167
Strike breaking, 115, 116; strike breakers (*crumiros*), 120, 121, 122, 125, 126, 143, 147, 152. *See also* Employers' groups; Free labor; Liga Patriótica Argentina
Strikes, 34, 38, 60, 63, 64, 66, 69, 81, 84, 91, 112, 117, 125, 126, 129, 135, 141, 142, 145, 147, 148, 149, 152, 173, 203; of December 1918, 73; end of Las

Palmas strike, 127; general strikes, 18, 19, 73, 118, 148, 177; general strike of 1919, 9, 73, 74, 76; meat packers' of 1917, 69, 76; of 1910, 35; port strike, River Plate, 127; taxi drivers' of Buenos Aires, 122; tenant farmers' of 1912, 25; tenant farmers' of 1919, 127, 128; tenant strike of 1907, 20. *See also* Employer groups; Labor
Suffrage, 16, 17, 27, 30, 31, 184, 238; law of 1912, 86; women's, 88, 238
Syndicalists, 19, 188. *See also* Federación Obrera Regional Argentina IX

Tariffs, 31, 69, 188, 189, 217, 218
Teachers, 107, 108, 115, 157; Patriotic League of Argentine Teachers, 91, 116; statutes, 257n.51
Territorial Workers' Federation (Federación Obrera Comarcal), 129
Tezanos Pinto, Fausto de, 219
Third International (Comintern), 114
Tierra del Fuego, 145
Tomaso, Antonio de, 140, 141
Torre, Lisandro de la, 31, 62
Torres, Francisco, 171
Tragic Week (Semana Trágica). *See* Semana Trágica
Tres Arroyos, Buenos Aires, 128
Troncoso, Máxima Calvo de, 166

UCR. *See* Unión Cívica Radical
Ugarte, Marcelino, 32
UGT. *See* Unión General de Trabajadores

Unión Cívica (Civic Union), 27, 28
Unión Cívica Nacional (National Civic Union), 28
Unión Cívica Radical (UCR) (Radical Civic Union), 28, 29, 49, 70, 71, 72, 76, 79, 97, 107, 111, 139, 202, 208, 213, 216, 223, 224; Antipersonalists, 80, 86, 190; Personalists, 190, 191, 203, 214; Radical Klan, 204; Radicalism and Radicals, 28–32, 59, 61, 69, 73, 75, 77, 82, 86, 96–100, 103, 114, 117, 119, 123, 126, 127, 130, 132, 133, 134, 136, 140, 147–50, 152, 154, 171, 183–86, 188–91, 198, 200, 203, 204, 209, 215, 219, 225, 231, 235, 240, 241; and Radical uprisings, 211, 213. *See also* Yrigoyen, Hipolito
Unión General de Trabajadores (UGT) (General Union of Workers), 17, 19, 34
Unión Gremial Femenina (Union of Feminine Trade Unions), 23
Unión Industrial Argentina (Argentine Industrial Union), 60
Union movement. *See* Labor
Unión Popular Católica Argentina (Argentine Catholic Popular Union), (UPCA), 154
Unión Sindical Argentina (Argentine Syndical Union), 127, 151
University reform movement, 189, 206; nationalist opposition to, 194, 198
Unzué, Saturnino, 93
Upper class, the, 39, 50, 61, 69, 82, 98, 102, 108, 111, 118, 150, 176, 180, 190, 206, 211, 215, 225, 234, 235, 236, 238; women of, 89, 238

Uriburu, Francisco, 70, 71, 75, 76, 198
Uriburu, José F., 40, 86, 121, 176, 198, 201, 202, 206–11, 213–16, 218, 219, 223, 224, 231
Urquiza, Justo José de, 136, 137
Uruguay, Entre Ríos, 129
Ushuaia, Tierra del Fuego, 146

Valle, Delfor del, 80
Vanguardia, La, 16, 17, 36, 98, 100, 105, 106, 113, 118, 131, 137, 210
Varela, Héctor, 147, 148, 149; assassination of, 150
Vasena company, 73, 106
Vásquez de Mella, Juan, 197
Vela, Sixto, 132, 137, 138, 139, 140, 184
Vergara, Valentín, 150
Vida Nuestra, 50
Videla, Jorge, 240
Vigilantes, 38, 77, 79, 98. *See also* Civil guard movement; Militias
Villa, Federico de la, 186
Villa Domínguez, Entre Ríos, 129, 130, 131
Villa Gobernador Gálvez, Santa Fe, 158
Villaguay, Entre Ríos, 129, 130–34, 139, 177; protest of imprisonments in, 130–31; brigade, 133
Villalta, Blanco, 176
Villar Sáenz Peña, Mariano, 70, 71, 77, 80
Viñas, Alberto, 206
Viola, Roberto, 241

Weber, Eugen, 233, 239
Weimar Republic, 234
Welles, Sumner, 85, 99
Wilken, Kurt Gustav, 150

Women: lower-class, 57; phil-
anthropists, 21; in politics,
89, 201, 225, 238; recruited by
League, 87–92; rights of, 16,
159; upper-class, 57; workers,
15, 20, 23, 55. *See also* Catho-
lics; Feminism; Liga Patriótica
de Señoras; Liga Patriótica de
Señoritas; Partido Socialista;
"Social housekeepers"
Workers. *See* Labor
Workers' Circles. *See* Círculos de
Obreros
World War I, 67, 178

Yalour, Jorge, 76, 77, 81, 98, 111,
171

Young, Robert, 124, 125
Youth Committee. *See* Comité
Nacional de la Juventud
Yrigoyen, Hipólito, 28–32, 59,
63, 68, 69, 70, 71, 73–79, 86,
93, 98, 99, 101, 120, 127, 144,
148, 149, 152, 153, 175, 186,
188–91, 201–6, 209, 217, 224,
235; Yrigoyenism, 187, 198,
214, 225

Zárate, 114, 134
Zeballos, Estanislao, 82, 176
Zuberbühler, Luis, 79, 175
Zuleta Alvarez, Enrique, 6, 223,
235
Zwi Migdal, 221